The Thoughtful Reader

AUTHOR/TITLE INDEX

The Thoughtful Reader

Fourth Edition

Mary C. Fjeldstad
LaGuardia Community College
City University of New York

THOMSON

WADSWORTH

Australia • Canada • Mexico • Singapore • Spain • United Kingdom • United States

THOMSON

WADSWORTH

The Thoughtful Reader, Fourth Edition
Mary C. Fjeldstad

Publisher: Michael Rosenberg
Acquisitions Editor: Stephen Dalphin
Managing Development Editor: Karen Judd
Editorial Assistant: Cheryl Forman
Technology Project Manager: Joe Gallagher
Senior Marketing Manager: Mary Jo Southern
Marketing Assistant: Dawn Giovanniello
Associate Marketing Communications
   Manager: Patrick Rooney
Senior Project Manager, Editorial Production:
   Samantha Ross

Manufacturing Manager: Marcia Locke
Permissions Editor: Sarah Harkrader
Compositor/Production Service: International
   Typesetting and Composition
Photo Manager: Sheri Blaney
Photo Researcher: Sharon Donahue
Cover Designer: Diana Coe
Cover/Text Printer: Malloy Incorporated
Cover Art: © Images.com/CORBIS

For more information about our products, contact us at:
Thomson Learning Academic Resource Center
1-800-423-0563
For permission to use material from this text or product, submit a request online at
http://www.thomsonrights.com
Any additional questions about permissions can be submitted by e-mail to
thomsonrights@thomson.com

Library of Congress Control Number: 2005924513

ISBN 1-4130-0941-7

Credits appear on pages 441–444, which constitute a continuation of the copyright page.

Thomson Higher Education
25 Thomson Place
Boston, MA 02210-1202
USA

Asia (including India)
Thomson Learning
5 Shenton Way
#01-01 UIC Building
Singapore 068808

Australia/New Zealand
Thomson Learning Australia
102 Dodds Street
Southbank, Victoria 3006
Australia

Canada
Thomson Nelson
1120 Birchmount Road
Toronto, Ontario M1K 5G4
Canada

UK/Europe/Middle East/Africa
Thomson Learning
High Holborn House
50–51 Bedford Road
London WC1R 4LR
United Kingdom

Contents

UNIT ONE
READING AND THINKING ABOUT EDUCATION

Learning without thought is labor lost.
—Confucius

UNIT TWO
READING AND THINKING ABOUT CULTURE

Culture is that which binds men together.
—Ruth Benedict

UNIT THREE
READING AND THINKING ABOUT LANGUAGE

All words are pegs to hang ideas on.
—Henry Ward Beecher

UNIT FOUR
READING AND THINKING ABOUT WORK AND
THE WORLD OF BUSINESS

The more I want to get something done, the less I call it work.
—Delacorte

UNIT FIVE
CRITICAL READING AND THINKING ABOUT CONTROVERSIAL ISSUES

He who knows only his own side of the cause knows little.
—John Stuart Mill

UNIT SIX
READING AND THINKING ABOUT TEXTBOOKS

Knowledge itself is power.
—Francis Bacon

LEARNING STRATEGIES

Alternate Contents

VIII.   America—Past and Future

A Note to the Instructor

Can you imagine a life without reading? Without the consolation of a good book to crawl into after a disheartening day? Without that thrill of picking up the morning newspaper and, for just a moment, feeling the whole world in your hands? To us avid readers, a life without reading is nearly unimaginable.

What Are You Reading?

If you're like me, you've got at least one book going, probably two. The morning newspaper. A weekly news magazine. I'm studying Spanish, so I'm also in the middle of a novel by a young Argentinean writer. Oh, and a short story by García Márquez. A new *Atlantic Monthly* is due but I haven't finished last week's *New Yorker* yet. But I do want to check out that great BBC news website before I do anything else. . . . What does your list look like? If it's even longer than this, I envy and pity you—there aren't enough hours in the day to read all we want to read and need to read.

But now let's ask our students the same question: what are you reading? Some will say, nothing. Some, too few, will say the newspaper. Others are reading a book for their English classes. Textbooks will probably fill out the list. What's the point? Reading is like any other skill—you have to practice it to improve it. Over the years we avid readers have become effortless, fluent readers. We don't think about the process of reading, only the product— "The President said WHAT??" "A new drug is being developed for arthritis. . . . Hope it will be out in time for me." "Hopeful news from Haiti? At last. . . ." "Only three more weeks 'til spring training!" "Tuition is going up again??"

For our students, the experience is vastly different. For them the **process** is all-important and sometimes so exhausting it overwhelms the **product.** They struggle through a page, a chapter, encountering unfamiliar words, unfamiliar names, titles, events, and allusions. By the time they finish, they are too overwhelmed to make use of the ideas in the text.

When we avid readers read, we unconsciously call into play all we've read before. If we read a sociology text, we already have a vast store of knowledge about the nature of society and societies, human behavior, the debate over nature versus nurture, and a million other things we read in the past. When we read about business, we call on our knowledge of different forms of economic systems, the structure of capitalism, the impact of technology, the debate over free trade, and a million other things. Now think about reading without the benefit of all this background knowledge. Every article you read, every chapter you studied, every story, would be a heroic task: every unfamiliar word would have to be puzzled out, its definition laboriously considered, its context analyzed; every fact would have to be painstakingly decoded, examined, and somehow integrated with others being learned at the same time. This daunting task is what faces our students in much of their college work and, of course, in their outside reading.

How can we help our students to be more fluent readers? The first and most obvious answer is to ask them to read. The more they read, the better they will read. Just try to improve your tennis game, your golf stroke, your skills in the kitchen without practice. Why should reading be any different? So let's have our students read a lot. But unlike what many of them have experienced, let's not make reading a chore, a boring assignment, a frustrating exercise with no benefit other than a grade. Let's try to make reading for them what it is for us—an exhilarating part of our lives.

This book is full of interesting relevant stories, essays, and articles. The reading selections and the exercises that accompany them are geared to adults and adult interests. They treat issues important to all of us—education, our life as human beings living in societies, language, work, and topics of current controversy. Students will enjoy reading, thinking, talking, and writing about the stories. The book is organized according to themes. Because students don't have stores of background knowledge, they rarely experience the joy of reading fluently. Because most of what they read is unfamiliar, they constantly struggle as novices rather than fluent readers. But by reading deeply in one theme, students can build a fund of knowledge which will allow them to read at a higher, more sophisticated level.

The Fourth Edition

The philosophy of the text remains the same as in previous editions—thematic organization, high-interest readings, challenging exercises, and an emphasis on the connection between reading and writing. The fourth edition features a new emphasis on **learning strategies** that will help students cope with college level reading. These important strategies are placed in a special section at the back of the book, so the instructor can introduce and reinforce them whenever she feels it appropriate. **Marking text** is more fully explained and demonstrated, and model marking is shown for several of the reading selections. Definitions and uses of **direction words** are greatly expanded. Steps in **summary writing** are more clearly defined and demonstrated. In both old and new readings there is a stronger emphasis on **making connections** between new and previously read material. As in past editions, the last unit contains **excerpts from widely used college textbooks**. Three of the chapters—on the topics of education, business, and computers—are new, reflecting recent developments in the fields.

Several new reading selections appear. Stories about Afghan women learning, at last, to read, stories about a group of African refugees coming to America and having to learn everything—from how to flush a toilet to how to drive a car. There are more stories about cultural understanding and misunderstanding, a discussion of the issue of grade inflation—and more.

Why These Themes?

The five themes—education, culture, language, work, and controversial issues—were selected for five reasons. First, they are topics our students already know about; second, they are interesting—students like to read about them; third, connections can easily be drawn between the information in one section and that in another, as well as to what students read in newspapers and magazines; fourth, each theme lends itself to exposition in a variety of sources and styles—in each unit you will find selections from newspapers, magazines, essays, narratives, and textbooks; fifth, the content is presented in a way similar to that of college texts—for example, a history, psychology or business course. Thus the skills students learn here easily transfer to their other courses.

Many of the reading selections in this book are challenging. Students are insulted and demeaned when they are given materials they see as childish. They are challenged and engaged when presented with work they see as college level.

Writing and Reading

An important assumption of this book is that reading and writing are inextricably linked. Writing helps students become co-creators of the texts they read. In creating their own written versions and interpretations of, and reactions to, the content, they become masters of what they read. Writing about what they read allows them to monitor their own progress, to check whether they really understand what they read. It forces them to infer structure and make connections between the varying levels of information in the selection itself and their own background knowledge. In simple terms, writing can help readers make sense of what they read.

The book is also meant to be a "course model." Much as in a textbook for history, literature, sociology, or business, the reading selections contain information that students are expected to master; they read and study the selections with several goals similar to those of a college content course: learning vocabulary and information specific to a field, producing reaction and argumentation papers, and, finally, passing exams. The major difference is that, in the reading course, students are given more support from the textbook and from the teacher. The strategies and knowledge that students gain can transfer immediately to their primary concern—the concepts and processes of their content courses.

Organization

The readings in this book are not arranged in an artificial sequence of increasing complexity—does that happen in real life? Rather, they are arranged in a logical order one might expect in a college textbook. The ideas in each selection build upon those that came before. To provide the greatest support to students as they read these real and challenging materials, each unit contains the following features:

Thinking about the Theme. Each unit begins by inviting students to think about the subject they are about to read. There are pertinent quotations, a brief introduction to the theme, and some questions to engage students' interest. They are challenged to remember what they already know about the topic, to imagine some new aspect of the topic, and to think about how the topic affects them personally. In short, they are helped to "turn on the engines" of their minds and get ready to read.

Introduction to the Reading Selection. Each selection is briefly introduced—first to encourage students to activate the knowledge they already have about the specific subject at hand; second, in some cases, to provide them with crucial information they may lack; and finally, to stimulate their interest in what they are about to read.

Vocabulary. Because they are drawn from real sources, many of the selections contain fairly complex language. Students will be able to figure out many of the words from their context, but they will need the dictionary for many others. Several words from each reading are targeted, and students are asked to use a special vocabulary strategy to figure out its meaning: read the word in context, try to guess its meaning, evaluate the guess, and, finally, confirm the guess by checking the dictionary or other source. This strategy most closely resembles the way fluent readers naturally learn new words. Students are also encouraged to target other words they may find hard to understand and use the same strategy.

Guide Questions. The questions have several goals. First, they guide students to a basic understanding of the major ideas presented in the text. Thus some questions are aimed at the lowest levels of cognitive activity—knowledge and comprehension. Second, students are asked to apply the new ideas presented to their own experiences or to other situations they may read or hear about. Students then may be asked to synthesize the new information with ideas they had before or, where appropriate, evaluate the new ideas. The main ideas are generally attacked in the same sequence in which they appear, thus students discern text organization in a natural way.

Application. The themes addressed in this book are of high interest to most college students and lend themselves to application to students' own lives and experiences. Transferring information to novel situations is an excellent way to promote and demonstrate mastery of the content. Application questions are personal, interesting, and even enjoyable ways of stretching the mind.

Marking Text. Marking text is one of the most valuable learning strategies a student can use to master the ideas in his textbooks. Marking text means to underline important ideas and make notes in the margins to label those ideas and also write personal comments and questions. Marking text is explained in the special "Learning Strategies" section at the back of the book.

Learning Strategies. Students learn to identify, underline, and annotate. This ensures that they understand what they have read; it helps them to remember what they've learned, and is a big help when exam time comes along—they have their very own personalized study guide to study from—making test prep a breeze.

Writing. Students should be encouraged to see the connections among all the communication skills, but there is a special emphasis here on writing. The guide questions are meant to be answered in writing and discussed and argued about in class. Some of the readings naturally lend themselves to creative writing assignments, others to summary writing. Summary writing is explained and modeled in the special "Learning Strategies" section at the back of the book.

Collaborative Learning

At the end of Units One through Four are two reading selections with no attached exercises. Students are asked to work in small groups to master the information on their own. Following the model of the earlier chapters, students create their own exercises—vocabulary, guide questions, writing. This kind of collaborative activity reinforces active learning.

Special Projects

At the end of Units Two through Five are projects which will allow students to use the knowledge they've gained by reading the unit and to investigate topics independently.

Short Takes

Sprinkled through the book are short readings—little stories, examples, or explanations—related to ideas presented in the unit. They are included for their high interest, because they add to the topic, or just because they'll elicit a smile.

Unit 5

This unit, *Critical Reading and Thinking about Controversial Issues*, presents several topics of current controversy, interesting and stimulating issues for students to learn about and discuss. At the end of the unit, students are asked to work in groups to research and write an essay arguing for or against a position on a particular issue. This kind of concluding exercise calls on students to use higher level thinking skills, including synthesis, evaluation, and application, and encourages them to operate as fluent readers and thinkers.

Unit 6

This unit, *Reading and Thinking about Textbooks*, is different from the first five. Here, students tackle real college textbook chapters. Instructions guide them through previewing, reading, and marking the chapters. Then actual review, discussion, and exam questions are presented. Students can see what they will face in a college content course.

Please note that the answers to the exam questions in Unit Six can be found in the instructor's manual that accompanies this textbook.

Flexibility

An important feature of this book is its flexibility. Instructors may choose any theme they wish. It is not necessary to complete the first unit in order to understand the following units. If a particular reading selection does not appeal to the instructor, it can be skipped without any significant problem. (Note, however, that after the first reading in each unit, the directions for vocabulary and guide questions are abbreviated.) Learning strategies such as previewing, using direction words, marking text, summarizing, and others are taught in a separate section at the back of the book and may be presented at any point the teacher considers appropriate. Too often, textbooks are set up so rigidly that instructors have very little say in their own curricula and are forced to teach topics that bore them or that they don't feel confident teaching. This book offers a wide range of subjects that can be organized to suit the individual teacher and class. In addition, it offers both collaborative and independent activities that can be assigned to accommodate the learning styles of individual students.

Acknowledgments

Teaching is hard work. Writing textbooks is hard work. Sometimes there are not enough hours, not enough energy; sometimes the obstacles seem overwhelming. When disheartening feelings steal in, I think of my students. They come to class after working all day (or all night), after caring for their children, after cleaning the house and cooking the dinner. They struggle with the language, with exhausting class schedules, with the constant pressure of tests, and with financial worries I can only imagine. But come to class they do, and work they do, and succeed they do. If this book is of some small help to them, all the effort is more than worthwhile. They are my heroes.

A Note to the Student

Are you a good basketball player? Or a good singer? Can you cook well? Perhaps you are a computer whiz? Great! Now, answer this: How did you get so good at what you do? That's right—you practiced. No one ever got to be a good tennis player, golfer, swimmer, singer, or photographer without endless hours of practice.

Now here's another question: are you a good reader? Could you be better? How do you think you could become a better reader? Right again—by practicing. Reading is a skill like any other—you improve by practice. So, if you want to improve as a reader, you must read. But just like your tennis game or your computer skills, the practice can be fun. And the better you get, the more fun it is. If you get into the habit of reading, if you expand your vocabulary so that you are not running to the dictionary constantly, if you build enough background knowledge so that your reading is fast and fluent, then you will find that reading is not work, not a boring school requirement, but rather one of life's great pleasures.

In this book, you can read about many subjects that you are already familiar with—education, people and their customs, language, work, and careers, and some of the controversial issues of our time. You will find these topics interesting and entertaining to read. You will also learn things that will help you in the other courses you take in college and things that will be useful in your life.

How to Use This Book

Themes

This book is organized around five themes: (1) education, (2) culture, (3) language, (4) work and the world of business, and (5) controversial issues.

Thinking About

Each of the five thematic units of this book begins with a section called *Thinking About.* In this introductory section, ideas are presented to get you thinking about what you will be reading and studying. Often, you will find questions to stimulate you to remember what you already know about the subject the unit will cover. These questions will help you "turn on the engine" of your mind and get ready to learn.

Introduction

A short introduction precedes each reading selection. You should read it and answer any questions it contains. This will help you get ready to read.

The Reading

The reading selection itself then follows. You should read it straight through one time without stopping. Then go back and read it a second time, underlining important ideas, making notes and marking any words you don't know.

Vocabulary

Each reading selection is followed by a list of important words selected from the text and instructions to help you figure out their meanings. These words were chosen because they are crucial to your understanding of the selection.

Guide Questions

Each reading selection is also followed by guide questions. Their purpose is to "guide" your understanding of the text. Some of the questions are simple fact questions, meant to ensure that you understand the basic information the author is trying to get across. Other questions are more sophisticated and ask you to *analyze* information, to *synthesize* information, to *evaluate* information.

Application

Following the guide questions in each chapter are one or more questions that ask you to take some of the things you have learned and apply them to some different situation or to your own life. The ability to apply information to new situations is a high-level thinking skill. It proves that you truly comprehend what you have read.

Writing

Because reading and writing are closely linked, each chapter includes one or more writing assignments. Writing is the skill most college students need to develop.

Writing about what you have read is an interesting and valuable way to make the new information truly yours. As with all the features above, your instructor will select which exercises you are to do and will give you all the support you need to complete them successfully.

Preparation

With this book and with all your textbooks, it is important to get ready to read. A good way to do this is to preview the book before you consider any chapters you are assigned. To learn how to preview, turn to the back of the book and read the section titled "Learning Strategy I—Previewing." Then do the exercise "Previewing a Textbook" on page 417.

Just as you previewed the textbook, it is also helpful to preview each chapter. So before we discuss the first selection "What True Education Should Do," preview the reading by answering the questions on page 418, "Previewing a Chapter."

When you have finished previewing, return here and we'll take a look at the first unit.

The first unit focuses on the theme of *education*. This seems an appropriate topic to begin with—you may be in college for the first time or returning to school after some time away. Thinking about goals and how education can help achieve them is something all students ought to do. Read the selection called "Thinking about Education." It poses a number of questions. Think about them and try to answer them. Write your answers in a notebook. It is useful to discuss your answers with friends and classmates—this kind of give-and-take will help to clarify your reasons for being in school.

Now go to the first selection in Unit One, "What True Education Should Do" by Sydney Harris. Note the introduction before the reading selection. Always read these introductions and, if there are questions, answer them. This will help you prepare to read with understanding. In this case, we learn that the author compares students to both *sausages* and *oysters*. Does this seem strange to you? How can a student, a person, be like a sausage? What do you already know about sausages? Well, they are often tasty—no, that's probably not what the author is getting at. Just what is a sausage anyway? It is a casing stuffed with chopped meat and other filler. How could this be like a student? What could "stuff" a student? With this question in mind, read the selection.

Remember: Read the selection through quickly one time without worrying about unfamiliar words or whether you understand everything. This "once-over" will give you a good picture of what the selection is saying. Then return and read it carefully, noting any unfamiliar words. Mark any ideas that you think are important or that you want to ask your teacher about. Jot them down in the margin of the text. When you get to class, your notes will remind you to ask your teacher to explain.

When you finish reading the selection, go to the vocabulary section. Read the directions carefully. The directions are reproduced here:

Vocabulary

Directions: Find each of the **key words** in the reading selection. Study each word in its context and try to determine its meaning. Write what you think it means in the margin of the text, near the word. Then read over the sentence, mentally substituting your guess for the key word. Does the sentence still make sense? Does it retain its original meaning? If it does, you've probably figured out the key word correctly. In any case, confirm your guess by checking a dictionary or thesaurus.

If you take your meaning from a dictionary or thesaurus, be sure the definition includes words you already know and feel comfortable using. If it doesn't, you will be worse off than when you started—you will have begun with one word you didn't know and ended with *two* words you don't know!

Record the new words you've learned. (Note: After the first reading in each unit, instructions for the vocabulary section appear in abbreviated form.)

The key words in the chart were chosen because they are necessary to fully understand the chapter and also because they are words you will find valuable to have in your working vocabulary. Be sure to mark the words in the margin of the text. This marking of text is one of many ways you interact with the words on the page and thus become an active reader.

Let's do the first vocabulary word as an example. The word *animate* can be found in paragraph 1. Return to the paragraph and reread it:

> When most people think of the word *education*, they think of a pupil as a sort of animate sausage casing. Into this empty casing, the teachers are supposed to stuff "education."

The author is comparing a pupil to a "sort of animate sausage casing" into which teachers stuff education. What kind of sausage casing could "animate" be? Empty? A good guess—the sentence would then read ". . . they think of a pupil as a sort of [empty] sausage casing." Could be right. But then note the following sentence: "Into this empty casing, the teachers are supposed to stuff 'education.'" Why would the author repeat this notion of "empty"? No, *animate* probably means something else. If you are stuck, your next move should be to the dictionary, where you will find something like "alive" or "living" as meanings of *animate*. Does this make sense? Read the sentence again: ". . . they think of a pupil as a sort of [living] sausage casing." Sounds good, makes sense—it's probably right. Write it in the margin of the text. Then be sure to confirm your definition or synonym by looking up the word in a dictionary or thesaurus. When you get to class, check your meanings with your instructor. Then enter your correct words in the chart in the book.

If you find other words you don't know, follow the same procedure with them. A box at the end of the vocabulary chart says "Others?". Enter any other unfamiliar words you've found, and check their meanings in the same way you would the key words. For example, you may want to check the meaning of the word *cultivate* in paragraph 10.

Remember to write the meanings of all the new words in the margin of the text. When you finish the vocabulary section, your text should look something like this:

In the following reading selection, the author says students are usually treated as if they were sausages to be "stuffed" with information. He urges, instead, that students be treated as oysters—that is, something that education should "open" to reveal the riches within.

WHAT TRUE EDUCATION SHOULD DO

Sydney J. Harris

empty
living

1   When most people think of the word *education,* they think of a pupil as a sort of animate sausage casing. Into this empty casing, the teachers are supposed to stuff "education."

drawing out

2   But genuine education, as Socrates knew more than two thousand years ago, is not inserting the stuffings of information into a person, but rather eliciting knowledge from him; it is the drawing out of what is in the mind.

I think
elicit is
explained
here

3   "The most important part of education," once wrote William Ernest Hocking, the distinguished Harvard philosopher, "is this instruction of a man in what he has inside of him."

4   And as Edith Hamilton has reminded us, Socrates never said, "I know, learn from me." He said, rather, "Look into your own selves and find the spark of truth that God has put into every heart, and that only you can kindle to a flame."

5   In the dialogue called the "Meno," Socrates takes an ignorant slave boy, without a day of schooling, and proves to the amazed observers that the boy really "knows" geometry—because the principles and axioms of geometry are already in his mind, waiting to be called out.

useless

6   So many of the discussions and controversies about the content of education are futile and inconclusive because they are concerned with what should "go into" the student rather than with what should be taken out, and how this can best be done.

briefly
+
clearly

7   The college student who once said to me, after a lecture, "I spend so much time studying that I don't have a chance to learn anything" was succinctly expressing his dissatisfaction with the sausage-casing view of education.

8   He was being so stuffed with miscellaneous facts, with such an indigestible mass of material, that he had no time (and was given no encouragement) to draw on his own resources, to use his own mind for analyzing and synthesizing and evaluating this material.

not yet
developed

9   Education, to have any meaning beyond the purpose of creating well-informed dunces, must elicit from the pupil what is latent in every human being—the rules of reason, the inner knowledge of what is proper for men to be and do, the ability to sift evidence and come to conclusions that can generally be agreed to by all open minds and warm hearts.

make them
grow

10   Pupils are more like oysters than sausages. The job of teaching is not to stuff them and then seal them up, but to help them open and reveal the riches within. There are pearls in each of us, if only we knew how to cultivate them with ardor and persistence.

Key Word	Paragraph	Meaning
1. animate	1	*living/alive*
2. eliciting	2	*drawing out/bringing out*
3. futile	6	*useless*
4. succinctly	7	*briefly and clearly*
5. latent	9	*not yet developed/potential*
Others?		
cultivate	*10*	*make something grow*

When you have completed the vocabulary section, go on to the next section, *Guide Questions.* Again, read the directions carefully:

Guide Questions

Directions: The purpose of guide questions is to "guide" your analysis of the text. Your thoughtful answers will ensure that you understood the main ideas the author wanted to convey. Some questions require that you simply find the stated facts in the reading selection; others ask you to do more difficult tasks, such as paraphrasing information (putting the author's ideas into your own words), synthesizing several ideas into one complex thought, evaluating (making judgments about) an idea, or taking information from the reading and applying it to a new situation or to your own life.

Write answers to the questions in your notebook or on a separate sheet of paper if your instructor wishes to collect it. Your answers will form the basis of class discussion. (Note: After the first reading in each unit, directions for guide questions appear in abbreviated form.)

Notice that some of the questions are quite simple and straightforward, while others are much more demanding. Some may ask you to consider your own experience or knowledge of the world in answering, not just to consider ideas from the text.

Read the first guide question:

1. Write what you think is Harris's definition of a "true education."

No one sentence in the selection directly states Harris's definition of a true education, but it is certainly clear that he expects true learning to come from within the student rather than to be imposed by the teacher. The comments he makes in paragraph 9 begin to answer the question:

Education, to have any meaning beyond the purpose of creating well-informed dunces, must elicit from the pupil what is latent in every human being—the rules of reason, the inner knowledge of what is proper for men to be and do, the ability to sift evidence and come to conclusions that can generally be agreed to by all open minds and warm hearts.

But to properly answer, you should create your own conclusion of *what you think Harris would say if he were asked this question.* In other words, draw an inference based on all the information in the selection.

Complete the guide questions. Note that the third question asks you to take the ideas from the chapter and apply them to your own life.

Go on to the next section, called "Application." This section will vary with each selection. Here, you will be asked to think about the education you have received so far and discuss with your classmates what you would still like to learn.

Last is a section called "Writing." Here, you have two questions to consider. Your instructor will tell you whether to do one or both. In one, you are asked to write a short essay based on the ideas you generated in the Application section. In the second, you are asked to *react* to Harris's view of education. To *react* means to respond with your point of view and the reasons you feel the way you do.

Many of the questions in this book begin with special *direction words.* These are words you see frequently on college assignments and exams. Some examples are *cite, define, paraphrase, summarize,* and so on. It is important to respond accurately to these words. Turn to page 430 to study and practice using direction words.

Special Projects

At the end of Units Two through Five in the text you will find a special project. The goal of each project is to allow you to use the knowledge and skills you have gained from reading extensively about one particular topic.

Unit Six

Unit Six of the text, *Reading and Thinking about Textbooks,* is different from the first five parts. Here, you will work with actual excerpts from college textbooks. With these chapters, you can practice your reading and studying skills with "the real thing." An important feature of this section is the inclusion of test questions given to students who use these texts.

UNIT ONE

READING AND THINKING ABOUT EDUCATION

Think about the kind of world you want to live and work in. What do you need to know to build that world? Demand your teachers teach you that.

—Prince Kropotkin

In oneself lies the whole world, and if you know how to look and learn, then the door is there and the key is in your hand. Nobody on earth can give you either that key or the door to open, except yourself.

—J. Krishnamurti

Thinking about Education

As you begin this new chapter in your college career, take a moment to reflect. Why are you in college? You may answer that you are "getting an education." But what does the word *education* really mean? Do you envision learning lots of new facts, memorizing them, and repeating them back to the instructor on exams? Is the possession of a piece of paper (a degree or certificate) your only goal? Is education simply a stepping-stone to a well-paying job? Or is it the key to becoming a happier, more fulfilled person? Perhaps education means something different to you. Take a few moments to think about your definition of education before you read this section of the book.

In the following reading selection, the author says students are usually treated as if they were sausages to be "stuffed" with information. He urges, instead, that students be treated as oysters—that is, something that education should "open" to reveal the riches within.

WHAT TRUE EDUCATION SHOULD DO

Sydney J. Harris

1   When most people think of the word *education,* they think of a pupil as a sort of animate sausage casing. Into this empty casing, the teachers are supposed to stuff "education."

2   But genuine education, as Socrates knew more than two thousand years ago, is not inserting the stuffings of information into a person, but rather eliciting knowledge from him; it is the drawing out of what is in the mind.

3   "The most important part of education," once wrote William Ernest Hocking, the distinguished Harvard philosopher, "is this instruction of a man in what he has inside of him."

4   And as Edith Hamilton has reminded us, Socrates* never said, "I know, learn from me." He said, rather, "Look into your own selves and find the spark of truth that God has put into every heart, and that only you can kindle to a flame."

5   In the dialogue called the "Meno," Socrates takes an ignorant slave boy, without a day of schooling, and proves to the amazed observers that the boy really "knows" geometry—because the principles and axioms of geometry are already in his mind, waiting to be called out.

6   So many of the discussions and controversies about the content of education are futile and inconclusive because they are concerned with what should "go into" the student rather than with what should be taken out, and how this can best be done.

7   The college student who once said to me, after a lecture, "I spend so much time studying that I don't have a chance to learn anything" was succinctly expressing his dissatisfaction with the sausage-casing view of education.

8   He was being so stuffed with miscellaneous facts, with such an indigestible mass of material, that he had no time (and was given no encouragement) to draw on his own resources, to use his own mind for analyzing and synthesizing and evaluating this material.

---

*Socrates (469–399 BC) was a Greek philosopher who profoundly affected Western thought. Socrates believed that *discussion* and *self-examination* were the best ways to develop the mind and the spirit. He spent most of his life engaging in dialogue and argument with anyone who would listen and would engage in his question-and-answer form of teaching. He believed he could best serve his country as a teacher, encouraging the people of Athens to engage in self-examination and in tending to their souls.

Socrates believed that discussion was more important than writing, and so we have no written record of his thinking. Most of what we know about him we learn through the writings of his famous student, the philosopher Plato.

Education, to have any meaning beyond the purpose of creating well-informed dunces, must elicit from the pupil what is latent in every human being—the rules of reason, the inner knowledge of what is proper for men to be and do, the ability to sift evidence and come to conclusions that can generally be agreed to by all open minds and warm hearts.   9

Pupils are more like oysters than sausages. The job of teaching is not to stuff them and then seal them up, but to help them open and reveal the riches within. There are pearls in each of us, if only we knew how to cultivate them with ardor and persistence.   10

Vocabulary

Directions: Find each of the key words in the reading selection. Study each word in its context and try to determine its meaning. Write what you think it means in the margin of the text, near the word. Then read over the sentence, mentally substituting your guess for the key word. Does the sentence still make sense? Does it retain its original meaning? If it does, you've probably figured out the meaning of the key word correctly. In any case, confirm your guess by checking a dictionary or thesaurus.

If you take your meaning from a dictionary or thesaurus, be sure the definition includes words you already know and feel comfortable using. If it doesn't, you will be worse off than when you started—you will have begun with one word you didn't know and ended with *two* words you don't know!

Record the new words you've learned below.

Key Word	Paragraph	Meaning
1. animate	1	
2. eliciting	2	
3. futile	6	
4. succinctly	7	
5. latent	9	
Others?		

Guide Questions

Directions: The purpose of these questions is to guide your analysis of the text. Your thoughtful answers will ensure that you understood the main ideas the author wanted to convey. Some questions require that you simply find the stated facts in the reading selection; others ask you to do more difficult tasks, such as paraphrasing information (putting the author's ideas into your own words), synthesizing several ideas into one complex thought, evaluating (making judgments about) an idea, or taking information from the reading and applying it to a new situation or to your own life.

Write answers to the questions in your notebook or on a separate sheet of paper if your instructor wishes to collect it. Your answers will form the basis of class discussion.

1. Write what you think is Harris's definition of a "true education."
2. Explain what Harris means by his comparison of students to sausages and oysters.
3. Have teachers treated you like a sausage or like an oyster? Would a different comparison better describe your personal experience? Explain.

Application

Directions: Read the following observations by Alan Watts on what he feels would have been an ideal education for him; then answer the questions that follow.

It is perhaps idle to wonder what, from my present point of view, would have been an ideal education. If I could provide such a curriculum for my own children they, in their turn, might find it all a bore. But the fantasy of what I would have liked to learn as a child may be revealing, since I feel unequipped by education for problems that lie outside the cloistered, literary domain in which I am competent and at home. Looking back then, I would have arranged for myself to be taught survival techniques for both natural and urban wildernesses. I would want to have been instructed in self-hypnosis; in *aikido* (the esoteric and purely self-defensive style of judo); in elementary medicine; in sexual hygiene; in vegetable gardening; in astronomy, navigation, and sailing; in cookery and clothesmaking; in metalwork and carpentry; in drawing and painting; in printing and typography; in botany and biology; in optics and acoustics; in semantics and psychology; in mysticism and yoga; in electronics and mathematical fantasy; in drama and dancing; in singing and in playing an instrument by ear; in wandering; in advanced daydreaming; in prestidigitation; in techniques of escape from bondage; in disguise; in conversation with birds and beasts; in ventriloquism; in French and German conversation; in planetary history; in morphology; and in classical Chinese. Actually, the main thing left out of my education was a proper love for my own body, because one feared to cherish anything so obviously mortal and prone to sickness.

1. What do you think Watts does for a living? What evidence in the paragraph supports your guess?
2. When Watts says there is one area in which he feels competent and at home, what does he mean by "at home"?

3. In a small group, discuss the ideas addressed in this essay. Choose a director for your group whose job is to ask group members to discuss their own personal lists of: (1) the areas where they feel "competent and at home"; and (2) things they wish they had been taught. At the end of the discussion, each person should have two lists that can be developed into the essay described in writing assignment 1 below.

Writing

Directions: Choose one of the following assignments.

1. Write a short essay similar to the one by Alan Watts. In the first paragraph, describe, as Watts does, the areas in which you feel "competent." In the second paragraph, name and describe the things you wish you had been taught.
2. React to the argument presented in Sydney J. Harris's "What True Education Should Do." Do you agree or disagree with the author? Write one paragraph stating your reaction, giving reasons to support your opinion.

SHORT TAKE

Hope Helps

Just beginning college? Just sent your son or daughter off to school? Here is a scary statistic: there is approximately a 50% chance that you (or your beloved child) will drop out, most likely in the first year.

Is there anything that can help to improve your odds?

Research has shown that high hopes can make a difference. The students who scored "most hopeful" on tests tended to stay in school and to do better academically than those who described themselves as more pessimistic. In fact, students' perceptions of their likelihood of success were better predictors of success than standardized tests. Students with low expectations generally achieved averages of C while those with higher hopes averaged Bs.

More students who began with high hopes graduated at a higher rate than others.

So, look on the bright side—it couldn't hurt and may well help.

Mortimer Adler was well known for many things: he was the chairman of the Board of Editors of Encyclopaedia Britannica; *he was a prolific writer, perhaps most famous for his series of "Great Ideas" books in which he discussed six ideas—truth, beauty, equality, justice, goodness, and liberty—in ways that every reader could understand and enjoy. He originated the "Great Books" program in which people from all backgrounds met to read and discuss the classics. Dr. Adler was a philosopher who believed that "philosophy is everybody's business" and that a better understanding of great ideas is essential if we are to cope with the political, moral, and social issues that we all confront.*

Dr. Adler, who died in 2001 at the age of 98, wrote extensively about the joys of reading and the "how-to's" of reading. In this essay, which appeared in the Saturday Review of Literature *in 1940, he offers timeless advice on how to "own" a book.*

HOW TO MARK A BOOK

Mortimer Adler

1   You know you have to read "between the lines" to get the most out of anything. I want to persuade you to do something equally important in the course of your reading. I want to persuade you to "write between the lines." Unless you do, you are not likely to do the most efficient kind of reading.

2   I contend, quite bluntly, that marking up a book is not an act of mutilation but of love.

3   You shouldn't mark up a book which isn't yours. Librarians (or your friends) who lend you books expect you to keep them clean, and you should. If you decide that I am right about the usefulness of marking books, you will have to buy them. Most of the world's great books are available today, in reprint editions.

4   There are two ways in which one can own a book. The first is the property right you establish by paying for it, just as you pay for clothes and furniture. But this act of purchase is only the prelude to possession. Full ownership comes only when you have made it a part of yourself, and the best way to make yourself a part of it is by writing in it. An illustration may make the point clear. You buy a beefsteak and transfer it from the butcher's icebox to your own. But you do not own the beefsteak in the most important sense until you consume it and get it into your bloodstream. I am arguing that books, too, must be absorbed in your bloodstream to do you any good.

5   Confusion about what it means to *own* a book leads people to a false reverence for paper, binding, and type—a respect for the physical thing—the craft of the printer rather than the genius of the author. They forget that it is possible for a man to acquire the idea, to possess the beauty, which a great book contains, without staking his claim by pasting his bookplate inside the cover. Having a fine library doesn't prove that its owner has a mind enriched by books; it proves nothing more than that he, his father, or his wife, was rich enough to buy them.

6   There are three kinds of book owners. The first has all the standard sets and best-sellers—unread, untouched. (This deluded individual owns woodpulp and ink, not books.) The second has a great many books—a few of them read

through, most of them dipped into, but all of them as clean and shiny as the day they were bought. (This person would probably like to make books his own, but is restrained by a false respect for their physical appearance.) The third has a few books or many—every one of them dog-eared and dilapidated, shaken and loosened by continual use, marked and scribbled in from front to back. (This man owns books.)

Is it false respect, you may ask, to preserve intact and unblemished a beautifully printed book, an elegantly bound edition? Of course not. I'd no more scribble all over a first edition of *Paradise Lost* than I'd give my baby a set of crayons and an original Rembrandt! I wouldn't mark up a painting or a statue. Its soul, so to speak, is inseparable from its body. And the beauty of a rare edition or of a richly manufactured volume is like that of a painting or a statue.

But the soul of a book *can* be separated from its body. A book is more like the score of a piece of music than it is like a painting. No great musician confuses a symphony with the printed sheets of music. Arturo Toscanini reveres Brahms, but Toscanini's score of the C-minor Symphony is so thoroughly marked up that no one but the maestro himself can read it. The reason why a great conductor makes notations on his musical scores—marks them up again and again each time he returns to study them—is the reason why you should mark your books. If your respect for magnificent binding or typography gets in the way, buy yourself a cheap edition and pay your respects to the author.

Why is marking up a book indispensable to reading? First, it keeps you awake. (And I don't mean merely conscious; I mean wide awake.) In the second place, reading, if it is active, is thinking, and thinking tends to express itself in words, spoken or written. The marked book is usually the thought-through book. Finally, writing helps you remember the thoughts you had, or the thoughts the author expressed. Let me develop these three points.

If reading is to accomplish anything more than passing time, it must be active. You can't let your eyes glide across the lines of a book and come up with an understanding of what you have read. Now an ordinary piece of light fiction, like say, *Gone with the Wind,* doesn't require the most active kind of reading. The books you read for pleasure can be read in a state of relaxation, and nothing is lost. But a great book, rich in ideas and beauty, a book that raises and tries to answer great fundamental questions, demands the most active reading of which you are capable. You don't absorb the ideas of John Dewey the way you absorb the crooning of Mr. Vallee. You have to reach for them. That you cannot do while you're asleep.

If, when you've finished reading a book, the pages are filled with your notes, you know that you read actively. The most famous active reader of great books I know is President Hutchins, of the University of Chicago. He also has the hardest schedule of business activities of any man I know. He invariably reads with a pencil, and sometimes, when he picks up a book and pencil in the evening, he finds himself, instead of making intelligent notes, drawing what he calls "caviar factories" on the margins. When that happens, he puts the book down. He knows he's too tired to read, and he's just wasting time.

12   But, you may ask, why is writing necessary? Well, the physical act of writing, with your own hand, brings words and sentences more sharply before your mind and preserves them better in your memory. To set down your reaction to important words and sentences you have read, and the questions they have raised in your mind, is to preserve those reactions and sharpen those questions.

13   Even if you wrote on a scratch pad, and threw the paper away when you had finished writing, your grasp of the book would be surer. But you don't have to throw the paper away. The margins (top and bottom, as well as side), the endpapers, the very space between the lines, are all available. They aren't sacred. And, best of all, your marks and notes become an integral part of the book and stay there forever. You can pick up the book the following week or year, and there are all your points of agreement, disagreement, doubt, and inquiry. It's like resuming an interrupted conversation with the advantage of being able to pick up where you left off.

14   And that is exactly what reading a book should be: a conversation between you and the author. Presumably, he knows more about the subject than you do; naturally, you'll have the proper humility as you approach him. But don't let anybody tell you that a reader is supposed to be solely on the receiving end. Understanding is a two-way operation; learning doesn't consist in being an empty receptacle. The learner has to question himself and question the teacher. He even has to argue with the teacher, once he understands what the teacher is saying. And marking a book is literally an expression of your differences, or agreements of opinion, with the author.

15   There are all kinds of devices for marking a book intelligently and fruitfully. Here's the way I do it:

1. *Underlining:* of major points, of important or forceful statements.
2. *Vertical lines at the margin:* to emphasize a statement already underlined.
3. *Star, asterisk, or other doo-dad at the margin:* to be used sparingly, to emphasize the ten or twenty most important statements in the book. (You may want to fold the bottom corner of each page on which you use such marks. It won't hurt the sturdy paper on which most modern books are printed, and you will be able to take the book off the shelf at any time and, by opening it at the folded-corner page, refresh your recollection of the book.)
4. *Numbers in the margin:* to indicate the sequence of points the author makes in developing a single argument.
5. *Numbers of other pages in the margin:* to indicate where else in the book the author made points relevant to the point marked; to tie up the ideas in a book, which, though they may be separated by many pages, belong together.
6. *Circling of key words or phrases.*
7. *Writing in the margin, or at the top or bottom of the page, for the sake of:* recording questions (and perhaps answers) that a passage raised in your mind; reducing a complicated discussion to a simple statement; recording the sequence

of major points right through the books. I use the end-papers at the back of the book to make a personal index of the author's points in the order of their appearance.

The front end-papers are, to me, the most important. Some people reserve   16
them for a fancy bookplate. I reserve them for fancy thinking. After I have finished reading the book and making my personal index on the back end-papers, I turn to the front and try to outline the book, not page by page, or point by point (I've already done that at the back), but as an integrated structure, with a basic unity and an order of parts. This outline is, to me, the measure of my understanding of the work.

If you're a die-hard anti-book-marker, you may object that the margins, the   17
space between the lines, and the end-papers don't give you room enough. All right. How about using a scratch pad slightly smaller than the page-size of the book—so that the edges of the sheets won't protrude? Make your index, outlines, and even your notes on the pad, and then insert these sheets permanently inside the front and back covers of the book.

Or, you may say that this business of marking books is going to slow up   18
your reading. It probably will. That's one of the reasons for doing it. Most of us have been taken in by the notion that speed of reading is a measure of our intelligence. There is no such thing as the right speed for intelligent reading. Some things should be read quickly and effortlessly, and some should be read slowly and even laboriously. The sign of intelligence in reading is the ability to read different things according to their worth. In the case of good books, the point is not to see how many of them you can get through, but rather how many can get through you—how many you can make your own. A few friends are better than a thousand acquaintances. If this be your aim, as it should be, you will not be impatient if it takes more time and effort to read a great book than it does a newspaper.

You may have one final objection to marking books. You can't lend them   19
to your friends because nobody else can read them without being distracted by your notes. Furthermore, you won't want to lend them because a marked copy is a kind of intellectual diary, and lending it is almost like giving your mind away.

If your friend wishes to read your *Plutarch's Lives,* Shakespeare, or *The Feder-*   20
alist Papers, tell him gently but firmly to buy a copy. You will lend him your car or your coat—but your books are as much a part of you as your head or your heart.

Vocabulary
Directions: Locate each of the key words in the reading selection. Try to figure out each word's meaning by using the context. Confirm your guess by checking the dictionary or thesaurus. Write the meanings of the words in the margin of the text. Then record the meanings in the following chart.

Key Word	Paragraph	Meaning
1. mutilation	2	
2. intact	7	
3. indispensable	9	
4. invariably	11	
5. die-hard	17	
Others?		

Guide Questions

Directions: These questions will guide your understanding of what you have read. Write your answers in your notebook, or on a separate sheet of paper if your instructor wishes to collect it. Your answers to these questions will be the basis of class discussion.

1. Cite two ways to "own" a book, according to Adler.
2. List the three types of book owners.
3. Explain Adler's statement: "the soul of a book *can* be separated from its body."
4. Why is marking indispensable?
5. React to Adler's statement: "Reading a book should be a conversation between you and the author."
6. Which of the seven devices for marking a book do you think would be valuable to you?
7. Explain why Adler says that even though marking books will slow up your reading, that's ok.
8. Explain how you would mark these books differently:
   a. a romance novel
   b. a psychology textbook
   c. a "how-to" manual for using a digital camera
   d. a philosophy textbook
9. Assume you are still a die-hard anti-book marker. Can you think of any other ways to get the benefits of marking text? (Hint: Think *Post-Its.*)

Application

Use the tips in Adler's essay to mark his essay.

Making Connections
Consider the first reading selection in this unit, "What True Education Should Do" by Sydney J. Harris (pages 2–3). Which do you think Mortimer Adler would support—the "sausage" or "oyster" view of education?

SHORT TAKE

The First Book

Rita Dove

Open it.

Go ahead, it won't bite.
Well, maybe a little.

More a nip, like. A tingle.
It's pleasurable, really.

You see, it keeps on opening.
You may fall in.

Sure, it's hard to get started;
Remember learning to use

Knife and fork? Dig in:
You'll never reach bottom.

It's not like it's the end of the world—
Just the world as you think

You know it.

Richard Wright's story of his life caused a sensation when it was first published in 1937. Until then it had been unthinkable that a black man would dare to tell the truth about the poverty, hunger, fear, and hatred that dominated the lives of black Americans in the racially segregated South. In his book, Wright describes his own reaction to the brutality that surrounded him. He tells how he learned to hate, lie, steal, drink, and perhaps worst of all, to pity himself.

Eventually, through reading, Wright learned to understand himself and his situation. Through his writing, he helped the world understand the cruel society bred by racism.

BLACK BOY

Richard Wright

1 I entered the library as I had always done when on errands for whites, but I felt that I would somehow slip up and betray myself. I doffed my hat, stood a respectful distance from the desk, looked as unbookish as possible, and waited for the white patrons to be taken care of. When the desk was clear of people, I still waited. The white librarian looked at me.

2 "What do you want, boy?"

3 As though I did not possess the power of speech, I stepped forward and simply handed her the forged note, not parting my lips.

4 "What books by Mencken does he want?" she asked.

5 "I don't know, ma'am," I said, avoiding her eyes.

6 "Who gave you this card?"

7 "Mr. Falk," I said.

8 "Where is he?"

9 "He's at work, at the M——— Optical Company," I said. "I've been in here for him before."

10 "I remember," the woman said. "But he never wrote notes like this."

11 Oh, God, she's suspicious. Perhaps she would not let me have the books? If she had turned her back at that moment, I would have ducked out the door and never gone back. Then I thought of a bold idea.

12 "You can call him up, ma'am," I said, my heart pounding.

13 "You're not using these books, are you?" she asked pointedly.

14 "Oh, no, ma'am. I can't read."

15 "I don't know what he wants by Mencken," she said under her breath.

16 I knew now that I had won; she was thinking of other things and the race question had gone out of her mind. She went to the shelves. Once or twice she looked over her shoulder at me, as though she was still doubtful. Finally she came forward with two books in her hand.

17 "I'm sending him two books," she said. "But tell Mr. Falk to come in next time, or send me the names of the books he wants. I don't know what he wants to read."

18 I said nothing. She stamped the card and handed me the books. Not daring to glance at them, I went out of the library, fearing that the woman would call

me back for further questioning. A block away from the library I opened one of the books and read a title: *A Book of Prefaces*. I was nearing my nineteenth birthday and I did not know how to pronounce the word "preface." I thumbed the pages and saw strange words and strange names. I shook my head, disappointed. I looked at the other book; it was called *Prejudices*. I knew what that word meant; I had heard it all my life. And right off I was on guard against Mencken's books. Why would a man want to call a book *Prejudices*? The word was so stained with all my memories of racial hate that I could not conceive of anybody using it for a title. Perhaps I had made a mistake about Mencken? A man who had prejudices must be wrong.

When I showed the books to Mr. Falk, he looked at me and frowned.   19

"That librarian might telephone you," I warned him.   20

"That's all right," he said. "But when you're through reading those books, I want you to tell me what you get out of them."   21

That night in my rented room, while letting the hot water run over my can of pork and beans in the sink, I opened *A Book of Prefaces* and began to read. I was jarred and shocked by the style, the clear, clean, sweeping sentences. Why did he write like that? And how did one write like that? I pictured the man as a raging demon, slashing with his pen, consumed with hate, denouncing everything American, extolling everything European or German, laughing at the weaknesses of people, mocking God, authority. What was this? I stood up, trying to realize what reality lay behind the meaning of the words . . . Yes, this man was fighting, fighting with words. He was using words as a weapon, using them as one would use a club. Could words be weapons? Well, yes, for here they were. Then, maybe, perhaps, I could use them as a weapon? No. It frightened me. I read on and what amazed me was not what he said, but how on earth anybody had the courage to say it.   22

Occasionally I glanced up to reassure myself that I was alone in the room. Who were these men about whom Mencken was talking so passionately? Who was Anatole France? Joseph Conrad? Sinclair Lewis, Sherwood Anderson, Dostoyevsky, George Moore, Gustave Flaubert, Maupassant, Tolstoy, Frank Harris, Mark Twain, Thomas Hardy, Arnold Bennett, Stephen Crane, Zola, Norris, Gorky, Bergson, Ibsen, Balzac, Bernard Shaw, Dumas, Poe, Thomas Mann, O. Henry, Dreiser, H. G. Wells, Gogol, T. S. Eliot, Gide, Baudelaire, Edgar Lee Masters, Stendhal, Turgenev, Huneker, Nietzsche, and scores of others? Were these men real? Did they exist or had they existed? And how did one pronounce their names?   23

I ran across many words whose meanings I did not know, and I either looked them up in a dictionary or, before I had a chance to do that, encountered the word in a context that made its meaning clear. But what strange world was this? I concluded the book with the conviction that I had somehow overlooked something terribly important in life. I had once tried to write, had once reveled in feeling, had let my crude imagination roam, but the impulse to dream had been slowly beaten out of me by experience. Now it surged up again and I hungered for books, new ways of looking and seeing. It was not a matter of believing or disbelieving   24 what I read, but of feeling something new, of being affected by something that made the look of the world different.

25   As dawn broke I ate my pork and beans, feeling dopey, sleepy. I went to work, but the mood of the book would not die; it lingered, coloring everything I saw, heard, did. I now felt that I knew what the white men were feeling. Merely because I had read a book that had spoken of how they lived and thought, I identified myself with that book. I felt vaguely guilty. Would I, filled with bookish notions, act in a manner that would make the whites dislike me?

26   I forged more notes and my trips to the library became frequent. Reading grew into a passion. My first serious novel was Sinclair Lewis's *Main Street.* It made me see my boss, Mr. Gerald, and identify him as an American type. I would smile when I saw him lugging his golf bags into the office. I had always felt a vast distance separating me from the boss, and now I felt closer to him, that I could feel the very limits of his narrow life. And this had happened because I had read a novel about a mythical man called George F. Babbitt.

27   The plots and stories in the novels did not interest me so much as the point of view revealed. I gave myself over to each novel without reserve, without trying to criticize it; it was enough for me to see and feel something different. And for me, everything was something different. Reading was like a drug, a dope. The novels created moods in which I lived for days. But I could not conquer my sense of guilt, my feeling that the white men around me knew that I was changing, that I had begun to regard them differently.

28   Whenever I brought a book to the job, I wrapped it in newspaper—a habit that was to persist for years in other cities and under other circumstances. But some of the white men pried into my packages when I was absent and they questioned me.

29   "Boy, what are you reading those books for?"

30   "Oh, I don't know, sir."

31   "That's deep stuff you're reading, boy."

32   "I'm just killing time, sir."

33   "You'll addle your brains if you don't watch out."

34   I read Dreiser's *Jennie Gerhardt* and *Sister Carrie* and they revived in me a vivid sense of my mother's suffering; I was overwhelmed. I grew silent, wondering about the life around me. It would have been impossible for me to have told anyone what I derived from these novels, for it was nothing less than a sense of life itself. All my life had shaped me for the realism, the naturalism of the modern novel, and I could not read enough of them.

35   Steeped in new moods and ideas, I bought a ream of paper and tried to write; but nothing would come, or what did come was flat beyond telling. I discovered that more than desire and feeling were necessary to write and I dropped the idea. Yet I still wondered how it was possible to know people sufficiently to write about them? Could I ever learn about life and people? To me, with my vast ignorance, my Jim Crow station in life, it seemed a task impossible of achievement. I now knew what being a Negro meant. I could endure the hunger. I had learned to live with hate. But to feel that there were feelings denied me, that the very

breath of life itself was beyond my reach, that more than anything else, hurt, wounded me. I had a new hunger.

In buoying me up, reading also cast me down, made me see what was possible, what I had missed. My tension returned, new, terrible, bitter, surging, almost too great to be contained. I no longer *felt* that the world about me was hostile, killing; I *knew* it. A million times I asked myself what I could do to save myself, and there were no answers. I seemed forever condemned, ringed by walls.   36

I did not discuss my reading with Mr. Falk, who had lent me his library card; it would have meant talking about myself and that would have been too painful. I smiled each day, fighting desperately to maintain my old behavior, to keep my disposition seemingly sunny. But some of the white men discerned that I had begun to brood.   37

"Wake up there, boy!" Mr. Olin said one day.   38

"Sir!" I answered for the lack of a better word.   39

"You act like you've stolen something," he said.   40

I laughed in the way I knew he expected me to laugh, but I resolved to be more conscious of myself, to watch my every act, to guard and hide the new knowledge that was dawning within me.   41

If I went north, would it be possible for me to build a new life then? But how could a man build a life upon vague, unformed yearnings? I wanted to write and I did not even know the English language. I bought English grammars and found them dull. I felt that I was getting a better sense of the language from novels than from grammars. I read hard, discarding a writer as soon as I felt that I had grasped his point of view. At night the printed page stood before my eyes in sleep.   42

Mrs. Moss, my landlady, asked me one Sunday morning: 43

"Son, what is this you keep on reading?"   44

"Oh, nothing. Just novels."   45

"What you get out of 'em?"   46

"I'm just killing time," I said.   47

"I hope you know your own mind," she said in a tone which implied that she doubted if I had a mind.   48

I knew of no Negroes who read the books I liked and I wondered if any Negroes ever thought of them. I knew that there were Negro doctors, lawyers, newspapermen, but I never saw any of them. When I read a Negro newspaper I never caught the faintest echo of my preoccupation in its pages. I felt trapped and occasionally, for a few days, I would stop reading. But a vague hunger would come over me for books, books that opened up new avenues of feeling and seeing, and again I would forge another note to the white librarian. Again I would read and wonder as only the naïve and unlettered can read and wonder, feeling that I carried a secret, criminal burden about with me each day.   49

Vocabulary

Directions: Locate each of the key words in the reading selection. Try to figure out each word's meaning by using the context. Confirm your guess by checking the dictionary or thesaurus. Write the meanings of the words in the margin of the text. Then record the meanings in the chart below.

Key Word	Paragraph	Meaning
1. forged	3	
2. extolling	22	
3. reveled	24	
4. steeped	35	
5. buoying	36	
6. brood	37	
7. yearnings	42	
Others?		

Guide Questions

Directions: These questions will guide your understanding of what you have read. Write your answers in your notebook or on a separate sheet of paper if your instructor wishes to collect it. Your answers to these questions will be the basis of class discussion.

1. Jim Crow laws are not defined, but merely alluded to, in this story.
   a. Go through the story and find examples of unequal treatment of black Americans in the South during the first few decades of the twentieth century.
   b. Go to your encyclopedia or use the Internet to find a complete description of Jim Crow laws.
2. Blacks were forbidden to use public libraries, yet young Wright managed to get the books he so desperately wanted. How did he do this?
3. What can we infer about Mr. Falk and his attitude toward Wright's desire to read?
4. Wright managed to take out some books by H. L. Mencken. What effect did Mencken's words have on him?
5. In paragraph 23, Wright says, "Occasionally I glanced up to reassure myself that I was alone in the room." Why does he say this?

6. On a number of occasions, Wright refers to his "guilt" (see paragraph 27, for example). What does he feel guilty about?
7. In paragraph 35, Wright says, "I now knew what being a Negro meant." What do you think it meant to him?

Application

Wright makes extraordinary use of figurative language, for example in paragraph 22: "slashing with his pen," and "Could words be weapons?" How many other powerful examples of figurative language can you find in the story? Go through the story and note all the examples you find. Then compare your examples with those of your classmates. What effect does the use of this kind of language have on the reader? (Figurative language is introduced and explained on pages 434–436, Learning Strategy VI.)

Writing

Directions: Choose one of the assignments below.

1. Wright feels that he was "saved" by reading and writing. What might have happened to him if he had not discovered books? Write two or three paragraphs.
2. Imagine if the Richard Wright in this story were nineteen years old today. How would his life be different? Write two or three paragraphs.

SHORT TAKE

Examples of "Jim Crow" Laws

From the 1880s into the 1960s, a majority of American states enforced segregation through "Jim Crow" laws (so called after a black character in minstrel shows). From Delaware to California, and from North Dakota to Texas, many states (and cities, too) could impose legal punishments on people for associating with members of another race. The most common types of laws forbade intermarriage and ordered business owners and public institutions to keep their black and white clientele separated.

Here is a sampling of laws from various states.

Buses All passenger stations in this state operated by any motor transportation company shall have separate waiting rooms or space and separate ticket windows for the white and colored races. **Alabama**

Restaurants It shall be unlawful to conduct a restaurant or other place for the serving of food in the city, at which white and colored people are served in the same room, unless such white and colored persons are effectually separated by a solid partition extending from the floor upward to a distance of seven feet or higher, and unless a separate entrance from the street is provided for each compartment. **Alabama**

Toilet Facilities, Male Every employer of white or negro males shall provide for such white or negro males reasonably accessible and separate toilet facilities. **Alabama**

Intermarriage The marriage of a person of Caucasian blood with a negro, Mongolian, Malay, or Hindu shall be null and void. **Arizona**

Intermarriage All marriages between a white person and a negro, or between a white person and a person of negro descent to the fourth generation inclusive, are hereby forever prohibited. **Florida**

Education The schools for white children and the schools for negro children shall be conducted separately. **Florida**

Burial The officer in charge shall not bury, or allow to be buried, any colored persons upon ground set apart or used for the burial of white persons. **Georgia**

Amateur Baseball It shall be unlawful for any amateur white baseball team to play baseball on any vacant lot or baseball diamond within two blocks of a playground devoted to the Negro race, and it shall be unlawful for any amateur colored baseball team to play baseball in any vacant lot or baseball diamond within two blocks of any playground devoted to the white race. **Georgia**

Circus Tickets All circuses, shows, and tent exhibitions, to which the attendance of more than one race is invited or expected to attend shall provide for the convenience of its patrons not less than two ticket offices with individual ticket sellers, and not less than two entrances to the said performance, with individual ticket takers and receivers, and in the case of outside or tent performances, the said ticket offices shall not be less than twenty-five (25) feet apart. **Louisiana**

Promotion of Equality Any person . . . who shall be guilty of printing, publishing or circulating printed, typewritten, or written matter urging or presenting for public acceptance, or general information, arguments or suggestions in favor of social equality or of intermarriage between whites and negroes, shall be guilty of a misdemeanor and subject to fine not exceeding five hundred (500.00) dollars or imprisonment not exceeding six (6) months or both. **Mississippi**

Libraries The state librarian is directed to fit up and maintain a separate place for the use of the colored people who may come to the library for the purpose of reading books or periodicals. **North Carolina**

Lunch Counters No persons, firms, or corporations, who or which furnish meals to passengers at station restaurants or station eating houses, in times limited by common carriers of said passengers, shall furnish said meals to white and colored passengers in the same room, or at the same table, or at the same counter. **South Carolina**

Grace Paley (1922–   ) has long been one of America's most beloved writers. Best-known for her short stories, she has also written poetry, criticism and commentary. She has led what she calls "the push-pull life" of a wife, mother, professor, peace activist, and, of course, writer. Many call her a "great American writer" but as Jamaica Kincaid says, that is " . . . too specific; she is just simply great."

As you read this profoundly moving story, try to appreciate its simple, graceful language.

TRAVELING

Grace Paley

My mother and sister were traveling south. The year was 1927. They had begun their journey in New York. They were going to visit my brother, who was studying in the South Medical College of Virginia. Their bus was an express and had stopped only in Philadelphia, Wilmington, and now Washington. Here, the darker people who had gotten on in Philadelphia or New York rose from their seats, put their bags and boxes together, and moved to the back of the bus. People who boarded in Washington knew where to seat themselves. My mother had heard that something like this would happen. My sister had heard of it, too. They had not lived in it. This reorganization of passengers by color happened in silence. My mother and sister remained in their seats, which were about three-quarters of the way back.   1

When everyone was settled, the bus driver began to collect tickets. My sister saw him coming. She pinched my mother: Ma! Look! Of course, my mother saw him, too. What frightened my sister was the quietness. The white people in front, the black people in back—silent.   2

The driver sighed, said, You can't sit here, ma'am. It's for them waving over his shoulder at the Negroes, among whom they were now sitting. Move, please.   3

My mother said, No.   4

He said, You don't understand, ma'am. It's against the law. You have to move to the front.   5

My mother said, No.   6

When I first tried to write this scene, I imagined my mother saying, That's all right, mister, we're comfortable. I can't change my seat every minute. I read this invention to my sister. She said it was nothing like that. My mother did not try to be friendly or pretend innocence. While my sister trembled in the silence, my mother said, for the third time, quietly, No.   7

Somehow finally, they were in Richmond. There was my brother in school among so many American boys. After hugs and my mother's anxious looks at her young son, my sister said, Vic, you know what Mama did?   8

My brother remembers thinking, What? Oh! She wouldn't move? He had a classmate, a Jewish boy like himself, but from Virginia, who had had a public confrontation with a Negro man. He had punched that man hard, knocked him down. My brother couldn't believe it. He was stunned. He couldn't imagine a   9

Jewish boy wanting to knock anyone down. He had never wanted to. But he thought, looking back, that he had been set down to work and study in a nearly foreign place and had to get used to it. Then he told me about the Second World War, when the disgrace of black soldiers being forced to sit behind white German POWs shook him. Shamed him.

10   About fifteen years later, in 1943, in early summer, I rode the bus for about three days from New York to Miami Beach, where my husband in sweaty fatigues, along with hundreds of other boys, was trudging up and down the streets and beaches to prepare themselves for war.

11   By late afternoon of the second long day, we were well into the South, beyond Richmond, maybe South Carolina or Georgia. My excitement about travel in the wide world was damaged a little by a sudden fear that I might not recognize Jess or he, me. We hadn't seen each other for two months. I took a photograph out of my pocket; yes, I would know him.

12   I had been sleeping waking reading writing dozing waking. So many hours, the movement of the passengers was something like a tide that sometimes ebbed and now seemed to be noisily rising. I opened my eyes to the sound of new people brushing past my aisle seat. And looked up to see a colored woman holding a large sleeping baby, who with the heaviness of sleep, his arms so tight around her neck, seemed to be pulling her head down. I looked around and noticed that I was in the last white row. The press of travelers had made it impossible for her to move farther back. She seemed so tired and I had been sitting and sitting for a day and a half at least. Not thinking, or maybe refusing to think, I offered her my seat.

13   She looked to the right and left as well as she could. Softly said Oh no. I became fully awake. A white man was standing right beside her, but on the other side of the invisible absolute racial border. Of course, she couldn't accept my seat. Her sleeping child hung mercilessly from her neck. She shifted a little to balance the burden. She whispered to herself, Oh, I just don't know. So I said. Well, at least give me the baby. First, she turned, barely looking at the man beside her. He made no move. So, to my surprise, but obviously out of sheer exhaustion, she disengaged the child from her body and placed him on my lap. He was deep in child-sleep. He stirred, but not enough to bother himself or me. I liked holding him, aligning him along my twenty-year-old young woman's shape. I thought ahead to that holding, that breathing together that would happen in my life if this war would ever end.

14   I was so comfortable under his nice weight. I closed my eyes for a couple of minutes, but suddenly opened them to look up into the face of a white man talking. In a loud voice he addressed me. Lady, I wouldn't of touched that thing with a meat hook.

15   I thought, Oh, this world will end in ice. I could do nothing but look straight into his eyes. I did not look away from him. Then I held that boy a little tighter, kissed his curly head, pressed him even closer so that he began to squirm. So sleepy, he reshaped himself inside my arms. His mother tried to narrow herself

away from the dangerous border, too frightened at first to move at all. After a couple of minutes, she leaned forward a little, placed her hand on the baby's head, and held it there until the next stop. I couldn't look up into her mother face.

I write this remembrance more than fifty years later. I look back at that   16
mother and child. How young she is. Her hand on his head is quite small, though she tries by spreading her fingers wide to hide him from the white man. But the child I'm holding, his little face as he turns toward me, is the brown face of my own grandson, my daughter's boy, the open mouth of the sleeper, the full lips, the thick little body of a child who runs wildly from one end of the yard to the other, leaps from dangerous heights with certain experienced caution, muscling his body, his mind, for coming realities.

Vocabulary

Directions: Locate each of the key words in the reading selection. Try to figure out each word's meaning by using the context. Confirm your guess by checking the dictionary or thesaurus. Write the meanings of the words in the margin of the text. Then record the meanings in the chart below.

Key Word	Paragraph	Meaning
1. fatigues	10	
2. trudging	10	
3. ebbed	12	

Guide Questions

Directions: These questions will guide your understanding of what you have read. Write your answers in your notebook or on a separate sheet of paper if your instructor wishes to collect it. Your answers to these questions will be the basis of class discussion.

1. Paley recounts several anecdotes in "Traveling." What happened in each story? Who were the characters in each?

   a. The mother's story:
   b. The brother's story:
   c. The young wife's story:
   d. The grandmother's story:

2. Interpret the last sentence of "Traveling," especially the phrase "muscling his body, his mind, for coming realities."

Application

In paragraph 15, Paley writes, "I thought Oh, this world will end in ice." This is an allusion (a reference) to the famous poem by Robert Frost called *Fire and Ice*:

> Some say the world will end in fire,
> Some say in ice.
> From what I've tasted of desire
> I hold with those who favor fire.
> But if it had to perish twice,
> I think I know enough of hate
> To know that for destruction ice
> Is also great
> And would suffice.

What do you think Frost is saying in his poem? Do you think Paley shares Frost's meaning when she says, " . . . this world will end in ice"?

Making Connections

Make a connection between "Traveling" and "Black Boy." Both of the selections are narratives. Review the characteristics of a narrative on page 419. Then compare and contrast the two stories by analyzing the characters, setting, events, tone, and relevance of each story.

Barbara Jordan was born in Texas in 1936 and died there in 1996. She began her life in the largest black ghetto in the biggest state of the union. She graduated magna cum laude from Texas Southern University and went on to Boston University Law School. She was the first woman and the only black member of the Texas State Senate; she was the first woman and the only black member of the U.S. Congress from Texas; she was the first woman and the only black member of Congress from the entire South. To quote Molly Ivins's essay on Jordan, which appeared in The New York Times, *"The degree of prejudice she had to overcome by intelligence and sheer force of personality is impossible to overestimate. She wasn't just black and female: she was homely, she was heavy, and she was dark black. When she first came to the Texas Senate, it was considered a great joke to bring racist friends to the gallery when B. J. was due to speak. They would no sooner gasp, 'Who is that nigger?' than she would open her mouth and out would roll language Lincoln would have appreciated. Her personal dignity was so substantial even admirers hesitated to approach her. No one will ever know how lonely she was at the beginning." Jordan won national acclaim for her intelligence and oratory during the House Judiciary Committee's proceedings to impeach President Richard Nixon in 1974 and later for her keynote speech to the Democratic National Convention in 1976. She retired from Congress after three terms and became an immensely popular and respected teacher at the University of Texas. In 1992, Jordan returned to the podium of the Democratic National Convention and electrified the nation with her speech. She spoke of her fierce passion for her country and for its ideals. She proclaimed, "My faith in the Constitution is whole, it is complete, it is total." To quote Ivins again, "She sounded like God." Suffering from multiple sclerosis and other ailments, Barbara Jordan died on January 17, 1996. President Clinton called her death the "loss of a national treasure." Today, she is the first and only black woman buried in the Texas State Cemetery.*

In this excerpt from her autobiography, Jordan describes learning to "think and read and understand and reason."

BECOMING EDUCATED

Barbara Jordan

So I was at Boston University in this new and strange and different world, and it occurred to me that if I was going to succeed at this strange new adventure, I would have to read longer and more thoroughly than my colleagues at law school had to read. I felt that, in order to compensate for what I had missed in earlier years, I would have to work harder, and study longer, than anybody else. I still had this feeling that I did not want my colleagues to know what a tough time I was having understanding the concepts, the words, the ideas, the process. I didn't want them to know that. So I did my reading not in the law library, but in a library at the graduate dorm, upstairs where it was very quiet, because apparently nobody else there studied. So I would go there at night after dinner. I would load my books under my arm and go to the library, and I would read until the wee hours of the morning and then go to bed. I didn't get much sleep during those years. I was lucky if I got three or four hours a night, because I had to stay up. I had to.

1

The professors would assign cases for the next day, and these cases had to be read and understood or I would be behind, further behind than I was.

2   I was always delighted when I would get called upon to recite in class. But the professors did not call on the "ladies" very much. There were certain favored people who always got called on, and then on some rare occasions a professor would come in and would announce: "We're going to have Ladies Day today." And he would call on the ladies. We were just tolerated. We weren't considered really top drawer when it came to the study of the law.

3   At some time in the spring, Bill Gibson, who was dating my new roommate, Norma Walker, organized a black study group, as we blacks had to form our own. This was because we were not invited into any of the other study groups. There were six or seven in our group—Bill, and Issie, and I think Maynard Jackson—and we would just gather and talk it out and hear ourselves do that. One thing I learned was that you had to talk out the issues, the facts, the cases, the decisions, the process. You couldn't just read the cases and study alone in your library as I had been doing; and you couldn't get it all in the classroom. But once you had talked it out in the study group, it flowed more easily and made a lot more sense.

4   And from time to time I would go up to the fourth floor at 2 Rawley Street to check on how Louise was doing. She was always reading *Redbook.* Every time I was in there and wanted to discuss one of the cases with her, she was reading a short story in *Redbook.* I don't know how she could do that. She was not prepared in class when the professors would call on her to discuss cases, but that did not bother her. Whereas it was a matter of life and death with me. I had to make law school. I just didn't have any alternatives. I could not afford to flunk out. That would have been an unmitigated disaster. So I read all the time I was not in class.

5   Finally I felt I was really learning things, really going to school. I felt that I was getting educated, whatever that was. I became familiar with the process of thinking. I learned to think things out and reach conclusions and defend what I had said.

6   In the past I had got along by spouting off. Whether you talked about debates or oratory, you dealt with speechifying. Even in debate it was pretty much canned because you had, in your little three-by-five box, a response for whatever issue might be raised by the opposition. The format was structured so that there was no opportunity for independent thinking. (I really had not had my ideas challenged ever.) But I could no longer orate and let that pass for reasoning. Because there was not any demand for an orator in Boston University Law School. You had to think and read and understand and reason. I had learned at twenty-one that you couldn't just say a thing is so because it might not be so, and somebody brighter, smarter, and more thoughtful would come out and tell you it wasn't so. Then, if you still thought it was, you had to prove it. Well, that was a new thing for me. I cannot, I really cannot describe what that did to my insides and to my head. I thought: I'm being educated finally.

Vocabulary

Directions: Locate each of the key words in the reading selection. Then read and study each word in its context and try to determine its meaning. Use a dictionary or thesaurus to check your guess. Write the meanings of the words in the margin of the text.

Record the new words you've learned on the following lines.

Key Word	Paragraph	Meaning
1. compensate	1	
2. top drawer	2	
3. spouting off	6	
4. oratory	6	
Others?		

Guide Questions

Directions: The purpose of these guide questions is to ensure your understanding of what you have read. They also will help you to analyze and evaluate the author's ideas and apply them to the real world and your own life.

Write answers to the questions in your notebook or on a separate sheet of paper if your instructor wishes to collect them. Your answers will form the basis of class discussion.

1. What can you infer from this story about the status of women and minorities in law schools at the time Barbara Jordan attended Boston University?
2. What did Jordan learn about the value of studying with a group of fellow students while she was at Boston University?
3. At the end of the piece, Jordan says, "I'm being educated finally." What had happened to make her feel this way?

Application

Directions: Learn a little more about this interesting American, Barbara Jordan. Visit these websites: http://www.elf.net/bjordan, http://www.pbs.org/newshour/bb/remember/jordan_1-17.html, or any of the hundreds of sites devoted to Barbara Jordan. Share what you discover with your classmates.

Writing

Directions: Complete the two assignments below.

1. Do you ever feel discouraged about school? Many students juggle work and family responsibilities as well as college. Many students find their course work just plain hard! Try this mental exercise: Write a letter to Barbara Jordan. Describe the problems you are having. Try to be specific: Is scheduling a problem? Do you have difficulty finding enough time to study? Are your classes extremely difficult? Is the material too advanced? Is there a problem with an instructor? Or with other students? Are your grades lower than you would like? Try to define and describe any trouble you are having. Write at least a page—you may need to write more.

2. Put the letter you wrote in assignment 1 above in a drawer for a few days. Then take it out and read it carefully. Imagine you are Barbara Jordan and write an answer to your letter. What do you think she might say in response to you?

Making Connections

Read the selection "Darkness at Noon" by Harold Krents on page 244. Write a letter to yourself from Mr. Krents in which he responds to the letter you wrote in the first writing assignment above.

This story appeared in The New York Times *in May 2000.*

AN UNRELENTING DRIVE, AND A HARVARD DEGREE

Jacques Steinberg

CAMBRIDGE, Mass., May 15—The honors thesis that Brooke Ellison presented earlier this spring at Harvard University, "The Element of Hope in Resilient Adolescents," was a scientific analysis steeped in data.   1

But her own story would have made a good case study.   2

Struck by a car on her first day in the seventh grade and given little chance of survival, Ms. Ellison awoke, after 36 hours in a coma, as a quadriplegic, one whose first words included the questions, "When can I get back to school?" and "Will I be left back?"   3

Though she would regain no sensation below her neck, Ms. Ellison never missed a grade, and early next month she will cap her improbable educational odyssey by graduating from Harvard with an A⁻ average and a bachelor's degree in psychology and biology.   4

A smiling 21-year-old woman with a strong, sometimes scratchy voice, Ms. Ellison said there is nothing extraordinary about her accomplishments, whether it is piloting her wheelchair (as well as the cursor on her computer screen) by touching her tongue to a keypad in a retainer on the roof of her mouth, or being selected by her peers to address them on senior class day on June 7.   5

And do not even try to tell her that she is, as near as university officials can tell, the first quadriplegic to graduate from Harvard.   6

"This is just the way my life is," Ms. Ellison said over the clicking of a ventilator that forces air through her trachea and into her lungs 13 times a minute. "I've always felt that whatever circumstances I confront, it's just a question of continuing to live and not letting what I can't do define what I can."   7

Those looking for a hero in this story, Ms. Ellison suggested, should focus on her mother, Jean Marie, 48, who has sat at her daughter's side in every class since the eighth grade.   8

After Ms. Ellison was admitted to Harvard, the family decided, reluctantly, that Mrs. Ellison would temporarily leave her husband and teenage son in Stony Brook, N.Y., and move into a dormitory suite with her daughter. The two have hardly been out of earshot, for even a moment, since.   9

"If I'm with friends or want to be alone," Ms. Ellison said, "she knows when to give me my space."   10

Mrs. Ellison, whose first—and last—day as a special education teacher was the day of her daughter's accident, has been much more than a 24-hour nurse. Though Ms. Ellison dictated her term papers into a voice-activated computer and did whatever research she could on the Internet, her mother turned the pages of books like "Heart of Darkness" ("I don't have a particular signal," Ms. Ellison said, "I just say, 'Mom, turn the page now.'"), and served as her   11 daughter's surrogate right hand, raising hers high when Ms. Ellison had something to say in class.

12   As a tribute, the mother received a mock degree in "virtual studies" from the seniors in her daughter's house.

13   "I'm the brawn," Mrs. Ellison said. "She's the brains."

14   The mother added that her daughter "can't understand what all the hoopla is about, which is refreshing."

15   Though she has never known the freedom of tossing a Frisbee across the Yard, Ms. Ellison insisted that hers had been a fairly typical Harvard existence. She has, for example, occasionally sipped a beer at Brew Moon in Harvard Square, though she has hardly made a habit of it.

16   "I'd be drinking and operating my wheelchair at the same time," she said. "That would classify me as a d.w.i."

17   Ms. Ellison lived on campus all four years (the last three in the boxy, 30-year-old Currier House), studied with renowned professors such as Alan Dershowitz and Stephen Jay Gould, founded a student advocacy group on behalf of the disabled and attended her house's senior formal.

18   But she is the first to say that her mother—as well as her father, younger brother and older sister—were only the starting lineup on a team deep in talent that made her graduation possible.

19   Her dormitory room was custom-fitted by Harvard technicians with a hospital bed, small hydraulic lift, panic button and electronic door opener. When she signed up for a class on the history of opera, it had to be moved because the building was inaccessible with a wheelchair.

20   And though she and her date stayed at the senior formal well past midnight, they had to be chaperoned by her mother (Ms. Ellison's brother, Reed, was his mother's escort) and were ferried from the party not in a white limousine but a white van with an open cargo bay.

21   Kevin Davis, a retired Cambridge police detective who would often drive Ms. Ellison to class, said: "Brooke's captured my heart. It's inspiring to know a person of her character."

22   Like one of her idols, the actor Christopher Reeve, Ms. Ellison conceded that she does have moments of sadness, particularly when her sleep is interrupted by dreams of the dance classes that were her childhood passion. (A poster in her dorm room, brought from home, showed five pint-size ballerinas at a dance bar, the middle girl desperately trying to stretch to reach as high as the other four.)

23   She said she has never wanted to meet the man whose car hit her as she walked home from school, an accident that fractured her skull, her spine and almost every major bone in her body. But she said she holds no grudge.

24   "If I were to harbor anger for 10 years," she said, "it'd be too exhausting."

25   Even though she was a formidable student in high school who scored 1510 out of a possible 1600 on her College Board exams (she filled in the bubbles by dictating to a teacher), Ms. Ellison never expected to get into Harvard, which was the only college to which she applied other than the State University of

New York at Stony Brook. "I thought if I got accepted, I would put the letter in a frame," she said.

But once she was admitted, she said, Harvard, which costs more than $30,000 a year, made herculean efforts to ensure that she would attend. The university provided her with scholarships not only to supplement her father's salary as an administrator in a Social Security office but also to pay for her costly medical needs.   26

Ms. Ellison is keeping the text of her class day address a secret, but does allow that it will touch on the many friendships she forged in Cambridge. Among the first to approach her, on the way to an early morning language class, was Neil Holzapfer, 22, then a freshman from Kingston, N.H., who majored in government and Russian studies.   27

"I was struck by the courage that it would take for her to be in this kind of atmosphere, which is stressful and intense under the best conditions," Mr. Holzapfer recalled.   28

Four years later, Mr. Holzapfer said that his friend had become his role model, her love of the bubble gum rocker Bryan Adams notwithstanding. "Brooke is living a life that is out there," he said, "instead of closing up and looking inward."   29

After spending the summer getting to know her family again, Ms. Ellison intends to write her autobiography (she already has an agent at William Morris) and hopes to travel as a motivational speaker.   30

"Anywhere people feel they need encouragement," she said, "that's where I hope to be."   31

Vocabulary

Directions: Locate each of the key words in the reading selection. Try to figure out each word's meaning by using the context. Confirm your guess by checking the dictionary or thesaurus. Write the meanings of the words in the margin of the text. Then record the meanings in the chart below.

Key Word	Paragraph	Meaning
1. resilient	1	
2. odyssey	4	
3. brawn	13	
4. advocacy	17	
5. formidable	25	
6. herculean	26	

Key Word	Paragraph	Meaning
Others?		

Guide Questions

Directions: These questions will guide your understanding of what you have read. Write your answers in your notebook or on a separate sheet of paper if your instructor wishes to collect it. Your answers to these questions will be the basis of class discussion.

1. "An Unrelenting Drive . . ." is the story of an extraordinary young woman and her family. Summarize the major facts of their story.
2. Each of the major characters in this story shows remarkable determination and effort. Think about each and describe their contributions to the "happy ending" of a Harvard degree.
   a. Brooke Ellison
   b. Ms. Ellison's mother, Jean
   c. Ms. Ellison's father, brother, and sister
   d. Harvard University
3. Imagine you are the person at *The New York Times* who writes the headlines. Write your own headline for this story.

Application/Writing

1. The following two letters appeared in *The New York Times* in response to "An Unrelenting Drive, and a Harvard Degree." Each focuses on a different aspect of the story. Write one sentence for each letter, summarizing its main point.

Disabled in America, Beyond Harvard

To the Editor:

Re "An Unrelenting Drive, and a Harvard Degree" (front page, May 17):

It seems that you missed the real significance of this story. The fact that Brooke Ellison is a quadriplegic who is graduating from Harvard, and that her story is worthy of coverage, tells us a lot about the general lack of equal opportunity for disabled people in this country.

The fact that her mother had to quit work to become her daughter's full-time attendant through high school and college demonstrates the appalling lack of support given to disabled people.

What if her mother had been unable or unwilling to do so? What would have become of Ms. Ellison then?

Douglas Baynton
Iowa City, May 18, 2000
The writer is an assistant professor of history at the University of Iowa.

A Student's Promise

To the Editor:

Re "An Unrelenting Drive, and a Harvard Degree" (front page, May 17):

The beautiful thing about inclusion of people with disabilities is that it is a classic "win–win" situation. Brooke Ellison gets to fulfill her fullest potential; Harvard gets to cultivate a broader intellectual and social climate than would otherwise be the case, benefiting everyone.

Ms. Ellison's classmates obviously recognize the degree to which their lives are enriched by exposure to her unique ideas, abilities and perspective; I presume that is why they voted for her to present a senior class day speech.

Harvard is to be commended for recognizing why inclusion of Ms. Ellison was a win-win. (Now it should make sure that all of its buildings are accessible to wheelchairs.)

Other institutions should take note of the fact that everyone benefits from an inclusive policy toward people with disabilities.

Barbara Quackenbos
Maplewood, N.J., May 17, 2000

2. Write your own letter, either to the *Times* or to Brooke Ellison, reacting to the story.

Making Connections

Compare and contrast the stories of Richard Wright ("Black Boy") and Brooke Ellison ("An Unrelenting Drive, and a Harvard Degree"). How are they similar? How are they different?

After decades of war and years of oppression by the Taliban in Afghanistan, attention is beginning to be paid to the education of women. Literacy classes are opening all over the country and the long-denied students are responding with enthusiasm.
This story appeared in The New York Times *in September 2002.*

LONG IN DARK, AFGHAN WOMEN SAY TO READ IS FINALLY TO SEE

Carlotta Gall

1   MAZAR-I-SHARIF, Afghanistan, Sept. 19—The female voices ring out clear and confident across the courtyard as a class recites the Afghan alphabet, "Alef, Be, Te. . . ." But the surprise is that inside the simple mud-brick house, the pupils sitting on the floor before their teacher are adult women, some nursing babies or pushing aside noisy toddlers.

2   In their greedy embrace of the government's back-to-school campaign after the prohibitive years under the Taliban, Afghanistan's women are as eager to get an education for themselves as for their children. Hundreds of women's literacy classes are forming in the back streets of this town in northern Afghanistan— faster than the government can register them—as women meet in neighborhood houses to learn to read and write.

3   "I wanted to know something and help my children," said Mahgul, 45, a widow and mother of six. "I have no knowledge, and so I am not a useful person. If I can get some knowledge, I can help my children more."

4   Zainab, 50, sitting next to her, said it was watching her own children read and write that made her want to learn, too. Her husband, sick with tuberculosis and also illiterate, urged her to come to the free lessons starting in the neighborhood. "He said, 'You are getting older, and you should know something and help your children so they do not grow up blind like you,'" she said.

5   "Blind" is the word many of these illiterate women use to describe themselves, and it speaks to the confusion and difficulties that they encounter as uneducated members of a society already harshly discriminatory against women.

6   "Without knowledge, I am blind; I do not know white from black," said Torpikay, 30. "In town, I do not know where is the hospital, or the baths or the washroom, and I will take my dishes into the wrong place, because we just follow other women and don't know where we are going." That last comment raised laughter from the entire class.

7   The women most often complain of not being able to decipher street signs, even for the bathroom, and not being able to understand medical prescriptions, says Mariya, one of the teachers who have started literacy classes for adult women in an impoverished neighborhood known as Ali Chupan, on the east side of Mazar-i-Sharif.

8   Silent, shadowy figures in public, Afghan women, dressed in the all-encompassing burka, often are too timid to approach strangers to ask for directions.

One woman said she could not tell the difference between government money and the money widely used in the north, which looks almost the same but is worth half the value. "She was sometimes cheated because of that," Mariya said.

And the women, especially those without men in the family, say they are ill equipped to manage the daily difficulties of running the household and feeding their families.

In each of four classes visited in Ali Chupan, there were widows and young women fending for themselves, and they all said they wanted to become literate so they could find employment.

Three sisters, who live alone with their widowed mother, said they made a living weaving carpets, but could barely earn enough to survive. "I really want to learn and get work, maybe in an office," said Nasi, 20. Tears welled up as she described her life, how she had never been to school and how the family fled to the mountains when the Taliban came. But after only a few days of classes, she and her sister, Shaqila, 18, were rapidly writing down the alphabet.

Another reason the women often gave for attending classes is that they wanted to read letters from members of the family who because of the years of conflict, often live miles apart, or abroad as refugees.

Basira, 17, said her in-laws, who live with her, had urged her to come to classes because her father-in-law, the only one in the family who can read and write, was having trouble with his eyes.

"He suggested I learn to read so I could read the letters when they come," she said. "My mother-in-law becomes happy when I read something to them. She says, 'When we have a problem, you are the youngest of this house, and you will be able to solve the problem.'"

Some of the older women stare uncomprehendingly at the makeshift blackboards that teachers have arranged in their houses, one on the bare plastered wall, one on an old broken door.

But some women are fascinated and clearly hungry to learn. When they received new notebooks, they huddled in groups and helped each other write the letters.

"The best thing is being able to write my name," says Siddiqa, 18, who studied the Koran in her village but never went to school.

Some estimates have put women's illiteracy in Afghanistan as high as 85 percent, and the new government has begun a broad program not only to get all children back to school, but also to address the adult literacy problem by paying schoolteachers in the cities to instruct adults in their homes after school lets out.

Mazar-i-Sharif already has 172 registered adult literacy classes, and more are opening all the time as teachers hope to earn some extra pay, and women pile in to receive the free lessons. "We are happy about this, a lot of people want to come to the classes," said Palwasha Rafat of U.N.-Habitat, a United Nations aid organization that works with the Afghan government on education.

Governments that preceded the Taliban had organized women's literacy classes, but the surge of interest now after years of women's exclusion has surpassed anything before, she said. "People realized that the reason for all these years of war was the lack of education in the country," she said. "Both the men and the women realize this now and want to change that."

Vocabulary

Directions: Locate each of the key words in the reading selection. Try to figure out each word's meaning by using the context. Confirm your guess by checking the dictionary or thesaurus. Write the meanings of the words in the margin of the text. Then record the meanings in the chart below.

Key Word	Paragraph	Meaning
1. decipher	7	
2. fending	11	
3. makeshift	16	
Others?		

Guide Questions

Directions: These questions will guide your understanding of what you have read. Write your answers in your notebook or on a separate sheet of paper if your instructor wishes to collect it. Your answers to these questions will be the basis of class discussion.

1. In a sentence or two, summarize the main points of this article.
2. Explain what Torpikay means what she describes herself as "blind."
3. Relate the women's description of being blind to the title of the article.
4. What kinds of problems do the women encounter because of their illiteracy?
5. What are some of the goals the women have?
6. What is your reaction to the story? Write a few sentences.

Application

What is the illiteracy rate of women in Afghanistan? Use the Internet to find the overall illiteracy rate of both women and men and the illiteracy rate in the United States. If you are from another country, check the statistics from your home country.

Making Connections

Imagine that Richard Wright ("Black Boy," page 12) visited one of the women's literacy classes in Afghanistan. Write what you think he would say to the Afghan women in the class.

In recent years, the number of older people returning to school has grown enormously. Many return to improve their employment potential. Others return simply for the pleasure of learning. In the essay below, we learn of a thirty-year-old woman who feels handicapped by her lack of education—and of her determination to help herself overcome it.

OVERCOMING AN INVISIBLE HANDICAP

Thomas J. Cottle

On her thirtieth birthday, Lucille Elmore informed her husband that she was going through a crisis. "I was thirty years old, active, in good health—and I was illiterate," she recalls. "I didn't know books, I didn't know history, I didn't know science. I had the barest understanding of the arts. Like a physical condition, my knowledge limped, my intelligence limped." 1

She was not only the mother of two young children but also was working full time as an administrative assistant in a business-consulting firm. Nevertheless, at age thirty, with her husband's agreement, Lucille Elmore enrolled in college. "I thought getting in would be difficult," she says. "It was easy. I thought I couldn't discipline myself, but that came. Half the people in the library the first day thought I was the librarian, but that didn't deter me." 2

For Lucille, the awareness of her invisible limp came only gradually. As a young woman, she had finished high school, but she had chosen not to go on with her education. Her parents, who had never completed high school themselves, urged her to go to college but she refused. At the time, she was perhaps a bit timid and lacked a certain confidence in her own intellectual or academic abilities. Besides, a steady job was far more important at that point to Lucille than schooling; she felt she could read on her own to make up for any lack of education. 3

At twenty, working full time, she married Ted Elmore, a salesman for a food-store chain, a man on his way to becoming more than modestly successful. There was no need for her to work, but she did so until her first child was born; she was then twenty-two. A second child was born two years later, and three years after that, she went back to work. With her youngest in a day-care program, she felt no reservations about working, but her lack of education began to nag at her as she approached the age of thirty. She thus gave up her job, entered a continuing-education program at a nearby university, and began what she likens to a love affair. 4

"I'm carrying on an open affair with books, but like a genuinely good lover, I'm being guided. Reading lists, suggested reading, recommended readings—I want them all. I must know what happened in the twelfth, thirteenth, and eighteenth centuries. I want to know how the world's major religions evolved. Papal history, I know nothing of papal history and succession, or the politics involved. I read the Bible, but I never studied it. It's like music: I listened, but it wasn't an informed listening. Now all of this is changing. 5

6   "I must tell you, I despise students when they talk about 'the real world,' as if college were a dream world. They simply don't understand what the accumulation of knowledge and information means. Maybe you have to be thirty at least, and going through a personal crisis, to fully appreciate what historical connections are.

7   "A line of Shakespeare challenges me more than half the jobs I'll be equipped for when I'm finished. I'm having an affair with him, too, only it's called Elizabethan Literature 606. I think many people prefer the real world of everyday work because it's less frightening than the larger-than-life world of college.

8   "There's a much more important difference between the rest of the students and me. We don't agree at all on what it means to be a success. They think in terms of money, material things. I suppose that's normal. They don't understand that, with a nice home, and decent job prospects, and two beautiful children, I know I am a failure. I'm a failure because I am ignorant. I'm a failure until I have knowledge, until I can work with it, be excited by and play with ideas.

9   "I don't go to school for the rewards down the line. I want to reach the point at which I don't measure knowledge by anything but itself. An idea has value or it doesn't. This is how I now determine success and failure.

10   "'How can I use it?' That's what students ask. 'What good will this do me?' They don't think about what the question says about them, even without an answer attached to it. Questions like that only build up competition. But competition is the bottom line for so many students, I guess, getting ahead, getting a bit of a step up on the other guy. I know, it's my husband's life.

11   "I'll tell what I think I like most about my work: the library. I can think of no place so exclusive and still so open and public. Millions of books there for the taking. A chair to sit in, a row of books, and you don't need a penny. For me, the library is a religious center, a shrine.

12   "Students talk about the real world out there. What about the free world in here? Here, no one arrests you for what you're thinking. In the library, you can't talk, so you have to think. I never knew what it meant to think about something, to really think it through. I certainly never understood what you had to know to even begin to think. I always thought it was normal to limp."

Vocabulary

Directions: Locate each of the key words in the reading selection. Then read and study each word in its context and try to determine its meaning. Use a dictionary or thesaurus to check your guess. Write the meanings of the words in the margin of the text.

Record the new words you've learned below.

Key Word	Paragraph	Meaning
1. deter	2	
2. shrine	11	

Key Word	Paragraph	Meaning
Others?		

Guide Questions

Directions: The purpose of these guide questions is to ensure your understanding of what you have read. They will also help you to analyze and evaluate the author's ideas and apply them to the real world and your own life.

Write answers to the questions in your notebook or on a separate sheet of paper if your instructor wishes to collect them. Your answers will form the basis of class discussion.

1. Define the word *illiterate* as it is generally used; then define *illiterate* as it is used by Elmore in this essay.
2. Why did half of the people in the library on the first day think Elmore was the librarian?
3. In this essay, Elmore uses powerful comparisons in describing her return to school: a "handicap," or "limp," and a "love affair." Explain each of these comparisons.
4. In paragraph 8, Elmore describes herself as a failure. Why does she say this? Do you agree that she was a failure?
5. Contrast Elmore's view of what it means to be a success with the view of her fellow students.
6. a. Why does Elmore say she despises students when they talk about "the real world"?
   b. List some of the other differences of opinion between Elmore and her younger classmates.
7. a. Why does Elmore describe the library as "a religious center"?
   b. Compare and contrast your opinion of the library with Elmore's.

Making Connections

Compare Lucille Elmore's view of education with that of Sydney Harris's ("What True Education Should Do"). Would they agree on the purpose of education? Give evidence to support your answer. Write at least one paragraph.

Writing

If you are a "returning student" (say, returning to school after an absence of five or more years), discuss your view of education with a younger student (someone who came to college directly from high school). If you are a young student, discuss education with an older classmate. Then write one or two paragraphs comparing and contrasting your views.

COLLABORATIVE LEARNING

Working in Groups to Guide Your Own Reading

All of the reading selections so far in this unit have been accompanied by questions and exercises that are meant to help you understand and use what you've read. However, in much of your college reading (not to mention in your real life), you will be expected to master the material on your own.

Research has shown that one of the most effective ways to learn is in *groups*. In college, working with classmates can help you to master the material of a college course. The give-and-take that comes naturally when working with other people helps us to avoid falling into bad habits like *passive reading*. (We have all had the awful experience of reading a whole chapter, then realizing that we don't remember one single thing we've read.) Working with other students will help you to avoid such problems. For this assignment, form groups of approximately four students. In your group, read and think about the two following reading selections, "The Teacher Who Changed My Life" by Nicholas Gage and "When Gadgets Get in the Way" by Lisa Guernsey. Then, create your own vocabulary chart, guide questions, and application and writing assignments.

Follow these steps to complete the assignment:

1. Preview the selection before you read—look at and think about the title, any headings or subheadings, the first paragraph, the last paragraph, and the first sentence of each paragraph.
2. Read through the selection one time quickly.
3. Read the selection a second time, more carefully. This time mark the text. Review how to do this by turning to page 421, "Learning Strategy III—Marking Text."
4. Brainstorm with your group. Ask yourselves: What important issues is the author discussing? What new information did you learn? Can the issues discussed in the selection be connected to those you have already studied? Can any of the information here be applied to situations in your own life?
5. Now, create a set of exercises similar to those you have completed in previous chapters of this book:
   a. **Vocabulary**. Make a list of key words from the text. Set them up in chart format as on page 3.
   b. **Guide Questions**. Write questions that will guide understanding of the major ideas in the reading.
   c. **Application**. Prepare an application exercise that takes one or more of the important ideas in the reading and relates it to real life.
   d. **Writing**. Create a writing assignment to conclude the chapter.

Before you begin, it would be a good idea to review the questions and exercises in the previous reading selections in this book for reference.

When you are finished, submit your work to your instructor. Your instructor may review and combine the work of all the groups and return the exercise to the class. You will then have the opportunity to *answer* the questions you and your classmates have developed.

Now, use your skills as an active, independent reader to tackle the following reading selections. Good luck!

"If it weren't for her . . ." says Nicholas Gage as he speaks of Miss Hurd, the English teacher and school newspaper-club advisor who changed the whole course of his life. She was "the catalyst that sent me into journalism and indirectly caused all the good things that came after." This powerful and emotional story comes from Gage's book, A Place for Us. *In it, he describes his life after coming to the United States at the age of nine. Earlier, during the Greek civil war, Gage's mother had been captured and killed for sending her children to safety and freedom in America. It was Miss Hurd who "directed [his] grief and pain into writing," inspired him to become an investigative reporter, foreign correspondent, and writer of the much-acclaimed book about his mother's life,* Eleni. *Can you recall a teacher who had a special effect on your life?*

THE TEACHER WHO CHANGED MY LIFE

Nicholas Gage

The person who set the course of my life in the new land I entered as a young war refugee—who, in fact, nearly dragged me onto the path that would bring all the blessings I've received in America—was a salty-tongued, no-nonsense school-teacher named Marjorie Hurd. When I entered her classroom in 1953, I had been to six schools in five years, starting in the Greek village where I was born in 1939. 1

When I stepped off a ship in New York Harbor on a gray March day in 1949, I was an undersized nine-year-old in short pants who had lost his mother and was coming to live with the father he didn't know. My mother, Eleni Gatzoyiannis, had been imprisoned, tortured, and shot by Communist guerrillas for sending me and three of my four sisters to freedom. She died so that her children could go to their father in the United States. 2

The portly, bald, well-dressed man who met me and my sisters seemed a foreign, authoritarian figure. I secretly resented him for not getting the whole family out of Greece early enough to save my mother. Ultimately, I would grow to love him and appreciate how he dealt with becoming a single parent at the age of fifty-six, but at first our relationship was prickly, full of hostility. 3

As Father drove us to our new home—a tenement in Worcester, Massachusetts—and pointed out the huge brick building that would be our first school in America, I clutched my Greek notebooks from the refugee camp, hoping that my few years of schooling would impress my teachers in this cold, crowded country. They didn't. When my father led me and my eleven-year-old sister to Greendale Elementary School, the grim-faced Yankee principal put the two of us in a class for the mentally retarded. There was no facility in those days for non-English-speaking children. 4

By the time I met Marjorie Hurd four years later, I had learned English, been placed in a normal, graded class and had even been chosen for the college preparatory track in the Worcester public school system. I was thirteen years old when our father moved us yet again, and I entered Chandler Junior High shortly after the beginning of seventh grade. I found myself surrounded by richer, smarter, and better-dressed classmates who looked askance at my strange clothes and heavy accent. Shortly after I arrived, we were told to select a hobby to pursue 5 during "club hour" on Fridays. The idea of hobbies and clubs made no sense to my immigrant ears, but I decided to follow the prettiest girl in my class—the blue-eyed daughter of the local Lutheran minister. She led me through the door marked "Newspaper Club" and into the presence of Miss Hurd, the newspaper advisor and English teacher who would become my mentor and my muse.

6   A formidable, solidly built woman with salt-and-pepper hair, a steely eye, and a flat Boston accent, Miss Hurd had no patience with layabouts. "What are all you goof-offs doing here?" she bellowed at the would-be journalists. "This is the Newspaper Club! We're going to put out a *newspaper.* So if there's anybody in this room who doesn't like work, I suggest you go across to the Glee Club now, because you're going to work your tails off here!"

7   I was soon under Miss Hurd's spell. She did indeed teach us to put out a newspaper, skills I honed during my next twenty-five years as a journalist. Soon I asked the principal to transfer me to her English class as well. There, she drilled us on grammar until I finally began to understand the logic and structure of the English language. She assigned stories for us to read and discuss; not tales of heroes, like the Greek myths I knew, but stories of underdogs—poor people, even immigrants, who seemed ordinary until a crisis drove them to do something extraordinary. She also introduced us to the literary wealth of Greece—giving me a new perspective on my war-ravaged, impoverished homeland. I began to be proud of my origins.

8   One day, after discussing how writers should write about what they know, she assigned us to compose an essay from our own experience. Fixing me with a stern look, she added, "Nick, I want you to write about what happened to your family in Greece." I had been trying to put those painful memories behind me and left the assignment until the last moment. Then, on a warm spring afternoon, I sat in my room with a yellow pad and pencil and stared out the window at the buds on the trees. I wrote that the coming of spring always reminded me of the last time I said good-bye to my mother on a green and gold day in 1948.

9   I kept writing, one line after another, telling how the Communist guerrillas occupied our village, took our home and food, how my mother started planning our escape when she learned that the children were to be sent to re-education camps behind the Iron Curtain and how, at the last moment, she couldn't escape with us because the guerrillas sent her with a group of women to thresh wheat in a distant village. She promised she would try to get away on her own, she told me to be brave, and hung a silver cross around my neck, and then she kissed me. I watched the line of women being led down into the ravine and up the other side, until they disappeared around the bend—my mother a tiny brown figure at the end who stopped for an instant to raise her hand in one last farewell.

10   I wrote about our nighttime escape down the mountain, across the minefields, and into the lines of the Nationalist soldiers, who sent us to a refugee camp. It was there that we learned of our mother's execution. I felt very lucky to have come to America, I concluded, but every year, the coming of spring made me feel sad because it reminded me of the last time I saw my mother.

I handed in the essay, hoping never to see it again, but Miss Hurd had it published in the school paper. This mortified me at first, until I saw that my classmates reacted with sympathy and tact to my family's story. Without telling me, Miss Hurd also submitted the essay to a contest sponsored by the Freedoms Foundation at Valley Forge, Pennsylvania, and it won a medal. The Worcester paper wrote about the award and quoted my essay at length. My father, by then a "five-and-dime-store chef," as the paper described him, was ecstatic with pride, and the Worcester Greek community celebrated the honor to one of its own.

For the first time I began to understand the power of the written word. A secret ambition took root in me. One day, I vowed, I would go back to Greece, find out the details of my mother's death and write about her life, so her grandchildren would know of her courage. Perhaps I would even track down the men who killed her and write of their crimes. Fulfilling that ambition would take me thirty years.

Meanwhile, I followed the literary path that Miss Hurd had so forcefully set me on. After junior high, I became the editor of my school paper at Classical High School and got a part-time job at the Worcester *Telegram and Gazette.* Although my father could only give me $50 and encouragement toward a college education, I managed to finance four years at Boston University with scholarships and part-time jobs in journalism. During my last year of college, an article I wrote about a friend who had died in the Philippines—the first person to lose his life working for the Peace Corps—led to my winning the Hearst Award for College Journalism. And the plaque was given to me in the White House by President John F. Kennedy.

For a refugee who had never seen a motorized vehicle or indoor plumbing until he was nine, this was an unimaginable honor. When the Worcester paper ran a picture of me standing next to President Kennedy, my father rushed out to buy a new suit in order to be properly dressed to receive the congratulations of the Worcester Greeks. He clipped out the photograph, had it laminated in plastic and carried it in his breast pocket for the rest of his life to show everyone he met. I found the much-worn photo in his pocket on the day he died twenty years later.

In our isolated Greek village, my mother had bribed a cousin to teach her to read, for girls were not supposed to attend school beyond a certain age. She had always dreamed of her children receiving an education. She couldn't be there when I graduated from Boston University, but the person who came with my father and shared our joy was my former teacher, Marjorie Hurd. We celebrated not only my bachelor's degree but also the scholarships that paid my way to Columbia's Graduate School of Journalism. There, I met the woman who would eventually become my wife. At our wedding and at the baptisms of our three children, Marjorie Hurd was always there, dancing alongside the Greeks.

By then, she was Mrs. Rabidou, for she had married a widower when she was in her early forties. That didn't distract her from her vocation of introducing young minds to English literature, however. She taught for a total of forty-one years and continually would make a "project" of some balky student in whom she

11

12

13

14

15

16

spied a spark of potential. Often these were students from the most troubled homes, yet she would alternately bully and charm each one with her own special brand of tough love until the spark caught fire. She retired in 1981 at the age of sixty-two but still avidly follows the lives and careers of former students while overseeing her adult stepchildren and driving her husband on camping trips to New Hampshire.

17   Miss Hurd was one of the first to call me on December 10, 1987, when President Reagan, in his television address after the summit meeting with Gorbachev, told the nation that Eleni Gatzoyiannis's dying cry, "My children!" had helped inspire him to seek an arms agreement "for all the children of the world."

18   "I can't imagine a better monument for your mother," Miss Hurd said with an uncharacteristic catch in her voice.

19   Although a bad hip makes it impossible for her to join in the Greek dancing, Marjorie Hurd Rabidou is still an honored and enthusiastic guest at all family celebrations, including my fiftieth birthday picnic last summer, where the shish kebab was cooked on spits, clarinets and *bouzoukis* wailed, and costumed dancers led the guests in a serpentine line around our Colonial farmhouse, only twenty minutes from my first home in Worcester.

20   My sisters and I felt an aching void because my father was not there to lead the line, balancing a glass of wine on his head while he danced, the way he did at every celebration during his ninety-two years. But Miss Hurd was there, surveying the scene with quiet satisfaction. Although my parents are gone, her presence was a consolation, because I owe her so much.

21   This is truly the land of opportunity, and I would have enjoyed its bounty even if I hadn't walked into Miss Hurd's classroom in 1953. But she was the one who directed my grief and pain into writing, and if it weren't for her I wouldn't have become an investigative reporter and foreign correspondent, recorded the story of my mother's life and death in *Eleni*, and now my father's story in *A Place for Us*, which is also a testament to the country that took us in. She was the catalyst that sent me into journalism and indirectly caused all the good things that came after. But Miss Hurd would probably deny this emphatically.

22   A few years ago, I answered the telephone and heard my former teacher's voice telling me, in that won't-take-no-for-an-answer tone of hers, that she had decided I was to write and deliver the eulogy at her funeral. I agreed (she didn't leave me any choice), but that's one assignment I never want to do. I hope, Miss Hurd, that you'll accept this remembrance instead.

Vocabulary

Directions: Mark any important words in the reading selection that you don't know. Then list them in the following chart along with their paragraph numbers. Try to figure out each word's meaning by reading over the context carefully for clues to help you guess the meaning of the unfamiliar word. Check your dictionary or thesaurus to confirm your guess. After you discuss the words with your group members, write the meanings in the margin of the text, near the word. Then enter them in the chart as well.

Key Word	Paragraph	Meaning

Guide Questions

Directions: Develop a list of questions that elicit the important ideas in the reading selection. Start at the beginning and work your way sequentially through the text until you have addressed all of the author's major ideas.

Application

Directions: When you have a list of guide questions, read through the selection again. This time, write one or more questions that require application of the information in the text to a situation in the real world.

Writing

Directions: Your last task is to prepare a writing assignment. For example, you might ask for a paragraph in which the writer comments on the ideas in the reading selection. You might also ask for a summary of the selection.

Competing with cell phones and laptops for students' attention, teachers are fighting back.

WHEN GADGETS GET IN THE WAY

Lisa Guernsey

1   Now that computers are a staple in schools around the country, perhaps the machines should come with a warning label for teachers: "Beware: Students may no longer hear a word you say."

2   Today 80 percent of public schools have high-speed Internet access in at least one classroom, according to Market Data Retrieval, an education research company. Among colleges, 69 percent have classroom Internet access and 70 percent have wireless networks. Students start tapping away behind laptop lids with no way for professors to know if they are taking notes or checking Hotmail.

3   "I've never been in a lecture where I haven't seen someone checking their e-mail when they were supposed to be doing stuff," said Bill Walsh, a student at the Massachusetts Institute of Technology. Instant messages, news tickers and games like solitaire beckon too.

4   Joe Huber, the technology coordinator for the public schools in Greenwood, Indiana., said that teachers routinely complain about gadget-distraction among students. "It is a huge problem with anyone who teaches with any kind of technology," he said.

5   Even in rooms without computers or Internet access, students have other devices to draw their attention away from academics. Cellphones may be prohibited at many schools, but that doesn't stop students from putting them on vibrate and trading text messages under their desks. That is, when they aren't fiddling with their organizers or music players.

6   Teachers have started to fight back. All agree that the best weapon against attention deficit is the same one that worked before the dawn of computers: strong teaching. But new strategies don't hurt, either. Some teachers have found, in fact, that the best defense against the distractions of technology is other technology. Here are five examples of teachers who are fighting fire with fire.

Polishing Skills through Games

7   Anyone who stepped into Mark Greenberg's class at Camelback High School in Phoenix last year probably saw an entire class of students immersed in computer games. That's the way Mr. Greenberg wanted it: He designed the games to keep his students focused.

8   Mr. Greenberg, who will teach English at North High School in Phoenix this fall, has written dozens of games. He said that when he gave them to his remedial students last year, their scores improved on the state's English test. His library also includes Jeopardy-like games to train students for the Academic Decathlon, a student contest.

9   Mr. Greenberg said he had heard the criticism that educational games are nothing more than "drill and kill."

"But now we're finding we're not drilling the kids enough, because they don't   10
know the vocabulary or don't have the computational skills," he said. "So there is
a resurgence back to drill and practice."

When he sees a skill in need of polishing, he works over the weekend to pro-   11
gram a new game, like a multimedia quiz on comma placement or the multiplica-
tion of polynomials. One of his early creations required students to fill in blank
speech balloons from Calvin and Hobbes comic strips, as a way of teaching dialogue.

One of his newest games is based on the role-playing card game called   12
Magic: The Gathering. It requires students to "dress" historical figures with
qualities that best fit their names (like adding the "poet" quality to John Keats).
The game then pits one student's character against another to do battle and see
whose attire wins the day.

He can almost understand, he said, when students get distracted in com-   13
puter labs where the machine is reduced to a "really expensive typewriter." "There
are a lot more discipline problems when you tell kids, 'Now type this up on the
computer,'" he said. "I mean, how boring can that be?"

Vintage Curiosities

Nancy Kemp, a drafting teacher at Cairo High School in Cairo, Ga., has been   14
known to haul out some old technology to seize her students' attention.

A few years ago she set up a film projector and showed a 1956 film about the   15
basics of drafting. She advanced the frames slowly, projecting the images onto a
white board, pointing out techniques and making annotations with dry-erase
markers. "These kids had never seen film strips," she said. "I had that whole class
in the palm of my hand for an hour and a half."

"I don't think I could do it as a steady diet because the newness wears off,"   16
she added. But for those three days, she said, "it was just wonderful."

A teacher for 30 years, Ms. Kemp said she doesn't put much credence in   17
PowerPoint—all pomp with no circumstance," she calls it—and she avoids showing anything on video. "They'll tune it out," she said, adding that the students are
already inundated with television images, including scrolling announcements on
the monitors at school.

She acknowledges, however, that computers are a must these days. The ma-   18
chines in her room feature AutoCad 12, a program used by architects and designers.
Of course, the computers also offer the enticement of the Internet.

"I have to be vigilant," Ms. Kemp said. When she notices students using in-   19
stant messaging software, she waits to make sure that they have closed the program instead of simply minimizing it. But her most effective tactic, she said, is
to threaten to reboot the computer without giving the student a chance to hit
Save and keep the day's schoolwork. "I'll walk over and say, 'Do I need to reboot?'
And they say, 'No, no,' and they do the right thing."

Round Tables and Loud Noises

To keep his students focused, Eric Hudson, an assistant professor of physics at   20
the Massachusetts Institute of Technology, has an ally in his classroom's layout.

Instead of tiers of seats, they are all on one level, arranged around 12 round tables. Each table seats nine students and holds three wireless laptops.

21 If those laptops were used in a conventional lecture hall, students could hide behind the screens. But in this room, professors and teaching assistants wander, keeping an eye out for students opening Yahoo! Mail or 3D Pinball.

22 "Stealth works," Professor Hudson said.

23 The classroom layout is part of a larger education project called Technology Enabled Active Learning, which was organized by another M.I.T. professor, John Belcher, two years ago. TEAL, as the project is known, uses collaborative work groups, hands-on experiments, computer simulations and remote controls for instantaneous quizzes and class-wide feedback sessions. Hanging on the walls are white boards and projection screens for discussions and presentations.

24 Professor Hudson said he also deploys a high-paced lecture style. "I'll try to cover topics in five-to 10-minute chunks," he said. Anything longer, he added, and "there is more of a chance that they'll lose what you're talking about and will turn to IM-ing their friends."

25 Sometimes in his demonstrations he will make a capacitor blow up, with its bang reverberating down the hall.

26 "You have to make loud noises once or twice to snap them back to attention," he said.

27 Large physics lectures typically have a high rate of failing students, partly because so many enrollees never bother to show up. "It used to be that the fail rate for this course was 15 percent," he said. "When we went to this format, it dropped to 1 percent to 2 percent." And what about attendance? It's up to 100 percent, he said.

An Onscreen 'No No'

28 It doesn't take long for the students in Donna Lee's class at the North Gulfport Seventh and Eighth Grade School in Gulfport, Miss., to realize that the computers at their desks are not under their control.

29 Ms. Lee, who teaches keyboarding and Microsoft Office skills, uses networked software called NetOp to take over a student's computer screen whenever she sees fit. Her desktop computer has a master control panel that enables her to see thumbnail images of every screen in her lab. If she spots an unauthorized Web site, she clicks a button to freeze the student's screen, Using her mouse like a red pen, she writes "No No" across the screen. The scolding suddenly appears on the student's screen too.

30 "The kids turn around and look at me," she said. "I give them a look, and they get off there real quick."

31 Ms. Lee also uses the software to rein in all of her students at once. "If I want to explain something, I can freeze every screen," she said, "And in big neon letters I say, 'Pay Attention.'" Without the software, she said, she could ask students to turn to face her and turn off their monitors, but not everyone would obey.

To Ms. Lee, the Web demons that beckon to her students are online chat rooms—"the horrible, horrible teenage chat rooms"—where people can post anonymous notes, sometimes in foul or graphic language, about anyone they know. 32

Using NetOp, she can record exactly what a student has been viewing and for how long. "I save it to my hard drive and put 'No No' on it and call a parent conference, with the student there," she said. A student might plead that he just looked for a second. But, Ms. Lee said, she can open the file and say, "Let's look where you went." 33

Zooming In on Details

When Greg Malone takes charge of his science classroom at Capital High School in Santa Fe, N.M., he takes a tip from talk show hosts. With a tiny microphone pinned to his collar, he walks between tables, asking questions about what he has projected on a six-foot-wide screen in front. 34

"If you can amplify your voice but still speak in a normal conversational voice, the children can actually concentrate better," he said. "There is a focus." 35

He carries a cordless keyboard and mouse so that he can project new images from his desktop computer no matter where he is standing. Using a list of Web sites that he calls up before class, he bounces from one site to another. 36

The projector's zoom function is a favorite tool. Mr. Malone said he pulls up images from the Hubble Space Telescope and zooms in on tiny galaxies that would be a strain for the students to see otherwise. In texts on the screen, he zooms in on numbers and words. "I watch their faces," he said. "They are absolutely riveted." 37

Mr. Malone, who used to work in the computer gaming industry, hands out remote controls, too. By pressing buttons, students can respond immediately and simultaneously to quizzes on the day's lesson. Their answers are tabulated wirelessly, and the totals are projected for all to see. 38

"We'll suddenly stop, and I'll flash a question on the screen and I'll say 'Respond to this,'" he said. "If there is anything that these kids relate to, it's holding a remote control in their hands." 39

Still, Mr. Malone said that working in a classroom with computers creates problems that even high-tech props cannot solve. Teachers, he said, have to be constantly watching for students who "drift off." 40

"It's more than just e-mail. It's looking at Web sites with cars, with sports, playing games," he said. "As a teacher, you have to have those antennas up." 41

Vocabulary

Directions: Mark any important words in the reading selection that you don't know. Then list them in the following chart along with their paragraph numbers. Try to figure out each word's meaning by reading over the context carefully for clues to help you guess the meaning of the unfamiliar word. Check your dictionary or thesaurus to confirm your guess. After you discuss the words with your group members, write the meanings in the margin of the text, near the word. Then enter them in the chart as well.

Key Word	Paragraph	Meaning

Guide Questions

Directions: Develop a list of questions that elicit the important ideas in the reading selection. Start at the beginning and work your way sequentially through the text until you have addressed all of the author's major ideas.

Application

Directions: When you have a list of guide questions, read through the selection again. This time, write one or more questions that require application of the information in the text to a situation in the real world.

Writing

Directions: Your last task is to prepare a writing assignment. For example, you might ask for a paragraph in which the writer comments on the ideas in the reading selection. You might also ask for a summary of the selection.

UNIT TWO

READING AND THINKING ABOUT CULTURE

As the traveler who has once been from home is wiser than he who has never left his own doorstep, so a knowledge of one other culture should sharpen our ability to scrutinize more steadily, to appreciate more lovingly, our own.

—Margaret Mead

Culture regulates our lives at every turn. From the moment we are born until we die there is, whether we are conscious of it or not, constant pressure upon us to follow certain types of behavior that other men have created for us.

—Clyde Kluckhohn

Thinking about Culture

Before you begin this part of the textbook, think about the brief descriptions below. Then answer the question at the end.

A small group of people called *hijras* live in India. *Hijras* are men who live as women. They wear female clothing and jewelry and their body language is feminine. They earn their living by asking for alms and receiving pay for blessing newborn babies. They believe in a goddess named Bahuchara Mata and identify with her totally. They undergo emasculation as a way of expressing their devotion to the goddess.

The Mundugumor people of New Guinea live a life of extreme individualism and hostility. They live in subdivided households and there is little community life. Babies are kept in hard uncomfortable baskets. When they cry, the mothers do not pick them up and hold them. Instead, they make scratching noises on the side of the basket. If the child continues to cry, the mother will feed it, standing up, in an awkward manner. As soon as the child has eaten, it is immediately returned to the basket.

The Wodaabe of West Africa hold a celebration every year before which the unmarried men spend days styling their hair, donning elegant robes, and applying elaborate and enormous amounts of make-up. As a result they are transformed into very feminine-looking young men. Nevertheless, the young women of the village are enchanted by the sight of these men, who most Americans would take for women. A beauty contest is then held to choose the most "beautiful" man. Then, if they agree, the winner and the most eligible young woman of the village may wed.

These are snapshots of people living in various cultures. Do these people seem very different from you and your family? Can you imagine that they would find *your* customs to be strange indeed? How can we account for the great differences that exist among human beings all over the world? After all, we are all basically the same animal, with a few differences in skin color, height, hair texture, eye shape, and so on. The major differences seem to be in the *culture* each group has developed. Think about this question:

What is culture?

Now, write your own definition or explanation of culture.

Anthropologist Clifford Geertz says in his book The Interpretation of Cultures, *"There is no such thing as a human nature independent of culture. Men without culture . . . would be unworkable monstrosities with very few useful instincts, fewer recognizable sentiments, and no intellect: mental basket cases."*

In this section, you will be introduced to the basic elements of culture and will take a look at different groups of people to see how they are different from us—and how they are the same.

CULTURE

Clyde Kluckhohn

Why do the Chinese dislike milk and milk products? Why would the Japanese die willingly in a Banzai charge [in World War II] that seemed senseless to Americans? Why do some nations trace descent through the father, others through the mother, still others through both parents? Not because different peoples have different instincts, not because they were destined by God or Fate to different habits, not because the weather is different in China and Japan and the United States. Sometimes shrewd common sense has an answer that is close to that of the anthropologist: "because they were brought up that way." By *culture,* anthropology means the total life way of a people, the social legacy the individual acquires from his group. Or *culture* can be regarded as that part of the environment that is the creation of man.

This technical term has a wider meaning than the *culture* of history and literature. A humble cooking pot is as much a cultural product as is a Beethoven sonata. In ordinary speech a man of culture is a man who can speak languages other than his own, who is familiar with history, literature, philosophy, or the fine arts. In some cliques that definition is still narrower. The cultured person is one who can talk about James Joyce, Scarlatti, and Picasso. To the anthropologist, however, to be human is to be cultured. There is culture in general, and then there are the specific cultures, such as Russian, American, British, Hottentot, Inca. The general abstract notion serves to remind us that we cannot explain acts solely in terms of the biological properties of the people concerned, their individual past experience, and the immediate situation. The past experience of other men in the form of culture enters into almost every event. Each specific culture constitutes a kind of blueprint for all of life's activities.

One of the interesting things about human beings is that they try to understand themselves and their own behavior. While this has been particularly true of Europeans in recent times, there is no group which has not developed a scheme or schemes to explain man's actions. To the insistent human query "why?" the most exciting illumination anthropology has to offer is that of the concept of culture. Its explanatory importance is comparable to categories such as evolution in biology, gravity in physics, disease in medicine. A good deal of human behavior can be understood and, indeed, predicted, if we know a people's design for living. Many acts are neither accidental nor due to personal peculiarities nor caused by supernatural forces nor simply mysterious. Even those of us who pride ourselves on our individualism follow most of the time a pattern not of our own making. We brush our teeth on arising. We put on pants—not a loincloth or a grass skirt. We eat three meals a day—not four or five or two. We sleep in a bed—not in a hammock or on a sheep pelt. I do not have to know the individual and his life history to be able to predict these and countless other regularities, including many in the thinking process, of all Americans who are not incarcerated in jails or hospitals for the insane.

4   To the American woman a system of plural wives seems "instinctively" abhorrent. She cannot understand how any woman can fail to be jealous and uncomfortable if she must share her husband with other women. She feels it "unnatural" to accept such a situation. On the other hand, a Koryak woman of Siberia, for example, would find it hard to understand how a woman could be so selfish and so undesirous of feminine companionship in the home as to wish to restrict her husband to one mate.

5   Some years ago I met in New York City a young man who did not speak a word of English and was obviously bewildered by American ways. By "blood" he was American, for his parents had gone from Indiana to China as missionaries. Orphaned in infancy, he was reared in a remote village. All who met him found him more Chinese than American. The facts of his blue eyes and light hair were less impressive than a Chinese style of gait, Chinese arm and hand movements, Chinese facial expression, and Chinese modes of thought. The biological heritage was American, but the cultural training had been Chinese. He returned to China.

6   Another example of another kind: I once knew a trader's wife in Arizona who took a somewhat devilish interest in producing a cultural reaction. Guests who came her way were often served delicious sandwiches filled with a meat that seemed to be neither chicken nor tuna fish yet was reminiscent of both. To queries she gave no reply until each had eaten his fill. She then explained that what they had eaten was not chicken, not tuna fish, but the rich, white flesh of freshly killed rattlesnakes. The response was instantaneous—vomiting, often violent vomiting. A biological process is caught in a cultural web.

7   A highly intelligent teacher with long and successful experience in the public schools of Chicago was finishing her first year in a [North American] Indian school. When asked how her Navaho pupils compared in intelligence with Chicago youngsters, she replied, "Well, I just don't know. Sometimes the Indians seem just as bright. At other times they just act like dumb animals. The other night we had a dance in the high school. I saw a boy who is one of the best students in my English class standing off by himself. So I took him over to a pretty girl and told them to dance. But they just stood there with their heads down. They wouldn't even say anything." I inquired if she knew whether or not they were members of the same clan. "What difference would that make?"

8   "How would you feel about getting into bed with your brother?" The teacher walked off in a huff, but, actually, the two cases were quite comparable in principle. To the Indian, the type of bodily contact involved in our social dancing has a directly sexual connotation. The incest taboos between members

of the same clan are as severe as between true brothers and sisters. The shame of the Indians at the suggestion that a clan brother and sister should dance and the indignation of the white teacher at the idea that she should share a bed with an adult brother represent equally nonrational responses, culturally standardized unreason.

All this does not mean that there is no such thing as raw human nature. The very fact that certain of the same institutions are found in all known societies indicates that, at bottom, all human beings are very much alike. The files of the Cross-Cultural Survey at Yale University are organized according to categories, such as "marriage ceremonies," "life crisis rites," "incest taboos." At least seventy-five of these categories are represented in every single one of the hundreds of cultures analyzed. This is hardly surprising. The members of all human groups have about the same biological equipment. All men undergo the same poignant life experiences, such as birth, helplessness, illness, old age, and death. The biological potentialities of the species are the blocks with which cultures are built. Some patterns of every culture crystallize around focuses provided by the inevitables of biology: the difference between the sexes, the presence of persons of different ages, the varying physical strength and skill of individuals. The facts of nature also limit culture forms. No culture provides patterns for jumping over trees or for eating iron ore.

9

Vocabulary

Directions: Find each of the key words in the reading selection. Study the word in its context and try to determine its meaning. Write your guess in the margin of the text, near the word. Then read over the sentence, mentally substituting your guess for the key word. Does the sentence still make sense? Does it retain its original meaning? If it does, you've probably figured out the meaning of the key word correctly. In any case, confirm your guess by checking a dictionary or thesaurus.

If you take your meaning from a dictionary or thesaurus, be sure the definition includes words you already know and feel comfortable using. If it doesn't, you will be worse off than when you started—you will have begun with one word you didn't know and ended with *two* words you don't know!

Record the new words you've learned in the following chart.

Key Word	Paragraph	Meaning
1. legacy	1	
2. cliques	2	
3. insistent	3	
4. abhorrent	4	
5. gait	5	

Key Word	Paragraph	Meaning
6. instantaneous	6	
7. poignant	9	
Others?		

Guide Questions

Directions: The purpose of these questions is to guide your analysis of the text. Your thoughtful answers will ensure that you have understood the main ideas the author wanted to convey. Some of the questions require that you simply find the stated facts in the reading selection; others will ask you to do more difficult tasks, such as paraphrasing information (putting the author's ideas into your own words), synthesizing several ideas into one complex thought, evaluating (making judgments about) an idea, or taking information from the reading and applying it to a new situation or to your own life.

Write answers to the questions in your notebook or on a separate sheet of paper if your instructor wishes to collect it. Your answers will form the basis of class discussion.

1. Kluckhohn states that the term *culture* can have two different meanings, depending on the context. What does *culture* mean in ordinary speech? What does *culture* mean to an anthropologist?
2. a. Many people feel that the way we eat, drink, marry, walk, and talk are somehow "instinctual" or "natural." Give some examples from the text that contradict this.
   b. Explain what Kluckhohn means by his description of people's reaction to eating rattlesnake: "A biological process is caught in a cultural web."
3. Kluckhohn cites many institutions that have been found in every single one of the hundreds of cultures that have been studied. How does he explain the presence of so many similarities among the peoples of the world?
4. Explain what Kluckhohn means by his final point, "the facts of nature also limit culture forms."

Application

Directions: Consider each of the following little stories, which describe the traditional behavior of a group of people in a certain situation. Compare and contrast these with how you and the members of your culture would act in the same situation.

Work in small groups to complete this assignment. First, choose a *group leader,* who will be responsible for directing the conversation and ensuring that every member participates. Next, choose a *reader,* who will read each of the stories out loud before the group discusses it. Next, choose a *secretary,* who will record the group's answers to the questions following each story. Finally, choose a *timekeeper,* whose job is to "keep the ball rolling" and make sure the group works efficiently. When you finish, your instructor may want you to hand in your answers.

1. *Finding a Wife.* A Chiricahua man, young and unmarried, goes to visit an old woman, the grandmother of an unmarried girl:

> I went to her place that night. I had heard the old lady had some *tiswin* (a fermented liquor made of corn). When I got there she told me to have a drink. As we talked she told me that I was single and needed a wife. She mentioned this girl (her grandchild) and said it was worth two horses to get her. I had never seen the girl before. When I got home I started to think about it seriously. I talked it over with my relatives. An uncle of mine gave me a mule, and a cousin gave me a horse.
>
> The next day I went to the home of a certain woman, a middle-aged woman. She was eating when I arrived. I called her outside and hired her to speak for me to this girl's grandmother. This woman lived just on the other side of a stream from the girl and her grandmother. The next day my go-between demanded two good horses. My go-between thanked the grandmother and came to tell me what had been said. I gave her the horse and the mule to lead to the old woman, and the next day I went to the girl.

Morris E. Opler, *An Apache Life-Way,* p. 157

Describe how a member of your culture finds a wife. List the similarities and differences between the way you would do it and the way the Chiricahua did it. (The Chiricahua are North American Indians.)

2. *A Husband Discovers His Wife Has Been Unfaithful.* A Chiricahua man is expected to take drastic action:

> A wronged husband who does not show some rancor is considered unmanly. . . . The woman, since she is close at hand, is likely to be the first to feel the husband's wrath. A beating is the least punishment she suffers. If there is no one to intercede for her, her very life may be forfeit, or she may be subjected to mutilation. . . . The husband is just as insistent that the man who has disrupted his home be punished. After the husband has punished or killed his wife, he will go after the man and kill him.

An Apache Life-Way, p. 410

List the similarities and differences between how a member of your culture would handle this situation and how the Chiricahua behaved.

3. *A Wedding in Tahiti.*

> Tahitian weddings generally last two days, the law allowing two days off from work, with pay. The civil ceremony takes place at the mayor's office. If there is a religious ceremony, it takes place later at the church. The reception is usually at the home of a family member. The decorations include a temporary covered terrace (in case of rain), posts wrapped in coconut leaves with flowers inserted into them; flowers and greenery everywhere. The bride and groom are welcomed to the reception with flower garlands and leis. Tahitians do not serve a wedding cake or throw a wedding bouquet or the garter. The festivities include eating, storytelling, singing, spoontapping, and dancing. At the reception the couple is given their new name, the "marriage name" by which they will henceforth be called. Usually the name is selected by the family and is the name of an ancestor or a name from the Bible. The names of the couple's first and second children are also selected.

Describe the similarities and differences between a wedding in Tahiti and a wedding in your culture.

4. *A Funeral among the Teton-Dakota Indians.*

> At the death of an individual, his relatives and friends gathered at his tepee to mourn. The women spent four days in intermittent wailing. Parents often gashed themselves or severed a finger to express their grief. A bereaved father might wander from camp, singing a death song, to shoot down the first person whom he met and then kill himself. A give-away of the family's property to the mourners was part of the funeral ceremony, and another give-away ended the year of mourning.

> Gordon MacGregor, *Warriors without Weapons: Society and Personality Development of the Pine Ridge Sioux*, p. 94

Describe a funeral ritual in your society. How is it similar to and different from a funeral among the Teton-Dakota Indians? (The Teton-Dakotas are North American Indians.)

5. *Birth Ceremonies of the Hmong.*

> Hmong women try not to cry or show pain during labor. Moments after birth, the baby is given a silver necklace to warn away bad spirits. In some Hmong communities, women make caps with flower designs to fool the spirits into thinking the baby is a flower.
>
> The placenta is buried beneath the central pole of the house. If the firstborn is a boy, the umbilical cord is dried and boiled with a piece of oak. It is then used as medicine.
>
> For the first month of life, the new mother eats only freshly killed chicken, boiled, with broth and rice three times a day.

When the baby is three days old, a naming ceremony takes place. The family calls back the child's soul, which may have been frightened away during birth. White strings are tied around the baby's wrist to protect him or her from the spirits. The strings prevent the soul from being stolen, and they remain in place until they fall off or disintegrate. Traditionally, the Hmong do not compliment a baby, believing evil spirits will then take the baby away.

Describe the rituals surrounding the birth of a child in your culture. Compare and contrast them with the traditions of the Hmong. (The Hmong live in Southeast Asia, principally in Laos and Cambodia.)

Writing

Directions: Return to the definition of culture that you were asked to write on page 50, "Thinking about Culture." Evaluate your definition in light of what you learned from this selection. Compare your definition to Kluckhohn's explanation of *culture*. Is your definition sufficient? Is it accurate? How would you rewrite it? Write a few sentences in response to these questions.

In Japan, when two businessmen meet, they automatically bow to one another; in the United States, two men in the same situation would shake hands. In Iran, men and women eat separately, while in most Western countries, men and women have their meals together. Fish is used as a food by most American Indian tribes, but some, including the Navajos and Apaches of New Mexico, consider it nauseating and unfit for human consumption. The aboriginal tribes of Australia and the Indians of Tierra del Fuego wear almost no clothing at all; the Baganda people of East Africa must be fully clothed from neck to ankles. Among the Navajos of the American Southwest, a man was not supposed to speak to or even look at his wife's mother. In northwestern India, married older brothers were not expected to show jealousy when younger brothers slept with their brides. Countless other cultural differences exist among human societies. When asked, for example, why they eat with knives and forks rather than with chopsticks, most Americans would reply, "Because that's the way we do it," or perhaps "Because it's the 'right' way to eat," or even "I don't know." Such answers are not very informative. Most people don't think about these common patterns of social behavior—they simply obey the rules. As anthropologist Clyde Kluckhohn says, "Culture regulates our lives at every turn. From the moment we are born until we die there is, whether we are conscious of it or not, constant pressure on us to follow certain types of behavior that other men have created for us."

In this selection we learn about the rules—imposed by culture—called norms.

NORMS

Mary Fjeldstad

1   Why do we behave in controlled and predictable ways? Because we are members of a society of human beings, our actions are controlled by *norms*—shared guidelines that prescribe the appropriate behavior in a particular situation. Norms define how we are expected to behave in specific circumstances in a specific society. Many norms are unwritten rules that regulate even the smallest details of social life. Usually, we are not even aware that we are obeying norms; they are simply a part of us. Such norms include knowing when to speak, how to address other people (Sir, Mr. Jones, or Bobby), when to sit or stand and when to leave. We learn these norms through the process of *socialization*—the education of individuals in society's customs and beliefs through the family, the school, professional organizations, and so on.

2   We generally only think about a norm when someone departs from it. For example, if, in a restaurant, someone were to suddenly begin eating with his hands, we would all be surprised, or distressed, or even amused by this departure from the American norm of using silverware to eat. Our criticism of the person, or ridicule, or even request for him to leave would be our way of applying sanctions to him. When we visit people from other cultures, we quickly become aware that they do things according to their own set of rules, which may be very different from ours. If we were to visit a village in Burkina Faso in Africa,

---

*This selection is based in part on information in Ian Robertson's *Sociology*.

for example, we would probably find ourselves the victim of sanctions if we did not use our hands to eat, as is the custom there.

What is the purpose of norms? Norms help society to function smoothly. They give guidelines to follow in our own behavior and help us anticipate how others will behave. Imagine how difficult life would be if we had no norms! Each time you encountered a novel situation, you'd have to figure out anew how you were going to act. Take a job interview, for example: should you wear a T-shirt or a jacket? Should you stand or sit? Or why not kneel down or lie on the floor? How can you expect the interviewer to act? Will he or she speak first? Or wait for you to begin? Will the interviewer direct the conversation? Shake your hand or bow? Or perhaps kiss your cheek? All of these questions are answered by our knowledge of the rules of our society. Life would indeed be stressful if we could not rely on norms. 3

The function of norms—regulating social behavior—is so crucial to day-to-day life that there is always pressure on people to conform. 4

There are two major types of norms. The first, *folkways,* are the ordinary rules of everyday life. We expect conformity to folkways, but accept a great deal of nonconformity. For example, in the United States, we expect people to bathe frequently, speak quietly in a library, wait for their turn in line. If people do not follow such rules, they are sanctioned, or "punished," by being criticized, or laughed at, but they are not considered criminal or depraved. Society is generally not outraged when someone violates a folkway. 5

On the other hand, *mores,* much more powerful norms, are treated more seriously. Rules against theft, murder, and rape are examples of mores. People believe that their mores are crucial to the decent and orderly functioning of society and are deeply outraged by violations of them. Penalties for those who disobey mores are serious and can range from monetary fines to physical attack to imprisonment or commitment to a mental institution. 6

One special type of more is the *taboo*—a powerful prohibition against acts that society considers loathsome. In most cultures, for example, the eating of human flesh is a taboo, one that is rarely broken. 7

Most mores are formally encoded and thus are also laws. A law is simply a rule of conduct that a society has officially recorded and that is enforced by the power of the state. Laws are written to codify existing norms, to specify the requirements and the exact penalties for violations of them. Penalties can vary widely both within a culture and from one culture to another. For example, in Iran, adultery may be punished by death, while in the United States violations of this law are usually ignored by the authorities. Within the United States the penalties for violations of laws vary from state to state. For example, drug abuse in certain states, such as Texas, is punished more severely than in many other states. The penalty for speeding while driving in New York is a heavy fine, as much as $500, while in the state of Montana the fine was only $5, no matter how fast the driver was going. The penalty for drunk driving can be as severe as a $1,000 fine plus a year in jail (in South Dakota) or as light as a $100 fine and ten days in jail (in Oklahoma). 8

9   Sometimes legislators introduce new laws in an attempt to alter existing norms. For example, in 1919 a constitutional amendment outlawing the manufacture and sale of alcoholic beverages was passed. Such laws are often ineffective if they run counter to a society's norms. In this case, the prohibition law was routinely violated until it was repealed fourteen years later. Other examples of ineffective laws are those prohibiting stores from being open on Sunday and those forbidding the personal use of certain drugs.

10   Norms are not fixed, however. Social protest and political movements may bring about changes in social norms—for example, abortion-law reform, treatment of homosexuals by society, and changes in the roles of women. Unlike Prohibition, certain laws that oppose social norms have survived. A notable example is the civil-rights laws passed in the 1960s and 1970s, which were aimed at changing the traditional behaviors of white-dominated society, especially in the South. Laws that required equal access to public facilities for people of all races ran counter to traditional norms and provoked great resistance. Eventually, however, the norms began to change to conform to the civil rights laws and great differences in folkways and mores have occurred in the past few decades. Traditional modes of behavior in the South, such as requiring blacks to sit at the rear of public buses, use separate public toilet facilities, or eat at lunch counters reserved for "colored," have changed through the strict enforcement of new laws as well as the efforts of civil rights groups.

Vocabulary

Directions: Find each of the key words in the reading selection. Study the word in its context and try to determine its meaning. Write your guess in the margin of the text, near the word. Then read over the sentence, mentally substituting your guess for the key word. Does the sentence still make sense? Does it retain its original meaning? If it does, you've probably figured out the meaning of the key word correctly. In any case, confirm your guess by checking a dictionary or thesaurus.

If you take your meaning from a dictionary or thesaurus, be sure the definition includes words you already know and feel comfortable using. If it doesn't, you will be worse off than when you started—you will have begun with one word you didn't know and ended with *two* words you don't know!

Record the new words you've learned in the following chart.

Key Word	Paragraph	Meaning
1. sanctions	2	
2. conform	4	
3. depraved	5	
4. crucial	6	

Key Word	Paragraph	Meaning
5. loathsome	7	
6. run counter to	9	
Others?		

Guide Questions

Directions: The purpose of these questions is to guide your analysis of the text. Your thoughtful answers will ensure that you have understood the main ideas the author wanted to convey. Some of the questions require that you simply find the stated facts in the reading selection; others will ask you to do more difficult tasks, such as paraphrasing information (putting the author's ideas into your own words), synthesizing several ideas into one complex thought, evaluating (making judgments about) an idea, or taking information from the reading and applying it to a new situation or to your own life.

Write answers to the questions in your notebook or on a separate sheet of paper if your instructor wishes to collect them. Your answers will form the basis of class discussion.

1. Define the term *norms*.
2. It is a norm in American society for men to shake hands upon meeting one another. Give an example of a different norm in some other society that regulates the same situation.
3. How do we learn the norms of our society?
4. Explain the purpose of norms.
5. Give some examples of what your day-to-day life would be like if we did not have norms.
6. List the two major types of norms discussed in the text.
7. a. Give an example of a folkway mentioned in the text.
   b. Give an example of a folkway not mentioned in the text.
8. Describe the type of pressure that is put on people to conform to folkways.
9. How do mores differ from folkways?
10. Give some examples of mores in American society.
11. Describe the type of pressure that society puts on people to conform to mores.
12. What are taboos?
13. Define the term *laws*.
14. Explain why the Prohibition amendment was not effective.
15. What can cause the norms of a society to change?

Application

1. Norms vary from society to society (as you probably already know if you are from another country or if you know people from other countries). One example of this variation in norms is that, in the United States, marriage is thought of as a private arrangement between a man and a woman who are motivated by romantic love. Do you know of other cultures where marriage is *not* a product of romantic love? Where the bride and groom have no control over whom or when they marry? If you do, write a paragraph describing this different kind of marriage. Be sure to name the society you are describing. You may need to visit the library and research marriage customs in the culture you choose.

2. Choose a social situation (other than marriage), and in two paragraphs describe how it is articulated in two different societies: the United States and some other society. In the first paragraph, describe the situation and the norm that regulates it in the United States; in the second paragraph, describe how the situation is regulated in some other society. For example, you might write one paragraph describing how Americans eat dinner using plates, knives, forks, and spoons, and a second paragraph describing how the Chinese use different utensils for their meals.

3. Write at least one paragraph in response to the following statement: Norms are constantly changing, especially in a dynamic society such as the United States. List as many norms as you can that have changed in your lifetime, or since your parents' youth. Then explain *how* each norm has changed. For example, you might consider how norms regarding premarital sex, smoking, or dress have changed in the past several years.

Marking Text

Turn to page 421, "Learning Strategy III—Marking Text." Read and study the information on how to mark your text. Then mark the selection "Norms" using what you've learned. To get you started, here is a model of how you might mark the first section of the selection. Finish marking the selection on your own.

NORMS

Mary Fjeldstad

1   Why do we behave in controlled and predictable ways? Because we are members of a society of human beings, our actions are controlled by *norms*—shared guidelines that prescribe the appropriate behavior in a particular situation. Norms define how we are expected to behave in specific circumstances in a specific society. Many norms are unwritten rules that regulate even the smallest details of social life. Usually, we are not even aware that we are obeying norms; they are simply a part of us. Such norms include knowing when to speak, how to address other people (Sir, Mr. Jones, or Bobby), when to sit or stand and when to leave. We learn these norms through the process of *socialization*—the education of individuals in

Norms definition

Socialization defined

society's customs and beliefs through the family, the school, professional organizations, and so on.

We generally only think about a norm when someone departs from it. For example, if, in a restaurant, someone were to suddenly begin eating with his hands, we would all be surprised, or distressed, or even amused by this departure from the American norm of using silverware to eat. Our criticism of the person, or ridicule, or even request for him to leave would be our way of applying sanctions to him. When we visit people from other cultures, we quickly become aware that they do things according to their own set of rules, which may be very different from ours. If we were to visit a village in Burkina Faso in Africa, for example, we would probably find ourselves the victim of sanctions if we did not use our hands to eat, as is the custom there.

Sanctions?

2

What is the purpose of norms? Norms help society to function smoothly. They give guidelines to follow in our own behavior and help us anticipate how others will behave. Imagine how difficult life would be if we had no norms! Each time you encountered a novel situation, you'd have to figure out anew how you were going to act. Take a job interview, for example: should you wear a T-shirt or a jacket? Should you stand or sit? Or why not kneel down or lie on the floor? How can you expect the interviewer to act? Will he or she speak first? Or wait for you to begin? Will the interviewer direct the conversation? Shake your hand or bow? Or perhaps kiss your cheek? All of these questions are answered by our knowledge of the rules of our society. Life would indeed be stressful if we could not rely on norms.

Why do we have norms?

3

(I never thought of this before!)

The function of norms—regulating social behavior—is so crucial to day-to-day life that there is always pressure on people to conform.

4

There are two major types of norms. The first, *folkways,* are the ordinary rules of everyday life. We expect conformity to folkways, but accept a great deal of non-conformity. For example, in the United States, we expect people to bathe frequently, speak quietly in a library, wait for their turn in line. If people do not follow such rules, they are sanctioned, or "punished," by being criticized, or laughed at, but they are not considered criminal or depraved. Society is generally not outraged when someone violates a folkway.

5 2 Types:
1-folkways

Exs of folkways

?

On the other hand, *mores,* much more powerful norms, are treated more seriously. Rules against theft, murder, and rape are examples of mores. People believe that their mores are crucial to the decent and orderly functioning of society and are deeply outraged by violations of them. Penalties for those who disobey mores are serious and can range from monetary fines to physical attack to imprisonment or commitment to a mental institution.

6

2-mores

Exs of mores

Now, finish, marking the chapter yourself.

Which is more important to you—winning that tennis game or making sure your friend has a good time playing? Both reflect values important to most Americans—winning and friendship. Sometimes we must decide between two equally desirable things, and it can be tough!

Most Americans would say they value honesty very highly. But what if it comes into conflict with some other value, like friendship? For example, if you saw your friend cheating on an exam, and he begged you not to tell, would you? You are caught in a conflict of two important values. What would you do?

Many Americans expect to work hard, overtime if necessary, to make decisions fast, and implement them quickly. If Americans try to work "as usual" in another culture where a long, relaxed lunch is the norm, and speedy implementation of decisions is unknown, they may become upset and frustrated because their values conflict with those of their new culture. Which values are at work here?

In this excerpt from a textbook chapter we learn about values, the principles that underlie a society's ideas and behavior.

VALUES

Ian Robertson

1   The norms of a society are ultimately an expression of its values—socially shared ideas about what is good, right, and desirable. The difference between values and norms is that values are abstract, general concepts, whereas norms are specific guidelines for people in particular kinds of situations.

Importance of Values

2   The values of a society are important because they influence the content of its norms. If a society values education highly, its norms will make provision for mass schooling. If it values a large population, its norms will encourage big families. In principle at least, all norms can be traced to a basic social value. For example, the norms that require a student to be more polite and formal to a professor than to other students express the value our society places on respect for authority and learning. The mid-20th century norms that insisted on short hair for men reflected the high value placed on men's "masculinity" in American culture—a value that was threatened by long hair because it was regarded as "effeminate."

3   Although all norms express social values, many norms persist long after the conditions that gave rise to them have been forgotten. The folkway that requires us to shake hands, especially when greeting a stranger, seems to have originated long ago in the desire to show that no weapon was concealed in the right hand. The folkway of throwing rice or confetti over a bride and groom may seem rather meaningless, but it actually stems from an ancient practice of showering newly-weds with nuts, fruits, and seeds as symbols of fertility.

American Values

Unlike norms, whose existence can easily be observed in everyday behavior, values are often more difficult to identify. The values of a society have to be inferred from its norms, so that any analysis of social values relies heavily on the interpretations of the observer. The United States presents a particular problem, for it has a heterogeneous culture drawn from many different racial, ethnic, religious, and regional traditions, and so lacks the unquestioned consensus on values that smaller, traditional communities tend to display. Sociologists have therefore concentrated on detecting "core" values that appear to be shared by the majority of Americans. The most influential of these attempts is that of Robin Williams, who found fifteen basic value orientations in the United States:

1. *Achievement and success.* The society is highly competitive, and great value is placed on the achievement of power, wealth, and prestige.
2. *Activity and work.* Regular, disciplined work is highly valued for its own sake; those who do not work are considered lazy and even immoral.
3. *Moral orientation.* Americans tend to be moralists, seeing the world in terms of right and wrong and constantly evaluating the moral behavior of others.
4. *Humanitarianism.* Americans regard themselves as a kindly, charitable people, always ready to come to the aid of the less fortunate or the underdog.
5. *Efficiency and practicality.* Americans believe that problems have solutions, and they are an intensely practical people; the ability to "get things done" is widely admired.
6. *Progress.* Americans look to the future rather than the past, sharing a conviction that things can and should get better; their outlook is fundamentally optimistic.
7. *Material comfort.* Americans value the "good life," which they define in terms of a high standard of living and the possession of material goods.
8. *Equality.* Americans claim to believe in human equality, particularly in equality of opportunity; they generally relate to one another in an informal, egalitarian way.
9. *Freedom.* The freedom of the individual is regarded as one of the most important values in American life; Americans believe devoutly that they are and should remain "free."
10. *External conformity.* Despite their expressed belief in "rugged individualism," Americans tend to be conformist and are suspicious of those who are not.
11. *Science and rationality.* Americans believe deeply in a scientific rational approach to the world and in the use of applied science to gain mastery over the environment.
12. *Nationalism–patriotism.* Americans are proud of their country and its achievements; the "American way of life" is highly valued and assumed to be the best in the world.

13. *Democracy.* Americans regard their form of government as highly democratic, and believe that every citizen should have the right of political participation.

14. *Individual personality.* To be a responsible, self-respecting individual is very important, and Americans are reluctant to give the group priority over the individual.

15. *Group-superiority themes.* A strong countervalue to that of individual personality is the one that places a higher value on some racial, ethnic, class, or religious groups than on others.

6   It is obvious that some of these values are not entirely consistent with one another. Many of them, too, are accepted by some Americans but rejected by others. Also, Williams's list does not exhaust all the possibilities, and other writers have identified rather different values. James Henslin, for example, includes several items on Williams's list but adds others, such as education, religiosity, male supremacy, romantic love, monogamy, and heterosexuality. Moreover, values change over time, and some of those listed by Williams may be eroding. Questions have been raised, for example, about the meaning of "progress," and about new problems posed by science and technology, such as pollution of the environment. There is perhaps less insistence now on the value of conformity, and certainly less emphasis on group superiority, than there was a few decades ago.

Vocabulary

Directions: Locate each of the key words in the reading selection. Then read and study each word in its context and try to determine its meaning. Use a dictionary or thesaurus to check your guess. Write the meanings of the words in the margin of the text.

Record the new words you've learned.

Key Word	Paragraph	Meaning
1. inferred	4	
2. heterogeneous	4	
3. consensus	4	
4. eroding	6	
Others?		

Guide Questions

Directions: The purpose of these guide questions is to ensure your understanding of what you have read. They also will help you to analyze and evaluate the author's ideas and apply them to the real world and your own life.

Write answers to the questions in your notebook or on a separate sheet of paper if your instructor wishes to collect them. Your answers will form the basis of class discussion.

1. Contrast the definitions of *values* and *norms* according to the information given in the first paragraph.
2. Give two examples of values that you personally hold.
3. a. Cite a few of the examples of values from the selection and the norms that result from them.
   b. Based on your understanding of question 3a, how would you describe the *relationship* between values and norms?
4. In paragraph 3 of the selection, the author states that some norms persist despite the fact that the conditions that produced them have disappeared. Give one of the examples from the paragraph. Then think of another example from your own knowledge and experience.
5. Discuss the point made in paragraph 4 of the selection: "The United States presents a particular problem, for it has a heterogeneous culture. . . ." What does the author mean by "a heterogeneous culture"? How can we account for the fact that the United States is so heterogeneous?
6. In the introduction and in paragraph 6, you read that we often must choose between two values in the same situation—for example, between honesty and friendship when your friend asks you to help her cheat on an exam. Can you think of some other situations in which two values are in conflict?
7. It is important to remember that values are different in different societies. The Tangu, a group of people who live in New Guinea, play a game called *taketak,* which is similar to bowling. The goal of the game is not for one team to score more points than the other, but rather for both sides to score the *same* number of points. The Tangu place a high value on *equivalence* and think that winning generates ill will. In fact, when the Europeans introduced soccer to New Guinea, the Tangu changed the rules so that the object of the game was for the two teams to score the same number of goals. Sometimes their soccer games went on for days! Americans, of course, value competition and winning and insist on winners and losers. Living among the Tangu would certainly be very different from living in the United States. What might be some of the *advantages* of living in a society where equivalence is valued and winning is disapproved of? What might the *disadvantages* be?
8. A major distinction between values and norms is that values are abstract concepts and norms are concrete rules for behavior. Using the chart that follows, give several examples of abstract values and some of the concrete norms that are derived from them. Some information is already filled in to get you started.

The Value	The Norm
Honesty	*I pay my taxes.*
	I will not cheat on Tuesday's exam.
Efficiency	*I make a list of "things to do" every day.*
Thrift	

Application

Directions: Choose one of the following exercises.

1. Did you know that in Mexico clocks do not "run," they "walk"? And that Mexicans do not say they "missed" the bus, but rather the bus "left" them? In three or four sentences, explain what you think these two examples tell us about the differing values of the United States and Mexico.

2. Work in small groups to complete this exercise. Below are brief descriptions of people in specific situations. Read the descriptions out loud, then discuss with your group members which American value is reflected in each little story.

    a. A mother says angrily to her young child, "You march right back to that bathroom—and this time use soap!"

    b. A boss looks at the clock as an employee arrives at work. The clock says 9:25 A.M. The boss says, "Well, good *afternoon!*"

    c. A girl wins an essay-writing contest sponsored by a nearby university. When told of her prize, she smiles and says, "Oh, it was nothing—anyone could have done it."

    d. A father takes his young daughter outside to practice baseball every night, rain or shine. When the girl is beaten by another child in a ballgame, they increase the length of their practice sessions. When the girl is chosen "Most Valuable Player" of her league, the father and daughter are happy and proud.

e. A male executive hears there may be layoffs in his company, so he decides to look for another job. Before going on his first interview, he visits a hair-styling salon to have his gray hair dyed back to its original
brown color.

Add the values you identify in this question to the chart of values and
norms you created for guide question 8.

Marking Text
Mark the chapter, "Values." (Marking text is explained on page 421.)

Making Connections
Connect the ideas in "Values" with those in the previous selection, "Norms." How did the
information in "Norms" help you to understand "Values"? What did you learn in "Values"
that clarified or enhanced your understanding of "Norms?"

The diversity of behavior among the peoples of the world is tremendous. For example, in some societies, bending your finger toward your body means "come here," while in other cultures, it means "go away." In India, cows wander freely through the streets, something Americans find offensive; in the United States, dogs run freely in homes, something visitors from India would find disgusting. Most Americans teach their children not to fight. "Solve your problems with words, not fists," they counsel. Among the Yanomamo of South America, a father deliberately teases and goads his son until the child, in desperation, strikes him in the face. The father cries out in approval. Why have humans all over the world, who are so similar physically, developed such different ways of living? Cultural anthropologists try to discover why people behave as they do. In this chapter we learn that our culture is only one alternative among the many designs for living. No one group of people has developed the "right" way of living. "Other fields, other grasshoppers," say the Javanese.

UNITY IN DIVERSITY

Donald Light and Suzanne Keller

1   What is more basic, more "natural" than love between a man and woman? Eskimo men offer their wives to guests and friends as a gesture of hospitality; both husband and wife feel extremely offended if the guest declines. The Banaro of New Guinea believe it would be disastrous for a woman to conceive her first child by her husband and not by one of her father's close friends, as is their custom.

2   The real father is a close friend of the bride's father. . . . Nevertheless the first-born child inherits the name and possessions of the husband. An American would deem such a custom immoral, but Banaro tribesmen would be equally shocked to discover that the first-born child of an American couple is the offspring of the husband.

3   The Yanomamo of northern Brazil, whom anthropologist Napoleon A. Chagnon named "the fierce people," encourage what we would consider extreme disrespect. Small boys are applauded for striking their mothers and fathers in the face. Yanomamo parents would laugh at our efforts to curb aggression in children, much as they laughed at Chagnon's naiveté when he first came to live with them. To be officially considered a man, a Yanomamo boy must compile a record of successful battles, and if he is to be taken seriously, by the time he reaches puberty his body must be covered with scars. Older men, hardened to injury, duel with each other constantly in an effort to prove which man has the greater capacity to bear pain. Even women do not escape tribal savagery since men will frequently prove just how fierce they are by beating, mutilating, or wounding their wives. A wife cannot even escape to her family because, to the family, the husband's behavior is simply part of a long tradition.

4   The variations among cultures are startling, yet all peoples have customs and beliefs about marriage, the bearing and raising of children, sex, and hospitality—to name just a few of the universals anthropologists have discovered in their

cross-cultural explorations. But the details of cultures do indeed vary: in this country, not so many years ago, when a girl was serious about a boy and he about her, she wore his fraternity pin over her heart; in the Fiji Islands, girls put hibiscus flowers behind their ears when they are in love. The specific gestures are different but the impulse to symbolize feelings, to dress courtship in ceremonies, is the same. How do we explain this unity in diversity?

Cultural Universals

Cultural universals are all of the behavior patterns and institutions that have been found in all known cultures. Anthropologist George Peter Murdock identified over sixty cultural universals, including a system of social status, marriage, body adornments, dancing, myths and legends, cooking, incest taboos, inheritance rules, puberty customs, and religious rituals.   5

The universals of culture may derive from the fact that all societies must perform the same essential functions if they are to survive—including organization, motivation, communication, protection, the socialization of new members, and the replacement of those who die. In meeting these prerequisites for group life, people inevitably design similar—though not identical—patterns for living. As Clyde Kluckhohn wrote, "All cultures constitute somewhat distinct answers to essentially the same questions posed by human biology and by the generalities of the human situation."   6

The way in which a people articulate cultural universals depends in large part on their physical and social environment—that is, on the climate in which they live, the materials they have at hand, and the peoples with whom they establish contact. For example, the wheel has long been considered one of humankind's greatest inventions, and anthropologists were baffled for a long time by the fact that the great civilizations of South America never discovered it. Then researchers uncovered a number of toys with wheels. Apparently the Aztecs and their neighbors did know about the wheel; they simply didn't find them useful in their mountainous environment.   7

Adaptation, Ethnocentrism, and Cultural Relativity

Taken out of context, almost any custom will seem bizarre, perhaps cruel, or just plain ridiculous. To understand why the Yanomamo encourage aggressive behavior in their sons, for example, you have to see things through their eyes. The Yanomamo live in a state of chronic warfare; they spend much of their time planning for and defending against raids with neighboring tribes. If Yanomamo parents did not encourage aggression in a boy, he would be ill-equipped for life in their society. Socializing boys to be aggressive is **adaptive** for the Yanomamo because it enhances their capacity for survival. "In general, culture is . . . adaptive because it often provides people with a means of adjusting to the physiological needs of their own bodies, to their physical–geographical environment and to their social environments as well."   8

9   In many tropical societies, there are strong taboos against a mother having sexual intercourse with a man until her child is at least two years old. As a Hausa woman explains,

> A mother should not go to her husband while she has a child she is suckling. . . . [I]f she only sleeps with her husband and does not become pregnant, it will not hurt her child, it will not spoil her milk. But if another child enters in, her milk will make the first one ill.

10   Undoubtedly, people would smirk at a woman who nursed a two-year-old child in our society and abstained from having sex with her husband. Why do Hausa women behave in a way that seems so overprotective and overindulgent to us? In tropical climates protein is scarce. If a mother were to nurse more than one child at a time, or if she were to wean a child before it reached the age of two, the youngster would be prone to kwashiorkor, an often fatal disease resulting from protein deficiency. Thus, long post-partum sex taboos are adaptive. In a tropical environment a post-partum sex taboo and a long period of breast-feeding solve a serious problem.

11   **Ethnocentrism** is the tendency to see one's own way of life, including behaviors, beliefs, values, and norms as the only right way of living. Robin Fox points out that "any human group is ever ready to consign another recognizably different human group to the other side of the boundary. It is not enough to possess culture to be fully human, you have to possess our culture." Although the error of this way of thinking about culture may seem self-evident today, it is a lesson that anthropologists and the missionaries who often preceded them to remote areas learned the hard way, by observing the effects their best intentions had on peoples whose way of life was quite different from their own. In an article on the pitfalls of trying to "uplift" peoples whose ways seem backward and inefficient, Don Adams quotes an old Oriental story:

> Once upon a time there was a great flood, and involved in this flood were two creatures, a monkey and a fish. The monkey, being agile and experienced, was lucky enough to scramble up a tree and escape the raging waters. As he looked down from his safe perch, he saw the poor fish struggling against the swift current. With the very best intentions, he reached down and lifted the fish from the water. The result was inevitable.

12   No custom is good or bad, right or wrong in itself; each one must be examined in light of the culture as a whole and evaluated in terms of how it works in the context of the entire culture. Anthropologists and sociologists call this **cultural relativity.**

13   The Tangu, who live in a remote part of New Guinea, play a game called *taketak,* which, in many ways, resembles bowling. The game is played with a top that has been fashioned from a dried fruit and with two groups of coconut stakes that are driven into the ground (more or less like bowling pins). The players divide into two teams. Members of the first team take turns throwing the top into

the batch of stakes; every stake the top hits is removed. Then the second team steps to the line and tosses the top into their batch of stakes. The object of the game, surprisingly, is not to knock over as many stakes as possible. Rather, the game continues until both teams have removed the same number of stakes. Winning is completely irrelevant.

In a sense, games are practice for "real life"; they reflect the values of the culture in which they are played. **Values** are the criteria people use in assessing their daily lives, arranging their priorities, measuring their pleasures and pains, choosing between alternative courses of action. The Tangu value equivalence: the idea of one individual or group winning and another losing bothers them, for they believe winning generates ill will. In fact, when Europeans brought soccer to the Tangu, they altered the rules so that the object of the game was for two teams to score the same number of goals. Sometimes their soccer games went on for days! American games, in contrast, are highly competitive; there are always winners and losers. Many rule books include provisions for overtime and "sudden death" to prevent ties, which leave Americans dissatisfied. World Series, Superbowls, championships in basketball and hockey, Olympic gold medals are front-page news in this country. In the words of the late football coach Vince Lombardi, "Winning isn't everything, it's the only thing."

14

Norms

Norms, the rules that guide behavior in everyday situations, are derived from values, but norms and values can conflict, as we have seen. You may recall a news item that appeared in American newspapers in December 1972, describing the discovery of survivors of a plane crash twelve thousand feet high in the Andes. The crash had occurred on October 13; sixteen of the passengers (a rugby team and their supporters) managed to survive for sixty-nine days in near-zero temperatures. The story made headlines because, to stay alive, the survivors had eaten parts of their dead companions. Officials, speaking for the group, stressed how valiantly the survivors had tried to save the lives of the injured people and how they had held religious services regularly. The survivors' explanations are quite interesting, for they reveal how important it is to people to justify their actions, to resolve conflicts in norms and values (here, the positive value of survival versus the taboo against cannibalism). Some of the survivors compared their action to a heart transplant, using parts of a dead person's body to save another person's life. Others equated their act with the sacrament of communion. In the words of one religious survivor, "If we would have died, it would have been suicide, which is condemned by the Roman Catholic faith."

15

Vocabulary

Directions: Locate each of the key words in the reading selection. Then read and study each word in its context and try to determine its meaning. Use a dictionary or thesaurus to check your guess. Write the meanings of the words in the margin of the text.

Record the new words you've learned in the chart that follows.

Key Word	Paragraph	Meaning
1. derive	6	
2. baffled	7	
3. chronic	8	
4. smirk	10	
5. wean	10	
6. pitfalls	11	
Others?		

Guide Questions

Directions: The purpose of these guide questions is to ensure your understanding of what you have read. They also will help you to analyze and evaluate the authors' ideas and apply them to the real world and your own life.

Write answers to the questions in your notebook or on a separate sheet of paper if your instructor wishes to collect them. Your answers will form the basis of class discussion.

1. Why did the Yanomamo laugh at Chagnon when he first went to live with them? Why did they think he was "naive"?
2. Define *cultural universal.*
3. Cite several examples of cultural universals.
4. The authors state that the *details* of cultural universals may vary from society to society. Give examples of cultural universals that are acted out differently in different cultures.
5. Explain why cultural universals exist.
6. According to the authors of the selection, what determines the way people articulate cultural universals?
7. Define or describe the concept of *adaptation.*
8. Explain why the Hausa post-partum sex taboo is *adaptive.*
9. Define *ethnocentrism.*
10. What moral or lesson can we learn from the Oriental story quoted in the selection?
11. Define *cultural relativity.*
12. Explain the conflict of values and norms cited in the story of the Andes plane-crash survivors.

Application

Directions: Read the following excerpt from the essay "Body Ritual among the Nacirema" by anthropologist Horace Miner:

> The Nacirema have an almost pathological horror of and fascination with the mouth, the condition of which is believed to have a supernatural influence on all social relationships. Were it not for the ritual of the mouth, they believe that their teeth would fall out, their gums bleed, their jaws shrink, their friends desert them, and their lovers reject them. They also believe that a strong relationship exists between oral and moral characteristics. For example, there is a ritual ablution of the mouth for children which is supposed to improve their moral fiber. 1
>
> The daily body ritual performed by everyone includes a mouth-rite. Despite the fact that these people are so punctilious about care of the mouth, this rite involves a practice which strikes the uninitiated stranger as revolting. It was reported to me that the ritual consists of inserting a small bundle of hog hairs into the mouth, along with certain magical powders, and then moving the bundle in a highly formalized series of gestures. 2
>
> In addition to the private mouth-rite, the people seek out a holy mouth-man twice a year. These practitioners have an impressive set of paraphernalia, consisting of a variety of augers, awls, probes, and prods. The use of these objects in the exorcism of the evils of the mouth involves almost unbelievable ritual torture of the client. The holy mouth-man opens the client's mouth and, using the above-mentioned tools, enlarges any holes which decay may have created in the teeth. Magical materials are put into these holes. If there are not naturally occurring holes in the teeth, large sections of one or more teeth are gouged out so that the supernatural substance can be applied. In the client's view, the purpose of these ministrations is to arrest decay and to draw friends. The extremely sacred and traditional character of the rite is evidenced by the fact that the natives return to the holy mouth-man year after year, despite the fact that their teeth continue to decay. 3

If you feel that living among the people who practice such bizarre customs would be strange and horrifying, then reexamine the excerpt *after* you read the name of the tribe—Nacirema—backwards!

Note the formal, highly technical language used to describe ordinary, everyday things. In order to understand the passage, "translate" the following phrases into everyday language.

   1. In paragraph 2:
      mouth-rite—
      small bundle of hog hairs—
      magical powders—
      moving the bundle in a highly formalized series of gestures—

2. In paragraph 3:
   holy mouth-man—
   exorcism of the evils of the mouth—
   magical materials are put into these holes—
   large sections . . . are gouged out—
3. In paragraph 1:
   What is Miner referring to at the end of paragraph 1 when he says "there is a ritual ablution of the mouth for children which is supposed to improve their moral fiber"?

Why does Miner describe our dental habits in such a "foreign" way? What point is he making here?

Writing

1. a. Consider this custom of the Thompson Indians (a North American Indian tribe): Their puberty ritual includes a long period of fasting, sweating, and beating of the teenaged boys to prepare them to take on the responsibilities of manhood. Write a few sentences describing the reactions of ethnocentric individuals upon learning of this ritual. How would they feel about it? What would they say? What might they do about it?
   b. Now write a similar short paragraph from the perspective of a person who believes in the concept of cultural relativity.
2. The authors tell us in paragraph 6 that cultural universals developed from the requirements for survival in group life. Why do they specify *group* life? Why would these concepts not apply to *individual* life—say, to a hermit living alone on a deserted island?
3. In order to fully understand the important concepts presented in "Unity in Diversity," you must make the ideas your own. In your own words, write definitions of the key concepts: cultural universals, adaptation, ethnocentrism, cultural relativity, norms, and values.

Marking Text

Mark the chapter "Unity in Diversity." (Marking text is explained on page 421.)

Making Connections

Return to the selection "Culture" and reread paragraph 9. Compare the information in paragraph 9 to the information in paragraphs 5, 6, and 7 in "Unity in Diversity." What are the similarities? Are there any differences?

Anthropologists generally devote their careers to studying people in "exotic" cultures. Well, what makes a culture "exotic"? In truth, it simply means it is a culture different from our own. No doubt the members of these so-called exotic societies feel their ways are "normal" and would view our habits as mystifyingly strange. In this July 2000 Associated Press article, we read about a small group of anthropologists who have turned their attention to a new group of exotic humans—the American middle class.

EVERYDAY PEOPLE

Matt Crenson

A small man paces back and forth and chants into a metal stick. He wears a black-and-white costume. A half a dozen similarly dressed minions scan the packed crowd as the chanting man's voice intensifies. People in the crowd flash signals that drive the man's chanting to an even greater frenzy.   1

Brian Hoey watches this spectacle from one side of the airless room, his back pressed against a cool cinder-block wall. What strange ritual is this? The black mass of a twisted cult? A warrior band's preparations for battle?   2

No, it's a real estate auction.   3

American Anthropology

Hoey is an anthropologist. For him, the event offers an opportunity to delve into an almost unknown culture—the American middle class.   4

After dedicating their careers to studying exotic cultures in faraway lands, a few anthropologists are coming home. They're taking research techniques they once used in African shantytowns and Himalayan villages to Knights of Columbus halls, corporate office buildings and suburban shopping centers.   5

The idea is to study American culture with fresh eyes unclouded by preconceived notions—to study "us" the way anthropologists used to look at "them."   6

Cruising the 'Burbs

"I've seen a line coming out of that Dairy Queen that goes down the block," Conrad Kottak says.   7

He's cruising a Michigan suburb, pointing out cultural landmarks. The high school. A satellite dish. Fast food joints. Video rental stores. Newspaper boxes that indicate which residents are reading what.   8

Kottak, the chairman of the University of Michigan anthropology department, works with research fellow Lara Descartes on a project titled "The Relationship of Media to Work and Family Issues Among the Middle Class." They interview people about their viewing habits and spend evenings watching television in suburban homes.   9

After 38 years of research in Brazil, Kottak now finds himself pondering the mysterious allure of the Jerry Springer show.   10

"I think it's very interesting," he says.   11

He's not kidding.   12

Their Own Backyard

13   Traditionally, American anthropologists have been reluctant to study their own cultures. They've preferred remote subjects not yet gripped by Hollywood, pop music and the other tentacles of Western culture.

14   Even when they do work in the United States, most anthropologists concentrate on subcultures: drug addicts, streetwalkers, transvestites.

15   Rebecca Upton recently completed a classic anthropology Ph.D. in Botswana. Now she does much of her research at an Ann Arbor, Michigan, playground.

16   Upton introduces herself to parents and interviews them about their lives for a project on young families that have just had or are considering a second child.

17   "There's all this study about what happens at the first child," Upton says. "There's nothing about what happens with the second."

18   In Africa, Upton could start from scratch, learning about the culture as if she were a child. In Ann Arbor, the first thing she has to do is forget everything she thought she knew.

19   "Suddenly I'm questioning my observations and assumptions about everything," Upton says.

A Dramatic Change

20   "Something dramatic is happening here. Something is changing," says University of Michigan anthropologist Tom Fricke.

21   America, he says, is going through the most profound social upheaval since the Industrial Revolution, when a rural nation of farmers became a country of factory towns and cities. Dual-career families, single parenthood and divorce are supplanting the traditional model of family. Factory work has given way to high-tech jobs that require college and graduate degrees. The mass media saturate our lives.

22   Everybody knows all this is happening, but there has been little research on how these changes affect the way Americans think about their lives.

23   To that end, the Alfred P. Sloan Foundation has funded two research centers to do anthropological studies of the relationship between work and family life in middle-class America. Fricke heads the Center for the Ethnography of Everyday Life, based at the University of Michigan. The other one, based at Emory University in Atlanta, is called the Center for Myth and Ritual in American Life.

24   Anthropologists at the centers study American families the same way they would Polynesian cargo cults or Mongolian nomads—by inserting themselves into the daily lives of their subjects. So a few months out of the year, Fricke lives and works on a farm in Richardton, North Dakota, half way around the world from the Himalayan village where he has conducted most of his life's work. Fricke occupies a spare bedroom in the home of Cal and Julie Hoff. They introduce him to friends and neighbors as "our anthropologist."

25   The Hoffs' 18-year-old son Casey would like to be a farmer too, but in a land of failing farms and dying towns, the prospects are bleak.

"You get this litany of despair out there," Fricke says. "People are really leaving this part of the countryside."   26

Fricke spends a lot of time in Richardton simply listening to people's stories about life on the prairie. Later, he plans to interview people who left town after high school to see how they relate to Richardton.   27

"If you move out at 18 you're marked by that place," Fricke says.   28

Farm life is hardly alien to Fricke; he and his five brothers grew up in Bismarck, about an hour's drive to the east. Now all six of them have scattered to distant cities in pursuit of their careers.   29

So it's not hard to figure out how Fricke came up with the idea for his project, "Rural Parents & Urban Children: Place, Work, Migration, and the Natal Home."   30

"I've always been studying myself," Fricke says. "Even in Nepal."   31

Hoey has taken it a step further—he has practically gone native. In December he and his wife moved to Traverse City, a town of 15,000 nestled into a bay of Lake Michigan. His research project—to study people who have recently moved to Traverse City.   32

In recent years, urbanites have flocked to Traverse City in search of a low-stress life. Hoey has met dozens of these middle-class refugees who sacrifice salary and first-run movies for a slower pace and natural beauty.   33

The Piemaker

Everybody who moves to Traverse City seems to have a similar story. Take Mike Busley. He moved here from San Diego, where he worked as an engineer for General Dynamics. He made good money, but he was growing tired of the corporate jungle.   34

So on his 40th birthday, Busley quit his job, moved his family to Traverse City and opened the Grand Traverse Pie Company on Front Street.   35

"I had never baked a pie in my life," Busley says.   36

He's telling his tale in the coffee-shop part of his store, the smell of pies in the air and the jingle-bells on the door ringing whenever a customer walks in. Hoey sips a cup of decaf as he listens.   37

To Hoey, a Grand Traverse Pie Company pie is more than cherries and filling and crust. It is a powerful symbol in a tumultuous world, an edible icon of the good life.   38

Hoey tries to explain this all in complex academic jargon, then suddenly pauses and smiles.   39

"He's selling an image," Hoey says. "He's selling a piece of the pie!"   40

Vocabulary

Directions: Locate each of the key words in the article. Try to figure out each word's meaning by using the context. Confirm your guess by checking the dictionary or thesaurus. Write the meanings of the words in the margin of the text. Then record the meanings in the following chart.

Key Word	Paragraph	Meaning
1. minions	1	
2. shantytowns	5	
3. allure	10	
4. saturate	21	
5. cults	24	
6. litany	26	
7. tumultuous	38	
8. icon	38	
Others?		

Guide Questions

Directions: These questions will guide your understanding of what you have read. Write your answers in your notebook or on a separate sheet of paper if your instructor wishes to collect it. Your answers to these questions will be the basis of class discussion.

1. Why do you think the author begins with the story of the small man pacing back and forth chanting into a metal stick?
2. What is so unusual about what these researchers into "American Anthropology" are doing?
3. Explain the author's comment "He's not kidding" in paragraph 12.
4. What does Rebecca Upton say she must do before she can learn about her own culture? Does her comment make sense to you?
5. Describe the "dramatic" change that anthropologist Tom Fricke states is happening in the United States.
6. Describe the specific groups of people that are being studied by:
   a. Tom Fricke
   b. Brian Hoey

Application/Writing

Directions: Turn to the Application exercise on pages 75–76. Reread Horace Miner's description of the "bizarre" body ritual of the Nacirema (aka American). Now choose another "ritual" performed by Americans, and write a paragraph or two describing it. Do as the anthropologists in the article "Everyday People" do—start from scratch. Describe the ritual as if you were writing for someone from another planet, someone who knows nothing about our culture and customs. Here are a few suggestions of rituals you could describe:

1. cooking a meal
2. going to a movie
3. riding a bus
4. going to the hair salon
5. going to the gas station
6. attending a church service
7. putting on makeup
8. eating a meal in a restaurant
9. buying groceries at the supermarket
10. playing basketball, football, etc.
11. and many, many other possibilities . . .

Imagine going from a life of slavery, a life so primitive that you had never seen a light bulb, flushed a toilet or eaten an apple to a life in twenty-first century America. Can you imagine having to learn to use a refrigerator, lock a door, take out a lease, use a cell phone, to name just a tiny part of a very long list? In this story, we learn about the Bantu people of Somalia who are hoping to leave a life of poverty and discrimination for a new life in the United States. They know they have a lot to learn.

AFRICA'S LOST TRIBE HOPES TO DISCOVER AMERICA

Rachel L. Swarns

1   KAKUMA, Kenya—The engines rumbled and the red sand swirled as the cargo plane roared onto the dirt airstrip. One by one, the dazed and impoverished refugees climbed from the belly of the plane into this desolate wind-swept camp.

2   They are members of Africa's lost tribe, the Somali Bantu, who were stolen from the shores of Mozambique, Malawi and Tanzania and carried on Arab slave ships to Somalia two centuries ago. They were enslaved and persecuted until Somalia's civil war scattered them to refugee camps in the 1990's.

3   Yet on this recent day, the Bantu people were rejoicing as they stepped from the plane into the blinding sun. They were the last members of the tribe to be transferred from a violent camp near the Somali border to this dusty place just south of Sudan. They knew their first trip in a flying machine was a harbinger of miracles to come.

4   Over the next two years, nearly all of the Somali Bantu refugees in Kenya— about 12,000 people—are to be flown to the United States. This is one of the largest refugee groups to receive blanket permission for resettlement since the mid-1990's, State Department officials say.

5   The refugees will be interviewed by American immigration officials in this camp, which is less violent than the camp near Somalia. The interview process has been slowed by security concerns in the aftermath of Sept. 11. Despite the repeated delays, the preparations for the extraordinary journey are already under way.

6   Every morning, dozens of peasant farmers take their seats in classrooms in a simple one-story building with a metal roof. They study English, hold their first notebooks and pens, and struggle to learn about the place called America. It is an enormous task.

7   The Bantu, who were often denied access to education and jobs in Somalia, are mostly illiterate and almost completely untouched by modern life. They measure time by watching the sun rise and fall over their green fields and mud huts.

8   As refugees, they have worked the soil, cooked, cleaned and labored in back-breaking construction jobs, filling about 90 percent of the unskilled jobs in the camp in Dadaab, Kenya, where most Bantu people lived until they were transferred here last year. But most have never turned on a light switch, flushed a toilet or held a lease.

9   So the students here study in a classroom equipped with all the trappings of modern American life, including a gleaming refrigerator, a sink, a toilet and a

bathtub. They are learning about paper towels and toilet cleanser and peanut butter and ice trays, along with English and American culture.

Refugee officials here fear that the Bantu's battle to adjust to a high-tech world will only be complicated by American ambivalence about immigrants since the terrorist attacks in the United States. 10

The Bantu are practicing Muslims. Women cover their hair with brightly colored scarves. Families pray five times a day. In Somalia, they were in a predominantly Muslim country often described as a breeding ground for terrorists. 11

The American government requires refugees from such hot spots to undergo a new series of security clearances before they can be resettled in the United States. The new system has delayed the arrival of thousands of refugees, leaving them to languish in camps where children often die of malnutrition. 12

But most people here are willing to do what it takes to live in a country that outlaws discrimination. While they wait, they learn about leases and the separation between church and state, and they practice their limited English. 13

About 700 Bantu have gone through this cultural orientation. By the end of September, State Department officials say, 1,500 are expected to be resettled in about 50 American cities and towns, including Boston; Charlotte, N.C.; San Diego; and Erie, Pa. 14

In America, the refugees tell each other, the Bantu will be considered human beings, not slaves, for the first time. 15

"It's scary," said Haw Abass Aden, a peasant farmer still trembling as she stepped off her first flight through the clouds. She clung tightly to a kerosene lamp with one hand and her little girl with the other. But she regained her composure as she considered her future. 16

"We are coming here to be resettled in the United States," said Ms. Aden, 20, speaking through a translator. "There, we will find peace and freedom." 17

After centuries of suffering, they are praying that America will be the place where they will finally belong. The United Nations has been trying to find a home for the Bantu for more than a decade because it is painfully clear they cannot return to Somalia. 18

In Somalia, the lighter-skinned majority rejected the Bantu, for their slave origins and dark skin and wide features. Even after they were freed from bondage, the Bantu were denied meaningful political representation and rights to land ownership. During the Somali civil war, they were disproportionately victims of rapes and killings. 19

The discrimination and violence continues in the barren camps today—even here—where the Bantu are often attacked and dismissed as Mushungulis, which means slave people. 20

But finding a new home for the Bantu refugees here has not been easy. First Tanzania and then Mozambique, the Bantu's ancestral homelands, agreed to take the tribe. Both impoverished countries ultimately reneged, saying they could not afford to resettle the group. 21

In 1999, the United States determined that the Somali Bantu tribe was a persecuted group eligible for resettlement. The number of African refugees approved 22 for admission in the United States surged from 3,318 in 1990 to 20,084 a decade later as the cold war ended and American officials focused on assisting refugees beyond those fleeing Communist countries.

23   "I don't think Somalia is my country because we Somali Bantus have seen our people treated like donkeys there," said Fatuma Abdekadir, 20, who was waiting for her class to start. "I think my country is where I am going.

24   "There, there is peace. Nobody can treat you badly. Nobody can come into your house and beat you."

25   The refugees watch snippets of American life on videos in class, and they marvel at the images of supermarkets filled with peppers and tomatoes and of tall buildings that reach for the clouds. But they know little about racism, poverty, the bone-chilling cold or the cities that will be chosen for them by refugee resettlement agencies.

26   What they know is this flat, parched corner of Africa, a place of thorn trees and numbing hunger where water comes from wells when it comes at all—a place of fierce heat and wind that whips the sand into biting and blinding storms.

27   In the classes, the teachers try to prepare the Bantu for a modern world. Issack Adan carefully guides his students through the lessons, taking questions from older men with graying beards, teenage girls with ballpoint pens tucked into their head scarves and young mothers with babies tied to their backs.

28   The lesson of the day: a white flush toilet. "Come close, come close," Mr. Adan said as the women approached the strange object doubtfully. "Mothers, you sit on it, you don't stand on it."

29   The women nodded, although they seemed uncertain. Mr. Adan showed them how to flush the toilet and how to clean it. "You wash with this thing and you will have a good smell," he said.

30   "A very nice smell," the students agreed.

31   Then Abubakar Saidali, a 30-year-old student, looked closely at the odd contraption and asked, "But where does that water go?" For an answer, Mr. Adan took the refugees outside to show them the pipes that carry the sewage.

32   Back in the classroom, the students spent the next few hours learning about the refrigerator, ice cubes and strawberry jam. They watched eagerly as Mr. Adan washed dishes in a sink and admired the bathtub and shower. One woman demurred, however, when he invited her to step into the tub.

33   "It is so clean," she said shyly. "Can I really step in it?"

34   Some students grumbled that the American appliances seemed more complicated than their ordinary ways of living. Why worry about cleaning a toilet, some refugees said aloud, when the bushes never need to be cleaned?

35   But Mr. Saidali said he was thrilled to learn about modern toilets after years of relying on smelly pit latrines.

36   "This latrine is inside the house," marveled Mr. Saidali, a lean man in tattered sneakers. "It's better than what we are now using. It has a seat for sitting and the water goes down.

"Even this sink—it's my first time," he said. "This sink is for washing. It cleans things very nicely."   37

Even with the lessons, some Bantu are worried about how they will cope in America. They know that blacks and Muslims are minorities there. Will Americans be welcoming? Will they learn English quickly enough? Will they find jobs and housing and friends? Some officials here worry, too.   38

"These people are from rural areas," Mr. Adan said. "They don't know much about modern life."   39

But the refugees who arrived on the plane here said they were eager for the challenge.   40

Uncertain of what might be needed in the United States, they carried most of their precious possessions—broken brooms, chipped mugs, metal plates—as they boarded a rattling bus that roared deep into the camp as the sun sank beyond the horizon.   41

The refugees knew they would be sleeping on the ground again and going hungry as they have often done. But they also knew that this was only the first phase of an incredible journey.   42

First stop, Kakuma. Next stop, America.   43

Vocabulary

Directions: Locate each of the key words in the reading selection. Try to figure out each word's meaning by using the context. Confirm your guess by checking the dictionary or thesaurus. Write the meanings of the words in the margin of the text. Then record the meanings in the chart below.

Key Word	Paragraph	Meaning
1. desolate	1	
2. harbinger	3	
3. ambivalence	10	
4. disproportionately	19	
5. snippets	25	
6. contraption	31	
Others?		

Guide Questions

Directions: These questions will guide your understanding of what you have read. Write your answers in your notebook, or on a separate sheet of paper if your instructor wishes to collect it. Your answers to these questions will be the basis of class discussion.

1. Who are the people referred to as "Africa's lost tribe"? Identify them and tell a bit about their history.
2. The people in the article are currently living in a refugee camp. What is their final destination?
3. Based on what you learned from reading the article, contrast the life the Somali Bantu have lived up until now with the life they will find in the U.S.
4. Assume you are in charge of teaching the Somali Bantu all about America. What would you teach them? Make a list of all the things they'll need to learn if they are to successfully adapt to their new culture. Include ordinary things like riding in an elevator and more complicated things like driving a car.
5. If you could talk with the Somali Bantu people in the refugee camp, what advice would you give them about America?

Application

Use the Internet or the library to find a map of Africa. Locate the countries mentioned in the article: (1) the people's home countries of Mozambique, Malawi, and Tanzania; (2) the country which enslaved them, Somalia; (3) Kenya, where the refugee camp is located.

To find out more about the Somali Bantu people, check the website http://www.somalibantu.com.

Making Connections

Read the following selection "Africa's Lost Tribe Discovers Its American Dream."

The previous reading selection "Africa's Lost Tribe Hopes to Discover America" was written in March 2003. It reported on the Somali Bantu people living in refugee camps, having escaped from wretched conditions in their homeland. They were eagerly anticipating and training for their new lives in America. In this article, which appeared in July 2004, we get an update on their amazing story.

AFRICA'S LOST TRIBE DISCOVERS ITS AMERICAN DREAM

William L. Hamilton

For Abkow Edow, a Bantu refugee from Somalia who now lives in Tucson, the Fourth of July was just another day. Though fireworks on the mountain and a reggae concert were scheduled, Mr. Edow was washing dishes at the Westin La Paloma Resort and Spa, wearing a baseball cap and thick rubber gloves that came up to his elbows. His wife, Madina Idle, was folding sheets and towels several corridors away in the vast underground complex below the desert views, the fountains and the valet golf carts.   1

But work is good. If the Fourth was just another day, it was a day in an extraordinary year for the couple, their two children and a grandson.   2

Mr. Edow, 57, and Ms. Idle, 42, have found themselves, after 12 years in refugee camps, at the end of the rainbow: America.   3

"In Somalia, I dreamed of the United States, even though I didn't know anything about it," Mr. Edow said, speaking through a translator like the other Bantu adults interviewed. America represents opportunity, Bantu refugees say, which involves hard work, struggles with English, discarding cultural ways— like the physical disciplining of children and arranged marriages—and a wary assimilation with Americans and other refugee groups in Tucson.   4

For them, independence is not a holiday but a daily engagement.   5

Mr. Edow (pronounced EE-doh) and Ms. Idle (pronounced EE-dalay) are part of a continuing resettlement of 13,000 Bantu people from Somalia, descendants of people kidnapped from southern Africa by Arab slave traders two centuries ago. As part of one of the most ambitious relocations of political refugees by the United States in recent history, the Bantu couple arrived in Tucson in May 2003 from a Kenyan camp. They were uneducated, unemployed and unfamiliar with basic facts of American life like electrical appliances and indoor plumbing.   6

Now Mr. Edow and Ms. Idle drive themselves to work in their own car, a Ford Escort they bought in September. They shop at 99-cent stores. They pay the $635 rent for their three-bedroom apartment. The children, a 15-year-old and two 8-year-olds, are in school, earning good grades and, like other Bantu children, school officials say, outperforming the general student population. Mr. Edow is saving money to buy a house.   7

"Every month I pay rent," he said, sitting in his kitchen with a bare foot propped on his seat, a cellphone in his hand and a videotape of "Shrek" entertaining his children in the next room. "It's good to own a house. It belongs to you."   8

9   Mr. Edow, who could not read numbers a year ago, knows what a down payment is. In May, he applied for a green card, celebrating his application with a red, white and blue cake.

10   The availability of entry-level jobs in the hospitality industry has made Tucson a popular destination for the resettlement of Bosnians, Afghans and Liberians. There are 71 Bantu people, and more than 100 are expected by the end of the year.

11   Mr. Edow and Ms. Idle escaped from Somalia to Kenya on foot, a 10-day walk without food. In Somalia, Mr. Edow said, he watched as his father was executed with a hammer and nails.

12   Now, in life-skill classes that supplement daily English classes, Bantu parents learn that hitting their children is discouraged, though that was how they were disciplined in Africa. They make a wary peace with African-Americans at home and at school who consider them foreign. They learn that Fourth of July fireworks are exploded to entertain, not kill, and that being hit by a water balloon, as Bantu children were in one incident at school, is a game and not a hateful fight.

13   At work, the Bantu refugees learn how to prepare hotel amenities, like placing courtesy soaps and folding the tips of the toilet tissue, though they used pit latrines in Kenya and Somalia and had never seen a toilet.

14   But caseworkers, school officials and employers say the Bantus are making the most remarkable progress of the refugee groups in Tucson, given that they arrived with the most remarkable disadvantages: the trauma of tribal war in Somalia, where the Bantus were considered low-caste and denied opportunities for education and employment, and a rural ignorance of Western culture and modern life.

15   The Bantu refugees had to be taught to tell time, an accomplishment that fills them with pride.

16   Wall clocks and calendars decorate many Bantu homes in Mission Vista, an 80-unit apartment complex where many, including Mr. Edow and Ms. Idle, live.

17   "I adjusted to time," said Makai Osman, 38, a Bantu friend of Ms. Idle's who lives in Mission Vista with her husband, Mudey Libange, 36, and their five children. "I was scared, but I'm punctual now."

18   Though job training required professional coaches, Karen Vallecillo, the director of human resources at the Westin La Paloma, gave the Bantu refugees high marks.

19   "They were a group that had been through pretty atrocious things, probably more than any other group," Ms. Vallecillo said. "Learning to trust authority again probably took them a little longer."

20   Twelve languages, including four Somali dialects, are spoken at the hotel, which has 500 employees, 25 percent of whom are refugees.

21   "We'd be lost without our partnerships with refugee agencies," Ms. Vallecillo said. "We don't seem to be able to raise American citizens to want to take these kinds of jobs."

22   The federal government organized the relocation effort but contracted with agencies, like the International Rescue Committee in Tucson, to provide financial support and social services to the refugees in each city.

At Mission Vista one Friday, Ms. Osman's son, Abdullahi Osman, 15, sat at home at the dining table, homework assignments and an English-Somali dictionary in his lap.

Several Bantu friends have taken jobs when they turned 16 to help their parents. Older children like Abdullahi's sister, Halima Osman, who is 13, run the home while their parents work, taking care of younger brothers and sisters and the children of other families as well.

"Until I finish my education, I don't want to do anything else," said Abdullahi, who dreams of becoming a doctor. He said that books were his most valued possessions, though he checks them out of the public library. Abdullahi's girlfriend, a Bantu he met in Kenya, was relocated to Salt Lake City. They speak on the telephone.

"If I stay for a long time and I have money, I want to go and meet, and see how she is," he said.

As Abdullahi spoke, children from other families entered or left the apartment, or opened the door to peek. Each Bantu family has its own apartment, but as is most familiar to them as villagers and camp internees, they visit frequently and without formality.

"I know in American culture, if someone is going to visit you, he's going to call, 'What time are you going to visit?'" said Ms. Osman, sitting forward with determination, legs apart, elbows on her knees, her sandaled feet embellished by designs in henna. "For us, it's not a big deal. People can visit us anytime."

Ms. Osman gave a brief tour of her apartment.

"I have a lot of stuff," she said, with a small laugh. "I don't want to move it somewhere."

Ever present is the memory, still as strong as reality, of the long relocation route. With arrival in America has come miles and miles of documentation, regulation, offices and appointments. In speaking with the Bantu refugees, in the patient looks in their faces and in the acceptance in their attitudes toward caseworkers, teachers, employers and even strangers, there is a palpable sense that the stop in Tucson could be a stage in an unending journey if they do not acquiesce to the bewildering bureaucracy.

"With most refugees, until they've gotten their citizenship, there's always that feeling that it's just not real," said Karen Bailey, the community resource coordinator with the International Rescue Committee.

Ms. Osman, who became eligible for a green card in July, said forcefully: "I want to be Tucsonian. I don't want to go back, no way. I don't dream at all of going back to Somalia."

But forgetting can be hard.

Outside, as the cool of the evening descended and the clouds above the desert blossomed in the sunset, four Bantu girls sat in a circle on the sidewalk playing shabko, a traditional game of tossing stones. Ms. Osman's daughter, Halima, who was shepherding the children, chased Mr. Abkow's son, Ahmed, 8, with a stick when he angered her by disobeying. Ahmed, crying, disappeared into the shadow of a building corridor, then returned silently to the group, like a shy dog, and sat behind a bush.

36   "In Somalia, we didn't know America," said Hamadi Musse, 16, whose best friend in Tucson is Hakim Rahimi, a 14-year-old Afghan boy.

37   Hakim and his family lived in Pakistan before being resettled here six months ago. Hakim worked from 4 a.m. until 8 p.m. laying floors in Pakistan.

38   "We saw on TV, the American people," he said.

39   Hamadi, who goes to school and helps his brother at his job at a Boston Market restaurant, said of his new life, "I don't have time for watching TV."

Vocabulary

Directions: Locate each of the key words in the reading selection. Try to figure out each word's meaning by using the context. Confirm your guess by checking the dictionary or thesaurus. Write the meanings of the words in the margin of the text. Then record the meanings in the chart below.

Key Word	Paragraph	Meaning
1. wary	4	
2. assimilation	4	
3. trauma	14	
4. atrocious	19	
Others?		

Guide Questions

Directions: These questions will guide your understanding of what you have read. Write your answers in your notebook, or on a separate sheet of paper if your instructor wishes to collect it. Your answers to these questions will be the basis of class discussion.

1. When the Bantu refugees say, "America represents opportunity," what do they mean?
2. The article describes some of the accomplishments of the former refugees. What things have they learned?
3. What lessons about America have the Bantu refugees learned in their life-skill classes?
4. Explain why caseworkers say the Bantu refugees have made "remarkable progress."

Writing

Write 1–2 paragraphs reacting to the story of the Bantu Somali refugees.

Most Americans (if they think about it at all) think of monogamy as "natural" and are surprised to learn that many other societies practice different forms of marriage. Problems can arise when people leave their home countries and immigrate to new lands with different values and norms. Should immigrants be allowed to bring their customs with them? What if those customs are illegal in their new countries? This article appeared in the international section of The New York Times *in January 1996.*

AFRICAN WOMEN IN FRANCE BATTLE POLYGAMY

Marlise Simons

1   Khadi Keita shifted in her chair in a Paris cafe as she described the day she became a stranger in her own home. That was the day in 1985 when her husband suddenly arrived here with a new wife.

2   He hung a curtain in the middle of the cramped bedroom and announced that, from now on, the two women would have to share him, the kitchen, the closets, everything.

3   The next four years became a nightmare of pregnancies, babies, nasty fights, and long, hostile silences, Mrs. Keita said. Then her husband, a Muslim, went home to his African village, married again and brought wife no. 3.

4   Mrs. Keita, who has since divorced—a rarity in polygamous marriages—and become a social worker, is an immigrant from Senegal. She is one of the African women in France who are now willing to speak openly about the secrets of polygamy and about the strains, the anger, and the humiliations of their marriages.

5   Long overshadowed by other immigrant problems of poverty and discrimination, the widespread practice of polygamy in France is coming to light because African women here are fighting the tradition. In the current anti-immigrant mood, the government has also decided to take a stand.

6   After quietly tolerating the Muslim male right to have up to four wives, the government has said France will recognize only one spouse and consider other marriages annulled.

7   The discussion of polygamy has raised anew the question of how a society should deal with immigrant customs that are unacceptable or against the law in a new land. There have already been heated debates about whether girls may wear Muslim headscarves, a religious symbol, in France's secular schools, and French prosecutors have gone to court to forbid the tradition of sexually mutilating Muslim girls.

A Custom Tolerated in the Homeland Turns Sour Abroad

8   "Polygamy may be as old as Africa, but it doesn't work in France," said Mrs. Keita, whose former husband could not be located.

9   "It's unbearable because there is no room for two or three wives and fifteen children in one small place. The women are rivals. The husband is never fair. He has a favorite, so there are horrible fights."

10   There is the wrenching lack of privacy. "You hear everything, your husband and the other wives," she said. "You hear how he behaves with his favorite, usually the new one. The women end up hating the man. Everyone feels bad inside."

11   The politics of polygamy is no less charged. Ivry, a Paris suburb, has some fifteen hundred African immigrants, and two out of three families are polygamous. "Consider the costs," a town official said. "One husband with three wives and a team of children may need government health care, education, and subsidies for up to twenty people. Is this fair?"

12   He said this question weighs heavily at a time when France's social welfare system is in the midst of an enormous debt crisis. In December, government plans to cut benefits caused three weeks of strikes and protests.

13   Polygamy has come to France with the tens of thousands of African immigrants from countries like Senegal, Mali, and Mauritania. The French Interior Ministry says there are no firm statistics because foreign wives are often in the country clandestinely and immigrants keep other wives back in Africa.

14   In the United States, the law bars polygamous immigrants and the authorities say they believe that such cases are rare.

15   In the Paris area alone, it is estimated that 200,000 people live in polygamous families. They live in the rickety neighborhoods behind Montmartre and in glum suburbs like Bobigny, St. Denis, and Creteil.

16   Moustafa Djaara, a construction worker from Mali, lives in Bobigny with his two wives and nine children. Both wives are pregnant. He wants to bring his young, third wife to France. His modest income is more than doubled by the generous benefits the French state pays to children and pregnant women, regardless of their status.

17   Mr. Djaara asserts that polygamy is hardest for the husband because his wives fight a lot, he has his job, and does all the shopping. He shops because he must control all the money, he said.

18   Given his complaints, why does he want more than one wife? "My father did, my grandfather did, so why shouldn't I?" Mr. Djaara said.

19   "When my wife is sick and I don't have another, who will care for me?" Besides, he said, "one wife on her own is trouble. When there are several, they are forced to be polite and well behaved. If they misbehave, you threaten that you'll take another wife."

20   Ruling at home may be one thing, but living with the neighbors is another.

21   Town officials and building owners have refused large tribal families on their premises. In St. Denis last year, a welfare office allocated a small apartment to a Mauritanian family of six. Two months later, thirty members of the same family had moved in. The French neighbors, outraged at the noise, pressed the town hall until the group was moved.

22   It was mainly the Socialist government in the 1980s that quietly admitted more than one wife per husband as part of its family-reunification policy. The argument was that immigrants had the right to a "normal" family life.

As a result, many immigrants brought not just their wives but, as their income improved, they went home to buy new, young brides, often still teenagers. Once the women gave birth in France, mother and child were allowed to stay. 23

"We've been telling the French for ten years that this was wrong, that polygamy couldn't work here because we saw the problems," said Madine Diallo, who was born in Mali and now heads an African women's health and family-planning group. 24

"In Africa there is space. Even if co-wives live around the same courtyard, at least each wife has her own room or her house. The man visits her there, in her own bed. Here two, three families are packed into two rooms." 25

It is a myth that African women like polygamy, she continued. "Our mothers and grandmothers and every woman before them would go to the witch doctor to get a potion or cast a spell if she knew her husband was going to take another wife. Many still do. And women do it even here." 26

Fatima Traoré, who came from Mali, said she sometimes feels she will lose her mind. Sometimes she and her two co-wives do not talk to each other for days. She and her husband had been in Paris for four years when he went "on holiday" and came back with another wife. 27

"From one day to the next, another wife comes and does what you do," Mrs. Traoré said. "She meddles in the house. She gets pregnant. You still get your turn with your husband, your nights with him. But he pays no attention to you. Just two, three minutes to satisfy himself. That's it. Whatever you do makes no difference. You can cry all you want. He doesn't care." 28

Women in polygamous marriages describe the marital routine like this: The husband spends two nights with one wife, then two nights with the next. The wife who has her turn in the marital bed does the cooking for the family. "If a woman says 'It's my turn in the kitchen,' then you know," Mrs. Traoré said. 29

Health workers say the feelings boiling in close quarters can make the women ill or violent. 30

"Sometimes the women go crazy, they attack each other," said Catherine Rixain, a family counselor who works in the suburbs. "Or they take it out on each other's children. We have seen children beaten by a desperate co-wife." 31

Hawa Koulibali is one of the women who feel trapped. She came as a young bride from Mali twenty years ago and now lives with her two co-wives and their fourteen children in Marne-la-Vallée, half an hour's train ride east of Paris. But she and the co-wives have never seen Paris. They cannot read. They speak no French. 32

Although their husband goes home every two years, he says a trip for all of them would be too expensive. Cut off from France and cut off from Mali, Mrs. Koulibali feels lost. She and the co-wives try to get along. But being friends is too difficult, she said. 33

Beyond the strains and rivalry at home, immigrant women can find moments of solidarity in the support groups formed by French and African social workers. One group met recently in a day-care center at Emerainville, east of Paris. 34

35   The center is a cheerful, airy place, festooned with toys and drawings. But in a back room, sixteen women, all in polygamous marriages, met around a small table. Ostensibly they met to discuss child care. But other questions seemed more haunting.

36   They denied that anyone liked polygamy. "We have no choice!" a woman in her thirties shouted. The consensus was that the immigrant women here had lost their dignity.

37   "If you don't get along with your co-wife in Africa, you do not pass by her door and she does not pass yours," a woman from Mauritania said. Another participant whispered: "An African woman will not sleep with her husband in a bed that another woman uses. Here we must take turns."

38   The anger quickly focused on the men. The women complained of injustices: husbands gave money to their favorite wife, usually the new one; husbands had used money a wife had earned in France in order to go to Africa and buy another wife. As humiliating, the women said, was when a husband took the wife's identity card to Africa and used it to bring in a new wife.

39   In the support groups, counselors have been prodding women to warn their husbands that they will denounce them if they beat their wives or if they seize their cards.

40   "We try to stop some of the dirty tricks," said Kani Sidibe, who used to work for Air Afrique and is now a social worker. "Some women are losing their fear. They come and talk to us. But we have a long way to go."

41   Some signs of change have appeared; for example, in the life of Moustafa Diop, an immigrant from Senegal who lives near Charles de Gaulle Airport. He does odd jobs driving a truck. One wife works as a part-time cleaner and one as a seamstress. The third does the home work. At night they look after the eighteen children.

42   He concedes that "the women are not content," but now outright rebellion looms. Two years ago Mr. Diop went back to Senegal and used the family savings to buy another bride. He paid for a dowry and a big wedding. "It gives a man great standing," he said.

43   While he prepared to bring his young bride from Dakar, his three wives in Paris banded together. They are furious because he wasted their hard-earned money on another wife.

44   "They say if the new one comes, they will all leave," Mr. Diop said. With three wives in France and one in Dakar, Mr. Diop said he has great prestige in his village, but he is unsure how to deal with the rebellion at home. The French government may settle that. The Interior Ministry has already said it will not give a residence permit to more than one wife.

Vocabulary

Directions: Locate each of the key words in the article. Try to figure out each word's meaning by using the context. Confirm your guess by checking the dictionary or thesaurus. Write the meanings of the words in the margin of the text. Then record the meanings in the following chart.

Key Word	Paragraph	Meaning
1. annulled	6	
2. wrenching	10	
3. clandestinely	13	
4. rickety	15	
5. meddles	28	
6. prodding	39	
Others?		

Guide Questions

Directions: These questions will guide your understanding of what you have read. Write your answers in your notebook or on a separate sheet of paper if your instructor wishes to collect it. Your answers to these questions will be the basis of class discussion.

1. Define the word *polygamy* and try to recall anything you may know about it.
2. According to the author, why is the practice of polygamy in France coming to the attention of the public at this time?
3. Cite some of the statistics on polygamy in France (and the difficulty of acquiring good statistics).
4. Beginning in paragraph 16, Moustafa Djaara gives the polygamous man's side of the story. What are the pros and cons of polygamy for Mr. Djaara?
5. Why do town officials, landlords, and neighbors oppose having polygamous families in their neighborhoods?
6. Describe some of the complaints voiced by the women in polygamous marriages in the article.
7. What are some strategies that African women in France are using to combat polygamy?
8. Explain the relationship between the practice of polygamy and the question of how a society should deal with immigrant customs that are unacceptable or illegal in a new land.

Application

1. We learned in the article that polygamy is practiced in Senegal, Mali, and Mauritania. Use the library or the Internet to research the issue further.

In what other countries is polygamy practiced? Is it legal or is it practiced illegally? Was polygamy ever practiced in the United States? Use the information you gather as a basis for a class discussion.

2. For an interesting look at polygamy from the perspective of a woman who favors it, read "In Defense of Polygamy" on page 276.

Writing

Imagine you are the husband of one of the women in the article "African Women in France Battle Polygamy." Write a letter to *The New York Times* reacting to the information in the article.

Making Connections

How did the information in the preceding chapters ("Culture," "Norms," "Values," "Unity in Diversity") affect your reading of this article?

Marking Text

Mark the article "African Women in France Battle Polygamy." Follow the directions for marking text on page 421.

SHORT TAKE

Marriage Takes Many Different Forms throughout the World

The number of spouses that are allowed varies from culture to culture. North Americans are most familiar with **monogamy** (from the Greek word part *mono* meaning *one* and *gamy* meaning *marriage*)—one man married to one woman. In reality, though, with the divorce rate in the United States hovering at around 50 percent, a system of **serial monogamy,** marriage to multiple spouses—but one at a time—is becoming the norm. Contrast this with the system in some Greek villages, where women have traditionally been socially prohibited from marrying again after the death of their husbands. Widows take on a sexually neutral status and are therefore free for the first time in their lives to go into male places such as coffeehouses. However, for the rest of their lives they must wear black clothes to indicate their widow status. In contrast, Greek men who become widowers are not similarly restricted nor are they stigmatized as being gender neutral.

Polygamy (from the Greek word parts *poly* meaning *many* and *gamy* meaning *marriage*) means any combination of multiple spouses. When most people think of polygamy, they assume a structure in which two or more women share one husband. Strictly speaking, though, this form of marriage is **polygyny** (from the Greek word part *poly* meaning *many* and *gyny* meaning *female*). In this form of marriage there is one husband and two or more wives. Polygyny is most common today in Moslem nations, among traditional cattle-herding societies in East Africa, and in remnants of the old kingdoms of West Africa.

Among the polygamous Turkana of East Africa, a wife generally considers it an economic advantage for her family to have co-wives, because the women help each other with domestic chores and caring for the animals. They may even help their husband find a new bride. They interview prospective wives to find one who will be compatible and hard working. Usually the husband must have his current wives' approval before he can marry again.

Most Westerners view polygyny as advantageous for the husband only— more sexual partners, more children, and above all more prestige in society. However, multiple wives can be a disadvantage as well: the co-wives may gang up on him and force him to do things he may not want to do.

There is also a rarer structure called **polyandry** (from the Greek word part *poly* meaning *many* and *andr* meaning *male*). This form of marriage includes one wife and two or more husbands. Polyandry is very rare, found in less than 1 percent of societies. Polyandry is most often found in economically depressed societies. Since a woman can have only one child per year, this form of marriage keeps the birth rate down. Polyandry is found in some rural regions of the following: India, Sri Lanka, Nepal, and Tibet. Usually it is *fraternal polyandry,* that is, two brothers married to the same woman. This reduces the problem of determining what family their children belong to, since both potential fathers have the same parents. The younger brother usually marries the shared wife when he is in his early teens but often does not have sexual relations with her for years.

Polyandry has definite economic advantages for small-scale agricultural societies. It keeps the family farm in one piece. It allows one of the husbands to be away from the farm working for years at a time without disrupting the family. It provides economic security for the wife when one of her husbands dies. However, it also places an extra workload on her.

Over the past decade or so, the notion of romantic love has disrupted the tradition of polyandry, as men and women have begun to demand exclusive bonds with their spouse.

In the 1970s, as its population soared toward one billion, China began the implementation of strict family-planning measures. Over the next two decades the average number of babies per woman dropped from five or six to two or three. Without the controls, officials say, 240 million more babies would have been born. The goal of one child per family is now accepted in the cities and, even in the countryside, most people are having fewer children than their parents did. But an unforeseen problem has arisen: millions of children are growing up without siblings and are the sole object of their parents' affection. As a result, many Chinese say the children are growing up spoiled, selfish, and lazy. This article appeared in The New York Times *in 1996.*

AS A PAMPERED GENERATION GROWS UP, CHINESE WORRY

Patrick E. Tyler

1   It was just another school day for Liu Huamin when the father of one of her students burst through the classroom door and said his teen-age son was threatening to commit suicide by jumping off the fourth-floor balcony of the family's apartment building.

2   Why? asked Mrs. Liu, a chemistry teacher at Waluji Middle School here.

3   Because, the man replied, the boy's mother would not cook his favorite meat dumplings for breakfast.

4   He did not jump, but the story of his breathtaking display of willfulness incites a look of instant recognition across the faces of many Chinese teachers today.

5   Indeed, it seems at times as if the willfulness of China's generation of "little emperors"—children growing up without siblings under China's one-child population control policy—knows no bounds.

6   In Guangdong Province a power failure prevented a housewife from cooking dinner for her fourteen-year-old son, who flew into a rage and went out to watch television with a friend. When the boy returned, there was still no dinner, so he seized a meat cleaver and killed his mother with ten blows to the head. Then he hanged himself.

7   An extreme case, but the fact that China's government-run news organization gave it prominent display last year also illustrates the concern of many Chinese that its first generation of only children is rapidly maturing into a generation of spoiled, self-absorbed tyrants.

8   After decades of famine and political turmoil in China, parents who grew up in troubled and often violent times under Mao, suffering long periods of deprivation in the countryside and interrupted schooling, are now rearing—in many cases doting on—a generation of only children.

9   And these new parents are filled with anxiety about whether they are doing it right.

10   "This is a fixation," said James L. Watson, an anthropologist at Harvard University who has studied the Chinese family. "I would call it kind of a compensation complex. The generation of parents that we are dealing with now, many of

them are Cultural Revolution veterans who themselves did not have much of a childhood, and I think that many of them are trying hard to make sure that their own children get all the benefits and more that they missed out on."

But they are doing it with little cultural guidance. The current generation 11
of parents has been cut adrift from both the traditional Confucian values emphasizing reverence for elders that were once the foundation of China's extended families and from the Communist values imposed for three decades under Mao.

Neither has much credibility in China today. 12

Specialists say it is too early to say whether China's "little emperors" are 13
growing up to be a generation of self-centered autocrats, whose politics may be more aggressive than the generation that grew up under Mao, or whether they are so over-indulged at home that they will be ill prepared for the competitive pressures and harsh realities of China's market economy.

Off to Bad Start, Teachers Say

"Seems like it could go either way," said David Y. H. Wu, an anthropologist at 14
Chinese University of Hong Kong. "You could either raise a generation of rebels against the controls of the Communist party or you could raise a generation that would feel more nationalistic and assertive as Chinese.

"Talking about personality traits and trying to project to the whole nation 15
is very difficult, but I can see a whole generation perhaps more independent and willing to challenge authority, or simply more authoritative because of their intensified relationships with their parents, and the symbol of parents is government."

Either way, if today's teachers are any judge, the "little emperor" generation 16
is off to an inauspicious start.

"As life and economic conditions get better and better, the moral principles 17
of students and their sense of responsibility to society and family get worse and worse," said Mrs. Liu, the chemistry teacher, who has an eighteen-year-old son. "We teachers often wonder how these students can take up their social responsibility when they get older."

Teachers around the world have long complained about the quality of the 18
next generation. But in China, a generation of children is growing up in the midst of a profound economic revolution, where social and political values seem suspended in time as the country waits for the death of Deng Xiaoping,* the ninety-one-year-old paramount leader, not knowing whether that event will usher in a new era with a new value system.

"My most terrifying concern," said Zhang Xiaoyun, thirty-three, who 19
teaches literature at the China Youth Political College in Beijing, a former Communist party school, "is that you must raise a child within some system of beliefs, but our generation has no beliefs, so how can we educate our children?"

---

* Deng Xiaoping died on February 19, 1997.

20   The demographic shift from multi-child families under strong patriarchs to small, nuclear families centered on only children "is going to have a profound effect" on Chinese society, Professor Watson said.

Increased Spending on Toys and Books

21   One of the ways that Chinese are overcompensating in bringing up the country's only children is by spending the greatest portion of family income ever on toys, books, educational materials, personal computers, and food.

22   The national obsession with children is fostering multibillion-dollar opportunities for business.

23   Baby food, which barely existed in China a decade ago, is now a staple of family life and a major item in family budgets.

24   China's "little emperors" are the single greatest force in determining consumer decisions today, experts say.

25   "I met a woman who took her daughter to McDonald's in Beijing twice a week to give her modern nutrition," said Yan Yunxiang, a Chinese-born anthropologist at Johns Hopkins University, who frequently returns to examine the culture he grew up in.

26   When he asked the woman why she was spending as much as half a normal worker's income each month on McDonald's, she replied: "I want my daughter to learn more about American culture. She is taking English typing classes now, and next year I will buy her a computer."

27   Professor Watson said: "It turns out that most Chinese don't even like the food, but what they are buying is culture. They are buying connectedness to the world system.

28   "The idea is that if these kids can connect with McDonald's, they are going to end up at Harvard Law School."

29   One of China's most popular amusement parks, Window on the World in Shenzhen, has no rides and no arcades. Chinese come from all over the country to pay, in some cases a week's wages, to show their children miniatures of Manhattan Island, the Statue of Liberty, the Eiffel Tower, and the Taj Mahal.

A Generation Driven by Rewards

30   "Most of our time and money are spent on this child," said Wen Geli, the mother of a two-year-old boy who seems less attentive to the park's attractions than to gorging himself on ice cream. "We want to give him an introduction to the world and expand his outlook."

31   "My generation grew up with hardship," said her husband, Zhang Xinwen, a communications officer in the Chinese Army. "We were born in the 1960s, and that was a period of bitter shortage, but this generation is growing up in richer times and we want to take advantage of this better environment."

32   Not far away, a retired sports teacher, Cai Kunling, fifty-nine, was squiring his five-year-old granddaughter, Fu Hua, past the wonders of the world. "She should be in kindergarten today," he said, "but she wanted to take me to this place," he added in a tone that reflected who was in charge.

The two of them sat for their photo in front of a miniature of Niagara Falls   33
and then strolled over to the little Manhattan.

To Mr. Cai, who lived through the Mao period, it was like a dream world.   34

"My generation made a lot of sacrifices and had a lot of devotion to the coun-   35
try," he said. "But this generation needs a reward if you want them to do something. If there is no compensation, they don't want to do it."

Free-for-All Future Worries the Parents

Sitting around a dinner of baked carp with three other teachers one evening,   36
Mrs. Liu and some of her colleagues vented their anxieties.

Li Shunmei, thirty-one, a high-school teacher with a three-year-old daugh-   37
ter, said: "I worry a lot about my daughter's future, because I have doubts about
whether she can survive under the harsher and harsher competition of Chinese
society.

"Nowadays, there are many children who commit suicide. I think it is be-   38
cause parents obey their children's every demand, so they are not able to endure
any reversals or hard times."

This strain of anxiety is very prominent in Chinese families.   39

The old "iron rice bowl" society of cradle-to-grave social welfare protection   40
is giving way year by year to the new market economy, where life is beginning to
look like a terrifying free-for-all to many Chinese used to something more secure.

"The home can be very sweet and gentle for these toddlers, but the world out   41
there is a cruel world," said Jing Jun, a Beijing native who now teaches anthropology at City College in New York. "When we were growing up, the state
arranged everything for you, but now parents know the state is not going to do
anything for them and the job market is pretty grim."

Mr. Jing said he believed that China's "little emperors" would have to pass   42
through a tough period of adjustment. "They are under so much pressure," he
said, "and their parents have such great expectations for them. Whether they are
psychologically prepared for that, I cannot say."

Professor Watson said, "A lot of people, including Chinese psychologists, are   43
concerned whether the next generation is going to be able to 'eat bitterness,'
whether they are going to be able to work hard or whether they will be willing
to sacrifice themselves as was true under socialism."

Some Chinese feel that the "little emperors" will adjust.   44

"I'm optimistic," said Wang Xujin, a teacher at Beijing Business College   45
with a nine-year-old son.

But, he confessed, "although the students each year are smarter and smarter,   46
I like them less and less."

Vocabulary

Directions: Locate each of the key words in the article. Try to figure out each word's
meaning by using the context. Confirm your guess by checking the dictionary or
thesaurus. Write the meanings of the words in the margin of the text. Then record the
meanings in the chart that follows.

Key Word	Paragraph	Meaning
1. willfulness	4, 5	
2. fixation	10	
3. autocrats	13	
4. traits	15	
5. inauspicious	16	
6. overcompensating	21	
7. staple	23	
8. gorging	30	
Others?		

Guide Questions

Directions: These questions will guide your understanding of what you have read. Write your answers in your notebook or on a separate sheet of paper if your instructor wishes to collect it. Your answers to these questions will be the basis of class discussion.

1. Here, as in many news feature stories, the author begins with an example to illustrate his main point. Summarize the example and the point it illustrates.
2. Why are the children in the article described as "little emperors"?
3. Describe the differences in living conditions now and during the childhood of the parents of the "little emperors."
4. According to anthropologist James Watson, why are Chinese parents "doting on" their children now?
5. Explain the author's point in paragraph 11: "But they are doing it with little cultural guidance."
6. Anthropologist David Y. H. Wu says, "Seems like it could go either way." What does he mean?
7. Adults throughout history have complained about "the next generation." Judging from the information in this article and anything else you may know about the topic, do you think the next generation of Chinese children will have special problems? Explain.

8. React to the comments of the mother described in paragraph 25 who, among other things, took her child to McDonald's to give her "modern nutrition."

9. Do you see similarities between the treatment of Chinese children as described in the article and American children?

10. a. Explain what is meant by the old "iron rice bowl" society of China.
    b. Contrast the "iron rice bowl" society with the situation in China today.

Application

Directions: Choose one of the assignments below.

1. China's one-child policy was established in the 1970s. Use the Internet or the library to investigate the reasons for the policy and what the results have been.

2. If you read the selections "Norms" (page 58) and "Values" (page 64), try to make connections between what you learned from those selections and the problems facing the parents of China's current generation of children. Be sure to consider the information in paragraphs 10 through 12 of "As a Pampered Generation Grows Up, Chinese Worry."

Marking Text

Review how to mark your text on page 421. Then mark this article, "As a Pampered Generation Grows Up, Chinese Worry."

SHORT TAKE

A Nation of Lost Boys

Thomas Omestad

In China, they're called "bare branches"—young men who are unlikely to find a mate, have children, or settle into a stable, prosperous lifestyle. It's a population that's growing rapidly in countries like China and India, where traditional preferences for boys (who are expected to care for parents) have led to dramatically skewed male-to-female ratios. The fallout, says a new book, *Bare Branches: The Security Implications of Asia's Surplus Male Population:* an increased chance of internal turmoil and even war in such places, because men without family ties tend to be more aggressive. Coauthors Valerie Hudson and Andrea den Boer point to studies linking "bare branches" to greater criminal violence and also argue their presence can make war more likely, as governments look for ways to channel the energies of angry, nationalistic young men—often into the military.

In China, 117 boys are now born for every 100 girls. In India, the official rate is 113 to 100, though spot checks in some locales have turned up ratios as high as 156 to 100. The gender gap is fueled by several factors, including infanticide and withholding of healthcare from girls. The introduction of ultrasound machines, often wheeled into rural villages, accelerated the imbalance in the mid-1980s as some parents opted to abort female fetuses. Abortion for sex selection is illegal in both China and India, but the practice remains common in some areas; ultrasound practitioners, says coauthor Hudson, may *say* nothing but may light a cigarette to signal that the mother is carrying a boy—or stamp one out if it's a girl.

China perceives some risk in the trend: Last month, it announced that it will offer financial incentives to try to normalize gender ratios by 2010. But with the first big wave of bare branches turning 18 and 19, Hudson says, the world is already facing a new source of volatility.

Thirty years have passed since China implemented its one child policy. While it has been enormously successful in limiting the country's population growth, the policy has also had some unexpected and worrisome results.
This article was written for Radio Free Europe/Radio Liberty in January 2005.

CHINA: A FUTURE WITH A SHORTAGE OF BRIDES, AN ABUNDANCE OF ELDERLY

Daisy Sindelar

PRAGUE, 6 January 2005 — China today officially passed a population milestone — the birth of its 1.3 billionth baby. 1

A Chinese government official announced the news in Beijing after awarding a certificate to the infant's mother: "The 1.3 billionth citizen was born at 00:02 on January 6, 2005." 2

And the gender of the history-making baby? A boy. 3

That fact might not surprise China-watchers, who say the country's true population story is not its size, but its composition. 4

China's one-child family planning policy has largely succeeded in curbing the country's population growth over the past 25 years. 5

But Chinese officials are now faced with two resulting complications: dwindling numbers of marriageable women — and larger numbers of elderly born during a post-World War II baby boom. 6

The international programs division of the United States Census Bureau estimates that roughly seven out of 100 Chinese are currently over the age of 65. Within the next 30 years, that number is set to more than double. 7

By 2030, elderly Chinese will number some 240 million — slightly higher than the entire population of Indonesia. 8

The so-called "graying" trend is an issue facing many countries to varying degrees, including the United States and many in Western Europe. But unlike much of the West, the aging of China's population is taking place at a rapid rate — leaving the government little time to prepare. 9

Chinese society has traditionally depended on the family, rather than the state, to care for its elderly. In the past, couples would have as many as six children to ensure a comfortable old age. 10

But the one-child policy has dramatically reduced the number of offspring parents can count on to provide for them as they grow older. This has forced the state to begin experimenting with pension systems and other reforms. 11

Loraine West, an economist with the U.S. Census Bureau, says the real challenge will be changing the mindset of rural Chinese, who make up some two-thirds of the population: "The pension program still is largely an urban-based program. And that's where I think you see the change first. An increasing proportion of the elderly are no longer solely dependent on their children; they have a pension to rely on. The rural areas are still, I would say, relatively dependent on their children. But that's where it will be critical to see if the government can successfully expand this 12 program, or put in place something comparable for the rural population. They're going to have fewer dependents. As time passes, they'll be relying on one or two children and it will be increasingly important that they have some other resources available to them."

13   For young Chinese, an even more worrying trend is the prospect of a future with too many men and too few women.

14   The one-child policy, a traditional preference for sons, and accessibility to selective abortions have combined to leave China with a strongly skewed gender ratio. The underreporting of girls by families hoping to reserve their "official" spot for a boy is also cited as a cause for the imbalance—as are, to a lesser degree, adoption and infanticide.

15   Male babies naturally outnumber female babies throughout much of the world. But in China, the gap has grown unusually large.

16   In most societies, there are between 102 and 106 male births for every 100 female births. In China, that number is estimated to be as high as 117.

17   Census Bureau demographer Daniel Goodkind says surplus grooms will eventually number in the millions—a trend with significant social implications: "The most common one that demographers talk about is called 'marriage squeeze'—that is, when you have an imbalance in either potential husbands or wives. So that can affect the marital chances of the sex that's in greater supply—in this case, males. So if you're female in China over the next 20 years, in terms of the number of potential partners, you'll be doing pretty well, assuming it's a free market."

18   With the one-child policy hitting the quarter-century mark, the sex-ratio crisis is already being felt.

19   Chinese media increasingly cover cases of "bride stealing"—the kidnapping and trafficking of young single women for marriage. One recent television documentary profiled a police officer responsible for recovering more than 100 "stolen brides" over the past several years.

20   Chinese officials are attempting to counter the problem by relaxing some restrictions on the number of children a family can have—meaning less pressure on mothers to produce a son, and fewer selective abortions. They are also taking steps to criminalize abortions based on gender.

21   Other social trends may help balance the sex ratio as well. David Osterhout, a journalist living in Shanghai, says China's dramatic economic growth is slowly changing the way some Chinese look at their daughters.

22   He says with more and more women entering the workforce, daughters are no longer seen as a financial handicap: "The other thing is that I think girls are becoming more prized as society changes, and women are getting into jobs traditionally reserved for men, and are making salary levels comparable with the levels of men."

23   Not all Chinese men may be pleased with the idea of a future world inhabited by powerful working women and a shortage of wives. Chinese women, however, may see it in a different way.

Vocabulary

Directions: Locate each of the key words in the reading selection. Try to figure out each word's meaning by using the context. Confirm your guess by checking the dictionary or thesaurus. Write the meanings of the words in the margin of the text. Then record the meanings in the chart below.

Key Word	Paragraph	Meaning
1. milestone	1	
2. curbing	5	
3. dwindling	6	
4. skewed	14	
5. demographer	17	
Others?		

Guide Questions

Directions: These questions will guide your understanding of what you have read. Write your answers in your notebook, or on a separate sheet of paper if your instructor wishes to collect it. Your answers to these questions will be the basis of class discussion.

1. Explain the point of paragraph 4: "… the country's true population story is not its size, but its composition."
2. State the two complications that are the result of China's one-child policy.
3. Explain the problem that results from a "graying" population in China.
4. What "worrying trend" concerns young Chinese?
5. Are the potential results of China's one-child policy all bad? Are there any positive aspects?

Application

Directions: Compare China's population with that of the United States., India, and Indonesia. If you are from another country, include your native country. Use the Internet or the library to get the population statistics.

Making Connections

Directions: Reread the article "As a Pampered Generation Grows Up, Chinese Worry." Draw connections between that story, written in 1996 and this article written in 2005.

Writing

Directions: React to what you've read about Chinese population problems and policies. In your reaction, comment on the Chinese government's decision to enforce a one child policy. If you were in charge of China's government, what would you do? Write two or more paragraphs.

After twenty years of negotiation, the Inuit people of the Arctic have finally achieved their long-desired dream: a territory of their own. Carved out of northern Canada, it is home to the largest population of Inuit people in the world. But the past twenty years have seen enormous changes in the lives of these northern inhabitants. This article was researched and written by Yva Momatiuk and John Eastcott, a freelance photojournalist team. It appeared in The World and I *in July 2000 and focuses on the women of Nunavut, their sudden entry into the modern world, and their newfound independence.*

OUR LAND: NUNAVUT'S INUIT WOMEN

Yva Momatiuk and John Eastcott

Mabel Angulalik ties the dead bird's feet to the top of a makeshift post. She spreads its wings to warn other seagulls patrolling the beach: leave my drying fish alone. Around the post, wooden racks bend under slabs of Arctic char curing in the weak July sun. Its warmth has only just begun to melt the sea ice around Victoria Island in Canada's new territory of Nunavut, *Our Land* in Inktitut, the language of the Inuit.   1

Angulalik watches the shifting ice, and the lines in her old face deepen. After she was born, her mother—paralyzed from the waist down—put her baby daughter in the snow to freeze. "My mother was crawling on her hands and knew she couldn't look after me," Angulalik says quietly. "But another family camping nearby found me and took me in. And here I am."   2

Indeed she is. Yet her memories of the nomadic life following animals across tundra and ice are full of hardship: Hardly any food. No oil for lamps. A husband chosen for her, as required by custom. Babies born in snow houses. Caribou hides to sew, fish to dry, seal blubber to preserve.   3

Today Angulalik lives in a warm house in the nearby town of Ikaluktitiak, which means Good Fishing Place. She spends her summers in a cabin by the sea, tending to fish racks and smelling the salty air. But when a young relative arrives to collect her, she hikes up her wolverine-trimmed parka, climbs aboard the all-terrain vehicle, and holds tight as they bump back to Ikaluktitiak.   4

The town, like most Arctic settlements, has an airport, a nurses' station, several stores, schools, hotels, and churches. The political entity of Nunavut was created on April 1, 1999, and constitutes about one-fifth of Canada's landmass. Eighty-five percent of its inhabitants, some 17,500 people, are Inuit. It took them twenty years to negotiate independence, and now the Inuit want to plan the future on their terms. Yet things have changed in twenty years.   5

Change has brought forth a new Inuit woman. Today she is more likely to drive a truck than a dogsled, visit a tanning salon than her fishing net, and worry about her children's grades rather than food for them. If she is forty-five or older, she may be fluent in her ancestors' tongue as well as in English; if she is younger, her Inuktitut may be limited to a few phrases. She holds a job, travels south for holidays, and prefers Big Macs to blubber. She is a bridge between her traditional parents and the thoroughly modern youngsters. She is the glue of her family and at times the sole wage earner.   6

7   One of the earliest debates in Nunavut was over equal representation of women and men in the new government. It failed, but today the Pauktuutit Inuit Women's Association funds job-training programs, helps women fighting custody battles, and builds shelters for abused wives.

8   Eva Otokiak is the manager of Ikaluktitiak's seven-bed shelter and a former victim of domestic violence. "I endured because of my five children," she says, stroking her short hair. She explains that as families left the open land for settlements, many became troubled. The men discovered that their legendary survival and hunting skills were useless. Unless they attended school, learned English, and joined the market economy, they had to survive on government handouts. Welfare covered necessities but killed pride; alcohol and drugs obliterated pain but destroyed whole families. Nunavut's suicide rate is seven times that of southern Canada.

9   In some families, men who once hunted take care of the children while the women work. Women aren't just chasing better jobs, however; they have also emerged as a healing force. Most Inuit women try to ensure the kind of robust family life, communal ties, and connection to the land that social researchers say are necessary for emotional health.

10   "I have to say no to my children more often than if we still lived on the land," Otokiak says. "I say no to big parties, no to getting pregnant early." To cope with the new life, she learned to be more assertive than her ancestors, a difficult task if you come from an intrinsically cooperative culture.

11   Nunavut women credit the men with much of their strength. Brenda Jencke decided to return north from her husband's home province of Ontario, so their three children would grow up close to her Inuit roots. He supported her all the way, and today she heads their construction company in Ikaluktitiak.

12   A slender woman with a dazzling smile, Margo Kadlun works for a caribou research project. She remembers how much she wanted to go hunting when she was small. "My father warned me: 'You cannot go if you are whining, and I won't bring you back if you get tired,'" she recalls. "We walked miles and miles across the tundra until we got a couple caribou. Brought back several leg bones and cached the rest. But my father never told me I couldn't go because I was a girl. And he taught me not to whine but to stick to what I want to do. He gave me that."

Vocabulary

Directions: Locate each of the key words in the reading selection. Try to figure out each word's meaning by using the context. Confirm your guess by checking the dictionary or thesaurus. Write the meanings of the words in the margin of the text. Then record the meanings in the following chart.

Key Word	Paragraph	Meaning
1. makeshift	1	
2. tundra	3	

Key Word	Paragraph	Meaning
3. blubber	3	
4. robust	9	
5. intrinsically	10	
Others?		

Guide Questions

Directions: These questions will guide your understanding of what you have read. Write your answers in your notebook or on a separate sheet of paper if your instructor wishes to collect it. Your answers to these questions will be the basis of class discussion.

1. Compare and contrast the life of Inuit women today and their life of twenty years ago. Include information on where they live, the food they eat, the comforts of their homes, their worries, marriage, work, transportation, and language.
2. Describe the problems that resulted as families left the open land for settlements.
3. What have Inuit women learned in order to cope with their new life?
4. Explain what Margo Kadlun means when she speaks of her father: "He gave me that."

Application

Use the library or the Internet to do some research on this brand-new territory of Nunavut. One excellent source is www.facts.com, which is available through many libraries. Major newspapers and magazines are also excellent sources of information.

Marking Text

Review how to mark text on page 421. Mark this article "Our Land" and then compare your marked text to the model on page 112.

Writing

Directions: Now use your marked text to write a concise summary of this article. Summary-writing is explained on page 425.

Example of Marked Text

After twenty years of negotiation, the Inuit people of the Arctic have finally achieved their long-desired dream: a territory of their own. Carved out of northern Canada, it is home to the largest population of Inuit people in the world. But the past twenty years have seen enormous changes in the lives of these northern inhabitants. This article was researched and written by Yva Momatiuk and John Eastcott, a freelance photojournalist team. It appeared in The World and I in July 2000 and focuses on the women of Nunavut, their sudden entry into the modern world, and their newfound independence.

OUR LAND: NUNAVUT'S INUIT WOMEN

Yva Momatiuk and John Eastcott

Intro

1 Mabel Angulalik ties the dead bird's feet to the top of a makeshift post. She spreads its wings to warn other seagulls patrolling the beach: leave my drying fish alone. Around the post, wooden racks bend under slabs of Arctic char curing in the weak July sun. Its warmth has only just begun to melt the sea ice around Victoria Island in Canada's new territory of Nunavut, *Our Land* in Inktitut, the language of the Inuit.

2 Angulalik watches the shifting ice, and the lines in her old face deepen. After she was born, her mother—paralyzed from the waist down—put her baby daughter in the snow to freeze. "My mother was crawling on her hands and knew she couldn't look after me," Angulalik says quietly. "But another family camping nearby found me and took me in. And here I am."

Contrast past:

3 Indeed she is. Yet her memories of the nomadic life following animals across tundra and ice are full of hardship: Hardly any food. No oil for lamps. A husband chosen for her, as required by custom. Babies born in snow houses. Caribou hides to sew, fish to dry; seal blubber to preserve.

present:

4 Today Angulalik lives in a warm house in the nearby town of Ikaluktitiak, which means Good Fishing Place. She spends her summers in a cabin by the sea, tending to fish racks and smelling the salty air. But when a young relative arrives to collect her, she hikes up her wolverine-trimmed parka, climbs aboard the all-terrain vehicle, and holds tight as they bump back to Ikaluktitiak.

5 The town, like most Arctic settlements, has an airport, a nurses station, several stores, schools, hotels, and churches. The political entity of Nunavut was created on April 1, 1999, and constitutes about one-fifth of Canada's landmass. Eighty-five percent of its inhabitants, some 17,500 people, are Inuit. It took them twenty years to negotiate independence, and now the Inuit want to plan the future on their terms. Yet things have changed in twenty years.

a new nation
→ *Nunavut*

Inuit

MI → *
New roles for women

6 Change has brought forth a new Inuit woman. Today she is more likely to * drive a truck than a dogsled, visit a tanning salon than her fishing net, and worry about her children's grades rather than food for them. If she is forty-five or older, she may be fluent in her ancestors' tongue as well as in English; if she is younger, her Inuktitut may be limited to a few phrases. She holds a job, travels south for holidays, and prefers Big Macs to blubber. She is a bridge between her traditional

parents and the thoroughly modern youngsters. She is the glue of her family and at times the sole wage earner.

One of the earliest debates in Nunavut was over equal representation of women and men in the new government. It failed, but today the Pauktuutit Inuit Women's Association funds job-training programs, helps women fighting custody battles, and builds shelters for abused wives.   7

Eva Otokiak is the manager of Ikaluktitiak's seven-bed shelter and a former victim of domestic violence. "I endured because of my five children," she says, stroking her short hair. She explains that as families left the open land for settlements, many became troubled. The men discovered that their legendary survival and hunting skills were useless. Unless they attended school, learned English, and joined the market economy, they had to survive on government handouts. Welfare covered necessities but killed pride; alcohol and drugs obliterated pain but destroyed whole families. Nunavut's suicide rate is seven times that of southern Canada.   8

men lost their power ∴ problems

ex of "culture change"

In some families, men who once hunted take care of the children while the women work. Women aren't just chasing better jobs, however; they have also emerged as a healing force. Most Inuit women try to ensure the kind of robust family life, communal ties, and connection to the land that social researchers say are necessary for emotional health.   9

women support families + try to heal society

"I have to say no to my children more often than if we still lived on the land," Otokiak says. "I say no to big parties, no to getting pregnant early." To cope with the new life, she learned to be more assertive than her ancestors, a difficult task if you come from an intrinsically cooperative culture.   10

Nunavut women credit the men with much of their strength. Brenda Jencke decided to return north from her husband's home province of Ontario, so their three children would grow up close to her Inuit roots. He supported her all the way, and today she heads their construction company in Ikaluktitiak.   11

men support women emotionally

A slender woman with a dazzling smile, Margo Kadlun works for a caribou research project. She remembers how much she wanted to go hunting when she was small. "My father warned me: 'You cannot go if you are whining, and I won't bring you back if you get tired,'" she recalls. "We walked miles and miles across the tundra until we got a couple caribou. Brought back several leg bones and cached the rest. But my father never told me I couldn't go because I was a girl. And he taught me not to whine but to stick to what I want to do. He gave me that."   12

ex of man supporting woman's independence

Writer Esmeralda Santiago was thirteen when her mother decided to move from Puerto Rico to Brooklyn with her eight children. Santiago found the move frightening: New York was cold, dark, its language and customs incomprehensible. In her 1993 memoir, When I Was Puerto Rican, *Santiago describes the difficult transition between two cultures. The following is an excerpt from that book.*

A PUERTO RICAN STEW

Esmeralda Santiago

To Mami, the trip north made me "Americana."
But I found my own recipe for identity.

1   I'm in my kitchen, browsing through Puerto Rican cookbooks, when it hits me. These books are in English, written for people who don't know a *sofrito* from a *sombrero.* Then I remember the afternoon I returned to Puerto Rico for the summer after 15 years of living in the United States. The family gathered for dinner in my mother's house. The men settled in a corner of the living room, while Mami and my sisters chopped, washed, seasoned: I stood on the other side of the kitchen island, enjoying their Dance of the Stove with Pots and Pans—the flat metal sounds, the thud of the refrigerator door opening and closing, the swish of running water—a percussive accompaniment enhancing the fragrant sizzle of garlic and onions in hot oil.

2   "Do you cook Puerto Rican?" Norma asked as she cored a red pepper.

3   "No," I answered, "I never got the hang of it."

4   "How can you be Puerto Rican without your rice and beans?" joked Alicia.

5   "Easy," said Mami. "She's no longer Puerto Rican."

6   If she had stabbed me with the chicken-gutting knife in her hand it would have hurt less. I swallowed the pain. "Si, Mami," I said, "I have become Americana."

7   I parried with "Wasn't that what you wanted when you first brought us to New York?"

8   As Mami split the chicken, her voice rose, indignant: "I only wanted the best for you."

9   The dance was over, a knife suspended above tomato halves, rinse water running through rice clear as sunshine. I walked away, pushed by their silence—my mother, my sisters, my brothers-in law. No one followed me, or challenged her assessment of me as a turncoat who had abandoned her culture. I stood in the gravelly yard, the soles of my sandals separating me from the ground as if I were on stilts, unable to touch my native soil, unable to feel a connection. I wanted to cry, but would not give them nor myself the satisfaction of tears. Instead, I leaned against a fence and wondered if her words hurt so much because they were true.

10   Whatever I was, Puerto Rican or not, had been orchestrated by Mami. When I was 13, she moved us from rural Puerto Rico to Brooklyn. We were to learn English, to graduate from high school, to find jobs in clean offices not factories. We were to assimilate into American society to put an end to the poverty she was forced to endure for lack of an education.

I, the oldest, took up the challenge. I learned English so well that people told me I didn't "speak like a Puerto Rican." I gave up the bright, form-fitting clothes of my friends and relatives for drab loose garments that would not brand me as a "hot tomato." I developed a formal evasive manner when asked about my background. I would not admit to being poor, to living with my mother and 10 sisters and brothers in a three-room apartment. I would tremble with shame if newspapers identified a criminal as Puerto Rican.

Mami beamed when I got a job as a typist in Manhattan. She reminded me that I was to show my sisters and brothers the path to success without becoming "Americanized," a status that was never clearly defined but to be avoided at all costs.

That afternoon in her kitchen was the first time we had spoken in seven years. The grudge we held was so deep, neither could bridge it without losing *dignidad,* an imperative of Puerto Rican self-esteem. The break had come when I stopped being a "good" Puerto Rican girl and behaved like an American one.

At 21, I assumed I was old enough to live my life as I pleased. And what I pleased was a man a year older than Mami. I ran away with him, leaving a letter telling Mami I wouldn't be home after work because I was eloping. "Don't worry," I signed off, "I still love you."

She tracked me down to an apartment in Fort Lauderdale more luxurious than any we'd ever lived in, to say that if I returned home all would be forgiven. I refused. During those seven years, the man for whom I'd left my mother turned out to be as old-fashioned, possessive and domineering as she had seemed. From him, too, I ran away.

To question my Puerto Rican identity that afternoon in her kitchen was Mami's perfect comeback to what had surely been seven years of worry. It was also her way of recognizing her own folly. She had expected me to thrive in American culture, but I was to remain 100 percent Puerto Rican.

Mami came to realize the impossibility of such a demand, how difficult it is for someone from a "traditional" culture to achieve success in the United States without becoming something other than the person she set out to be. My one act of rebellion forced her to face what she had never expected. In the United States, her children would challenge her authority based on different rules of conduct. Within a year of my leaving home, she packed up the family and returned to Puerto Rico, where, she hoped, her children would be what they couldn't be in the United States: real Puerto Ricans.

I stayed behind, immersed in the American culture she feared. But I never considered myself any less Puerto Rican. I was born there, spoke its language, identified with its culture. But to Puerto Ricans on the island during my summer there, I was a different creature altogether. Employers complained that I was too assertive, men said I was too feminist, my cousin suggested I had no manners and everyone accused me of being too independent. Those, I was made to understand, were Americanisms.

Back in the United States, I was constantly asked where I was from, the comments about my not looking, behaving or talking like a Puerto Rican followed me into the era of political correctness, when it's no longer polite to say things like that.

20   I've learned to insist on my peculiar brand of Puerto Rican identity. One not bound by geographical, linguistic or behavioral boundaries, but rather, by a deep identification with a place, a people and a culture which, in spite of appearances, define my behavior and determine the rhythms of my days. An identity in which I've forgiven myself for having to look up a recipe for *arroz con pollo* in a Puerto Rican cookbook meant for people who don't know a *sombrero* from a *sofrito*.

Vocabulary

Directions: Locate each of the key words in the story. Try to figure out each word's meaning by using the context. Confirm your guess by checking the dictionary or thesaurus. Write the meanings of the words in the margin of the text. Then record the meanings in the chart below.

Key Word	Paragraph	Meaning
1. parried	7	
2. indignant	8	
3. turncoat	9	
4. assimilate	10	
5. evasive	11	
6. folly	16	
7. thrive	16	
Others?		

Guide Questions

Directions: These questions will guide your understanding of the story. Write your answers in your notebook or on a separate sheet of paper if your instructor wishes to collect it. Your answers to these questions will be the basis of class discussion.

1. Describe the scene at the beginning of the story: the setting, the characters, their actions.
2. Why did Santiago become upset and leave the kitchen?

3. Why did Santiago's mother decide to leave Puerto Rico and move to New York?
4. Describe Santiago's experiences after the move to New York.
5. What was Santiago's mother's impossible "demand"?
6. Describe Santiago's "peculiar brand of Puerto Rican identity."
7. Why do you think the author titled her story "A Puerto Rican Stew"?

Making Connections

Relate this story to what you learned in earlier parts of this unit. Give some examples of how the values and norms of Puerto Rico were different from those of the United States. Why did these differences cause Santiago to suffer? Have you ever experienced a culture conflict like this?

SHORT TAKE

Watch Your Language!

The world is becoming more homogeneous each day: American fast-food restaurants appear in the heart of Paris and the center of Beijing; teenagers in the farthest corners of the earth wear t-shirts by the same "hot" designers; pop music is heard blasting from short-wave radios in the middle of the Gobi desert and in ice-shrouded research stations in Greenland. But that doesn't mean there still aren't a few problems, a few misunderstandings along the way. Consider the messages on these signs found in businesses all over Europe and Asia.

"Please leave your values at the front desk," requests a Paris hotel. "Because of the impropriety of entertaining guests of the opposite sex in the bedroom, it is suggested that the lobby be used for this purpose," advises a hotel in Zurich. A Japanese hotel sign says "You are invited to take advantage of the chambermaid."

If all these moral dilemmas make you hungry, head for the restaurant in Poland whose menu features "roasted duck let loose" and "beef rashers beaten up in the country people's fashion." Or try the inn in Spain that offers "swerd cherde with anals."

Or try sightseeing. In Moscow, you might follow the suggestion of a hotel sign that reads, "You are welcome to visit the cemetery, where famous Russian and Soviet composers, artists, and writers are buried daily except Thursday."

But be careful if you are visiting a Bucharest zoo. A sign there reads: "Please do not feed the animals. If you have any suitable food, give it to the guard on duty."

If shopping in Sweden, by all means avoid the furrier who advertises "Fur coats made for ladies from their own skin." Or the Paris shop that sells "dresses for street walking."

But who needs clothes? Go to Bangkok where a dry cleaner says "Drop your trousers here for best results."

In this excerpt from the textbook Sociology, *we learn about one of the great distinguishing features of the United States—immigration. Few other nations have been so welcoming and at the same time so conflicted by the flow of immigrants from every corner of the world. They may not always be welcomed by those who preceded them (former immigrants themselves), but new arrivals have shaped this country and will continue to change it.*

THE UNITED STATES: LAND OF IMMIGRANTS

Henry Tischler

1   Since the settlement of Jamestown in 1607, well over 45 million people have immigrated to the United States. Up until 1882, the policy of the United States was almost one of free and unrestricted admittance. The country was regarded as the land of the free, a haven for those oppressed by tyrants, and a place of opportunity. The words of Emma Lazarus, inscribed on the Statue of Liberty, were indeed appropriate:

> Give me your tired, your poor,
> Your huddled masses yearning to breathe free,
> The wretched refuse of your teeming shore.
> Send these, the homeless, tempest-tost to me,
> I lift my lamp beside the golden door!

2   To be sure, there were those who had misgivings about the immigrants. George Washington wrote to John Adams in 1794, "My opinion with respect to immigration is that except for useful mechanics and some particular descriptions of men or professions, there is no need for encouragement." Thomas Jefferson was even more emphatic in expressing the wish that there might be "an ocean of fire between this country and Europe, so that it would be impossible for any more immigrants to come hither." Such fears, however, were not widely felt. There was the West to be opened, railroads to be built, and canals to be dug; there was land for the asking. People poured across the mountains, and the young nation was eager for population.

3   Immigration of white ethnics to the United States can be viewed from the perspective of old migration and new migration. The old migration consisted of people from northern Europe who came before the 1880s. The new migration was much larger in numbers and consisted of people from southern and eastern Europe who came between 1880 and 1920. The ethnic groups that made up the old migration included the English, Dutch, French, Germans, Irish, Scandinavians, Scots, and Welsh. The new migration included Poles, Hungarians, Ukrainians, Russians, Italians, Greeks, Portuguese, and Armenians.

4   Figure 1 on page 119 shows the number of immigrants who came to the United States in each decade from 1820 to 2000. The new migration sent far more immigrants to the United States than the old migration. The earlier immigrants felt threatened by the waves of unskilled and uneducated newcomers, whose

appearance and culture were so different from their own. Public pressure for immigration restriction increased. After 1921, quotas were established limiting the number of people who could arrive from any particular country. The quotas were designed specifically to discriminate against potential immigrants from the southern and eastern European countries. The discriminatory immigration policy remained in effect until 1965, when a new policy was established.

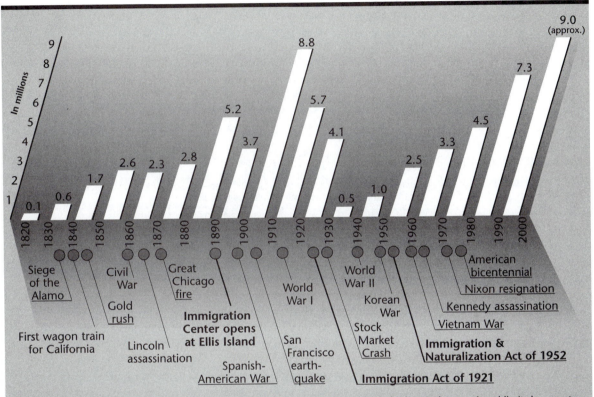

1882: Chinese immigration prohibited, more restrictions placed on immigration.

Immigration reached a peak between 1901 and 1910, when 8.8 million newcomers (8 million of them white Europeans) arrived in the United States.

1921: First immigration quotas (by country) announced.

1948: Refugee Relief Act brings in homeless Europeans and Soviets. Will be used later for Hungarians, Chinese, and Cubans.

1965: Quotas by hemisphere replaced limits by country.

Four out of five immigrants in the 1980s came from Asia, Latin America, and the Caribbean. Counting approximately 500,000 undocumented immigrants, there will be more newcomers in the United States in the 1990s than in any previous decade.

1986: Immigration and Refugee Control Act created means for immigrants in U.S. since 1962 to become citizens; led to legalization of many agricultural workers. Major beneficiaries: Mexicans (3 million have become legal residents since 1987), Cubans, Haitians.

Figure 1   Immigration to the United States, 1820–2000

TABLE 1   United States Immigration Restrictions

1769–1875	No restrictions; open-door policy
1875	No convicts; no prostitutes
1882	No idiots; no lunatics; no people likely to need public care Start of head tax
1882–1943	No Chinese
1885	No gangs of cheap contract laborers
1891	No immigrants with dangerous contagious diseases; no paupers; no polygamists Start of medical inspections
1903	No epileptics; no insane people; no betters; no anarchists
1907	No feeble-minded; no children under 16 unaccompanied by parents; no immigrants unable to support themselves because of physical or mental defects
1917	No immigrants from most of Asia or the Pacific islands; no adults unable to read or write Start of literacy tests
1921	No more than 3% of foreign-born of each nationality in U.S. in 1910; total about 350,000 annually
1924–1927	National Origins Quota Law; no more than 2% of foreign-born of each nationality already in U.S. in 1890; total about 150,000 annually
1940	Alien Registration Act; all aliens must register and be fingerprinted
1950	Exclusion and deportation of aliens dangerous to national security
1952	Codification, nationalization, and minor alterations of previous immigration laws
1965	National Origins Quota system abolished; no more than 20,000 from any one country outside the Western Hemisphere; total about 170,000 annually Start of restrictions on immigrants from other Western Hemisphere countries; no more than 120,000 annually Preference to refugees, aliens with relatives here, and workers with skills needed in the United States
1980	Congress passes the Refugee Act of 1980, repealing ideological and geographical preferences that had favored refugees fleeing communism and Middle Eastern countries
1986	The Immigration Reform and Control Act (IRCA) takes effect; grants amnesty to illegal immigrants residing in the United States since 1982; increases sanctions against employers for hiring illegal immigrants
1990	President George Bush increases immigration quotas

Source: Smithsonian Institution exhibit, Washington, DC.

5   In Table 1 you will see a list of the various peoples who were excluded from immigrating to the United States during each of the periods in its history. As you can see, we were much more lenient during the early days of our history. However, even with our periods of restrictive immigration, the United States has had one of the most open immigration policies in the world, and we continue to take in more legal immigrants than the rest of the world combined.

Immigration Today Compared with the Past

The past 30 years have seen a marked shift in United States immigration patterns. From the beginning of the country's birth until the 1960s, most immigrants were from European countries. Mexico, the Philippines, China, Korea, and Vietnam were the top five countries of origin for immigrants during the 1980s.   6

A huge wave of immigrants entered the United States in the late 1980s and early 1990s, peaking in 1991 with 1.8 million legal immigrants. Many of these "immigrants" had lived in the country for many years before becoming part of the government's statistics.   7

Today's immigrants are unique in their ethnic origins, education, and skills. The waves of immigration during earlier periods in our history were mostly from European countries. Today's immigrants are primarily from Latin American and Asian countries. Their education levels are at two extremes. While most native-born people have completed high school, immigrants are only half as likely to have done so. At the same time, many other immigrants are highly educated, and some immigrants are more likely than [the] native born to have advanced college degrees.   8

The Census Bureau projects that 880,000 legal immigrants per year will enter the country between 1997 and 2050. Thirty-seven percent of the immigrants will be Hispanic, 35% will be from Asian countries, approximately 23% will be white non-Hispanics, and 7% are expected to be black. With this type of immigration, non-Hispanic whites will account for barely half of the total U.S. population, while Asians and Hispanics will form nearly one-third. The African-American share of the population is expected to rise to 14% (see Figure 2 on page 122).   9

With the large number of people immigrating to the United States, nearly 1 in 10 U.S. residents (9.6%) was foreign born in 1997. This is the highest percentage of foreign-born residents since World War II and nearly double the 1970 level of 4.8%. Many of these people are recent arrivals. Of the 25.8 million foreign-born people living in the United States in March of 1997, 7.5 million had arrived during the previous 7 years. Nearly one-third of these new immigrants live in California, with New York and Florida attracting another 25% (U.S. Bureau of the Census, Current Population Survey, March 1997).   10

Illegal Immigration

Since 1970, illegal immigration has figured prominently in the ethnic makeup of certain regions of the United States. The U.S. Immigration and Naturalization Service (INS) estimates that currently, 3.5 million to 4 million people are residing in the country illegally and that the number is growing by 200,000 a year. There are two types of illegal immigrants: those who enter the United States legally but overstay their visa limits, and those who enter illegally to begin with. Those who migrate over the border each day to work must also be figured into the total.   11

Mexico, El Salvador, and Guatemala account for 44% of the total number of illegal immigrants (see Table 2 on page 123). Illegal immigrants tend to settle in certain states. California is home to 40% of the total, with New York, Florida, Texas, and   12

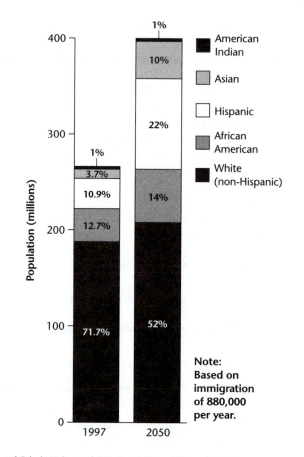

Figure 2   Racial and Ethnic Makeup of U.S. Population, 1997 and 2050

Illinois accounting for most of the rest. The vast majority (71%) of the illegal immigrants are between ages 15 and 39; very few are over 65.

13   In 1986, the Immigration Reform and Control Act (IRCA) was passed, a law designed to control the flow of illegal immigrants into the United States. The law makes it a crime for employers, even individuals hiring household help, to knowingly employ an illegal immigrant. Stiff fines and criminal penalties can be imposed if they do so. The law also provided legal status to illegal immigrants who entered the United States before 1982 and who have lived here continuously since then. Between 1989 and 1993, 2.7 million people were granted legal resident status under special provisions of the IRCA. These people had lived and worked in the country illegally during the 1980s. Interestingly, only 4% of those who applied for amnesty under the 1986 act worked in farming, fishing, or forestry, running counter to the perception that most illegal immigrants are migrant farm workers.

14   What is America's racial and ethnic composition today? As you can see in Figure 2, the United States is perhaps the most racially and ethnically diverse

	TABLE 2 · Top Ten Countries of Origin of Illegal Immigrants	

Country	Percent of Total
Mexico	31
El Salvador	9
Guatemala	4
Canada	3
Poland	3
Philippines	3
Haiti	3
Nicaragua	2
Colombia	2
Bahamas	2

Source: Immigration and Naturalization Service.

country in the world. Unlike many other countries, it has no ethnic group that makes up a numerical majority of the population.

Vocabulary

Directions: Locate each of the key words in the reading selection. Try to figure out each word's meaning by its context. Confirm your guess by checking the dictionary or thesaurus. Write the meanings of the words in the margin of the text. Then record the meanings in the chart below.

Key Word	Paragraph	Meaning
1. haven	1	
2. misgivings	2	
3. lenient	5	
Others?		

Guide Questions

Directions: These questions will guide your understanding of what you have read. Write your answers in your notebook or on a separate sheet of paper if your instructor wishes to collect it. Your answers to these questions will be the basis of class discussion.

1. a. Describe the attitudes toward immigration of two of America's Founding Fathers, George Washington and Thomas Jefferson.
   b. Were you surprised when you read their opinions?
2. Explain why the author says Washington's and Jefferson's fears "were not widely felt."
3. Contrast the "old immigration" with the "new immigration."
4. According to the text, why were quotas limiting immigration imposed after 1921?
5. Describe the change in immigration patterns that began in the 1960s. (Include information on ethnic origins, education, and skills.)
6. Summarize the Census Bureau's predictions of future immigration.
7. State the current estimates of the number of illegal residents in the United States today.
8. What are the "two types" of illegal immigration?
9. Summarize the key elements of the 1986 Immigration Reform and Control Act.

Working with Graphs

Directions: Answer the following questions based on the information in Figure 1 on page 119.

1. Which decade of the twentieth century experienced the greatest influx of immigrants?
2. Which decade of the twentieth century had the fewest immigrants?
3. Why do think there was so little immigration from approximately 1930 to the mid-1950s?

Use the information in Figure 2 on page 122 to answer these questions.

1. In 1997, what percentage of the U.S. population was the following:
   American Indian?
   Hispanic?
   African American?
2. Which group is expected to increase the most by the year 2050?
3. Is any group expected to decline in number?
4. What was the total population (approximately) of the United States in 1997?
5. What is the total population expected to be in 2050?

Application/Writing

1. Use the Internet or your library to research the current immigration situation in your state. Use the same racial/ethnic categories given in Figure 2 on page 122.
2. Prepare either a graph, a list, or a brief essay summarizing the racial/ethnic makeup of your state according to the latest census figures.

Suggested website: www.census.gov

An appreciation for cultural diversity is a good thing, right? What could be wrong with learning about other cultures, other ways of living, of looking? Well, maybe plenty. Read this witty story in which a mother describes the "celebration" of Cultural Diversity Month at her daughter's preschool.

This story first appeared in the National Review *in 1997.*

THEY'VE GOT TO BE CAREFULLY TAUGHT

Susan Brady Konig

At my daughter's preschool it's time for all the children to learn that they are different from one another. Even though these kids are at that remarkable age when they are thoroughly color blind, their teachers are spending a month emphasizing race, color, and background. The little tots are being taught in no uncertain terms that their hair is different, their skin is different, and their parents come from different places. It's Cultural Diversity Month. 1

I hadn't really given much thought to the ethnic and national backgrounds of Sarah's classmates. I can guarantee that Sarah, being two and a half, gave the subject absolutely no thought. Her teachers, however, had apparently given it quite a lot of thought. They sent a letter asking each parent to contribute to the cultural-awareness effort by "providing any information and/or material regarding your family's cultural background. For example: favorite recipe or song." All well and good, unless your culture isn't *diverse* enough. 2

The next day I take Sarah to school and her teacher, Miss Laura, anxious to get this Cultural Diversity show on the road, begins the interrogation. 3

"Where are you and your husband from?" she cheerily demands. 4

"We're Americans," I reply—less, I must confess, out of patriotism than from sheer lack of coffee. It was barely 9:00 A.M. 5

"Yes, of course, but where are you *from*?" I'm beginning to feel like a nightclub patron being badgered by a no-talent stand-up comic. 6

"We're native New Yorkers." 7

"But where are your *people* from?" 8

"Well," I dive in with sigh, "my family is originally Irish on both sides. My husband's father was from Czechoslovakia and his mother is from the Bronx, but her grandparents were from Ukraine." 9

"Can you cook Irish?" 10

"I could bring in potatoes and beer for the whole class." 11

Miss Laura doesn't get it. 12

"Look," I say, "we're Americans. Our kids are Americans. We tell them about American history and George Washington and apple pie and all that stuff. If you want me to do something American, I can do that." 13

She is decidedly unexcited. 14

A few days later, she tells me that she was trying to explain to Sarah that her dad is from Ireland. 15

"Wrong," I say, "but go on." 16

17   "He's *not* from Ireland?"

18   No, I sigh. He's from Queens. I'm from Ireland. I mean I'm Irish—that is my great-grandparents were. Don't get me wrong. I'm proud of my heritage—but that's entirely beside the point. I told you we tell Sarah she's American.

19   "Well, anyway," she smiles, "Sarah thinks her Daddy's from *Iceland!* Isn't that cute?"

20   Later in the month, Miss Laura admits that her class is not quite getting the whole skin-color thing. "I tried to show them how we all have different skin," she chuckled. Apparently, little Henry is the only one who successfully grasped the concept. He now runs around the classroom announcing to anyone who'll listen, "I'm white!" Miss Laura asked the children what color her own skin was. (She is a light-skinned Hispanic, which would make her skin color…what? Caramel? Mochaccino?). The kids opted for purple or orange. "They looked at me like I was crazy!" Miss Laura said. I just smile.

21   The culmination of Cultural Diversity Month, the day when the parents come into class and join their children in a glorious celebration of multicultural disparity, has arrived. As I arrive I see a large collage on the wall depicting the earth, with all the children's names placed next to the country they are from. Next to my daughter's name it says "Ireland." I politely remind Miss Laura that Sarah is, in fact, from America and suggest that, by insisting otherwise, she is confusing my daughter. She reluctantly changes Sarah's affiliation to USA. It will be the only one of its kind on the wall.

22   The mom from Brazil brings in a bunch of great music, and the whole class is doing the samba and running around in a conga line. It's very cute. Then I get up to teach the children an indigenous folk tune from the culture of Sarah's people, passed down through the generations from her grandparents to her parents and now to Sarah—a song called "Take Me Out to the Ballgame." First I explain to the kids that Sarah was born right here in New York—and that's in what country, Sarah? Sarah looks at me and says, "France." I look at Miss Laura, who just shrugs.

23   I stand there in my baseball cap and sing my song. The teacher tries to rush me off. I say, "Don't you want them to learn it?" They took long enough learning to samba! I am granted permission to sing it one more time. The kids join in on the "root, root, root" and the "1, 2, 3 strikes you're out," but they can see their teacher isn't enthusiastic.

24   So now these sweet, innocent babies who thought they were all the same are becoming culturally aware. Two little girls are touching each other's hair and saying, "Your hair is blonde, just like mine." Off to one side a little dark-haired girl stands alone, excluded. She looks confused as to what to do next. She knows she's not blonde. Sure, all children notice these things eventually, but, thanks to the concerted efforts of their teachers, these two- and three-year-olds are talking about things that separate rather than connect.

And Sarah only knows what she has been taught: Little Henry is white, her   25
daddy's from Iceland, and New York's in France.

Vocabulary

Directions: Locate each of the key words in the reading selection. Try to figure out each word's meaning by using the context. Confirm your guess by checking the dictionary or thesaurus. Write the meanings of the words in the margin of the text. Then record the meanings in the chart below.

Key Word	Paragraph	Meaning
1. badgered	6	
2. opted	20	
3. culmination	21	
4. disparity	21	
5. indigenous	22	
6. concerted	24	
Others?		

Guide Questions

Directions: These questions will guide your understanding of what you have read. Write your answers in your notebook, or on a separate sheet of paper if your instructor wishes to collect it. Your answers to these questions will be the basis of class discussion.

1. Ms. Konig and Miss Laura are obviously engaged in a disagreement about Cultural Diversity Month.
   a. What do you think are the school and teacher's goals in promoting Cultural Diversity Month?
   b. Why is Ms. Konig bothered by the Cultural Diversity Month activities?
2. What do you think Sarah learned from the activities during Cultural Diversity Month?
3. Your reaction? Write three or four sentences.

Application/Writing

Directions: Choose one of the following questions.

1. The title of this story is an allusion (a reference) to a well-known song from the musical *South Pacific* written by Rodgers and Hammerstein in 1949 and presented thousands of times over the years. The name of the song is "You've Got to Be Carefully Taught." Go to the internet and find the lyrics of the song (one site is <http://www.lyricskeeper.com/south_pacific_soundtrack-lyrics.htm>). Read the lyrics and think about this question: Do you agree with the ideas in the song? Write one or two paragraphs expressing your opinion.

2. Write a letter from Miss Laura to the mother in the story. In your letter, explain the reasons for Cultural Diversity Month and why Miss Laura thinks it is a good idea.

COLLABORATIVE LEARNING

Working in Groups to Guide Your Own Reading

All of the reading selections so far in this unit have been accompanied by questions and exercises that are meant to help you understand and use what you've read. However, in much of your college reading (not to mention in your real life), you will be expected to master the material on your own.

Research has shown that one of the most effective ways to learn is in *groups*. In college, working with classmates can help you to master the material of a college course. The give-and-take that comes naturally when working with other people helps us to avoid falling into bad habits like *passive reading*. (We have all had the awful experience of reading a whole chapter, then realizing that we don't remember one single thing we've read.) Working with other students will help you to avoid such problems. For this assignment, form groups of approximately four students. In your group, read and think about the two following reading selections, "Where We Stand" by Lisa Davis and "Mix and Match Society" by Sara Terry. Then, create your own vocabulary chart, guide questions, and application and writing assignments.

Follow these steps to complete this assignment:

1. Preview the selection before you read—look at and think about the title, any headings or subheadings, the first paragraph, the last paragraph, and the first sentence of each paragraph.
2. Read through the selection one time quickly.
3. Read the selection a second time, more carefully. This time mark the text. Review how to do this by turning to page 421, "Learning Strategy III—Marking Text."
4. Brainstorm with your group. Ask yourselves: What important issues is the author discussing? What new information did you learn? Can the issues discussed in the selection be connected to those you have already studied? Can any of the information here be applied to situations in your own life?
5. Now, create a set of exercises similar to those you have completed in previous chapters of this book:
   a. **Vocabulary**. Make a list of key words from the text. Set them up in chart format as on page 53.
   b. **Guide Questions**. Write questions that will guide understanding of the major ideas in the reading.
   c. **Application**. Prepare an application exercise that takes one or more of the important ideas in the reading and relates it to real life.
   d. **Writing**. Create a writing assignment to conclude the chapter.

Before you begin, it would be a good idea to review the questions and exercises in the previous reading selections in this book for reference.

When you are finished, submit your work to your instructor. Your instructor may review and combine the work of all the groups and return the exercise to the class. You will then have the opportunity to answer the questions you and your classmates have developed.

Now, use your skills as an active independent reader to tackle the following reading selections. Good luck!

Our culture affects us in many ways: our language, religion, the way we dress, the foods we eat. But have you noticed more subtle differences? The next time you strike up a conversation with someone from another culture, pay attention to where they stand as well as what they say.

This article appeared in the magazine In Health *in 1990*

WHERE DO WE STAND?

Lisa Davis

1 Call it the dance of the jet set, the diplomat's tango: A man from the Middle East, say, falls into conversation with an American, becomes animated, takes a step forward. The American makes a slight postural adjustment, shifts his feet, edges backward. A little more talk and the Arab advances; a little more talk and the American retreats.

2 "By the end of the cocktail party," says Middle East expert Peter Bechtold of the State Department's Foreign Service Institute, "you have an American in each corner of the room, because that's as far as they can back up."

3 What do you do when an amiable chat leaves one person feeling vaguely bullied, the other unaccountably chilled? Things would be simpler if these jetsetters were speaking different languages—they'd just get themselves a translator. But the problem's a little tougher, because they're using different languages of space.

4 Everyone who's ever felt cramped in a crowd knows that the skin is not the body's only boundary. We each wear a zone of privacy like a hoop skirt, inviting others in or keeping them out with body language—by how closely we approach, the angle at which we face them, the speed with which we break a gaze. It's a subtle code, but one we use and interpret easily, indeed automatically, having absorbed the vocabulary from infancy.

5 At least, we *assume* we're reading it right. But from culture to culture, from group to group within a single country, even between the sexes, the language of space has distinctive accents, confusing umlauts. That leaves a lot of room for misinterpretations, and the stakes have gotten higher as business has become increasingly international and populations multicultural. So a new breed of consultants has appeared in the last few years, interpreting for globe-trotters of all nationalities the meaning and use of personal space.

6 For instance, says international business consultant Sondra Snowdon, Saudi Arabians like to conduct business discussions from within spitting distance—literally. They bathe in each other's breath as part of building the relationship. "Americans back up," says Snowdon, "but they're harming their chances of winning the contracts." In seminars, Snowdon discusses the close quarters common in Middle Eastern conversations and has her students practice talking with each other at very chummy distances.

7 Still, her clients had better be careful where they take their shrunken "space bubble," because cultures are idiosyncratic in their spatial needs. Japanese subways bring people about as close together as humanly possible, for instance, yet

even a handshake can be offensively physical in a Japanese office. And, says researcher and writer Mildred Reed Hall, Americans can even make their business counterparts in Japan uncomfortable with the kind of direct eye contact that's normal here.

"Not only do most Japanese businessmen not look at you, they keep their eyes down," Hall says. "We look at people for hours, and they feel like they're under a searchlight."   8

The study of personal space got under way in the early 1950s, when anthropologist Edward Hall described a sort of cultural continuum of personal space. (Hall has frequently collaborated with his wife, Mildred.) According to Hall, on the "high-contact" side of the continuum—in Mediterranean and South American societies, for example—social conversations include much eye contact, touching and smiling, typically while standing at a distance of about a foot. On the other end of the scale, say in Northern European cultures, a lingering gaze may feel invasive, manipulative or disrespectful; a social chat takes place at a remove of about 2½ feet.   9

In the middle-of-the-road United States, people usually stand about 18 inches apart for this sort of conversation—unless we want to win foreign friends and influence people, in which case, research shows, we'd better adjust our posture. In one study, when British graduate students were trained to adopt Arab patterns of behavior (facing their partners straight on, with lots of eye contact and smiling), Middle Eastern exchange students found them more likable and trustworthy than typical British students.   10

In contrast, the misuse of space can call whole personalities into suspicion: When researchers seated pairs of women for conversation, those forced to talk at an uncomfortably large distance were more likely to describe their partners as cold and rejecting.   11

Don't snuggle up too fast, though. Men in that study were more irritated by their partners when they were forced to talk at close range. Spatially speaking, it seems men and women are subtly foreign to each other. No matter whether a society operates at arm's length or cheek-to-jowl, the women look at each other more and stand a bit closer than do the men.   12

Anthropologist Hall suggests that a culture's use of space is evidence of a reliance on one sense over another: Middle Easterners get much of their information through their senses of smell and touch, he says, which require a close approach; Americans rely primarily on visual information, backing up in order to see an intelligible picture.   13

Conversational distances also tend to reflect the standard greeting distance in each culture, says State Department expert Bechtold. Americans shake hands, and then talk at arm's length. Arabs do a Hollywood-style, cheek-to-cheek social kiss, and their conversation is similarly up close and personal. And, at a distance great enough to keep heads from knocking together—about two feet—the Japanese bow and talk to each other. On the other hand, the need for more or less space may reflect something of a cultural temperament. "There's no word for privacy in Arab cultures," says Bechtold. "They think it means loneliness."   14

15　　　Whatever their origin, spatial styles are very real. In fact, even those who set out to transgress find it uncomfortable to intrude on the space of strangers, says psychologist John Aiello at Rutgers University. "I've had students say, 'Boy, that was the hardest thing I ever had to do—to stand six inches away when I was asking those questions.'"

16　　　Luckily, given coaching and time, it seems to get easier to acculturate to foreign habits of contact. Says Bechtold, "You often see men holding hands in the Middle East and walking down the street together. It's just that they're concerned and don't want you to cross the street unescorted, but I've had American pilots come in here and say, 'I don't want some SOB holding my hand.' Then I see them there, holding the hand of a Saudi."

17　　　"Personal space isn't so hard for people to learn," Bechtold adds. "What is really much harder is the business of dinner being served at midnight."

Vocabulary

Directions: Mark any important words in the reading selection that you don't know. Then list them in the following chart along with their paragraph numbers. Try to figure out each word's meaning by reading over the context carefully for clues to help you guess the meaning of the unfamiliar word. Check your dictionary or thesaurus to confirm your guess. After you discuss the words with your group members, write the meanings in the margin of the text, near the word. Then enter them in the chart.

Key Word	Paragraph	Meaning

Guide Questions

Directions: Develop a list of questions that elicit the important ideas in the reading selection. Start at the beginning and work your way sequentially through the text until you have addressed all of the author's major ideas.

Application

Directions: When you have a list of guide questions, read through the selection again. This time, write one or more questions that require the application of the information in the text to a situation in the real world.

Writing

Directions: Your last task is to prepare a writing assignment. For example, you might ask for a paragraph in which the writer comments on the ideas in the reading selection. You might also ask for a summary of the selection.

Multiculturalism—the acceptance of, and celebration of, cultural heritages is the dominant and politically correct way of viewing ethnic identity in America today. But many see change approaching. They see the beginning of transculturalism—a melding or fusion of ethnic backgrounds and cultural experiences. As globalization spreads, people travel, move, and intermarry more. They may no longer define themselves by their racial, ethnic, or cultural heritage but rather by their own unique histories, by how they choose to live their lives.

This story appeared in the Christian Science Monitor *in August 2000.*

MIX AND MATCH SOCIETY: GOING "TRANSCULTURAL"

Sara Terry

1   Andrew Pham is on the cutting edge of culture.

2   Born in Vietnam. Escaped in 1977, at the age of 10, with his family. A boat person who wound up in Shreveport, La., before finally moving to California. A Buddhist who converted to Christianity. A sports fan who loves Italian food and gumbo. A man with an Asian face and family tree, who embraces Western values of independence and mobility.

3   He is, in other words, the very embodiment of "transcultural" identity. The term is increasingly being used—in literature, academia, even in public-policy discussions—to describe social changes wrought by globalization, increased mobility, and ethnic intermingling.

4   "We see ourselves in a different light," says Mr. Pham, referring to people whose sense of identity is being forged by a melding of cultures. "We don't say we have one foot in one world, and one in the other. We see ourselves as a bridge, or as a separate group, that can move back and forth.

5   "People are trying to redefine themselves," says Pham, whose recent memoir, "Catfish and Mandala," traces his bicycle journey through his homeland and illumines his attempts to define himself. "It isn't Asian-American anymore, or African-American. . . . It's a sense of identity defined through what a person does, through how he lives his life."

6   If this is the wave of the future, Pham is ahead of the curve. Multiculturalism—the acceptance of and celebration of distinct cultural heritages—continues to reign as the dominant, politically correct framework through which ethnic identity is examined. But beneath the radar screen of popular culture, some social observers have begun to argue that multiculturalism must give way to new views of self and community.

7   "It seems to have reached a limit," says Rey Chow, a Hong Kong-born and educated cultural theorist who teaches at Brown University in Providence, R.I. "The thing is, once you become aware of cultural differences, and respect and honor them, you can easily slide into a situation in which those differences become insurmountable. Every culture becomes an enclosure and no one else can touch it."

Transculturalism, on the other hand, casts identity in a new light: as a melding, or fusion, of ethnic backgrounds and cultural experiences. It's the kind of thing that has been almost inevitable for people like Pham, the Vietnamese-American engineer-turned-writer, who has drawn from a variety of cultural experiences. Or for the growing numbers of interracial couples whose children represent a literal blending of cultures.   8

"Transculturalism goes the other direction from multiculturalism," says Gregory Jay, director of the cultures and communities programs at the University of Wisconsin at Milwaukee. "It says, the only way I can understand myself is in part to get out of those boundaries, to see myself as made up of a confluence, a river of different things going through me."   9

A Matter of Degree

In one sense, transculturalism is a new name for an age-old phenomenon: Immigrants have always made new homes in new cultures, influencing those cultures even while assimilating values from them.   10

But what is different now, at the beginning of the 21st century, is a world that is more mobile—and more connected—than at any time in history. Today, cultural change happens more rapidly, and on a different scale.   11

In the past, immigrants may have made a small impact over time on the cultures they moved into. Today, it's more likely that mainstream culture itself will morph into new expressions, as people in essence create "fused" identities that mix and match cultural heritages.   12

"The important point is not that white people are going to be the minority in this country by 2050," says Mr. Jay of the University of Wisconsin. "The important fact is that racial categories as we know them will disappear. In fact, they will become incomprehensible as more and more people we meet are markedly fusion people. Those people will assert the right to identify themselves as they choose."   13

Resistance to Blending

Still, observers say transculturalism isn't likely to be embraced on a widespread basis anytime soon. Ethnic wars, such as those in the former Yugoslavia, are all too vivid a reminder that for many people, culture is a matter of ethnic purity, to be defended to the death. On a less tragic level, countries like France have become notorious for resisting imported intrusions, such as Hollywood films, into their own cultures.   14

Still, say these social observers, the forces of globalization that are transforming the world economically—creating free flows of capital and information through increasingly porous national boundaries—are also transforming the world culturally.   15

"These forces are with us. We're on a global ride, and it's only going to get more global," says Barbara Bundy, executive director of the Center for the Pacific Rim. "Transculturalism is the transformation of culture as we have known it and as we know it now. It's about working toward the new. And we don't have adequate terms and policies to deal with this phenomenon."   16

17   Steve Clemons, senior vice president of the New America Foundation, a centrist think tank in Washington, argues that public policymakers need to start thinking in terms of the forces of globalization—and how they will impact culture.

18   "When you get into these questions, you see that it's more than just Coca-Cola and McDonald's and MTV all around the world," says Mr. Clemons, who organized a recent conference in Washington on globalization and cultural identity, which brought together cultural thinkers from around the world and some 150 professionals interested in global policy issues.

19   "You've got to have deeper talk, more serious talk, about identity questions," he says. American public policymakers "are still assuming that everyone wants to be like us, when in fact the world is going in some really different directions, and that's something we need to consider."

20   Experts warn that globalization—and its domination by the United States—is already causing cultural inequities. They say the culture that is exported around the world, through Information Age technology, is all too frequently red, white, and blue.

21   And cultures of other countries can all too easily be turned into commodities—something for wealthy white people to buy and display at home. Such unchecked economic forces, warn these experts, work against true transculturalism.

22   In addition, they say, many people in poorer nations will remain locked in their cultures, financially unable to take advantage of the forces changing the world around them.

23   "Among many academics, there's a certain euphoria about transculturalism, about being mobile," says Ms. Chow, who teaches modern culture and media at Brown. "I'm not sure I like that. It's the euphoria of the privileged classes."

An Inevitable Change?

24   But like many of her colleagues, Chow believes that transculturalism is the next step in social change, an inevitable transformation in an increasingly interconnected—and interwoven—world.

25   "I think it will make us a better society," says Pham. "As is the case with any type of change, there's always growing pains. We will see great flashes of racism and violence and bigotry. But I have hope. I really believe this is the natural progression of society and the world. I think identity needs to be redefined for each group and for each time period of a society's history."

Vocabulary

Directions: Mark any important words in the reading selection that you don't know. Then list them in the following chart along with their paragraph numbers. Try to figure out each word's meaning by reading over the context carefully for clues to help you guess the meaning of the unfamiliar word. Check your dictionary or thesaurus to confirm your guess. After you discuss the words with your group members, write the meanings in the margin of the text, near the word. Then enter them in the chart.

Key Word	Paragraph	Meaning

Guide Questions
Directions: Develop a list of questions that elicit the important ideas in the reading selection. Start at the beginning and work your way sequentially through the text until you have addressed all of the author's major ideas.

Application
Directions: When you have a list of guide questions, read through the selection again. This time, write one or more questions that require the application of the information in the text to a situation in the real world.

Writing
Directions: Your last task is to prepare a writing assignment. For example, you might ask for a paragraph in which the writer comments on the ideas in the reading selection. You might also ask for a summary of the selection.

SPECIAL PROJECT

Exploring Your Own Culture

How much do you know about your own culture? As you have seen in the readings in this section of the text, every culture has its own set of traditions and beliefs. Investigate your roots by interviewing older family members and friends and by reading about your culture in the library.

Describe the rituals and traditions associated with

1. the birth of a child
2. a wedding
3. a funeral
4. a special holiday or event

Visit the library and use the Internet to find materials describing the traditions of your culture. List the books, periodicals, and other references you find at the end of your report.

Your report should consist of four sections. Give a title to each section; for example, you might name your first section "The Birth of a Child in Mexico." Then describe the rituals surrounding this event. For example, you may answer questions such as the following: Is it customary to have a party to celebrate the birth of a baby? Do friends and family bring gifts? Is a special type of gift traditional? Are special foods prepared? How long does the celebration last? Is the baby given a name at this time? How is the name chosen? Is special clothing worn? If there are other features to your culture's celebration, include them. Does your own family have any special customs?

Do the same with the other three sections of your report: a wedding, a funeral, a special holiday or event.

At the end of your report, include a list of references. Think of this list as a resource for someone who would like to learn more about your culture and its traditions.

UNIT THREE

READING AND THINKING
ABOUT LANGUAGE

All words are pegs to hang ideas on.

—Henry Ward Beecher

{It} is only through language that we enter fully into our human estate and culture, communicate freely with our fellows, acquire and share information. If we cannot do this, we will be bizarrely disabled and cut off—whatever our desires, or endeavors, or native capacities.

—Oliver Sacks

Thinking about Language

Before you begin this part of the text, think about and answer the questions below.

1. What is language? Write your own definition.
2. Do animals have language? If so, is it the same as human language? In what ways is it the same? In what ways is it different?
3. Many linguists, the people who study language, believe humans began using language about fifty thousand years ago. Before then, they relied on crude gestures and sounds for what communication did go on. Try to imagine that you are a "cave man" or a "cave woman." What are some gestures, signs, or sounds you would use to communicate?
4. How would your life be different if humans had never developed language? Imagine some of the events of a typical day and describe how you would communicate what you need to say, without words.

Everyone has a very personal interest in language. Because it is all around us and within us, too, we all feel that language belongs to us. And all of us, bank presidents, farmers, secretaries, and traffic cops, are language experts even though we don't often stop to think about it.

Before you read this selection, take a moment to think about language—its definition and its meaning in your life.

LANGUAGE

Mary Fjeldstad

Defining Language

1   What is language? If you asked five different people, you would probably get five different answers. So, before we can talk about language, we need to agree on its definition. Let's construct a definition by listing the *characteristics* of language. First, the most basic characteristic of language is that it is a means of *communication*. Language is what we use to get through the day, to buy a newspaper, order a cup of coffee, ask for directions on the street, or decide on a movie. Language lets us think about our desire for a better life, the love we feel for our family, the vacation we plan to take, and the sadness at the death of a friend. Language lets us dream about things that never were, and perhaps never will be. You can imagine a werewolf or a vampire because you have the language for it, even though such a thing never existed. If you see a picture of a handsome or beautiful person of the opposite sex, you can imagine or talk about meeting such a person in your future because you have language. The past and the future can be just as great a part of your reality as the present—because of language.

2   Without language we would be isolated from our fellow humans. Human societies as we know them never would have formed without language; cultures never would have developed. Language is essentially what made human civilization possible. It is language that has allowed us to produce literature, music, mathematics, and science. Language has allowed us to transmit knowledge, the sum of our stored experience in spoken or written form, from one generation to the next. Without language, life as we know it would not be possible.

Language Consists of Symbols

3   A second major characteristic of language is that it consists of *symbols*. A symbol is something that represents something else. A person can be a symbol. For example, Martin Luther King, Jr., stood for nonviolent opposition to racial discrimination. The Pope is a symbol of the Catholic church. *Gestures*, like the clenched fist, or a facial expression like a smile or a frown, can be symbols of attitudes or moods. *Objects* can be symbols. In the United States a woman may wear a diamond ring on her left hand as a symbol of her engagement to a man; in the Fiji Islands young women wore hibiscus flowers behind their ears to symbolize the fact they were in love.

But *words* are also symbols. The word *hamburger* is a symbol for that item of food Americans so love to eat, and while the word may set our mouths to watering, we do not start chewing on the word—we must wait until the thing it symbolizes is cooked and on the plate.

4

We live in two worlds at the same time: the real (or physical) world—the world we can see and touch and smell and taste—and the verbal (or symbolic) world—where we use language to name and talk about and think about all the things we experience in the physical world.

5

Imagine what it would be like if you did not have the ease of words or symbols to communicate with other people. Your conversation would be limited to the objects, or persons, or events actually present in your physical world at that moment in the conversation. People have long been fascinated by this notion of language as symbols. The writer Jonathan Swift, in his famous satire, *Gulliver's Travels,* plays with the possibility of nonsymbolic words:

6

> [This] was urged as a great advantage in point of health as well as brevity. For it is plain that every word we speak is, in some degree, a diminution of our lungs by corrosion, and consequently contributes to the shortening of our lives. An expedient was therefore offered that since words are only names for things it would be more convenient for all men to carry about with them such things as were necessary to express a particular business they are to discourse [speak] on. . . . Many of the most learned and wise adhere to the new scheme of expressing themselves by things, which has only this inconvenience attending it, that, if a man's business be very great, and of various kinds, he must be obliged, in proportion, to carry a greater bundle of things upon his back unless he can afford one or two strong servants to attend him. I have often beheld two of these sages [wise men] almost sinking under the weight of their packs, like peddlers among us; who, when they meet in the street, would lay down their loads, open their packs, hold conversation for an hour, and then put up their implements, help each other to resume their burdens, and take their leave.

Swift's comical description makes the importance of symbols in language clear—just imagine if the people in his story wished to talk about an elephant or the Empire State Building!

7

Is Language Unique to Humans?

People have long speculated that animals have their own languages and, of course, many animals do communicate with one another. Birds use sounds to warn other birds of danger or to announce "ownership" of a particular tree. Bees "dance" to inform other bees of food sources. Velvet monkeys make sounds that signal the proximity of predators. Certainly many pet owners swear that their dog or cat "talks" to them and understands them when they talk. But none of these examples of communication will fit our definition of language because they are not *symbolic*; that is, none has a one-to-one correlation to a specific object or concept.

8

9   Several years ago there was great excitement among language researchers when it was shown that the great apes (especially chimpanzees) could learn language to some extent. While they do not have the physical apparatus necessary for speech, apes do have the ability to understand the meanings of words as symbols for things and relationships. Apes have been taught a limited number of words through sign language and through the use of typewriters and other devices. A gorilla named Koko was taught more than three hundred words in American Sign Language. To the surprise of most scientists, she also was able to "invent" new words and phrases, a skill that was previously believed to be uniquely human. For example, she invented sign words for *ring* ("finger bracelet") and *mask* ("eye hat"). She was even able to use sign words to refer to abstract ideas, such as pain and fear. Although the success of Koko and other apes encouraged many scientists to believe that these animals are capable of sophisticated human language, it soon became apparent that the apes' abilities are severely limited. No ape has ever progressed beyond the level of that of a two-and-a-half-year-old child. Nor can apes produce sentences of more than two words. Human language, on the other hand, allows us to communicate an infinite number of thoughts and to preserve these thoughts over long periods of time and distance.

10   Language allows us to step out beyond the confinement of the immediate present. It means that people can, for example, talk about food to eat at the present time, and also food tomorrow and food yesterday. If you believe that your dog has a human-like language ability to communicate, try to talk to Spot about "dog food tomorrow." Another example is the important symbol of the personal name. While it seems clear that dogs understand names, their own, their masters', and others, they do not understand them in the same way humans do. If you say to Spot, "Sam is at work," how does Spot react? He will look for Sam, understanding *Sam* only as an immediate sign, exactly as he would react to his master's voice or the sound of his footsteps at the door. A human, on the other hand, will probably ask you something like, "When is Sam coming home?" or "How does he like his job?" or any of thousands of other thoughts that were stimulated by the symbol *Sam.* All of these thoughts are forever beyond the capabilities of the dog.

Symbols Are Not the Events They Symbolize

11   When you communicate with another person, you use symbols—words. However, the words you use to refer to objects, persons, events, situations, sensations, and feelings are not those *actual* objects, persons, events, situations, sensations, or feelings. For example, it is one thing to experience a toothache and quite another to comment "I have a toothache." Those words merely refer to your pain, but there is no way the other person can experience your toothache.

12   Have you ever tried to think about something—anything—without using its name? As Peter Farb says, "Try to think about the stars, a grasshopper, love or hate, pain, anything at all—and it must be done in terms of language. There is no other way; thinking is language spoken to oneself. Until language has made sense of experience, that experience is meaningless." Our ability to use the

symbol system of language is the main thing that distinguishes us from other animals and makes us human beings.

Language Is Systematic

A third characteristic of language is that it is a *system*. That system is called *grammar*. Grammar is a set of rules that defines how words may be combined. For example, because we know the grammar system of English, we understand the sentence *The man bit the dog* to mean one thing and *The dog bit the man* to mean something quite different. In both examples, the meanings of the five words are exactly the same. But the way they are combined changes the meaning of the sentence completely. Similarly, *The bit dog man the,* although using the same, easy-to-understand words, is meaningless—because it does not follow the rules of grammar we all carry around in our heads.

13

Language Is Limitless

The final characteristic of language is that it is infinitely creative. In fact, most of the sentences we utter are original, that is, we have never heard or read them before in exactly the same form. As Steven Pinker says in his book *The Language Instinct,* "Go into the Library of Congress and pick a sentence at random from any volume, and chances are you would fail to find an exact repetition no matter how long you continued to search. Estimates of the number of sentences that an ordinary person is capable of producing are breathtaking."

14

Definition of Language

To conclude, let's review the characteristics of language we have discussed: Language is communication. Language is symbolic. Language is systematic. Language is infinitely creative.

15

    Now we can write our definition: *Language is an infinitely creative system of communication, consisting of symbols.* Compare this definition to the one you wrote at the beginning of this selection, and think about what you've learned as you study the rest of this unit.

16

Vocabulary

Directions: Find each of the key words in the reading selection. Study each word in its context and try to determine its meaning. Write what you think it means in the margin of the text, near the word. Then read over the sentence, mentally substituting your guess for the key word. Does the sentence still make sense? Does it retain its original meaning? If it does, you've probably figured out the meaning of the key word correctly. In any case, confirm your guess by checking a dictionary or thesaurus.

    If you take your meaning from a dictionary or thesaurus, be sure the definition includes words you already know and feel comfortable using. If it doesn't, you will be worse off than when you started—you will have begun with one word you didn't know and ended with *two* words you don't know!

Record the new words you've learned below.

Key Word	Paragraph	Meaning
1. satire	6	
2. adhere	6	
3. speculated	8	
4. predators	8	
5. infinitely	14	
Others?		

Guide Questions

Directions: The purpose of these questions is to guide your analysis of the text. Your thoughtful answers will ensure that you have understood the main ideas the author wanted to convey. Some of the questions require that you simply find the stated facts in the reading selection; others will ask you to do more difficult tasks, such as paraphrasing information (putting the author's ideas into your own words), synthesizing several ideas into one complex thought, evaluating (making judgments about) an idea, or taking information from the reading and applying it to a new situation or to your own life.

Write answers to the questions in your notebook or on a separate sheet of paper if your instructor wishes to collect them. Your answers will form the basis of class discussion.

1. Define *symbol* and give some examples of symbols.
2. In the excerpt from Jonathan Swift's classic novel *Gulliver's Travels,* people supposedly believed speaking corroded their lungs and shortened their lives. So they decided it would be better for their health to stop using words, the symbols of things, and carry around the things themselves. Assume you did this in school tomorrow. What things would you have to carry with you? Imagine your participation in class, or a conversation with a friend in the cafeteria. What things would you pull out of your bag? How would you communicate your thoughts about those things without using any words? How would you feel about communicating like this? How does Swift's story reinforce the idea that words are symbols?
3. Do you agree with the statement made by the linguist Peter Farb in paragraph 12? Please explain.

4. Consider a famous example of two headlines of two different news stories:

   Dog Bites Man
   Man Bites Dog

   Each headline contains exactly the same words. Why, then, do the sentences have two very different meanings? Can you invent a similar example?

5. Following are some strings of words that, while containing easily comprehensible English words, are in some way "not quite right." Consider each example, and explain why it does not make sense; that is, explain how it violates the rules of grammar.

   This sentence no verb.
   This book has contains six units.
   Is raining.
   The car was put in the.
   Where did he put it the car?
   Please say those little three words.

   Can you invent some examples? Make up a "not quite right sentence" and show it to your classmates. See if they can figure out what is wrong.

Application

Work in groups to complete this exercise. Think of a simple everyday message you would like to convey to the members of another group in the class. Then try to communicate your message without using words.

Writing

Think about the exercise you did in the Application section above. What difficulties did you have communicating your message and understanding the messages of other groups? In a paragraph, describe your experience and how you felt about it. Relate your experience to what you learned when you read the selection "Language."

Marking Text

Turn to page 421 "Learning Strategy III—Marking Text." Read and study the information on how to mark your text. Then mark the chapter "Language" using what you've learned. To get you started, here is a model of how you might mark the first few paragraphs of the chapter. Finish marking it on your own.

1

LANGUAGE

Mary Fjeldstad

Defining Language

1   What is language? If you asked five different people, you would probably get five different answers. So, before we can talk about language, we need to agree on its definition. <u>Let's construct a definition by listing the *characteristics* of language.</u> <u>First the most basic characteristic of language is that it is a means of *communication.*</u> Language is what we use to get through the day, to buy a newspaper, order a cup of coffee, ask for directions on the street, or decide on a movie. Language lets us think about our desire for a better life, the love we feel for our family, the vacation we plan to take, and the sadness at the death of a friend. Language lets us dream about things that never were, and perhaps never will be. You can imagine a werewolf or a vampire because you have a name for it, even though such a thing never existed. If you see a picture of a handsome or beautiful person of the opposite sex, you can imagine or talk about meeting such a person in your future because you have language. The past and the future can be just as great a part of your reality as the present — because of language.

1st characteristic of L: means of communication

2   Without language we would be isolated from our fellow humans. Human societies never would have formed without language; cultures never would have developed. Language is essentially what made human civilization possible. It is language that has allowed us to produce literature, music, mathematics, and science. Language has allowed us to transmit knowledge, the sum of our stored experience in spoken or written form, from one generation to the next. Without language, life as we know it would not be possible.

Importance of language to humans

Language Consists of Symbols

3   <u>A second major characteristic of language is that it consists of *symbols*. A symbol is something that represents something else. A person can be a symbol.</u> For example, Martin Luther King, Jr., stood for nonviolent opposition to racial discrimination. The Pope is a symbol of the Catholic church. *Gestures,* like the clenched fist, or a facial expression like a smile or a frown, <u>can be symbols of attitudes or moods. *Objects* can be symbols.</u> In the United States a woman may wear a diamond ring on her left hand as a symbol of her engagement to a man; in the Fiji Islands young women wore hibiscus flowers behind their ears to symbolize the fact they were in love.

2nd characteristic: symbolic

Symbols can be
1—person
2—gesture
3—object
* 4—words

4   <u>But *words* are also symbols.</u> The word *hamburger* is a symbol for that item of food Americans so love to eat, and while the word may set our mouths to watering, we do not start chewing on the word — we must wait until the thing it symbolizes is cooked and on the plate. . . .

Helen Keller was born in 1880. At the age of nineteen months, she suffered an illness that left her both blind and deaf. Later she also became unable to speak. Her young years were indeed difficult as she raged against her forced isolation from the world, unable to communicate except by means of gestures and direct physical contact. Nevertheless, by age twenty-four, she had graduated cum laude *from Radcliffe College, where, in addition to mastering all her other subjects, she learned many different languages, including Latin and Greek. She went on to write many books and travel the country giving inspirational speeches, many on behalf of the handicapped—all with the help of her dedicated teacher, Anne Sullivan, who came to her when Keller was seven. In this excerpt from her autobiography, Keller takes the first indispensable step to thought and to learning—realizing that words are symbols.*

In the Beginning was the Word.

—St. John

THE KEY TO LANGUAGE

Helen Keller

The morning after my teacher came she led me into her room and gave me a doll. 1
The little blind children at the Perkins Institution had sent it and Laura Bridgman had dressed it; but I did not know this until afterward.

When I had played with it a little while, Miss Sullivan slowly spelled into 2
my hand the word "d-o-l-l." I was at once interested in this finger play and tried to imitate it. When I finally succeeded in making the letters correctly I was flushed with childish pleasure and pride. Running downstairs to my mother I held up my hands and made the letters for doll. I did not know that I was spelling a word or even that words existed; I was simply making my fingers go in monkey-like imitation. In the days that followed I learned to spell in this uncomprehending way a great many words, among them *pin, hat, cup,* and a few verbs like *sit, stand,* and *walk.* But my teacher had been with me several weeks before I understood that everything has a name.

One day, while I was playing with my new doll, Miss Sullivan put my big 3
rag doll into my lap also, spelled "d-o-l-l" and tried to make me understand that "d-o-l-l" applied to both. Earlier in the day we had had a tussle over the words "m-u-g" and "w-a-t-e-r." Miss Sullivan had tried to impress it upon me that "m-u-g" is *mug* and "w-a-t-e-r" is *water,* but I persisted in confounding the two. In despair she had dropped the subject for the time only to renew it at the first opportunity. I became impatient at her repeated attempts and, seizing the new doll, I dashed it upon the floor. . . .

We walked down the path to the well-house, attracted by the fragrance of the 4
honeysuckle with which it was covered. Someone was drawing water and my teacher placed my hand under the spout. As the cool stream gushed over one

hand she spelled into the other the word *water,* first slowly, then rapidly. I stood still, my whole attention fixed upon the motions of her fingers. Suddenly I felt a misty consciousness, as of something forgotten—a thrill of returning thought; and somehow the mystery of language was revealed to me. I knew then that "w-a-t-e-r" meant the wonderful cool something that was flowing over my hand. That living word awakened my soul, gave it light, hope, joy, set it free. There were barriers still, it is true, but barriers that could, in time, be swept away.

5   I left the well-house eager to learn. Everything had a name and each name gave birth to a new thought. As we returned to the house every object which I touched seemed to quiver with life. That was because I saw everything with the strange, new sight that had come to me. On entering the door I remembered the doll I had broken. I felt my way to the hearth and picked up the pieces. I vainly tried to put them together. Then my eyes filled with tears; for I realized what I had done, and for the first time I felt repentance and sorrow.

6   I learned a great many new words that day. I do not remember what they all were; but I do know that *mother, father, sister, teacher* were among them—words that were to make the world blossom for me, "like Aaron's rod, with flowers." It would have been difficult to find a happier child than I was as I lay in my crib at the close of that eventful day and lived over the joys it had brought me, and, for the first time, longed for a new day to come. . . .

7   I had now the key to all language and I was eager to learn to use it. Children who hear acquire language without any particular effort; the words that fall from others' lips they catch on the wing, as it were, delightedly, while the little deaf child must trap them by a slow and often painful process. But whatever the process, the result is wonderful. Gradually, from naming an object we advance step by step until we have traversed the vast distance between our first stammered syllable and the sweep of thought in a line of Shakespeare.

8   At first, when my teacher told me about a new thing I asked very few questions. My ideas were vague, and my vocabulary was inadequate, but as my knowledge of things grew, and I learned more and more words, my field of inquiry broadened, and I would return again and again to the same subject, eager for further information. Sometimes a new word revived an image that some earlier experiences had engraved on my brain.

9   I remember the morning that I first asked the meaning of the word *love.* This was before I knew many words. I had found a few early violets in the garden and brought them to my teacher. She tried to kiss me; but at that time I did not like to have anyone kiss me except my mother. Miss Sullivan put her arm gently around me and spelled into my hand "I love Helen."

10   "What is love?" I asked.

11   She drew me closer to her and said, "It is here," pointing to my heart, whose beats I was conscious of for the first time. Her words puzzled me very much because I did not then understand anything unless I touched it.

12   I smelt the violets in her hand and asked, half in words, half in signs, a question which means, "Is love the sweetness of flowers?"

13   "No," said my teacher.

Again I thought. The warm sun was shining on us.   14

"Is this not love?" I asked, pointing in the direction from which the heat   15
came, "Is this not love?"

It seemed to me that there could be nothing more beautiful than the sun,   16
whose warmth makes all things grow. But Miss Sullivan shook her head, and I
was greatly puzzled and disappointed. I thought it strange that my teacher could
not show me love.

A day or two afterward I was stringing beads of different sizes in symmetrical   17
groups—two large beads, three small ones, and so on. I had made many mistakes, and
Miss Sullivan had pointed them out again and again with gentle patience. Finally I
noticed a very obvious error in the sequence and, for an instant, I concentrated my
attention on the lesson and tried to think how I should have arranged the beads. Miss
Sullivan touched my forehead and spelled with decided emphasis, "Think."

In a flash, I knew that the word was the name of the process that was going   18
on in my head. This was my first conscious perception of an abstract idea.

Vocabulary

Directions: Locate each of the key words in the reading selection. Then read and study
each word in its context and try to determine its meaning. Use a dictionary or thesaurus
to check your guess. Write the meanings of the words in the margin of the text.

Record the new words you've learned below.

Key Word	Paragraph	Meaning
1. quiver	5	
2. hearth	5	
3. vainly	5	
4. repentance	5	
5. symmetrical	17	
Others?		

Guide Questions

Directions: The purpose of these guide questions is to ensure your understanding of what
you have read. They also will help you to analyze and evaluate the author's ideas and
apply them to the real world and your own life.

Write answers to the questions in your notebook or on a separate sheet of paper if your instructor wishes to collect them. Your answers will form the basis of class discussion.

1. Because most of us learned language at a very early age, we do not remember, nor were we old enough to comprehend, the power that the use of language gave to us. Describe the process that brought Keller to her exciting discovery that words are symbols.
2. Contrast the way hearing children learn language with the way deaf children learn it, according to Keller.
3. To Keller, was there a difference in learning that the word *doll* was a symbol for a doll and that the word *love* was a symbol for love? Explain why these are different concepts.

Application

Keller's discovery of the "key to language" was obviously one of the turning points in her life. Think about the turning points in your own life. What were they? What were their results? Describe one or more of the turning points in your life in a paragraph or two.

Writing

React to the fact that, despite her enormous handicaps, Keller managed to graduate from Radcliffe College and become a world-famous lecturer and scholar. Write a paragraph or two.

Making Connections

Return to the selection titled "Language" on page 140. What connections can you make between the information in "Language" and the story of Helen Keller's discovery of "The Key to Language"?

Amy Tan, the daughter of Chinese immigrants, was born and raised in California. Her first novel, The Joy Luck Club, *became an international favorite. Much of her writing focuses on the clash of Chinese and American cultures and on Tan's intense and complicated relationship with her mother. This essay first appeared in the* Threepenny Review *in 1989.*

MOTHER TONGUE

Amy Tan

I am not a scholar of English or literature. I cannot give you much more than personal opinions on the English language and its variations in this country or others.

I am a writer. And by that definition, I am someone who has always loved language. I am fascinated by language in daily life. I spend a great deal of my time thinking about the power of language—the way it can evoke an emotion, a visual image, a complex idea, or a simple truth. Language is the tool of my trade. And I use them all—all the Englishes I grew up with.

Recently, I was made keenly aware of the different Englishes I do use. I was giving a talk to a large group of people, the same talk I had already given to half a dozen other groups. The nature of the talk was about my writing, my life, and my book, *The Joy Luck Club*. The talk was going along well enough, until I remembered one major difference that made the whole talk sound wrong. My mother was in the room. And it was perhaps the first time she had heard me give a lengthy speech, using the kind of English I have never used with her. I was saying things like, "The intersection of memory upon imagination" and "There is an aspect of my fiction that relates to thus-and-thus"—a speech filled with carefully wrought grammatical phrases, burdened, it suddenly seemed to me, with nominalized forms, past perfect tenses, conditional phrases, all the forms of standard English that I had learned in school and through books, the forms of English I did not use at home with my mother.

Just last week, I was walking down the street with my mother, and I again found myself conscious of the English I was using, the English I do use with her. We were talking about the price of new and used furniture and I heard myself saying this: "Not waste money that way." My husband was with us as well, and he didn't notice any switch in my English. And then I realized why. It's because over the twenty years we've been together I've often used that same kind of English with him, and sometimes he even uses it with me. It has become our language of intimacy, a different sort of English that relates to family talk, the language I grew up with.

So you'll have some idea of what this family talk I heard sounds like, I'll quote what my mother said during a recent conversation which I videotaped and then transcribed. During this conversation, my mother was talking about a political gangster in Shanghai who had the same last name as her family's, Du, and how the gangster in his early years wanted to be adopted by her family, which was rich by comparison. Later, the gangster became more powerful, far richer than my mother's family, and one day showed up at my mother's wedding to pay his respects. Here's what she said in part:

6   "Du Yusong having business like fruit stand. Like off the street kind. He is Du like Du Zong—but not Tsung-ming Island people. The local people call pu-tong, the river east side, he belong to that side local people. That man want to ask Du Zong father take him in like become own family. Du Zong father wasn't look down on him, but didn't take seriously, until that man big like become a mafia. Now important person, very hard to inviting him. Chinese way, came only to show respect, don't stay for dinner. Respect for making big celebration, he shows up. Mean gives lots of respect. Chinese custom. Chinese social life that way. If too important won't have to stay too long. He come to my wedding. I didn't see, I heard it. I gone to boy's side, they have YMCA dinner. Chinese age I was nineteen."

7   You should know that my mother's expressive command of English belies how much she actually understands. She reads the *Forbes* report, listens to *Wall Street Week*, converses daily with her stockbroker, reads all of Shirley MacLaine's books with ease—all kinds of things I can't begin to understand. Yet some of my friends tell me they understand 50 percent of what my mother says. Some say they understand 80 to 90 percent. Some say they understand none of it, as if she were speaking pure Chinese. But to me, my mother's English is perfectly clear, perfectly natural. It's my mother tongue. Her language, as I hear it, is vivid, direct, full of observation and imagery. That was the language that helped shape the way I saw things, expressed things, made sense of the world.

8   Lately, I've been giving more thought to the kind of English my mother speaks. Like others, I have described it to people as "broken" or "fractured" English. But I wince when I say that. It has always bothered me that I can think of no way to describe it other than "broken," as if it were damaged and needed to be fixed, as if it lacked a certain wholeness and soundness. I've heard other terms used, "limited English," for example. But they seem just as bad, as if everything is limited, including people's perceptions of the limited English speaker.

9   I know this for a fact, because when I was growing up, my mother's "limited" English limited *my* perception of her. I was ashamed of her English. I believed that her English reflected the quality of what she had to say. That is, because she expressed them imperfectly her thoughts were imperfect. And I had plenty of empirical evidence to support me: the fact that people in department stores, at banks, and at restaurants did not take her seriously, did not give her good service, pretended not to understand her, or even acted as if they did not hear her.

10   My mother has long realized the limitations of her English as well. When I was fifteen, she used to have me call people on the phone to pretend I was she. In this guise, I was forced to ask for information or even to complain and yell at people who had been rude to her. One time it was a call to her stockbroker in New York. She had cashed out her small portfolio and it just so happened we were going to go

to New York the next week, our very first trip outside California. I had to get on the phone and say in an adolescent voice that was not very convincing, "This is Mrs. Tan."

And my mother was standing in the back whispering loudly, "Why he don't send me check, already two weeks late. So mad he lie to me, losing me money." 11

And then I said in perfect English, "Yes, I'm getting rather concerned. You had agreed to send the check two weeks ago, but it hasn't arrived." 12

Then she began to talk more loudly. "What he want, I come to New York tell him front of his boss, you cheating me?" And I was trying to calm her down, make her be quiet, while telling the stockbroker, "I can't tolerate any more excuses. If I don't receive the check immediately, I am going to have to speak to your manager when I'm in New York next week." And sure enough, the following week there we were in front of this astonished stockbroker, and I was sitting there redfaced and quiet, and my mother, the real Mrs. Tan, was shouting at his boss in her impeccable broken English. 13

We used a similar routine just five days ago, for a situation that was far less humorous. My mother had gone to the hospital for an appointment, to find out about a benign brain tumor a CAT scan had revealed a month ago. She said she had spoken very good English, her best English, no mistakes. Still, she said, the hospital did not apologize when they said they had lost the CAT scan and she had come for nothing. She said they did not seem to have any sympathy when she told them she was anxious to know the exact diagnosis, since her husband and son had both died of brain tumors. She said they would not give her any more information until the next time and she would have to make another appointment for that. So she said she would not leave until the doctor called her daughter. She wouldn't budge. And when the doctor finally called her daughter, me, who spoke in perfect English—lo and behold—we had assurances the CAT scan would be found, promise that a conference call on Monday would be held, and apologies for any suffering my mother had gone through for a most regrettable mistake. 14

I think my mother's English almost had an effect on limiting my possibilities in life as well. Sociologists and linguists probably will tell you that a person's developing language skills are more influenced by peers. But I do think that the language spoken in the family, especially in immigrant families which are more insular, plays a large role in shaping the language of the child. And I believe that it affected my results on achievement tests, IQ tests, and the SAT. While my English skills were never judged as poor, compared to math, English could not be considered my strong suit. In grade school I did moderately well, getting perhaps B's, sometimes B-pluses, in English and scoring perhaps in the sixtieth or seventieth percentile on achievement tests. But those scores were not good enough to override the opinion that my true abilities lay in math and science, because in those areas I achieved A's and scored in the ninetieth percentile or higher. 15

This was understandable. Math is precise; there is only one correct answer. Whereas, for me at least, the answers on English tests were always a judgment 16 call, a matter of opinion and personal experience. Those tests were constructed around items like fill-in-the-blank sentence completion, such as, "Even though Tom was————, Mary thought he was————." And the correct answer always seemed to be the most bland combinations of thoughts, for example, "Even though Tom was shy, Mary thought he was charming," with the grammatical structure "even though" limiting the correct answer to some sort of semantic opposites, so you wouldn't get answers like, "Even though Tom was foolish, Mary thought he was ridiculous." Well, according to my mother, there were very few limitations as to what Tom could have been and what Mary might have thought of him. So I never did well on tests like that.

17   The same was true with word analogies, pairs of words in which you were supposed to find some sort of logical, semantic relationship—for example, *"Sunset is to nightfall as* ————— *is to* —————.*" And here you would be presented with a list of four possible pairs, one of which showed the same kind of relationship: *red* is to *stoplight, bus* is to *arrival, chills* is to *fever, yawn* is to *boring*. Well, I could never think that way. I knew what the tests were asking, but I could not block out of my mind the images already created by the first pair, *"sunset is to nightfall"*—and I would see a burst of color against a darkening sky, the moon rising, the lowering of a curtain of stars. And all the other pairs of words—red, bus, stoplight, boring—just threw up a mass of confusing images, making it impossible for me to sort out something as logical as saying: "A sunset precedes nightfall" is the same as "a chill precedes a fever." The only way I would have gotten that answer right would have been to imagine an associative situation, for example, by being disobedient and staying out past sunset, catching a chill at night which turns into feverish pneumonia as punishment, which indeed did happen to me.

18   I have been thinking about all this lately, about my mother's English, about achievement tests. Because lately I've been asked, as a writer, why there are not more Asian Americans represented in American literature. Why are there few Asian Americans enrolled in creative writing programs? Why do so many Chinese students go into engineering? Well, these are broad sociological questions I can't begin to answer. But I have noticed in surveys—in fact, just last week—that Asian students, as a whole, always do significantly better on math achievement tests than in English. And this makes me think that there are other Asian-American students whose English spoken in the home might also be described as "broken" or "limited." And perhaps they also have teachers who are steering them away from writing and into math and science, which is what happened to me.

19   Fortunately, I happen to be rebellious in nature and enjoy the challenge of disproving assumptions made about me. I became an English major my first year in college, after being enrolled as pre-med. I started writing nonfiction as a freelancer the week after I was told by my former boss that writing was my worst skill and I should hone my talents toward account management.

But it wasn't until 1985 that I finally began to write fiction. And at first I wrote using what I thought to be wittily crafted sentences, sentences that would finally prove I had mastery over the English language. Here's an example from the first draft of a story that later made its way into *The Joy Luck Club*, but without this line: "That was my mental quandary in its nascent state." A terrible line, which I can hardly pronounce. 20

Fortunately, for reasons I won't get into today, I later decided I should envision a reader for the stories I would write. And the reader I decided upon was my mother, because these were stories about mothers. So with this reader in mind—and in fact she did read my early drafts—I began to write stories using all the Englishes I grew up with: the English I spoke to my mother, which for lack of a better term might be described as "simple"; the English she used with me, which for lack of a better term might be described as "broken"; my translation of her Chinese, which could certainly be described as "watered down"; and what I imagine to be her translation of her Chinese if she could speak in perfect English, her internal language, and for that I sought to preserve the essence, but neither an English nor a Chinese structure. I wanted to capture what language ability tests can never reveal: her intent, her passion, her imagery, the rhythms of her speech and the nature of her thoughts. 21

Apart from what any critic had to say about my writing, I knew I had succeeded where it counted when my mother finished reading my book and gave me her verdict: "So easy to read." 22

Vocabulary

Directions: Locate each of the key words in the reading selection. Try to figure out each word's meaning by using the context. Confirm your guess by checking the dictionary or thesaurus. Write the meanings of the words in the margin of the text. Then record the meanings in the chart below.

Key Word	Paragraph	Meaning
1. evoke	2	
2. belies	7	
3. vivid	7	
4. wince	8	
5. empirical	9	
6. guise	10	
7. insular	15	

Key Word	Paragraph	Meaning
8. bland	16	
9. hone	19	
Others?		

Guide Questions

Directions: These questions will guide your understanding of what you have read. Write your answers in your notebook or on a separate sheet of paper if your instructor wishes to collect it. Your answers to these questions will be the basis of class discussion.

1. From reading the introduction and the first few paragraphs of the essay, what do we learn about Amy Tan? Who is she? What does she do? How does she describe herself? Have you read any of her novels?
2. In paragraph 3, Tan describes giving a speech she'd given many times successfully. What went wrong this time?
3. There seems to be a big difference in Tan's mother's ability to read/understand English and her ability to speak "standard" English. Describe this difference.
4. What words does Tan use to describe her mother's English? Which of these words make her wince? Why?
5. Why was Tan ashamed of her mother's English when she was growing up?
6. What did Tan's mother think of her own English language skills?
7. Explain why Tan says she had trouble with analogies.
8. How does all this relate to Tan's questions about why there are not more Asian Americans represented in American literature?
9. When Tan first decided to write fiction she wrote some lines she calls "terrible." How did she solve this problem?
10. Amy Tan speaks about "different Englishes"? What does she mean by this? How many "different Englishes" does she talk about?
11. There are at least two ways you could define the term *mother tongue*. What would these two definitions be?

Writing

What is your mother tongue? Do you have more than one? Think about the way Amy Tan's world was affected by her mother tongue. How has your mother tongue affected you and the way you view yourself and your world? Have you had to struggle with or reject anything about your mother tongue?

SHORT TAKE

Is English Broken Here?

Consider the English sentences below, written by persons with, to say the least, an imperfect command of the language. Can you "translate" these fractured sentences into comprehensible English?

A warning to motorists by a Tokyo car rental agency: "When a passenger of the foot heave in sight, tootle the horn. Trumpet at him melodiously at first, but if he still obstacles your passage, then tootle him with vigor."

A sign at an Austrian ski resort: "Do not preambulate the corridors in the hours of repose in the boots of ascension."

A hotel in Acapulco boasted: "The manager has personally passed all the water served here."

A notice in a Norwegian cocktail lounge reads: "Ladies are requested not to have children in the bar."

An airline in Copenhagen promises to "take your bags and send them in all directions."

Instructions on a package of convenience food from Italy: "Besmear a backing pan, previously buttered with a good tomato sauce, and after, dispose the cannelloni, lightly distanced between them in a only couch."

A sign in a Tokyo hotel: "It is forbidden to steal hotel towels please. If you are not a person to do such thing please not to read notice."

A dentist in Hong Kong advertised tooth extractions: "using the latest Methodists."

Can your name have an effect on your life? Here are some actual names of real people for your consideration. Mrs. Screech was a singing teacher; Mr. Vroom was a motorcycle dealer; Justin Tune was a choir director; Wyre and Tapping were detectives; Groaner Digger was an undertaker; I. C. Shiver was—you guessed it—an iceman; Grecian T. Snooze was a university student, of course. Perhaps while on vacation he met July August September? Mr. Doctor, Mr. Bonecutter, Mr. Paine, and Mr. Butcher all became physicians, naturally. So did Mr. Rash: his speciality is dermatology. Is there a connection between Mr. Vice's name and the fact that he was arrested 890 times and convicted 421 times? What were Rapid Integration's parents thinking when they named their baby? Not to mention Ms. Virginia May Sweat Strong and Buncha Love. We leave without comment Mr. A. Moron, who was a Commissioner of Education in the Virgin Islands.[1]

WHAT'S IN A NAME?

Kiley Armstrong

1   Sticks and stones may break your bones, but the wrong name can land you in an asylum, a language expert says.

2   "You will have a higher chance of being in an asylum or jail if you have an unusual name," warns Leonard R. N. Ashley of Brooklyn College, past president of the American Name Society.

3   But if you are strong enough to overcome the stigma of a wrong name, you also have a higher chance of becoming a college president, a movie star, or even a religious leader, says Ashley.

4   Ashley, who has a doctorate in psychology, studies names as "an aspect of human behavior." He writes articles for professional journals and is working on an anthology of British names.

5   He contends that the "way you perceive people depends on their name. Have you ever met an Episcopal priest named Buck?"

6   And he believes an unusual name will have either a wonderful or a terrible effect on your life.

7   The late Ima Hogg, daughter of Texas Governor James Hogg, overcame an unusual name to become a prominent Houston socialite and philanthropist. Before she died in 1975, fictitious stories abounded about the existence of a sister named Ura.

8   Then there are names like "Oral Roberts or Hubert Humphrey. If you stand up to that, you can become unique instead of peculiar and can do very well," Ashley says.

9   A sense of humor can help, as in the case of Manila's archbishop—Cardinal Jaime Sin.

---

[1] All these names were taken from John Train, *Remarkable Names of Real People* (New York: Clarkson N. Potter, 1977).

The cardinal often tells in speeches how he enjoys inviting people to "the 10 house of sin," his official residence in a Manila suburb.

"When I was little I suppose you could call me a 'Venial Sin,' but after I die 11 people will realize I was a 'Mortal Sin,'" he adds.

Even ordinary names often imply something about their owners "whether it 12 is true or not," says Ashley.

"Everybody named Leonard wears glasses and is interested in the futures 13 market," says Leonard Ashley. "*George* means 'farmer' in Greek. But now it suggests someone who is a weak husband."

"Christopher suggests intellectuality and Katherine is determined and 14 strong," he says.

People's names, product names, place names, and the names of objects all are 15 scrutinized by the American Name Society, a group composed of linguists, psychologists, and other people who study names.

Its scholars have found that the origins of names often are clouded by 16 assimilation.

"Darren is an African name. But the British saw the TV show "Bewitched" 17 and thought it was an American name."

Some name guidelines for parents include: 18

—Pay attention to the initials. "When Arthur S. Sullivan grows up and gets a briefcase with his initials on it, he's going to be furious."

—Watch for double meanings. "I once had a student named Warren Peace. He signed his name W. Peace because he was embarrassed."

—Choose names that offer a lot of nicknames—such as Margaret, which yields Maggy, Peggy, Margie—so the child has an option.

—Keep "family heirloom" names. "If the name is ugly, just give the kid an extra name or two."

As for Leonard R. N. Ashley, call him Leonard or Tim. But don't ask what 19 the R. N. stands for—he won't tell.

Vocabulary

Directions: Locate each of the key words in the reading selection. Then read and study each word in its context and try to determine its meaning. Use a dictionary or thesaurus to check your guess. Write the meanings of the words in the margin of the text.

Record the new words you've learned.

Key Word	Paragraph	Meaning
1. stigma	3	
2. anthology	4	
3. philanthropist	7	

Key Word	Paragraph	Meaning
4. imply	12	
Others?		

Guide Questions

Directions: Answering these guide questions will help ensure that you understand what you have read. They also will help you to analyze and evaluate the author's opinions and apply the ideas contained in the article to the real world and your own life.

Write answers to the questions in your notebook or on a separate sheet of paper if your instructor wishes to collect them. Your answers will form the basis of class discussion.

1. a. Think about your own first name. Do you like it? Hate it? Why?
   b. Do you know the origin of your first name? (That is, where did it come from? Were you named after someone or something?)
2. Think about your surname. Do you know its derivation? What does it mean?
3. If you could change your name, what would you change it to? Why?
4. a. Identify the authority on names who is described in the article.
   b. What are his credentials?
5. State the main idea of the article.
6. How does the example of Ms. Hogg support the main idea of the article?
7. Give two examples from the article of the effect a name can have on a person's life.
8. Do you know anyone who changed his or her name? What was the reason? What if your parents had named you Pat Fanny? Rhoda Bike? Rock Pile? Robin Droppings? Doris Closed? Isabel Ringing? (All of these are real names of real people.) Would you have changed your name?

Application

Directions: Investigate your own name. Try to find the origin of your first and last names. Interview your family members. Visit the library or use the Internet. If you are not able to find information about your own name, investigate the name of a friend or some person who interests you. Discuss your findings with your classmates.

Marking Text

Mark the text "What's in a Name?" To review marking text turn to page 421.

Writing

Now use your marked text to write a summary of the article. Summary writing is explained on page 425.

SHORT TAKE

Update on the Name Game

One British couple named Beer chose the first name Bottled for their new son. Then there is the Wall family, who named their baby Stone and Mr. and Mrs. Jordan whose new addition is named River. Don't forget the Waters family: they named their daughter Mineral, or the Castle family and their new son, Windsor. All these come from the Registrar in the British town of Stafford, whose list also includes children named Rheumatism and Fatso. But all these pale when compared to the couple in Sweden who want to name their son the following: Brfxxccxxmnpcccclllmmnprxvclmnckssqlbb11116. (They pronounce it Albin.)

*"What's your name?" seems an innocent question, but these days, it can call up any num-
ber of confusing, comical, even baffling responses. Do you know anyone with an unusual
name? Can you imagine a reason to change your name?*

*Name changes, in New York City at least, are increasing, for both practical and per-
plexing reasons. This article appeared in* The New York Times *in September 2003.*

A BOY NAMED YO, ETC.

Tara Bahrampour

1   Under the grayish fluorescent lights of the Civil Court clerk's office on Centre
Street, Dalton Conley made his request: if no one objected, he wanted to change
his 4-year-old son's name to Yo Xing Heyno Augustus Eisner Alexander Weiser
Knuckles Jeremijenko-Conley.

2   It is the longest name in the city's files, at least according to the unofficial
tally kept by clerks at the office, where any New Yorker can go to legally change
his or her name. (Each borough has an office providing the service.)

3   The boy's name—which technically was just lengthened, not changed—was
the talk of the office for a few days this summer after Mr. Conley made the application. But by the time he returned, several weeks later, to pick up the judge's
order of approval, the clerks had accepted it as just another of the weird, intimate
fragments that surface when one tinkers with a name, that most basic measure of
identity, in a city famous as a place to remake oneself.

4   "We always compare stories," said Peter DiGenova, a clerk. "There was a
woman who was changing the name of her daughter. She had four very
Hispanic-sounding names and she wanted to add the name Claridge." After a
little questioning, the woman admitted, somewhat sheepishly, that the name
was a nod to the Claridge Hotel in Atlantic City, where her daughter had been
conceived.

5   Never have New Yorkers been reinventing themselves at the rate they are
now. The office, which has kept files on name changes since 1887, says the number of applications has nearly doubled citywide, to 4,233 last year from 2,449 in
1999. The clerks trace most of that increase to a simplification of the process in
late 2000.

6   Until then, the forms were so complicated that most people had to pay a
lawyer several hundred dollars to get a name change, Mr. DiGenova said. Now,
applicants merely fill out a two-page form and pay a $65 fee.

7   A judge must still approve the change, but 95 percent of the requests pass
muster.

8   Since Sept. 11, the process has actually become more time-consuming for
those who are not United States citizens. The clerk's office must now wait 30 days
while the federal officials check into an applicant's background.

9   But 9/11 also increased the number of applications from certain quarters. "A
lot of people with Muslim names come in asking to have them Americanized because of prejudice against them," Mr. DiGenova said.

A search of the office's database unearthed several recent applicants who said   10
they wished to change their Muslim names because they did not practice the religion. "So it's ridiculous for me to have an Islamic name," wrote one woman who
chose an English-sounding surname.

Another applicant, a Queens resident, said he had changed his surname from   11
one shared by a certain recently ousted dictator to something less Middle Eastern. "People are conditioned to think of and categorize you" on the basis of your
name, he said in an interview, adding that he did not want his new name printed
because he did not want his new friends to think he had deceived them.

For those seeking to make the switch, there are only a few restrictions. To   12
change a child's name, both parents must agree, and if the child is 14 or older, he
or she must also consent in writing.

Titles are not allowed. You cannot legally become the Sultan of Swing or the   13
Queen of Chelsea. And you cannot take the name of a public figure if it is likely
to cause confusion. "Nobody would let you call yourself George W. Bush," said
Ernesto Belzaguy, first deputy chief clerk of the civil court. "You would really
have to have a good reason for that."

Even for less recognizable names, applicants must state a reason. These range   14
from the practical to the unusual. Couples often change their names when they
marry, and transsexuals often change their names to match their sexual identity.
If a judge does not suspect the applicant of trying to commit fraud, he generally
signs an order for the change.

Recently, a gray-haired man named Mordechai Engelman stood in line to   15
apply to change his first name to Martin, the name on his driver's license and
other documents. "My mother told me my English name was Martin," said Mr.
Engelman, who grew up in Brooklyn with a mother who spoke Yiddish and
Hungarian. "She is deceased, but I'm sure she'd be fine with it."

A source book used by the court says names should not be changed for "triv-   16
ial, capricious, or vainglorious reasons." Apparently, that did not apply to A.
Fluffy Bunny, a man who worked with children in a hospital and legally changed
his name to match his professional persona.

Nor has it impeded other applicants with unorthodox requests. "Let's see,   17
there was Grey I's, and there was Human Being," said Nancy Santiago, a clerk,
giggling as she scanned a list on her computer.

The office also draws people who have been surprised to learn their actual   18
legal names. "Years ago, if a hospital didn't report a baby's name by a certain
amount of time, the first name would be recorded by the city as Male or Female,"
Mr. DiGenova said. "There are people who don't find out until they're in their
60's, and they go to apply for Social Security, that their name is Male Smith or
Female Smith."

As for Mr. Conley, the father of Yo Xing Heyno Augustus, etc., his son's   19
names all have specific intentions, from honoring deceased ancestors to upsetting
common expectations.

"I had wanted to do ethnic disassimilation," said Mr. Conley, who is a sociol-   20
ogist at New York University. "So getting this white kid and giving him a name,

Yo Xing, that belongs to this ethnicity that's really not his, it evens the score for the Howard and Robert Chins."

21   Mr. Conley and his wife, Natalie Jeremijenko, originally gave their son, who is called Yo for short, four middle names, and waited until now to append the three others. The son suggested two of them, including the name of his father's childhood dog, Knuckles. "I have my limits," Mr. Conley said. "I wouldn't name my kid after a dog." Still, he named his 5-year-old daughter E, after the letter, so she could complete the name when she got older.

22   After the judge signs a name change order, the final hurdle is to post a notice of the change in a local newspaper, a step intended to curtail fraud. So, after receiving his order, Mr. Conley took a cab up to *The Village Voice* to place a classified ad.

23   Karen McWharter, who takes ads there, saw the name and her eyes widened. "That's a handful," she said. "I'd say anyone who chooses to change his name to that has got to be masochistic."

24   Hearing that the name was for a preschooler, she softened. "Well," she said, "when he turns 18 he can change it to Joe Blow."

Vocabulary

Directions: Locate each of the key words in the reading selection. Try to figure out each word's meaning by using the context. Confirm your guess by checking the dictionary or thesaurus. Write the meanings of the words in the margin of the text. Then record the meanings in the chart below.

Key Word	Paragraph	Meaning
1. tally	2	
2. tinkers	3	
3. trivial	16	
4. capricious	16	
5. vainglorious	16	
6. impeded	17	
7. masochistic	23	
Others?		

Guide Questions

Directions: These questions will guide your understanding of what you have read. Write your answers in your notebook, or on a separate sheet of paper if your instructor wishes to collect it. Your answers to these questions will be the basis of class discussion.

1. The story of Yo begins this article. What is special about Yo's name?
2. What is the main point of this story?
3. According to the article, what are the reasons people change their names?
4. Did any of the name changes especially interest you? Why?
5. Would you ever change your name? Why?

Making Connections

Imagine that the boy in this story, Yo, met Leonard R. N. Ashley (cited in "What's in a Name?" page 158). Write an imaginary conversation between the two. What might Yo say? What kind of advice do you think Ashley would give to Yo?

Writing

The following letter appeared in *The New York Times* on September 27, 2003 in response to the article "A Boy Named Yo, Etc." Write a letter of your own responding to the story.

To the Editor:

Re: "A Boy Named Yo, Etc.":

I find it sad to think that those with Muslim-sounding names are changing them after the increase in prejudice directed at them since 9/11.

My father changed his first name before entering the Navy on the advice of his older brother, who feared that there would be harassment in the service because of a name that sounded too Jewish.

We seem to learn nothing from history.

Carol Chetrick
New York, Sept. 26, 2003

SHORT TAKE

What's in a Name?

The Associated Press (appeared in The New York Daily News *2/2/2004)*

Tacking "Jr." or "II" onto a boy's name is a tradition that's tired, a new father has decided. So, the self-described engineering geek took a software approach to naming his newborn son.

Jon Blake Cusack somehow talked his wife, Jamie, into naming their son Jon Blake Cusack 2.0.

Version 2.0 was born Tuesday at Holland Community Hospital and the proud parents took him home Friday.

"I wanted to find something different to name him besides Jon Blake," said the original Cusack version. He said he had the idea for a few months, and spent the better part of that time persuading his wife to go along. Because she had "picked out the theme of the baby's room and done other things, I decided to let Jon have this," Jamie said.

After 2.0's birth, the Cusacks sent out, naturally, an electronic birth announcement.

Santha Rama Rau has written widely: novels, essays, and travel articles. Often her work focuses on the clash of cultures that resulted from Britain's long economic and political control over India, which did not end until 1947. This excerpt from her 1951 novel Gifts of Passage *first appeared in the* New Yorker *magazine. In it, Rama Rau describes the first experience of an Indian child sent to attend a British-run school.*

BY ANY OTHER NAME

Santha Rama Rau

At the Anglo-Indian day school in Zorinabad to which my sister and I were sent when she was eight and I was five and a half, they changed our names. On the first day of school, a hot, windless morning of a north Indian September, we stood in the headmistress's study and she said, "Now you're the *new* girls. What are your names?"

My sister answered for us. "I am Premila, and she"—nodding in my direction—"is Santha."

The headmistress had been in India, I suppose, fifteen years or so, but she still smiled at her helpless inability to cope with Indian names. Her rimless half-glasses glittered, and the precarious bun on top of her head trembled as she shook her head. "Oh, my dears, those are much too hard for me. Suppose we give you pretty English names. Wouldn't that be more jolly? Let's see, now—Pamela for you, I think." She shrugged in a baffled way at my sister. "That's as close as I can get. And for *you*," she said to me, "how about Cynthia? Isn't that nice?"

My sister was always less easily intimidated than I was, and while she kept a stubborn silence, I said, "Thank you," in a very tiny voice.

We had been sent to that school because my father, among his responsibilities as an officer of the civil service, had a tour of duty to perform in the villages around that steamy little provincial town, where he had his headquarters at that time. He used to make his shorter inspection tours on horseback, and a week before, in the stale heat of a typically postmonsoon day, we had waved good-by to him and a little procession—an assistant, a secretary, two bearers, and the man to look after the bedding rolls and luggage. They rode away through our large garden, still bright green from the rains, and we turned back into the twilight of the house and the sound of fans whispering in every room.

Up to then, my mother had refused to send Premila to school in the British-run establishments of that time, because, she used to say, "you can bury a dog's tail for seven years and it still comes out curly, and you can take a Britisher away from his home for a lifetime, and he still remains insular." The examinations and degrees from entirely Indian schools were not, in those days, considered valid. In my case, the question had never come up, and probably never would have come up if Mother's extraordinary good health had not broken down. For the first time in my life, she was not able to continue the lessons she had been giving us every morning. So our Hindi books were put away, the stories of the Lord Krishna as a little boy were left in midair, and we were sent to the Anglo-Indian school.

7   That first day at school is still, when I think of it, a remarkable one. At that age, if one's name is changed, one develops a curious form of dual personality. I remember having a certain detached and disbelieving concern in the actions of "Cynthia," but certainly no responsibility. Accordingly, I followed the thin, erect back of the headmistress down the veranda to my classroom feeling, at most, a passing interest in what was going to happen to me in this strange, new atmosphere of School.

8   The building was Indian in design, with wide verandas opening onto a central courtyard, but Indian verandas are usually whitewashed, with stone floors. These, in the tradition of British schools, were painted dark brown and had matting on the floors. It gave a feeling of extra intensity to the heat.

9   I suppose there were about a dozen Indian children in the school—which contained perhaps forty children in all—and four of them were in my class. They were all sitting at the back of the room and I went to join them. I sat next to a small, solemn girl who didn't smile at me. She had long, glossy-black braids and wore a cotton dress, but she still kept on her Indian jewelry—a gold chain around her neck, thin gold bracelets, and tiny ruby studs in her ears. Like most Indian children, she had a rim of black kohl around her eyes. The cotton dress should have looked strange, but all I could think of was that I should ask my mother if I couldn't wear a dress to school, too, instead of my Indian clothes.

10   I can't remember too much about the proceedings in class that day, except for the beginning. The teacher pointed to me and asked me to stand up "Now, dear, tell the class your name."

11   I said nothing.

12   "Come along," she said frowning slightly. "What's your name, dear?"

13   "I don't know," I said, finally.

14   The English children in the front of the class—there were about eight or ten of them—giggled and twisted around in their chairs to look at me. I sat down quickly and opened my eyes very wide, hoping in that way to dry them off. The little girl with the braids put out her hand and very lightly touched my arm. She still didn't smile.

15   Most of that morning I was rather bored. I looked briefly at the children's drawings pinned to the wall, and then concentrated on a lizard clinging to the ledge of the high, barred window behind the teacher's head. Occasionally it would shoot out its long yellow tongue for a fly, and then it would rest, with its eyes closed and its belly palpitating, as though it were swallowing several times quickly. The lessons were mostly concerned with reading and writing and simple numbers—things that my mother had already taught me—and I paid very little attention. The teacher wrote on the easel blackboard words like "bat" and "cat," which seemed babyish to me; only "apple" was new and incomprehensible.

16   When it was time for the lunch recess, I followed the girl with braids out onto the veranda. There the children from the other classes were assembled. I saw Premila at once and ran over to her, as she had charge of our lunchbox. The children were all opening packages and sitting down to eat sandwiches. Premila and I were the only ones who had Indian food—thin wheat chapatties, some vegetable curry,

and a bottle of buttermilk. Premila thrust half of it into my hand and whispered fiercely that I should go and sit with my class, because that was what the others seemed to be doing.

The enormous black eyes of the little Indian girl from my class looked at my food longingly, so I offered her some. But she only shook her head and plowed her way solemnly through her sandwiches.   17

I was very sleepy after lunch, because at home we always took a siesta. It was usually a pleasant time of day, with the bedroom darkened against the harsh afternoon sun, the drifting off into sleep with the sound of Mother's voice reading a story in one's mind, and, finally, the shrill, fussy voice of the ayah waking one for tea.   18

At school, we rested for a short time on low, folding cots on the veranda, and then we were expected to play games. During the hot part of the afternoon we played indoors, and after the shadows had begun to lengthen and the slight breeze of the evening had come up we moved outside to the wide courtyard.   19

I had never really grasped the system of competitive games. At home, whenever we played tag or guessing games, I was always allowed to "win"—"because," Mother used to tell Premila, "she is the youngest, and we have to allow for that." I had often heard her say it, and it seemed quite reasonable to me, but the result was that I had no clear idea of what "winning" meant.   20

When we played twos-and-threes that afternoon at school, in accordance with my training, I let one of the small English boys catch me, but was naturally rather puzzled when the other children did not return the courtesy. I ran about for what seemed like hours without ever catching anyone, until it was time for school to close. Much later I learned that my attitude was called "not being a good sport," and I stopped allowing myself to be caught, but it was not for years that I really learned the spirit of the thing.   21

When I saw our car come up to the school gate, I broke away from my classmates and rushed toward it yelling, "Ayah! Ayah!" It seemed like an eternity since I had seen her that morning—a wizened, affectionate figure in her white cotton sari, giving me dozens of urgent and useless instructions on how to be a good girl at school. Premila followed more sedately, and she told me on the way home never to do that again in front of the other children.   22

When we got home we went straight to Mother's high, white room to have tea with her, and I immediately climbed onto the bed and bounced gently up and down on the springs. Mother asked how we had liked our first day in school. I was so pleased to be home and to have left that peculiar Cynthia behind that I had nothing whatever to say about school, except to ask what "apple" meant. But Premila told Mother about the classes, and added that in her class they had weekly tests to see if they learned their lessons well.   23

I asked, "What's a test?"   24

Premila said, "You're too small to have them. You won't have them in your class for donkey's years." She had learned the expression that day and was using it for the first time. We all laughed enormously at her wit. She also told Mother, in an aside, that we should take sandwiches to school the next day. Not, she said, that *she* minded. But they would be simpler for me to handle.   25

26   That whole lovely evening I didn't think about school at all. I sprinted bare-foot across the lawn with my favorite playmate, the cook's son, to the stream at the end of the garden. We quarreled in our usual way, waded in the tepid water under the lime trees, and waited for the night to bring out the smell of the jasmine. I listened with fascination to his stories of ghosts and demons, until I was too frightened to cross the garden alone in the semidarkness. The ayah found me, shouted at the cook's son, scolded me, hurried me into supper — it was an entirely usual, wonderful evening.

27   It was a week later, the day of Premila's first test, that our lives changed rather abruptly. I was sitting at the back of my class, in my usual inattentive way, only half listening to the teacher. I had started a rather guarded friend-ship with the girl with the braids, whose name turned out to be Nalini (Nancy, in school). The three other Indian children were already fast friends. Even at that age it was apparent to all of us that friendship with the English or Anglo-Indian children was out of the question. Occasionally, during the class, my new friend and I would draw pictures and show them to each other secretly.

28   The door opened sharply and Premila marched in. At first, the teacher smiled at her in a kindly and encouraging way and said, "Now, you're little Cynthia's sister?"

29   Premila didn't even look at her. She stood with her feet planted firmly apart and her shoulders rigid, and addressed herself directly to me. "Get up," she said. "We're going home."

30   I didn't know what had happened, but I was aware that it was a crisis of some sort. I rose obediently and started to walk toward my sister.

31   "Bring your pencils and your notebook," she said.

32   I went back for them, and together we left the room. The teacher started to say something just as Premila closed the door, but we didn't wait to hear what it was.

33   In complete silence we left the school grounds and started to walk home. Then I asked Premila what the matter was. All she would say was "We're going home for good."

34   It was a very tiring walk for a child of five and a half, and I dragged along behind Premila with my pencils growing sticky in my hand. I can still remem-ber looking at the dusty hedges, and the tangles of thorns in the ditches by the side of the road, smelling the faint fragrance from the eucalyptus trees and won-dering whether we would ever reach home. Occasionally a horse-drawn tonga passed us, and the women, in their pink or green silks, stared at Premila and me trudging along on the side of the road. A few coolies and a line of women carry-ing baskets of vegetables on their heads smiled at us. But it was nearing the hottest time of day, and the road was almost deserted. I walked more and more slowly, and shouted to Premila, from time to time, "Wait for me!" with increas-ing peevishness. She spoke to me only once, and that was to tell me to carry my notebook on my head, because of the sun.

When we got to our house the ayah was just taking a tray of lunch into   35
Mother's room. She immediately started a long, worried questioning about what
are you children doing back here at this hour of the day.

Mother looked very startled and very concerned, and asked Premila what had   36
happened.

Premila said, "We had our test today, and she made me and the other Indians   37
sit at the back of the room, with a desk between each one."

Mother said, "Why was that, darling?"   38

"She said it was because Indians cheat," Premila added. "So I don't think we   39
should go back to that school."

Mother looked very distant, and was silent a long time. At last she said, "Of   40
course not, darling." She sounded displeased.

We all shared the curry she was having for lunch, and afterward I was sent   41
off to the beautifully familiar bedroom for my siesta. I could hear Mother and
Premila talking through the open door.

Mother said, "Do you suppose she understood all that?"   42

Premila said, "I shouldn't think so. She's a baby."   43

Mother said, "Well, I hope it won't bother her."   44

Of course, they were both wrong. I understood it perfectly, and I remember   45
it all very clearly. But I put it happily away, because it had all happened to a girl
called Cynthia, and I never was really particularly interested in her.

Vocabulary

Directions: Locate each of the key words in the reading selection. Try to figure out each word's meaning by its context. Confirm your guess by checking the dictionary or thesaurus. Write the meanings of the words in the margin of the text. Then record the meanings in the chart below.

Key Word	Paragraph	Meaning
1. precarious	3	
2. insular	6	
3. detached	7	
4. veranda	7	
5. palpitating	15	
6. wizened	22	
7. tepid	26	

Key Word	Paragraph	Meaning
Others?		

Guide Questions

Directions: These questions will guide your understanding of what you have read. Write your answers in your notebook or on a separate sheet of paper if your instructor wishes to collect it. Your answers to these questions will be the basis of class discussion.

1. Summarize what we learn in the story about Rau and her family; for example, where does the story take place? why is the Rau family there, etc. Identify the major characters in the story.
2. Interpret Rau's mother's comment in paragraph 6: "you can bury a dog's tail for seven years and it still comes out curly, and you can take a Britisher away from his home for a lifetime, and he still remains insular."
3. Contrast the life and status of the girls at home and at school.
4. a. Describe the day of Premila's test, the day the sisters' lives changed. What caused the change?
   b. What effect did this crisis have on Santha?

Application/Writing

Directions: Choose one of the questions below and write a paragraph in response.

1. The old saying goes, "Sticks and stones can break my bones, but words can never hurt me." Do you agree?
2. Have you ever been called a derogatory name? What effect did it have on you?
3. Have you ever changed your name? Why? What was the result?
4. Do you think a person's name establishes his or her identity (or a part of it)? Why?

Making Connections

The title of the story, "By Any Other Name," is an allusion (a reference) to Shakespeare's play, *Romeo and Juliet*. Read the following excerpt from Act II: Scene II. Can you paraphrase what Juliet means? Compare the idea about names in Romeo and Juliet to the selection "By Any Other Name." Is the meaning the same?

> *Juliet*: O Romeo, Romeo! Wherefore art thou Romeo?
> Deny thy father and refuse thy name;
> Or, if thou wilt not, be but sworn, my love,
> And I'll no longer be a Capulet.
>   . . .

'Tis but thy name that is my enemy;
Thou art thyself, though not a Montague.
What's a Montague? It is nor hand, nor foot,
Nor arm, nor face, nor any other part
Belonging to a man. O, be some other name!
What's in a name? that which we call a rose
By any other name would smell as sweet;
So Romeo would, were he not Romeo call'd,
Retain that dear perfection which he owes
Without that title. Romeo, doff thy name,
And for that name which is no part of thee
take all myself.

Romeo: I take thee at thy word:
Call me but love, and I'll be new baptized;
Henceforth I never will be Romeo.

SHORT TAKE

Phraseology

Henry Alford

Actual Selections from Phrase Books
and Language Primers for Travelers

You're a tourist in Yemen. Upon awakening one morning, you stumble down to the lobby of your hotel, where the proprietor asks you in Yemeni Arabic how you slept. Unsure how best to articulate your response, you open a copy of "Spoken Yemeni Arabic." You turn to the appropriate section and recite the first thing that catches your eye, from page 148:

I did not sleep all night. The next time I want a drug.

You're visiting Japan, where you have befriended a native. He invites you to his home; you go, looking over his house with more than a little interest. Eager to make a good impression, you pull out your trusty "Complete Japanese Expression Guide," cast a glance at Example 4 on page 38 and say:

There is a big difference in our income levels.

You're in a cafe in Albania, talking in Albanian with a waitress. Casting about for something to say during a lull in the conversation, you glance at your copy of "Spoken Albanian" on the table in front of you. You read from Unit 17:

I wanted you to explain to me your customs concerning blood vengeance.

Language primers and phrase books for travelers can be an odd introduction to a foreign country. Blithely insensitive to the subtleties of polite conversation, these tiny manuals re-enforce the xenophobic notion that all foreign travel is rife with unpleasure and mishap. Sometimes the source of this unpleasure and mishap is unspecified—the reader of "Teach Yourself Catalan," for instance, can only wonder what dire circumstances will require the use of the phrase

I am prepared to raffle the goat.

Other times the source of unpleasure and mishap is all too clear, as in the phrase book from the Imperial Russia era that is mentioned in James Thurber's essay "There's No Place Like Home." There, the reader is supplied with the Russian for

Oh, dear, our postilion has been struck by lightning!

Indeed, vehicular calamity (a postilion is a person who rides the left-hand leading horse of a four- or two-horse carriage) is a veritable staple of the language guide for travelers. These books imply that when not crawling out of a Citröen that has skidded off the autobahn, you will probably be watching *others* crawling out of Citröens that have skidded off the autobahn. As a rather dispassionate exchange between two bystanders to a car crash in "Spoken Turkish" runs:

The poor people are covered with blood. I wonder if they're suffering much?
I don't think so, since they've fainted.

A less delicate reference to a car crash appears in the "Fanagalo Dictionary," which translates a crude lingua franca used mostly in the mines of South Africa:

One European is dead; another has a broken arm, and a baby is bleeding from the mouth and ears.

Of course, automobiles are not the only source of conflict in phrase book land. Each manual seems to tap a new vein of potential misfortune. The "Introductory Course in Spoken Hindi" cites weather conditions:

You seem to be off mood today, what happened?
It seems that I got fever and bad cold.
How did it happen all of a sudden?
I got wet in the rain yesterday.
Perhaps you got flu.
Oh! What a hell!

And "2001 French and English Idioms" invokes modern medicine:

After the injection, I felt funny.

As is only to be expected, however, the lion's share of phrase book opprobrium is directed at fellow humans. In phrase books, as in the work of Jean-Paul

Sartre, hell is other people. An exchange from "German Chit-Chat" puts it most succinctly:

Why did you not play with Willibald?
Because I don't like him.

When we are dealing with servants, clerks or waiters, phrase books would have us adopt a brisk, businesslike tone. Consider the "Tailor" section of the Baedeker "Traveler's Manual of Conversation," which deals in four languages:

Good morning to you; you have kept me waiting long enough.

A later episode in that book has us inform a merchant:

That is very dear. Such a price frightens me.

The appalling "Spoken Hawaiian" advocates outright hostility:

Slave, bring fish, taro and a squid. If you don't do this fast, you'll be a live sacrifice.

Whatever their deficiencies, however, phrase books cannot be accused of countenancing boredom. Blood vengeance, goat raffles, live sacrifice—this is a colorful and decisive, if somewhat mysterious, world. Those who fail to capture this sense of drama will have to answer to "The Complete Japanese Expression Guide":

Every comment you make is just so innocuous!

Do you ever go to the rest room to rest? Or to the powder room to powder? And just how often do you take a bath when you make a trip to the bathroom? *Did you know that in many parts of the southern United States people don't die? No, they pass away. Some even go to their reward. In other parts of the country, people just buy the farm or experience the end of the ball game. Shakespeare never said "die," his characters shuffled off this mortal coil. People who would be mortally ashamed to discuss being naked feel free to discuss their birthday suit, or being in the altogether. Aware of it or not, we all use euphemisms. Here, the author of* A Dictionary of Euphemisms and Other Doubletalk *introduces us to these "linguistic fig leaves and verbal flourishes for artful users of the English language."*

EUPHEMISMS

Hugh Rawson

1   Mr. Milquetoast gets up from the table, explaining that he has to go to the *little boys' room* or to *see a man about a dog;* a young woman announces that she is *enceinte.* A secretary complains that her boss is a pain in the *derriere;* an undertaker or *mortician* asks delicately where to ship the *loved one.* These are euphemisms—mild, agreeable, or roundabout words used in place of coarse, painful, or offensive ones. The term comes from the Greek *eu,* meaning "well" or "sounding good," and *pheme,* "speech."

2   Many euphemisms are so delightfully ridiculous that everyone laughs at them. (Well, almost everyone: The people who call themselves the National Selected Morticians usually manage to keep from smiling.) Yet euphemisms have very serious reasons for being. They conceal the things people fear the most—death, the dead, the supernatural. They cover up the facts of life—of sex and reproduction and excretion—which inevitably remind even the most refined people that they are made of clay, or worse. They are beloved by individuals and institutions (governments, especially) who are anxious to present only the handsomest possible images of themselves to the world. And they are embedded so deeply in our language that few of us, even those who pride themselves on being plain-spoken, ever get through a day without using them.

3   The same sophisticates who look down their noses at *little boys' room* and other euphemisms of that ilk will nevertheless say that they are going to the *bathroom* when no bath is intended; that Mary has been *sleeping around* even though she has been getting precious little shut-eye; that John has *passed away* or even *departed* (as if he'd just made the last train to Darien); and that Sam and Janet are *friends,* which sounds a lot better than "illicit lovers."

4   Thus, euphemisms are society's basic *lingua franca.* As such, they are outward and visible signs of our inward anxieties, conflicts, fears, and shames. They are like radioactive isotopes. By tracing them, it is possible to see what has been (and is) going on in our language, our minds, and our culture.

5   Euphemisms can be divided into two general types—positive and negative. The positive ones inflate and magnify, making the euphemized items seem

altogether grander and more important than they really are. The negative euphemisms deflate and diminish. They are defensive in nature, off-setting the power of tabooed terms and otherwise eradicating from the language everything that people prefer not to deal with directly.

Positive euphemisms include the many occupational titles, which salve the egos of workers by elevating their job status: *custodian* for janitor (itself a euphemism for caretaker), *counsel* for lawyer, the many kinds of *engineer* (*exterminating engineer, mattress engineer, publicity engineer,* ad infinitum), *help* for servant (itself an old euphemism for slave), *hooker* and *working girl* for whore, and so forth. A common approach is to try to turn one's trade into a profession, usually in imitation of the medical profession. *Beautician* and the aforementioned *mortician* are the classic examples, but the same imitative instinct is responsible for social workers calling welfare recipients *clients,* for football coaches conducting *clinics,* and for undertakers referring to corpses as *cases* or even *patients.*   6

Other kinds of positive euphemisms include personal honorifics such as *colonel,* the *honorable,* and *major,* and the many institutional euphemisms, which convert madhouses into *mental hospitals,* colleges into *universities,* and small business establishments into *emporiums, parlors, salons,* and *shoppes.* The desire to improve one's surroundings also is evident in geographical place names, most prominently in the case of the distinctly non-green *Greenland* (attributed to an early real-estate developer named Eric the Red), but also in the designation of many small burgs as *cities,* and in the names of some cities, such as *Troy,* New York (née Vanderheyden's Ferry, its name-change in 1789 began a fad for adopting classical place names in the United States).   7

Negative, defensive euphemisms are extremely ancient. It was the Greeks, for example, who transformed the Furies into the Eumenides (the "kindly ones"). In many cultures, it is forbidden to pronounce the name of God (hence, pious Jews say Adonai) or of Satan (giving rise to the *deuce,* the *good man,* the *great fellow,* the generalized *Devil,* and many other roundabouts). The names of the dead, and of animals that are hunted or feared, may also be euphemized this way. The bear is called *grandfather* by many peoples and the tiger is alluded to as the *striped one.* The common motivation seems to be a confusion between the names of things and the things themselves: The name is viewed as an extension of the thing. Thus, to know the name is to give one power over the thing (as in the Rumpelstiltskin story). But such power may be dangerous: "Speak of the Devil and he appears." For mere mortals, then, the safest policy is to use another name, usually a flattering, euphemistic one, in place of the supernatural being's true name.   8

As strong as—or stronger than—the taboos against names are the taboos against particular words, especially the infamous *four-letter words.* (According to a recent Supreme Court decision, the set of *four-letter words* actually contains some words with as few as three and as many as twelve letters, but the logic of Supreme Court decisions is not always immediately apparent). These words form part of the vocabulary of everyone above the age of six or seven. They are not slang terms, but legitimate Standard English of the oldest stock, and they are euphemized in many ways, typically by conversion into pseudo-Latin (e.g., *copulation, defecation,*   9 *urination*) into slang (*make love, number two, pee*), or into socially acceptable dashes (f—, s—, p—, etc.). In the electronic media, the function of the dash is fulfilled by the *bleep* (sometimes pronounced *blip*), which has completed the circle and found its way into print.

10   The taboo against words frequently degenerates into mere prudery. At least—though the defensive principle is the same—the primitive (or *preliterate*) hunter's use of *grandfather* seems to operate on a more elemental level than the excessive modesty that has produced *abdomen* for belly, *afterpart* for ass, *bosom* for breast, *limb* for leg, *white meat* for breast (of a chicken), and so on.

11   When carried too far, which is what always seems to happen, positive and negative euphemisms tend finally to coalesce into an unappetizing mush of elegancies and genteelism, in which the underlying terms are hardly worth the trouble of euphemizing, i.e., *ablutions* for washing, *bender* for knee, *dentures* for false teeth, *expectorate* for spit, *home* for house, *honorarium* for fee, *ill* for sick, *libation* for drink, *perspire* for sweat, *position* for job, etc., etc., etc.

Vocabulary

Directions: Locate each of the key words in the reading selection. Then read and study each word in its context and try to determine its meaning. Use a dictionary or thesaurus to check your guess. Write the meanings of the words in the margin of the text.

Record the new words you've learned.

Key Word	Paragraph	Meaning
1. enceinte	1	
2. ilk	3	
3. eradicating	5	
4. honorifics	7	
5. née	7	
6. infamous	9	
7. prudery	10	
8. coalesce	11	
Others?		

Guide Questions

Directions: The purpose of these guide questions is to ensure your understanding of what you have read. They also will help you to analyze and evaluate the author's ideas and apply them to the real world and your own life.

Write answers to the questions in your notebook or on a separate sheet of paper if your instructor wishes to collect them. Your answers will form the basis of class discussion.

1. Explain and give two examples of euphemisms.
2. Contrast the two types of euphemisms Rawson describes.
3. According to Rawson, what happens when the use of euphemisms is "carried too far"?
4. If you read the selection "Language" (page 140), relate the use of euphemisms to the notion of confusing symbols (in this case, words) with the actual things they symbolize.
5. Rawson gives many examples of euphemisms, but he does not exhaust the subject. Money is one of the subjects we tend to disguise with euphemisms. In many cases it is considered poor taste to ask people about their financial affairs; we don't usually ask casual acquaintances, "How much is your salary?" Bill collectors often use indirect ways of asking for payment: "We beg to call your attention to what might be an oversight on your part," or "We would appreciate your early attention to this matter," instead of "Send us the money you owe!" Can you think of any other topics that we discuss using euphemisms?

Application

Directions: Working in pairs or in small groups, collect euphemisms. You will find ads from magazines, newspapers, radio, and TV especially rich sources of euphemisms, but you can easily find them in magazine and newspaper articles as well as in day-to-day conversations. Prepare the chart below with your collection of euphemisms.

Cite the source for each euphemism (for example, a real estate ad or a television commercial). Copy the euphemism into the appropriate column. Then write the word you think the euphemism replaces in the last column. An example is done for you.

Source	The Euphemism	The Word(s) the Euphemism Replaces
A memo from the CEO of my company.	It said: "We are forced by a downturn in the economy to downsize our work force."	It meant that they are going to fire a lot of us.

Writing

Directions: Write a summary of the selection "Euphemisms." To review summary writing, turn to page 425. In this summary, you should include one or two examples of each of the key ideas in order to make the summary clear and complete.

SHORT TAKE

More Broken English

Here are a few more examples of how English takes a beating as it travels the world. Can you repair these sentences?

A doctor in Rome advertised his specialties as: "women and other diseases."

A hotel in Yugoslavia announced heartily: "The flattening of underwear with pleasure is the job of the chambermaid. Turn to her straightaway."

Beware of a tailor on the Greek island of Rhodes who couldn't guarantee he could finish summer suits ordered by tourists: "Because is big rush we will execute customers in strict rotation."

A laundry in Rome invites: "Ladies, leave your clothes here and spend the afternoon having a good time."

Good news for pregnant tourists: a Czech tourist agency advertises, "Take one of our horse-drawn city tours. We guarantee no miscarriages."

A note on a Swiss menu: "Our wines leave you nothing to hope for."

After that wine, maybe it's for the best: A Swiss inn advises, "Special today—no ice cream."

And a bottle of the Swiss wine, please. A Polish menu tempts us with "Salad a firm's own make; limpid red beet soup with cheesy dumplings in the form of a finger; roasted duck let loose; beef rashers beaten up in the country people's fashion."

Writing is written language. The earliest writing we know of is called cuneiform, which dates back to about 3500 B.C. in the valley of the Tigris and Euphrates Rivers. Within the next five hundred years or so the Egyptians developed a picture-writing system called hieroglyphics. Somewhere around 1800 B.C. it is believed the Phoenicians developed a phonetic alphabet—one based on sounds. All the phonetic alphabets of history, including that of English, are based on this great invention. In the following essay, the author helps us imagine the beginnings of writing.

Before you read "Symbols of Humankind," try to think of what prompted humans to invent writing.

1. *Why was spoken language insufficient for human needs? Think about the advantages that written language has over spoken language.*
2. *"Non-literate" societies (people who do not have a written language) still exist. Why do you suppose they have not developed writing?*
3. *Imagine how daily life would be if written language had never been developed. List some of the things you do each day that are completely dependent on writing.*

SYMBOLS OF HUMANKIND

Don Lago

Many thousands of years ago, a man quietly resting on a log reached down and picked up a stick and with it began scratching upon the sand at his feet. He moved the stick slowly back and forth and up and down, carefully guiding it through curves and straight lines. He gazed upon what he had made, and a gentle satisfaction lighted his face.   1

Other people noticed this man drawing on the sand. They gazed upon the figures he had made, and though they at once recognized the shapes of familiar things such as fish or birds or humans, they took a bit longer to realize what the man had meant to say by arranging these familiar shapes in this particular way. Understanding what he had done, they nodded or smiled in recognition.   2

This small band of humans didn't realize what they were beginning. The images these people left in the sand would soon be swept away by the wind, but their new idea would slowly grow until it had remade the human species. These people had discovered writing.   3

Writing, early people would learn, could contain much more information than human memory could and contain it more accurately. It could carry thoughts much farther than mere sounds could—farther in distance and in time. Profound thoughts born in a single mind could spread and endure.   4

The first written messages were simply pictures relating familiar objects in some meaningful way—pictographs. Yet there were no images for much that was important in human life. What, for instance, was the image for sorrow or bravery? So from pictographs humans developed ideograms to represent more abstract ideas. 5

An eye flowing with tears could represent sorrow, and a man with the head of a lion might be bravery.

6   The next leap occurred when the figures became independent of things or ideas and came to stand for spoken sounds. Written figures were free to lose all resemblance to actual objects. Some societies developed syllabic systems of writing in which several hundred signs corresponded to several hundred spoken sounds. Others discovered the much simpler alphabetic system, in which a handful of signs represented the basic sounds the human voice can make.

7   At first, ideas flowed only slightly faster when written than they had through speech. But as technologies evolved, humans embodied their thoughts in new ways: through the printing press, in Morse code, in electromagnetic waves bouncing through the atmosphere, and in the binary language of computers.

8   Today, when the earth is covered with a swarming interchange of ideas, we are even trying to send our thoughts beyond our planet to other minds in the universe. Our first efforts at sending our thoughts beyond earth have taken a very ancient form: pictographs. The first message, on plaques aboard the *Pioneer* spacecraft launched in 1972 and 1973, featured a simple line drawing of two humans, one male and one female, the male holding up his hand in greeting. Behind them was an outline of the *Pioneer* spacecraft, from which the size of the humans could be judged. The plaque also included the "address" of the two human figures: a picture of the solar system, with a spacecraft emerging from the third planet. Most exobiologists believe that when other civilizations attempt to communicate with us they too will use pictures.

9   All the accomplishments since humans first scribbled in the sand have led us back to where we began. Written language only works when two individuals know what the symbols mean. We can only return to the simplest form of symbol available and work from there. In interstellar communication, we are at the same stage our ancestors were when they used sticks to trace a few simple images in the sand.

10   We still hold their sticks in our hands and draw pictures with them. But the stick is no longer made of wood; over the ages that piece of wood has been transformed into a massive radio telescope. And we no longer scratch on sand; now we write our thoughts onto the emptiness of space itself.

Vocabulary

Directions: Locate each of the key words in the reading selection. Then read and study each word in its context and try to determine its meaning. Use a dictionary or thesaurus to check your guess. Write the meanings of the words in the margin of the text.

Record the new words you've learned in the following chart.

Key Word	Paragraph	Meaning
1. profound	4	
2. pictographs	5	

Key Word	Paragraph	Meaning
3. ideograms	5	
4. plaques	8	
5. interstellar	9	
Others?		

Guide Questions

Directions: The purpose of these guide questions is to ensure your understanding of what you have read. They also will help you to analyze and evaluate the author's ideas and apply them to the real world and your own life.

Write answers to the questions in your notebook or on a separate sheet of paper if your instructor wishes to collect them. Your answers will form the basis of class discussion.

1. Until humans invented writing, human societies relied upon an oral tradition to pass on their culture from one generation to the next. Older people told stories that explained their world and history to the children. What are some advantages that a system of writing has for humans?
2. Explain what Lago means when he says that the first systems of writing used *pictographs*, whereas more sophisticated writing systems developed *ideograms*. Be sure to explain the distinction the author makes between pictographs and ideograms.
3. Explain the next "leap" that occurred in the development of writing.
4. What kind of alphabetic system does English use: pictograph, ideogram, syllabic, or phonetic?
5. What new systems of writing have developed as technology has advanced?
6. Explain what the author means when he says, "All the accomplishments since humans first scribbled in the sand have led us back to where we began."

Application

1. Imagine you are the first person to use writing to communicate your thoughts. What would be the first ideas you would try to communicate to your fellow humans? Write the symbols you would use. Then write the same ideas in the writing system you use now.

2. Imagine again that you are one of the first people to use writing to communicate. What would you write to communicate the following ideas:

   a. fire
   b. stars
   c. snow
   d. happy
   e. fear
   f. Run! Danger!
   g. I'm hungry.
   h. I love my children.
   i. Meet me tomorrow at sunset.

   Did you find the last six ideas more difficult to represent than the first three? Explain why it is easier to write about a star than about love.

Making Connections

Return to guide question 2 of "Language" (page 144). Compare your experience answering that question to your experience answering Application questions 1 and 2 above.

Writing

Directions: Return to the questions in the introduction to "Symbols of Humankind" on page 181. Think again about your answers. Then choose one of the questions and write one or two paragraphs in response.

SHORT TAKE

Break It to Me Gently. . . .

Writers know that when they submit their work to publishers it is very likely to be rejected. Most American publishers simply return the manuscript along with a brief letter saying effectively, "Thanks, but no thanks." A Chinese journal of economics, however, found a way to say NO in an entirely new and marvelous way:

> *We have read your manuscript with boundless delight. If we were to publish your paper it would be impossible for us to publish any work of a lower standard. As it is unthinkable that, in the next thousand years, we shall see its equal, we are, to our regret, compelled to return your divine composition, and to beg you a thousand times to overlook our short sight and timidity.*

Cited in *The Times Diary,* July 9, 1982.

Can you remember an experience that affected you so strongly that it changed the entire direction of your life? Here a writer describes a turning point in his life, when, he says "at the eleventh hour as it were, I had discovered a calling."

LEARNING TO WRITE

Russell Baker

When our class was assigned to Mr. Fleagle for third-year English I anticipated   1
another grim year in that dreariest of subjects. Mr. Fleagle was notorious among
City students for dullness and inability to inspire. He was said to be stuffy, dull,
and hopelessly out of date. To me he looked to be sixty or seventy and prim to a
fault. He wore primly severe eyeglasses, his wavy hair was primly cut and primly
combed. He wore prim vested suits with neckties blocked primly against the collar buttons of his primly starched white shirts. He had a primly pointed jaw, a
primly straight nose, and a prim manner of speaking that was so correct, so gen-
tlemanly, that he seemed a comic antique.

I anticipated a listless, unfruitful year with Mr. Fleagle and for a long time   2
was not disappointed. We read *Macbeth.* Mr. Fleagle loved *Macbeth* and wanted us
to love it too, but he lacked the gift of infecting others with his own passion. He
tried to convey the murderous ferocity of Lady Macbeth one day by reading aloud
the passage that concludes

> . . . I have given suck, and know
> How tender 'tis to love the babe that milks me.
> I would, while it was smiling in my face,
> Have plucked my nipple from his boneless gums . . .

The idea of prim Mr. Fleagle plucking his nipple from boneless gums was   3
too much for the class. We burst into gasps of irrepressible snickering. Mr. Fleagle
stopped.

"There is nothing funny, boys, about giving suck to a babe. It is the very   4
essence of motherhood, don't you see."

He constantly sprinkled his sentences with "don't you see." It wasn't a   5
question but an exclamation of mild surprise at our ignorance. "Your pronoun
needs an antecedent, don't you see," he would say, very primly. "The purpose
of the Porter's scene, boys, is to provide comic relief from the horror, don't
you see."

Late in the year we tackled the informal essay. "The essay, don't you see, is   6
the. . . ." My mind went numb. Of all forms of writing, none seemed so boring as
the essay. Naturally we would have to write informal essays. Mr. Fleagle distributed a homework sheet offering us a choice of topics. None was quite so simple-
minded as "What I Did on My Summer Vacation," but most seemed to be almost
as dull. I took the list home and dawdled until the night before the essay was
due. Sprawled on the sofa, I finally faced up to the grim task, took the list out of

my notebook, and scanned it. The topic on which my eye stopped was "The Art of Eating Spaghetti."

7　　This title produced an extraordinary sequence of mental images. Surging up out of the depths of memory came a vivid recollection of a night in Belleville when all of us were seated around the supper table—Uncle Allen, my mother, Uncle Charlie, Doris, Uncle Hal—and Aunt Pat served spaghetti for supper. Spaghetti was an exotic treat in those days. Neither Doris nor I had ever eaten spaghetti, and none of the adults had enough experience to be good at it. All the good humor of Uncle Allen's house reawoke in my mind as I recalled the laughing arguments we had that night about the socially respectable method for moving spaghetti from plate to mouth.

8　　Suddenly I wanted to write about that, about the warmth and good feeling of it, but I wanted to put it down simply for my own joy, not for Mr. Fleagle. It was a moment I wanted to recapture and hold for myself. I wanted to relive the pleasure of an evening at New Street. To write it as I wanted, however, would violate all the rules of formal composition I'd learned in school, and Mr. Fleagle would surely give it a failing grade. Never mind. I would write something else for Mr. Fleagle after I had written this thing for myself.

9　　When I finished it the night was half gone and there was no time left to compose a proper, respectable essay for Mr. Fleagle. There was no choice next morning but to turn in my private reminiscence of Belleville. Two days passed before Mr. Fleagle returned the graded papers, and he returned everyone's but mine. I was bracing myself for a command to report to Mr. Fleagle immediately after school for discipline when I saw him lift my paper from his desk and rap for the class's attention.

10　　"Now, boys," he said, "I want to read you an essay. This is titled 'The Art of Eating Spaghetti.'"

11　　And he started to read. My words! He was reading my words out loud to the entire class. What's more, the entire class was listening. Listening attentively. Then somebody laughed, then the entire class was laughing, and not in contempt and ridicule, but with openhearted enjoyment. Even Mr. Fleagle stopped two or three times to repress a small prim smile.

12　　I did my best to avoid showing pleasure, but what I was feeling was pure ecstasy at this startling demonstration that my words had the power to make people laugh. In the eleventh grade, at the eleventh hour as it were, I had discovered a calling. It was the happiest moment of my entire school career. When Mr. Fleagle finished he put the final seal on my happiness by saying, "Now that, boys, is an essay, don't you see. It's—don't you see—it's the very essence of the essay, don't you see. Congratulations, Mr. Baker."

Vocabulary

Directions: Locate each of the key words in the reading selection. Then read and study each word in its context and try to determine its meaning. Use a dictionary or thesaurus to check your guess. Write the meanings of the words in the margin of the text.

Record the new words you've learned below.

Key Word	Paragraph	Meaning
1. grim	1	
2. prim	1	
3. listless	2	
4. dawdled	6	
5. reminiscence	9	
6. ecstasy	12	
7. calling	12	
Others?		

Guide Questions

Directions: The purpose of these guide questions is to ensure your understanding of what you have read. They also will help you to analyze and evaluate the author's ideas and apply them to the real world and your own life.

Write answers to the questions in your notebook or on a separate sheet of paper if your instructor wishes to collect them. Your answers will form the basis of class discussion.

1. a. In describing Mr. Fleagle, Baker uses the word *prim* over and over again. Surely you have been taught by your writing teachers not to constantly repeat words in your essays. Why does Baker do it here? What effect does it have on the reader?
   b. What other words or phrases are repeated in the story?
2. Describe your impression of Mr. Fleagle at the beginning of the story. Does your opinion of him change by the end? Explain.
3. When Mr. Fleagle first assigns the informal essay, Baker dreads having to write it. What makes him change his mind and get excited about writing an essay?
4. What does Baker mean when he says in the last paragraph "In the eleventh grade, at the eleventh hour as it were, I had discovered a calling"? Have you experienced a similar moment?

Application

Directions: Read the story below about the great Russian writer Anton Chekhov.

> Chekhov told the story of a kitten that was given to his uncle. Wanting to make a champion mouse-killer of the kitten, the uncle set out to train it when it was still very young. First he showed the kitten a live mouse in a cage. The kitten inspected the mouse curiously but without any hostility. The uncle, wanting the kitten to know the mouse was its enemy, slapped and scolded the kitten and sent it away in disgrace. The next day the uncle again showed the mouse to the kitten. This time the kitten looked at the mouse fearfully, but still did not show any signs of attack. Again the uncle slapped and scolded the kitten and sent it away. Day after day, the training went on until the kitten would begin to scream and cry the moment it saw the mouse. The uncle became furious and gave away the kitten, saying it would never learn. He did not realize that the kitten had indeed learned exactly what it had been taught. "I can sympathize with that kitten," said Chekhov, "because that same uncle tried to teach me Latin."

Describe your experience learning to write in elementary and high school. Was it similar to Russell Baker's experience? Or more like the experience of the kitten in Chekhov's story? Write one paragraph.

Writing

Directions: Write one or two paragraphs describing, as Baker does in his story, "the happiest moment of my entire school career."

Do you groan aloud when faced with the prospect of writing a personal letter? Does it seem like a burden and a chore? Or a pleasant opportunity to express yourself to a friend in a relaxed way? Why write a letter these days when it's so easy to pick up the telephone? How are letters and phone calls different? Would you rather have a call from an old friend or receive a letter? Garrison Keillor, the popular radio show host and writer, gives us some delightful insights on the value of letter writing, and some practical hints on how to write a good letter—"to be our own sweet selves, and express the music of our souls."

HOW TO WRITE A PERSONAL LETTER
Garrison Keillor

We shy persons need to write a letter now and then, or else we'll dry up and blow away. It's true. And I speak as one who loves to reach for the phone, dial the number, and talk. I say "Big Bopper here—what's shakin', babes?" The telephone is to shyness what Hawaii is to February, it's a way out of the woods, and yet: a letter is better. 1

Such a sweet gift—a piece of handmade writing, in an envelope that is not a bill, sitting in our friend's path when she trudges home from a long day spent among wahoos and savages, a day our words will help repair. They don't need to be immortal, just sincere. She can read them twice and again tomorrow: *You're someone I care about, Corinne, and think of often and every time I do you make me smile.* 2

We need to write, otherwise nobody will know who we are. They will have only a vague impression of us as A Nice Person, because frankly, we don't shine at conversation, we lack the confidence to thrust our faces forward and say, "Hi, I'm Heather Hooten, let me tell you about my week." Mostly we say "Uh-huh" and "Oh really." People smile and look over our shoulder, looking for someone else to talk to. 3

So a shy person sits down and writes a letter. To be known by another person— to meet and talk freely on the page—to be close despite distance. To escape from anonymity and be our own sweet selves and express the music of our souls. 4

Same thing that moves a giant rock star to sing his heart out in front of 123,000 people moves us to take ballpoint pen in hand and write a few lines to our dear Aunt Eleanor. *We want to be known.* We want her to know that we have fallen in love, that we quit our job, that we're moving to New York, and we want to say a few things that might not get said in casual conversation: *thank you for what you've meant to me, I am very happy right now.* 5

Skip the Guilt
The first step in writing letters is to get over the guilt of *not* writing. You don't "owe" anybody a letter. Letters are a gift. The burning shame you feel when you see unanswered mail makes it harder to pick up a pen and makes for a cheerless letter when you finally do. *I feel bad about not writing, but I've been so busy,* etc. Skip this. Few letters are obligatory, and they are *Thanks for the wonderful gift* and *I am* 6

terribly sorry to hear about George's death, and *Yes, you're welcome to stay with us next month,* and not many more than that. Write those promptly if you want to keep your friends. Don't worry about the others, except love letters, of course. When your true love writes *Dear Light of My Life, Joy of My Heart, O Lovely Pulsating Core of My Sensate Life,* some response is called for.

7   Some of the best letters are tossed off in a burst of inspiration, so keep your writing stuff in one place where you can sit down for a few minutes and *Dear Ray, I am in the middle of an essay for* International Paper *but thought I'd drop you a line. Hi to your sweetie too;* dash off a note to a pal. Envelopes, stamps, address book, everything in a drawer so you can write fast when the pen is hot.

8   A blank white 8″ by 11″ sheet can look as big as Montana if the pen's not so hot—try a smaller page and write boldly. Or use a note card with a piece of fine art on the front; if your letter ain't good, at least they get the Matisse. Get a pen that makes a sensuous line, get a comfortable typewriter, a friendly word processor— whichever feels easy to the hand.

9   Sit for a few minutes with the blank sheet in front of you, and meditate on the person you will write to, let your friend come to mind until you can almost see her or him in the room with you. Remember the last time you saw each other and how your friend looked and what you said and what perhaps was un- said between you, and when your friend becomes real to you, start to write.

Tell Us What You're Doing

10 Write the salutation—*Dear You*—and take a deep breath and plunge in. A simple declarative sentence will do, followed by another and another and another. Tell us what you're doing and tell it like you were talking to us. Don't think about grammar, don't think about lit'ry style, don't try to write dramatically, just give us your news. Where did you go? who did you see, what did they say, what do you think?

11   If you don't know where to begin, start with the present moment: *I'm sitting at the kitchen table on a rainy Saturday morning. Everyone is gone and the house is quiet.* Let your simple description of the present moment lead to something else, let the letter drift gently along.

Take It Easy

12 The toughest letter to crank out is one that is meant to impress, as we all know from writing job applications; if it's hard work to slip off a letter to a friend, maybe you're trying too hard to be terrific. A letter is only a report to someone who already likes you for reasons other than your brilliance. Take it easy.

13   Don't worry about form. It's not a term paper. When you come to the end of one episode, just start a new paragraph. You can go from a few lines about the sad state of rock 'n' roll to the fight with your mother to your fond memories of Mexico to your cat's urinary-tract infection to a few thoughts on personal indebtedness to the kitchen sink and what's in it. The more you write, the easier it gets, and when you have a True True Friend to write to, a *compadre,* a soul sibling, then it's

like driving a car down a country road, you just get behind the keyboard and press on the gas.

Don't tear up the page and start over when you write a bad line—try to write your way out of it. Make mistakes and plunge on. Let the letter cook along and let yourself be bold. Outrage, confusion, love—whatever is in your mind, let it find a way to the page. Writing is a means of discovery, always, and when you come to the end and write *Yours ever* or *Hugs and Kisses,* you'll know something you didn't when you wrote *Dear Pal.*   14

An Object of Art

Probably your friend will put your letter away, and it'll be read again a few years from now—and it will improve with age.   15

And forty years from now, your friend's grandkids will dig it out of the attic and read it, a sweet and precious relic of the ancient Nineties that gives them a sudden clear glimpse of you and her and the world we old-timers knew. You will then have created an object of art. Your simple lines about where you went, who you saw, what they said, will speak to those children and they will feel in their hearts the humanity of our times.   16

You can't pick up a phone and call the future and tell them about our times. You have to pick up a piece of paper.   17

Vocabulary

Directions: Locate each of the key words in the reading selection. Then read and study each word in its context and try to determine its meaning. Use a dictionary or thesaurus to check your guess. Write the meanings of the words in the margin of the text.

Record the new words you've learned.

Key Word	Paragraph	Meaning
1. trudges	2	
2. anonymity	4	
3. sensuous	8	
4. relic	16	
Others?		

Guide Questions

Directions: These questions will guide your understanding of what you have read. Write your answers in your notebook or on a separate sheet of paper if your instructor wishes to collect it. Your answers to these questions will be the basis of class discussion.

1. Garrison Keillor is probably America's best-known "shy person." Yet it seems that making a phone call or writing a letter is a pleasure for him. Why do you think that is true? If you are also a shy person, do you feel the same way that Keillor does about phoning and writing?
2. What does Keillor mean when he says in paragraph 8, "if your letter ain't good, at least they get the Matisse." Your answer must, of course, identify Matisse.
3. Summarize the hints Keillor gives for writing a good letter.
4. Look back over the selection. Note the many words that are printed in italic type. Italics are often used for emphasis, as in paragraph 5, where Keillor says with feeling, "We *want to be known.*" But why are italics used in other places, for example in paragraph 11, "*I'm sitting at the kitchen table...*"?

Application

Directions: In a small group, compare and contrast writing a letter to making a phone call. Discuss the advantages and disadvantages of each. Use the chart below to organize your ideas.

	Letters	**Phone Calls**
Advantages		
Disadvantages		

Writing

Directions: Choose one of the following assignments.

1. Write a letter to a friend you haven't seen for a long time. Use the advice Keillor gives you in this selection. At the end of the letter, write a paragraph describing how the advice helped you.
2. Using the advice Keillor gives in this essay, write a letter to one of your instructors. In your letter ask any questions you may have about any of

the topics in the course, the course itself, or school in general. You may have some comments you would like to express to the instructor that you prefer to do in writing rather than in person—use this letter as your opportunity to speak your mind. Your letter should be at least one page, preferably typewritten.

Marking Text

Mark this selection "How to Write a Personal Letter." Remember, marking text is explained on page 421.

Who would believe that a black South African boy so poor his family often had nothing to eat, who did not learn English until he was ten, who attended schools under the poorest possible conditions, would go on to graduate from an American university and write a best-selling autobiography? Here, Mark Mathabane, the author of Kaffir Boy, *tells how writing helped him to survive and to heal himself.*

KAFFIR BOY AT THE TYPEWRITER

Determination and a Creative Gift

Offer a Rescue from Hell

Mark Mathabane

1   I was born and raised in Alexandra township, a squalid one-square-mile ghetto just outside Johannesburg, South Africa, with a population of more than 150,000 blacks. The eldest of seven children—two boys and five girls—I lived with my parents and siblings in a shack made of crumbling bricks and rusted sheets of metal zinks. The shack measured roughly 15 × 15 feet. Till I was ten, my siblings and I slept on pieces of cardboard under the kitchen table. During the bitterly cold months of June and July my mother reinforced our flimsy blanket with pieces of old newspapers. My father, whose self-taught skills as a carpenter the Job Discrimination Act (an apartheid law) refused to recognize, earned about $10 a week as a menial laborer. He was often arrested for the "crime" of being unemployed.

2   Whenever my father was carted away to prison, the family, to stay alive, scavenged for half-eaten sandwiches thrown away by whites at the garbage dump. Sometimes we ate leech-like worms called *sonjas* or begged at the local abattoir for cattle blood, which we boiled as soup. During good times, our diet consisted mostly of cornmeal, chicken feet and heads, cattle intestines and greens. There were many days when nothing was available to eat, and we would simply stare at each other, at the empty pots, and at the sun going down.

3   My mother attempted to still our pangs of hunger with her mesmerizing storytelling. Her stories about black culture, traditions, magic, and heroes and heroines were the only books we had. By sharpening my sensibilities and firing my curiosity and imagination, these stories, almost Homeric in their vividness, drama, and invention, became the seeds of my own creativity.

4   To force blacks to leave Alexandra and move to their respective homelands—arid and impoverished reservations run by ruthless and corrupt tribal leaders—the government ordered the local *Peri-Urban* police to raid the ghetto frequently, making random arrests for Influx Control infractions. Under these Kafkaesque laws, my parents had to have a permit allowing them to live together as husband and wife under the same roof. They couldn't get it. So as a child I was awakened almost daily by brutal midnight police raids, which were launched amid a pandemonium of blaring sirens, barking dogs, and thumping feet. I would watch in horror as my parents were marched naked out of bed and interrogated in the middle of the shack.

Though illiterate, my mother, a woman of indomitable faith, courage, and   5
love, believed that an education might rescue me from the pit of poverty, suffering, and degradation into which I was born, and for all intents and purposes, into
which I was expected to die. The black educational system, known as *Bantu Education,* was designed in the '50s by Dr. H. Verwoerd, a fanatical believer in
apartheid. It was meant to reconcile us black children to our subjection and the
status quo, to keep us ignorant of our fundamental rights as human beings, and
to make us better servants of whites. That is why, on June 16, 1976, black students revolted against it.

My father was vehemently opposed to *Bantu Education*—partly because he   6
felt that it strained his meager wages at a time when survival was first priority;
partly because he saw many educated blacks working at menial jobs. It was left
to my mother to struggle almost singlehandedly to have me educated. Since
black education was not free or compulsory, it took her nearly six months to obtain the birth certificate and permits necessary to enroll me in the local tribal
school, which I refused to attend. On my first day of school, she and my grandmother had to literally bind me and drag me to school for the boys on the streets
had told me horror stories about teachers beating pupils for lacking books, uni-
forms, or school fees. My mother used food money to purchase me a slate and uniform, and to pay my school fees. This infuriated my father, who then beat my
mother. Witnessing my mother's abuse made me pledge to her that I would go to
school for as long as she wanted me to, despite the hardships of black education.
Through discipline, drive, and respect for teachers, I soon became the top student.

I began learning English, my fifth language, when I was about ten. When I   7
was eleven, my grandmother—who worked for a white family that didn't believe
in apartheid—took me to the white world for the first time in my life. I remember gaping with amazement at the large, beautiful homes with neat lawns
and beds of flowers, the many stores, the paved roads, the many cars, the neatly
dressed and happy-looking white schoolchildren, the tennis courts and swim-
ming pools. *Why is life for whites paradisiacal and for blacks hellish?* I began asking.
Granny's employer began giving me books that were only read in white schools.
These "revolutionary" books—*Treasure Island, David Copperfield,* and other
classics—changed my life. They convinced me that there was a world beyond
that of the violence, poverty, and suffering in which I was steeped. They helped
emancipate me from mental slavery and taught me to believe in my own worth
and abilities, despite apartheid's attempts to limit my aspirations and prescribe
my place in life.

When I was around thirteen, I began working for Granny's employer on   8
weekends. I mowed the lawn, washed cars, cleaned the pool, polished brass and
silver and shoes, and swept the driveway. One day I was given a slightly warped
tennis racket as extra payment for a day's work well done.

I took the racket back to the ghetto and began pounding balls against the   9
wall at the local stadium where there were a couple sand courts. In November
1973, nearly a year after I took up tennis, Arthur Ashe was finally allowed to set
foot on South African soil. Before that he had been *persona non grata* because of his

harsh criticism of apartheid. Like all black children in South Africa, I idolized black American athletes and entertainers, who, we assumed, were typical of blacks in America. I went to see Ashe play in Johannesburg, and he became my first positive role model. He was the first free black man I had ever seen. His intelligence, brilliant tennis skills, and confidence before whites filled me with a desire to come to America.

10   I realized that dream in 1977 when I met 1972 Wimbledon champion Stan Smith and his wife, Margie, during a tournament in which I was the only black playing. After listening to my life story, and my desire to attend college in America, Stan and Margie agreed to help. Upon returning to the States, Stan contacted college tennis coaches on my behalf. In the fall of 1978, I finally left South Africa on a full tennis scholarship to Limestone College in South Carolina.

11   Once in America, I realized how unrealistic my dream of becoming a professional athlete was. I began emphasizing my education. Culture shock, my refusal to allow coaches to exploit my athletic abilities at the expense of my education, and my desire to express my individuality rather than conform and blindly follow custom and authority, all combined to force me to transfer colleges three times, during which time I lost my scholarship and was supported by Stan Smith.

12   Shortly after transferring to Dowling College, my fourth school, I volunteered to become the first black editor of the college paper, even though I couldn't yet type properly. In life I have always taken risks. Working on the paper convinced me that, as my favorite novelist, Joseph Conrad, said, "The right accent and the right word can move the world." And his incredible story of not learning English until he was in his twenties, and of not writing a word until he was in his late thirties, inspired me to begin *Kaffir Boy*, especially since, a year earlier, I had become infected by the fiery eloquence of Richard Wright, and longed to write about black life in South Africa the way he wrote about black life in the South.

13   When I began writing *Kaffir Boy* one snowy winter morning during my junior year, when I was twenty-one, I hardly dreamed that my story would become a nationwide bestseller, reaching #1 on *The Washington Post* bestseller list and #3 on *The New York Times* list. I did not even think it would get published.

14   Many who heard that I was writing a book dismissed my attempt as futile. Some thought I was crazy. But I was undeterred. I was determined to prove them wrong. Though there were times when I despaired, when I thought of giving up, writing down the experiences that had once haunted me—the night I witnessed a grisly murder, the day I attempted suicide at age ten, the morning my mother and I discovered a dead baby while scavenging for food at the garbage dump (black mothers were sometimes driven to kill their babies so they would not lose their jobs)—gave me a feeling of being purged. I was finally able to fully accept who I was and where I came from. In short, I wrote to heal myself as well as inform others.

15   After graduating from Dowling College with a degree in economics, I wanted nothing more than to complete writing *Kaffir Boy*. I approached Stan Smith with the idea and he agreed to support me for a year while I completed the

book (under immigration laws, I wasn't allowed to work at the time). During this year of writing continuously, I was occasionally asked to speak publicly about my years in South Africa.

One day Oprah Winfrey saw the paperback version of *Kaffir Boy* prominently   16
displayed in a bookstore. She bought a copy. She was so moved by the story that she tracked me down and offered me an appearance on her show. When she learned that I had been separated from my family for nearly nine years, she helped bring several members to America. Our reunion on *Oprah* made nationwide headlines. Shortly thereafter the book became a bestseller in paperback, with more than 200,000 copies in print. It is required reading in many high schools across the nation. Most readers of *Kaffir Boy* wanted to know what happened to me and my family after I left South Africa in 1978. The results of those requests is *Kaffir Boy in America,* which was published in June [1989].

My advice to aspiring writers is never lose hope—keep writing and believ-   17
ing in yourself despite the rejection slips, despite what others may say. Something within compelled me to begin writing my book—an inner voice yearning to be heard; a need to understand myself and come to terms with my past; a longing to show the rest of the world the deplorable truths, in human terms, about the system of legalized segregation and racial discrimination in my homeland. Above all, I wanted to record how, through the support of my family, through clinging to the positive values I was taught when a child, through believing that education was a powerful weapon of hope, and through a determination never to give up the struggle to influence my own destiny, I was able to survive the raging hell of the ghetto with my soul and dignity largely intact.

Vocabulary

Directions: Locate each of the key words in the reading selection. Then read and study each word in its context and try to determine its meaning. Use a dictionary or thesaurus to check your guess. Write the meanings of the words in the margin of the text.

Record the new words you've learned below.

Key Word	Paragraph	Meaning
1. squalid	1	
2. scavenged	2	
3. mesmerizing	3	
4. pandemonium	4	
5. indomitable	5	
6. vehemently	6	

Key Word	Paragraph	Meaning
7. emancipate	7	
8. warped	8	
9. *persona non grata*	9	
10. eloquence	12	
11. deplorable	17	
Others?		

Guide Questions

Directions: The purpose of these guide questions is to ensure your understanding of what you have read. They also will help you to analyze and evaluate the author's ideas and apply them to the real world and your own life.

Write answers to the questions in your notebook or on a separate sheet of paper if your instructor wishes to collect them. Your answers will form the basis of class discussion.

1. Synthesize the information in the story with what you already know about South Africa and its system of apartheid. Paint a picture in words of life in South Africa for black people in the 1970s when Mathabane was growing up.
2. Describe the factors that helped Mathabane rise above what he describes as the "hell" of life in South Africa to become a success.
3. Mathabane describes such books as *Treasure Island* and *David Copperfield* as "revolutionary." Are these books considered "revolutionary" in the United States? Why do you think South Africa considered them "revolutionary"?
4. Mathabane tells us that entertainers and athletes like tennis star Arthur Ashe were assumed to be "typical of blacks in America." Why do you think he believed this? Was it true? Explain.
5. Mathabane says he wrote "to heal myself as well as to inform others." What does he mean by this?

Application

Directions: Mathabane makes allusions to several important writers in his story: Homer (in paragraph 3); Franz Kafka (in paragraph 4); Joseph Conrad (in paragraph 12); and Richard Wright (in paragraph 12). If you are not familiar with these men and their work, visit the library to learn about them. In small groups, discuss who they were and the importance of their work.

Writing

Directions: Does Mathabane's notion of the value of writing ring true to you? Can you imagine using writing to help yourself feel better? One study showed that college students who spent time writing about their thoughts and experiences had more positive feelings about school and fewer visits to the infirmary. Other studies found that writing can help people recover from personal tragedy. James Pennebaker, a professor of psychology at Southern Methodist University, says that "The act of writing helps label and organize stressful events, making them seem more manageable." Have you ever tried it? If you have, write a paragraph or two describing the experience and how you benefited from it.

If you have never tried it, try it now. Think about a problem you are currently struggling with. Write it down, describing it in detail. Then write as many possible solutions as you can to the problem. In your last few sentences, state whether this exercise helped you begin to solve the problem or made you feel better.

SHORT TAKE

Speaking Different Languages

Deborah Tannen

An American woman set out for a vacation cruise and landed in a Turkish prison. Reading her book *Never Pass This Way Again,* I could see that Gene LePere's ordeal was an extreme example of the disastrous consequences that can result from cross-cultural differences in what I term conversational style—ways of framing how you mean what you say, and what you think you are doing when you say it. LePere's experience also illustrates, in an unusually dramatic way, the dangers of trying to avoid conflict and say "no" in a polite way.

LePere left her cruise ship for a brief tour of ancient ruins in Turkey. At an archeological site, she fell behind her group as she became absorbed in admiring the ruins. Suddenly, her path was blocked by a man selling artifacts she had no interest in buying. Yet she found herself holding a stone head, and when she told him politely that she did not want it, he would not take it back. Instead, he thrust forward another one, which she also automatically accepted. Since the man would not take either head back, the only path to escape she could envision was offering to buy them. She cut his price in half and hoped he'd refuse so she could move on. Instead he agreed to drop the price, and she dropped the two heads into her tote. But as she handed him the money, he handed her a third head. Once more she insisted she did not want it, but he just stepped back to avoid repossessing it. Seeing no alternative, she paid for the third head and stalked off—shaken and angry.

When LePere tried to reboard her cruise ship, she showed her purchases to customs officials, who had her arrested and thrown into jail for trying to smuggle out a national treasure. The third head was a genuine antiquity.

Having lived in Greece and observed the verbal art of bargaining, I could see that talking to the vendor and saying she did not want the artifacts would mean to him that she might want them if the price were lower. If she really had no intention of buying, she would not have talked to him at all. She would have pushed her way past him and walked on, never establishing eye contact—and surely not taking possession of any heads, no matter how insistently he proffered them. Each time she accepted a head, he received evidence of her interest and encouragement to offer another. Each step in his increasingly aggressive sales pitch was a response to what likely appeared to him as her bargaining maneuvers. Refusing to look at or talk to him, or, as a last resort, placing the heads on the ground—these were unthinkable alternatives for a polite American woman.

COLLABORATIVE LEARNING

Working in Groups to Guide Your Own Reading

All of the reading selections so far in this unit have been accompanied by questions and exercises that are meant to help you understand and use what you've read. However, in much of your college reading (not to mention in your real life), you will be expected to master the material on your own.

Research has shown that one of the most effective ways to learn is in *groups*. In college, working with classmates can help you to master the material of a college course. The give-and-take that comes naturally when working with other people helps us to avoid falling into bad habits like *passive reading*. (We have all had the awful experience of reading a whole chapter, then realizing that we don't remember one single thing we've read.) Working with other students will help you to avoid such problems. For this assignment, form groups of approximately four students. In your group, read and think about the two following reading selections, "Rx: Translation, Please" by Perri Klass and "Translating America" by Chris Hedges. Then, create your own vocabulary chart, guide questions, and application and writing assignments.

Follow these steps to complete the assignment:

1. Preview the selection before you read—look at and think about the title, any headings or subheadings, the first paragraph, the last paragraph, and the first sentence of each paragraph.
2. Read through the selection one time quickly.
3. Read the selection a second time, more carefully. This time mark the text. Review how to do this by turning to page 421, "Learning Strategy III—Marking Text."
4. Brainstorm with your group. Ask yourselves: What important issues is the author discussing? What new information did you learn? Can the issues discussed in the selection be connected to those you have already studied? Can any of the information here be applied to situations in your own life?
5. Now, create a set of exercises similar to those you have completed in previous chapters of this book:
   a. **Vocabulary.** Make a list of key words from the text. Set them up in chart format as on page 144.
   b. **Guide Questions.** Write questions that will guide understanding of the major ideas in the reading.
   c. **Application.** Prepare an application exercise that takes one or more of the important ideas in the reading and relates it to real life.
   d. **Writing.** Create a writing assignment to conclude the chapter.

Before you begin, it would be a good idea to review the questions and exercises in the previous reading selections in this book for reference.

When you are finished, submit your work to your instructor. Your instructor may review and combine the work of all the groups and return the exercise to the class. You will then have the opportunity to *answer* the questions you and your classmates have developed.

Now, use your skills as an active independent reader to tackle the following reading selections. Good luck!

Perri Klass is both a doctor and a writer, so it is only natural she would take an interest in the special language of medicine. Many professions have their own jargon (if you have ever spent an evening with a group of computer specialists you know what true loneliness is), but Klass illustrates that the special idiom of medicine is especially fascinating—as well as confusing, frightening, useful, and . . . seductive.

RX: TRANSLATION, PLEASE?

Perri Klass

"Mrs. Tolstoy is your basic L.O.L. in N.A.D., admitted for a soft rule-out M.I.," the intern announces. I scribble that on my patient list. In other words Mrs. Tolstoy is a Little Old Lady in No Apparent Distress who is in the hospital to make sure she hasn't had a heart attack (rule out a myocardial infarction). And we think it's unlikely that she has had a heart attack (a *soft* rule-out). 1

If I learned nothing else during my first three months of working in the hospital as a medical student, I learned endless jargon and abbreviations. I started out in a state of primeval innocence, in which I didn't even know that "s̄ C.P., S.O.B., N/V" meant "without chest pain, shortness of breath, or nausea and vomiting." By the end I took the abbreviations so for granted that I would complain to my mother the English professor, "And can you believe I had to put down *three* NG tubes last night?" 2

"You'll have to tell me what an NG tube is if you want me to sympathize properly," my mother said. NG, nasogastric—isn't it obvious? 3

I picked up not only the specific expressions but also the patterns of speech and the grammatical conventions; for example, you never say that a patient's blood pressure fell or that his cardiac enzymes rose. Instead, the patient is always the subject of the verb: "He dropped his pressure." "He bumped his enzymes." This sort of construction probably reflects that profound irritation of the intern when the nurses come in the middle of the night to say that Mr. Dickinson has disturbingly low blood pressure. "Oh, he's gonna hurt me bad tonight," the intern may say, inevitably angry at Mr. Dickinson for dropping his pressure and creating a problem. 4

When chemotherapy fails to cure Mrs. Bacon's cancer, what we say is, "Mrs. Bacon failed chemotherapy." 5

"Well, we've already had one hit today, and we're up next, but at least we've got mostly stable players on our team." This means that our team (group of doctors and medical students) has already gotten one new admission today, and it is our turn again, so we'll get whoever is next admitted in emergency, but at least most of the patients we already have are fairly stable, that is, unlikely to drop their pressures or in any other way get suddenly sicker and hurt us bad. Baseball metaphor is pervasive: a no-hitter is a night without any new admissions. A player is always a patient—a nitrate player is a patient on nitrates, a unit player is a patient in the intensive-care unit, and so on, until you reach the terminal player. 6

It is interesting to consider what it means to be winning, or doing well, in this perennial baseball game. When the intern hangs up the phone and announces, 7

"I got a hit," that is not cause for congratulations. The team is not scoring points; rather, it is getting hit, being bombarded with new patients. The object of the game from the point of view of the doctors, considering the players for whom they are already responsible, is to get as few new hits as possible.

8 These special languages contribute to a sense of closeness and professional spirit among people who are under a great deal of stress. As a medical student, it was exciting for me to discover that I'd finally cracked the code, that I could understand what doctors said and wrote and could use the same formulations myself. Some people seem to become enamored of the jargon for its own sake, perhaps because they are so deeply thrilled with the idea of medicine, with the idea of themselves as doctors.

9 I knew a medical student who was referred to by the interns on the team as Mr. Eponym because he was so infatuated with eponymous terminology,* the more obscure the better. He never said "capillary pulsation" if he could say "Quincke's pulses." He would lovingly tell over the multinamed syndromes— Wolff–Parkinson–White, Lown–Ganong–Levine, Henoch–Schonlein—until the temptation to suggest Schleswig–Holstein or Stevenson–Kefauver or Baskin–Robbins became irresistible to his less reverent colleagues.

10 And there is the jargon that you don't ever want to hear yourself using. You know that your training is changing you, but there are certain changes you think would be going a little too far.

11 The resident was describing a man with devastating terminal pancreatic cancer. "Basically he's C.T.D.," the resident concluded. I reminded myself that I had resolved not to be shy about asking when I didn't understand things. "C.T.D.?" I asked timidly.

12 The resident smirked at me. "Circling The Drain."

13 The images are vivid and terrible. "What happened to Mrs. Melville?"

14 "Oh, she boxed last night." To box is to die, of course.

15 Then there are the more pompous locutions that can make the beginning medical student nervous about the effects of medical training. A friend of mine was told by his resident, "A pregnant woman with sickle-cell represents a failure of genetic counseling."

16 Mr. Eponym, who tried hard to talk like the doctors, once explained to me, "An infant is basically a brainstem preparation." A brainstem preparation, as used in neurological research, is an animal whose higher brain functions have been destroyed so that only the most primitive reflexes remain, like the sucking reflex, the startle reflex, and the rooting reflex.

17 The more extreme forms aside, one most important function of medical jargon is to help doctors maintain some distance from their patients. By reformulating a patient's pain and problems into a language that the patient doesn't even speak, I suppose we are in some sense taking those pains and problems under our jurisdiction and also reducing their emotional impact. This linguistic separation

---

* *Eponymous* means "named after"—in this case, diseases or syndromes are named after the scientists who discovered them.

between doctors and patients allows conversations to go on at the bedside that are unintelligible to the patient. "Naturally, we're worried about adeno-C.A.," the intern can say to the medical student, and lung cancer need never be mentioned.

I learned a new language this past summer. At times it thrills me to hear myself using it. It enables me to understand my colleagues, to communicate effectively in the hospital. Yet I am uncomfortably aware that I will never again notice the peculiarities and even atrocities of medical language as keenly as I did this summer. There may be specific expressions I manage to avoid, but even as I remark on them, promising myself I will never use them, I find that this language is becoming my professional speech. It no longer sounds strange in my ears—or coming from my mouth. And I am afraid that, as with any new language, to use it properly you must absorb not only the vocabulary but also the structure, the logic, the attitudes. At first you may notice these new alien assumptions every time you put together a sentence, but with time and increased fluency you stop being aware of them at all. And as you lose that awareness, for better or for worse, you move closer and closer to being a doctor instead of just talking like one.

18

Vocabulary

Directions: Mark any important words in the reading selection that you don't know. Then list them in the chart below along with their paragraph numbers. Try to figure out each word's meaning by reading over the context carefully for clues to help you guess the meaning of the unfamiliar word. Check your dictionary or thesaurus to confirm your guess. After you discuss the words with your group members, write the meanings in the margin of the text, near the word. Then enter them in the chart.

Key Word	Paragraph	Meaning

Guide Questions

Directions: Develop a list of questions that elicit the important ideas in the reading selection. Start at the beginning and work your way sequentially through the text until you have addressed all of the author's major ideas.

Application

Directions: When you have a list of guide questions, read through the selection again. This time, write one or more questions that require the application of the information in the text to a situation in the real world.

Writing

Directions: Your last task is to prepare a writing assignment. For example, you might ask for a paragraph in which the writer comments on the ideas in the reading selection. You might also ask for a summary of the selection.

This article, which appeared in The New York Times, *points out one of the less-noted features of immigration: the newcomers often do not speak English. As most grown-ups are painfully aware, it is very difficult to learn a new language as an adult. On the other hand, children soak up their new language like a sponge, leaving them to assume the difficult role of translator in their families. This story focuses on an elementary school in Queens, New York.*

TRANSLATING AMERICA

Chris Hedges

It was an elementary school summit meeting. Crammed around the low table in the first-grade classroom sat the parents (fidgeting nervously), the principal, the first-grade teacher, the speech therapist and the 11-year-old translator, who had been hauled out of her sixth-grade class for the meeting.   1

The news was not unexpected. Eduardo Barros, who like nearly 80 percent of the incoming students in Public School 139 arrived speaking no English, needed to spend another year in first grade to improve his language and comprehension skills.   2

"Mommy," said Edda Barros, who translated the news about her brother to her parents, "they are saying that Eduardo has too much trouble reading and understanding. They do not want to put him in second grade and then move him back down. It is better if he does another year."   3

Edda's was not an unfamiliar role. She accompanies her parents, who were born in Ecuador, to the bank, to the doctor and on shopping trips, as well as to all school functions. It is her job to make sure her brother understands and completes his homework and to riffle through electric and gas bills, business letters, rent notices and school and community announcements. Edda's cousins, some in their 20's, often call with questions about English phrasing. One, who is 30, has used her help to get through a computer course. After learning about American traditions for holidays like Thanksgiving and Easter, Edda explained the customs to her family and insisted that her mother stuff and bake a turkey in November and hide candy eggs around the apartment in April.   4

Like millions of young children in immigrant families, Edda is much more than a translator for first-generation parents who speak little English. She interprets American culture, customs and mores for her parents, at times gently correcting and advising them. She plays a vital and at times nerve-racking role, navigating the complex and intimidating world of hospitals, law offices and officialdom. One slip, she knows, could mean disaster.   5

She assumes, as do more than half the students in her class, responsibilities and duties usually left to parents in English-speaking families. Along the way, she must listen to unvarnished and unsettling accounts of her father's illnesses and looming financial difficulties. It can be, she says, overwhelming.   6

"There are times, especially with doctors, when I have no idea what they are talking about," Edda said in English, seated in her Queens apartment with her parents.   7

"But I have to translate something. My parents rely on me. I have to keep asking and asking what it means, what they are talking about. And sometimes l have my own life, my own work to do, but I have to stop to help my brother or leave to go with mother or father. It is tiring."

8   Teachers and administrators in schools like P.S. 139, where 36 different languages are spoken and 77 of the 100 children in kindergarten come from homes in which the parents speak a foreign language, say young children must often mediate with parents to get them to conform to American society. And each new hurdle loads more onto the children.

9   "It is often too much for their fragile nervous systems," said Khanna Borukhov, a teacher in the English as a Second Language program at P.S. 139.

10   "They want to be leaders, but they do not have the capacity. They struggle to validate themselves, going from family appointment to family appointment. It leads to a kind of role reversal. Parents can begin to resent the power the child assumes. The parent wants to be a parent and the child wants to be a child, but because of the circumstances they cannot. With all that pressure it is hard for the child to function academically."

11   Dr. Gary D. Goldenback, the supervisor of the E.S.L. program for District 28, which includes P.S. 139, says that when children are taken out of school to accompany parents to appointments or on routine chores, the missed classes can affect homework and test scores.

12   "When this is done excessively, it can even harm chances for promotion," he said. "One should remember that some of these parents do not even have the English facility to buy a subway token or ask directions, so they must take the child along.

13   Conflict often comes in later years, when parents try to reclaim the authority they have ceded.

14   "This has contributed to the gang culture," said Frayda Sharaby, an E.S.L. teacher at P.S. 139. "These older children look for other avenues where they can again exercise authority."

15   Conflict also often erupts around benign and simple tasks. Many immigrant parents will not sign school permission slips or allow their children to go on overnight trips.

16   "A lot of these families live in fear of deportation," said Dr. Goldenback. "They fear that something could happen to the child if they sign anything, even a report card. At school, a child may be told every day to get his parents to sign a slip, and at home, his parents may be steadfastly refusing to cooperate. It is a lot of pressure."

17   And there is pressure on these students to Americanize their parents. "Bangladeshi women will typically not leave their homes, day or night, unescorted," said Dr. Goldenback. "The school can call, say a child is sick, but it does not mean the mother can come. She may have to wait for her husband. What looks like negligence is not."

18   Just as parents fight to grasp the new world, teachers fight to comprehend the old. Discussions about summer camps, for example, have disturbed children

from the former Yugoslavia, where families were held in detention centers. Simple rituals, such as fire drills, have sent some children into hysterics.

"We had a child who thought we were being bombed," said Steven C. Rosenberg, the principal of P.S. 139.   19

And school officials, as well as parents, can become perplexed by it all.   20

Cristina Chin, the co-president of the P.S. 139 parents' association, said she resorted at one point to speaking with a parent in an improvised sign language. And Mr. Rosenberg's best efforts to bridge the language gap have sometimes backfired. "I brought a boy in the office to help translate for a couple that did not speak English," he said. "He listened and told me, 'That's not my kind of Chinese.'"   21

Classrooms must also adjust to new traditions, such as allowing Muslims to skip lunch during Ramadan, and new cultural sensitivities.   22

BREAKDOWN

Melting Pot

Primary home language of students attending Public School 139 in Queens.

	Number of Students		Number of Students
Russian	200	Ukrainian	5
English	189	Bengali	4
Spanish	174	Polish	4
Mandarin	53	Portuguese	4
Cantonese	44	Georgian	3
Korean	40	Serbo-Croatian	3
Hindi	30	French	2
Chinese, other or unidentified dialects	21	Japanese	2
Pilipino	10	Khoisan	2
Hebrew	8	Czech	1
Indonesian	8	French-Khmer	1
Romanian	8	Greek	1
Urdu	8	Hungarian	1
Dari/Farsi/Persian	7	Malayalam	1
Albanian	6	Sinhalese	1
Arabic	6	Slovenian	1
Bulgarian	6	Tamil	1
Gujarati	5	Yonba	1

Source: P.S. 139 Queens

23   "I had a child from Iran in my class," said Ms. Sharaby, the E.S.L. teacher. "One day Mitre did something I perceived as brilliant. I said it was not just one thumb up, but two thumbs up. She fell to the floor laughing." The thumbs up sign, it turns out, is a foul insult in Iran.

24   The new wave of immigrants is so diverse that it is also impossible to keep up with the plethora of languages, even in schools such as P.S. 139, where teachers or administsrators speak Spanish, Korean and Russian.

25   The parents-night meetings are broken down into clusters, so children can translate what is being discussed. Newsletters go out in Russian, Spanish, Korean and Chinese, in an effort to reach at least some of the community in their own tongue. And teachers, dizzy with the infusion of cultures, customs and languages, look for ways to make the American experience relevant.

26   "How are the Pilgrims like Russians?" Jackie A. Neuwirt, the first grade teacher in classroom 1-229, asked her pupils one morning last week.

27   Mrs. Neuwirt, whose parents did not speak English when they arrived in Queens in 1959 from Israel, explained to her pupils that the Russians came to the United States to escape religious persecution and find freedom. She pointed to a bulletin board in her classroom labeled "We are the children of the world" that had 15 figures, labeled with names of countries like Peru, Azerbaijan, Nepal and Taiwan, that represented the cultural backgrounds of her 20 students.

28   "How many other people came for this reason?" she asked.

29   The music teacher at P.S. 139, Fern Nash, has the school choral group do songs in Spanish, Portuguese, Russian, Yiddish, French, Korean, German and Mandarin.

30   "We incorporate the school's diversity into the program," she said. "I have Chinese kids who know songs in Yiddish and have danced in Indian costumes. It is all here."

31   Years later, some who assumed the role of interlocutors say it was not only burdensome but uncomfortable.

32   Mrs. Neuwirt's sister, Zeporah Brecker-Gonzalez, a fifth-grade teacher at John I. Smith Elementary in Miami, remembers what it felt like to be the family translator.

33   "I was often embarrassed that my parents could not speak English or assimiliate," she said. "I wanted to be just like the other kids. I wanted to be an American."

34   One way she rebelled was by refusing to respond in Hebrew when her parents spoke to her. Despite the family tensions, she said she believed she was a stronger person for the experience.

35   "They could not help me with my homework," she said of her parents. "I had to do it myself. I could not depend on them to help me as much as other parents that spoke English. It made me more self-reliant than other children."

Vocabulary

Directions: Mark any important words in the reading selection that you don't know. Then list them in the following chart along with their paragraph numbers. Try to figure out each word's meaning by reading over the context carefully for clues to help you guess the meaning of the unfamiliar word. Check your dictionary or thesaurus to confirm your guess. After you discuss the words with your group members, write the meanings in the margin of the text, near the word. Then enter them in the chart.

Key Word	Paragraph	Meaning

Guide Questions
Directions: Develop a list of questions that elicit the important ideas in the reading selection. Start at the beginning and work your way sequentially through the text until you have addressed all of the author's major ideas.

Application
Directions: When you have a list of guide questions, read through the selection again. This time write one or more questions that require the application of the information in the text to a situation in the real world.

Writing
Directions: Your last task is to prepare a writing assignment. For example, you might ask for a paragraph in which the writer comments on the ideas in the reading selection. You might also ask for a summary of the selection.

SPECIAL PROJECT

LANGUAGE

A Personal Mini-Dictionary

Many of the new words you will encounter in your college reading will not be words used in everyday speaking and writing. Rather, they will be specific to your major field of study, to your future career. For example, terms such as *double-entry system, trial balance,* and *amortization* are generally used in the accounting field and not by the general public. Science and technology abound with vocabulary unique to their fields. For example, *hardware, software, boot,* and *byte* are words used in the computer field.

For this project you will create a mini-dictionary of words you need to know in your major field. Find the words in newspapers or magazines, not in your textbooks or dictionaries. For example, if you are a business major, you should be reading a periodical such as *The Wall Street Journal* and one of the major business journals. When you come across a technical term you don't know, enter it in your mini-dictionary according to the following format:

WORD:

DEFINITION:

CONTEXT SENTENCE:

SOURCE:

1. Enter the word.
2. Write the definition of the word. Try to figure out the definition by using the context. If you can't, use a dictionary. If the word is not in the dictionary, you will have to consult a professional dictionary or ask a teacher or someone in the field.
3. Copy the context sentence from the newspaper, periodical, or other source.
4. Name the source of the word—that is, the name of the magazine or newspaper where you found the word.

Follow this procedure for at least ten words each week.

UNIT FOUR

READING AND THINKING ABOUT WORK AND THE WORLD OF BUSINESS

Working hours are never long enough. Each day is a holiday and ordinary holidays . . . are grudged as enforced interruptions in an absorbing vacation.

—Winston Churchill

Thinking about Working

Before you begin to read about the world of work, take a few minutes to consider your own attitudes toward working. Read the questions below, think about them, then write down answers. Write freely—there are no "right" or "wrong" answers.

1. Consider former British Prime Minister Winston Churchill's attitude toward work (in the above quotation). Write a sentence or two summarizing how you feel about working.
2. What factors about a job can make you feel happy and satisfied?
3. What factors will enable you to achieve success in your career?
4. If you are unhappy or dissatisfied with your job, what can you do to change things (besides quit)?
5. If you had enough money so that you did not need to work, would you work anyway? Why or why not?
6. Imagine it is your retirement day. What would be the one thing you would want to be able to say about your job? About yourself?

The first day on the job can be terrifying, but imagine how very terrifying it would be if another person's life depended on you doing that job, and doing it right, the first time! In this frightening, comical, and touching chapter from his book The Making of a Surgeon, *doctor and writer William Nolen tells of his first day on the job—as a surgeon.*

THE FIRST APPENDECTOMY

William A. Nolen, M.D.

1   The patient, or better, victim, of my first major surgical venture was a man I'll call Mr. Polansky. He was fat, he weighed one hundred and ninety pounds and was five feet eight inches tall. He spoke only broken English. He had had a sore abdomen with all the classical signs and symptoms of appendicitis for twenty-four hours before he came to Bellevue.

2   After two months of my internship, though I had yet to do anything that could be decently called an "operation," I had had what I thought was a fair amount of operating time. I'd watched the assistant residents work, I'd tied knots, cut sutures, and even, in order to remove a skin lesion, made an occasional incision. Frankly, I didn't think that surgery was going to be too damn difficult. I figured I was ready, and I was chomping at the bit to go, so when Mr. Polansky arrived I greeted him like a long-lost friend. He was overwhelmed at the interest I showed in his case. He probably couldn't understand why any doctor should be so fascinated by a case of appendicitis: wasn't it a common disease? It was just as well that he didn't realize my interest in him was so personal. He might have been frightened, and with good reason.

3   At any rate, I set some sort of record in preparing Mr. Polansky for surgery. He had arrived on the ward at four o'clock. By six I had examined him, checked his blood and urine, taken his chest x-ray and had him ready for the operating room.

4   George Walters, the senior resident on call that night, was to "assist" me during the operation. George was older than the rest of us. I was twenty-five at this time and he was thirty-two. He had taken his surgical training in Europe and was spending one year as a senior resident in an American hospital to establish eligibility for the American College of Surgeons. He had had more experience than the other residents and it took a lot to disturb his equanimity in the operating room. As it turned out, this made him the ideal assistant for me.

5   It was ten o'clock when we wheeled Mr. Polansky to the operating room. At Bellevue, at night, only two operating rooms were kept open—there were six or more going all day—so we had to wait our turn. In the time I had to myself before the operation I had reread the section on appendectomy in the *Atlas of Operative Technique* in our surgical library, and had spent half an hour tying knots on the bedpost in my room. I was, I felt, "ready."

6   I delivered Mr. Polansky to the operating room and started an intravenous going in his arm. Then I left him to the care of the anesthetist. I had ordered a

sedative prior to surgery, so Mr. Polansky was drowsy. The anesthetist, after checking his chart, soon had him sleeping.

Once he was asleep I scrubbed the enormous expanse of Mr. Polansky's abdomen for ten minutes. Then, while George placed the sterile drapes, I scrubbed my own hands for another five, mentally reviewing each step of the operation as I did so. Donning gown and gloves I took my place on the right side of the operating-room table. The nurse handed me the scalpel. I was ready to begin. 7

Suddenly my entire attitude changed. A split second earlier I had been supremely confident; now, with the knife finally in my hand, I stared down at Mr. Polansky's abdomen and for the life of me could not decide where to make the incision. The "landmarks" had disappeared. There was too much belly. 8

George waited a few seconds, then looked up at me and said, "'Go ahead." 9
"What?" I asked. 10
"Make the incision," said George. 11
"Where?" I asked. 12
"Where?" 13
"Yes," I answered, "where?" 14
"Why, here, of course," said George and drew an imaginary line on the abdomen with his fingers. 15

I took the scalpel and followed where he had directed. I barely scratched Mr. Polansky. 16

"Press a little harder," George directed. I did. The blade went through the skin to a depth of perhaps one-sixteenth of an inch. 17

"Deeper," said George. 18
There are five layers of tissue in the abdominal wall: skin, fat, fascia (a tough membranous tissue), muscle, and peritoneum (the smooth, glistening, transparent inner lining of the abdomen). I cut down into the fat. Another sixteenth of an inch. 19

"Bill," said George, looking up at me, "this patient is big. There's at least three inches of fat to get through before we even reach the fascia. At the rate you're going we won't be into the abdomen for another four hours. For God's sake, will you cut?" 20

I made up my mind not to be hesitant. I pressed down hard on the knife, and suddenly we were not only through the fat but through the fascia as well. 21

"Not that hard," George shouted, grabbing my right wrist with his left hand while with his other hand he plunged a gauze pack into the wound to stop the bleeding. "Start clamping," he told me. 22

The nurse handed us hemostats and we applied them to the numerous vessels I had so hastily opened. "All right," George said, "start tying." 23

I took the ligature material from the nurse and began to tie off the vessels. Or rather, I tried to tie off the vessels, because suddenly my knot-tying proficiency had melted away. The casual dexterity I had displayed on the bedpost a short hour ago was nowhere in evidence. My fingers, greasy with fat, simply would not perform. My ties slipped off the vessels, the sutures snapped in my 24 fingers, at one point I even managed to tie the end of my rubber glove into the wound. It was, to put it bluntly, a performance in fumbling that would have made Robert Benchley blush.

25   Here I must give my first paean of praise to George. His patience during the entire performance was nothing short of miraculous. The temptation to pick up the catgut and do the tying himself must have been strong. He could have tied off all the vessels in two minutes. It took me twenty.

26   Finally we were ready to proceed. "Now," George directed, "split the muscle. But gently, please."

27   I reverted to my earlier tack. Fiber by fiber I spread the muscle which was the last layer but one that kept us from the inside of the abdomen. Each time I separated the fibers and withdrew my clamp, the fibers rolled together again. After five minutes I was no nearer the appendix than I had been at the start.

28   George could stand it no longer. But he was apparently afraid to suggest I take a more aggressive approach, fearing I would stick the clamp into, or possibly through, the entire abdomen. Instead he suggested that he help me by spreading the muscle in one direction while I spread it in the other. I made my usual infinitesimal attack on the muscle. In one fell swoop George spread the rest.

29   "Very well done," he complimented me. "Now let's get in."

30   We each took a clamp and picked up the tissue-paper-thin peritoneum. After two or three hesitant attacks with the scalpel I finally opened it. We were in the abdomen.

31   "Now," said George, "put your fingers in, feel the cecum (the portion of the bowel to which the appendix is attached) and bring it into the wound."

32   I stuck my right hand into the abdomen. I felt around—but what was I feeling? I had no idea.

33   It had always looked so simple when the senior resident did it. Open the abdomen, reach inside, pull up the appendix. Nothing to it. But apparently there was.

34   Everything felt the same to me. The small intestine, the large intestine, the cecum—how did one tell them apart without seeing them? I grabbed something and pulled it into the wound. Small intestine. No good. Put it back. I grabbed again. This time it was the sigmoid colon. Put it back. On my third try I had the small intestine again.

35   "The appendix must be in an abnormal position," I said to George. "I can't seem to find it."

36   "Mind if I try?" he asked.

37   "Not at all," I answered. "I wish you would."

38   Two of his fingers disappeared into the wound. Five seconds later they emerged, cecum between them, with the appendix flopping from it.

39   "Stuck down a little," he said kindly. "That's probably why you didn't feel it. It's a hot one," he added. "Let's get at it."

40   The nurse handed me the hemostats, and one by one I applied them to the mesentery of the appendix—the veil of tissue in which the blood vessels run. With George holding the veil between his fingers I had no trouble; I took the

ligatures and tied the vessels without a single error. My confidence was coming back.

"Now," George directed, "put in your purse string." (The cecum is a portion 41
of the bowel which has the shape of half a hemisphere. The appendix projects
from its surface like a finger. In an appendectomy the routine procedure is to tie
the appendix at its base and cut it off a little beyond the tie. Then the remaining
stump is inverted into the cecum and kept there by tying the purse-string stitch.
This was the stitch I was now going to sew.)

It went horribly. The wall of the cecum is not very thick—perhaps one-   42
eighth of an inch. The suture must be placed deeply enough in the wall so that
it won't cut through when tied, but not so deep as to pass all the way through the
wall. My sutures were alternately too superficial or too deep, but eventually I got
the job done.

"All right," said George, "let's get the appendix out of here. Tie off the base."   43
I did.   44
"Now cut off the appendix."   45

At least in this, the definitive act of the operation, I would be decisive. I took   46
the knife and with one quick slash cut through the appendix—too close to the
ligature.

"Oh oh, watch it," said George. "That tie is going to slip."   47
It did. The appendiceal stump lay there, open. I felt faint.   48
"Don't panic," said George. "We've still got the purse string. I'll push the   49
stump in—you pull up the stitch and tie. That will take care of it."

I picked up the two ends of the suture and put in the first stitch. George   50
shoved the open stump into the cecum. It disappeared as I snugged my tie.
Beautiful.

"Two more knots," said George. "Just to be safe."   51

I tied the first knot and breathed a sigh of relief. The appendiceal stump re-   52
mained out of sight. On the third knot—for the sake of security—I pulled a little tighter. The stitch broke; the open stump popped up; the cecum disappeared
into the abdomen. I broke out in a cold sweat and my knees started to crumble.

Even George momentarily lost his composure. "For Christ's sake, Bill," he   53
said, grasping desperately for the bowel, "what did you have to do that for?" The
low point of the operation had been reached.

By the time we had retrieved the cecum, Mr. Polansky's peritoneal cavity had   54
been contaminated. My self-confidence was shattered. And still George let me
continue. True, he all but held my hand as we retied and resutured, but the in-
struments were in my hand.

The closure was anticlimactic. Once I had the peritoneum sutured, things   55
went reasonably smoothly. Two hours after we began, the operation was over.
"Nice job," George said, doing his best to sound sincere.

"Thanks," I answered, lamely.   56
The scrub nurse laughed.   57
Mr. Polansky recovered, I am happy to report, though not without a long and   58
complicated convalescence. His bowel refused to function normally for two

weeks and he became enormously distended. He was referred to at our nightly conferences as "Dr. Nolen's pregnant man." Each time the reference was made, it elicited a shudder from me.

59   During his convalescence I spent every spare moment I could at Mr. Polansky's bedside. My feelings of guilt and responsibility were overwhelming. If he had died I think I would have given up surgery for good.

Vocabulary

Directions: Find each of the key words in the reading selection. Study each word in its context and try to determine its meaning. Write what you think it means in the margin of the text, near the word. Then read over the sentence, mentally substituting your guess for the key word. Does the sentence still make sense? Does it retain its original meaning? If it does, you've probably figured out the meaning of the key word correctly. In any case confirm your guess by checking a dictionary or thesaurus.

If you take your meaning from the dictionary or thesaurus, be sure the definition contains words you already know and feel comfortable using. If it doesn't, you will be worse off than when you started—you will have begun with one word you didn't know and ended with *two* words you don't know!

Record the new words you've learned below.

Key Word	Paragraph	Meaning
1. chomping at the bit	2	
2. equanimity	4	
3. donning	7	
4. dexterity	24	
5. infinitesimal	28	
6. contaminated	54	
7. distended	58	
8. convalescence	59	
Others?		

Guide Questions

Directions: The purpose of these questions is to guide your analysis of the text. Your thoughtful answers will ensure that you have understood the main ideas the author wanted to convey. Some of the questions require that you simply find the stated facts in the reading selection; others will ask you to do more difficult tasks, such as paraphrasing information (putting the author's ideas into your own words), synthesizing several ideas into one complex thought, evaluating (making judgments about) an idea, or taking information from the reading and applying it to a new situation or to your own life.

Write answers to the questions in your notebook or on a separate sheet of paper if your instructor wishes to collect them. Your answers will form the basis of class discussion.

1. Dr. Nolen had studied hard and prepared abundantly for the appendectomy. Why do you think he had so much trouble when the time came to actually do the job?
2. Why do you think George (Dr. Walters) allowed Nolen to continue when he was making such a mess of things?
3. The story of the operation has many elements of humor despite the tone of nervousness, even terror. Cite a few points in the narrative that are funny.
4. How do you think Nolen's next operation went?

Application

Directions: In small groups, discuss a point in your life when you did something for a terrifying "first time"—your first day on a job, or perhaps the first time you drove a car, or gave a speech.

Writing

Directions: Choose one of the writing assignments below.

1. Using the ideas you generated in the Application exercise above, write a story describing your first time, using "The First Appendectomy" as a model. Write at least 250 words.
2. Rewrite the story "The First Appendectomy" from the perspective of either the scrub nurse or George. Write at least 250 words.

K. C. Cole is a writer who devotes herself mainly to science and women's issues. In this essay, which first appeared in The New York Times *in 1981, she explores the reasons that very few women choose science as a career.*

WOMEN IN SCIENCE

K. C. Cole

1   I know few other women who do what I do. What I do is write about science, mainly physics. And to do that, I spend a lot of time reading about science, talking to scientists, and struggling to understand physics. In fact, most of the women (and men) I know think me quite queer for actually liking physics. "How can you write about that stuff?" they ask, always somewhat askance. "I could never understand that in a million years." Or more simply, "I hate science."

2   I didn't realize what an odd creature a woman interested in physics was until a few years ago when a science magazine sent me to Johns Hopkins University in Baltimore for a conference on an electrical phenomenon known as the Hall effect. We sat in a huge lecture hall and listened as physicists talked about things engineers didn't understand, and engineers talked about things physicists didn't understand. What *I* didn't understand was why, out of several hundred young students of physics and engineering in the room, less than a handful were women.

3   Sometime later, I found myself at the California Institute of Technology reporting on the search for the origins of the universe. I interviewed physicist after physicist, man after man. I asked one young administrator why none of the physicists were women. And he answered: "I don't know, but I suppose it must be something innate. My seven-year-old daughter doesn't seem to be much interested in science."

4   It was with that experience fresh in my mind that I attended a conference in Cambridge, Massachusetts, on science literacy, or rather the worrisome lack of it in this country today. We three women—a science teacher, a young chemist, and myself—sat surrounded by a company of august men. The chemist, I think, first tentatively raised the issue of science illiteracy in women. It seemed like an obvious point. After all, everyone had agreed over and over again that scientific knowledge these days was a key factor in economic power. But as soon as she made the point, it became clear that we women had committed a grievous social error. Our genders were suddenly showing; we had interrupted the serious talk with a subject unforgivably silly.

5   For the first time, I stopped being puzzled about why there weren't any women in science and began to be angry. Because if science is a search for answers to fundamental questions then it hardly seems frivolous to find out why women are excluded. Never mind the economic consequences.

6   A lot of the reasons women are excluded are spelled out by the Massachusetts Institute of Technology experimental physicist Vera Kistiakowsky in a recent article in *Physics Today* called "Women in Physics: Unnecessary, Injurious, and Out of Place?" The title was taken from a nineteenth-century essay written in

opposition to the appointment of a female mathematician to a professorship at the University of Stockholm. "As decidedly as two and two make four," a woman in mathematics is a "monstrosity," concluded the writer of the essay.

Dr. Kistiakowsky went on to discuss the factors that make women in science 7 today, if not monstrosities, at least oddities. Contrary to much popular opinion, one of those is *not* an innate difference in the scientific ability of boys and girls. But early conditioning does play a stubborn and subtle role. A recent *Nova* program, "The Pinks and the Blues," documented how girls and boys are treated differently from birth—the boys always encouraged in more physical kinds of play, more active explorations of their environments. Sheila Tobias, in her book *Math Anxiety,* showed how the games boys play help them to develop an intuitive understanding of speed, motion, and mass.

The main sorting out of the girls from the boys in science seems to happen 8 in junior high school. As a friend who teaches in a science museum said, "By the time we get to electricity, the boys already have had some experience with it. But it's unfamiliar to the girls." Science books draw on boys' experiences. "The examples are all about throwing a baseball at such and such a speed," said my stepdaughter, who barely escaped being a science drop-out.

The most obvious reason there are not many more women in science is that 9 women are discriminated against as a class, in promotions, salaries, and hirings, a conclusion reached by a recent analysis by the National Academy of Sciences.

Finally, said Dr. Kistiakowsky, women are simply made to feel out of place 10 in science. Her conclusion was supported by a Ford Foundation study by Lynn H. Fox on the problems of women in mathematics. When students were asked to choose among six reasons accounting for girls' lack of interest in math, the girls rated this statement second: "Men do not want girls in the mathematical occupations."

A friend of mine remembers winning a Bronxwide mathematics competi- 11 tion in the second grade. Her friends—both boys and girls—warned her that she shouldn't be good at math: "You'll never find a boy who likes you." My friend continued nevertheless to excel in math and science, won many awards during her years at the Bronx High School of Science, and then earned a full scholarship to Harvard. After one year of Harvard science, she decided to major in English.

When I asked her why, she mentioned what she called the "macho mores" of 12 science. "It would have been O.K. if I'd had someone to talk to," she said. "But the rules of comportment were such that you never admitted you didn't understand. I later realized that even the boys didn't get everything clearly right away. You had to stick with it until it had time to sink in. But for the boys, there was a payoff in suffering through the hard times, and a kind of punishment—a shame—if they didn't. For the girls it was O.K. not to get it, and the only payoff for sticking it out was that you'd be considered a freak."

Science is undeniably hard. Often, it can seem quite boring. It is unfortunately 13 too often presented as laws to be memorized instead of mysteries to be explored.

It is too often kept a secret that science, like art, takes a well-developed esthetic sense. Women aren't the only ones who say, "I hate science."

14   That's why everyone who goes into science needs a little help from friends. For the past ten years, I have been getting more than a little help from a friend who is a physicist. But my stepdaughter—who earned the highest grades ever recorded in her California high school on the math Scholastic Aptitude Test—flunked calculus in her first year at Harvard. When my friend the physicist heard about it, he said, "Harvard should be ashamed of itself."

15   What he meant was that she needed that little extra encouragement that makes all the difference. Instead, she got that little extra discouragement that makes all the difference.

16   "In the first place, all the math teachers are men," she explained. "In the second place, when I met a boy I liked and told him I was taking chemistry, he immediately said: 'Oh, you're one of those science types.' In the third place, it's just a kind of a social thing. The math clubs are full of boys and you don't feel comfortable joining."

17   In other words, she was made to feel unnecessary, injurious, and out of place.

18   A few months ago, I accompanied a male colleague from the science museum where I sometimes work to a lunch of the history of science faculty at the University of California. I was the only woman there, and my presence for the most part was obviously and rudely ignored. I was so surprised and hurt by this that I made an extra effort to speak knowledgeably and well. At the end of the lunch, one of the professors turned to me in all seriousness and said: "Well, K. C., what do the women think of Carl Sagan?" I replied that I had no idea what "the women" thought about anything. But now I know what I should have said: I should have told him that his comment was unnecessary, injurious, and out of place.

Vocabulary

Directions: Locate each of the key words in the reading selection. Try to figure out each word's meaning by using the context. Confirm your guess by checking the dictionary or thesaurus. Write the meanings of the words in the margin of the text. Then record the meanings in the following chart.

Key Word	Paragraph	Meaning
1. askance	1	
2. innate	3	
3. august	4	
4. frivolous	5	
5. esthetic (often spelled aesthetic)	13	

Key Word	Paragraph	Meaning
Others?		

Guide Questions

Directions: These questions will guide your understanding of what you have read. Write your answers in your notebook or on a separate sheet of paper if your instructor wishes to collect it. Your answers to these questions will be the basis of class discussion.

1. What do you think prompted the author to write this article? Would you be surprised to find an article titled "Men in Science" in a magazine or newspaper? Why?
2. According to the essay, what are some of the reasons women are excluded from the field of science?
3. Cole describes a friend who excelled in science but, after studying at Harvard for a year, changed her major to English. What reason does Cole's friend give for dropping science?
4. Cole states that "science is undeniably hard" (paragraph 13) and that men also say "I hate science." If these things are true, what explains the fact that women tend to drop out of science while men are much more likely to continue?

Application

Directions: Interview four adults. Try to find one person working in the field of science, one in math, and two from other fields. Ask them if their gender made a difference in which profession they chose and, if so, why. Compare their answers to the ideas in the essay. Use your interviews as a basis for a class discussion.

Writing

Directions: Describe your own experience studying science and math. Were boys and girls treated equally? Were there equal opportunities and encouragement for both boys and girls? Think about why you did or did not continue studying science. Are your experiences similar to those you read about in "Women in Science"? Write at least two paragraphs.

Making Connections

Directions: Read the following selection, "Sex and Science."

In January 2005, the president of Harvard University, Lawrence Summers, created a furor when he stated that genetic differences between men and women might explain why fewer women succeed in science and math careers. When a firestorm of angry reaction resulted, Summers quickly apologized, evidently hoping that would end the brouhaha. But reactions to his comments continued to appear in the media and be discussed in universities, boardrooms, and around kitchen tables. In his speech, Summers offered at least two explanations for the shortage of women in senior posts in science and engineering: first, their reluctance to work long hours because of child care responsibilities and second, genetic difference. As an example, Dr. Summers cited his daughter who had received two trucks as gifts. She treated them like dolls, and named them "mummy" and "daddy" trucks.

Hundreds, perhaps thousands, of news stories appeared about the controversy over the following several weeks. This article appeared on the MSNBC website and in Newsweek *magazine in January 2005.*

SEX AND SCIENCE

Barbara Kantrowitz

1   When Amber Post started grad school in physics at Princeton, her goal was the same as her male colleagues': a tenure-track job at a major university. Now with her Ph.D. just a year away, Post is thinking instead about working for a policy-making agency in Washington. Even though Princeton is generally welcoming to female scientists (the president, Shirley Tilghman, is a molecular biologist), Post, 25, senses that her reception in the larger academic world might be chillier. At elite universities, the percentage of women earning doctorates in science and engineering is considerably higher than the percentage of women professors—which means that a lot of talented women Ph.D.s like Post leave campus for jobs in government or industry instead of climbing the faculty ladder.

2   Stopping this female brain drain has been a challenge for years, and universities from MIT to Stanford are pushing hard with mentoring programs and stepped-up recruitment efforts. But Harvard president Lawrence Summers inadvertently threw the issue into the national spotlight when he suggested, at a recent academic conference, that women aren't succeeding because they lack "innate ability" in math and science. Scientists have uncovered some subtle differences in male and female brains, but it's unclear how these differences affect aptitude, and it certainly doesn't explain why there were only four women among 32 Harvard faculty members offered tenure last year. Around the country, women account for nearly half the bachelor's degrees in chemistry and math but only about 10 percent of the faculty. Summers's comments drew immediate criticism from women scientists at Harvard and elsewhere, and he issued a quick apology. "The human potential to excel in science is not somehow the province of one gender or another," he said in a statement.

3   But for many women scientists, the damage was done. "We all know that when we walk into a classroom or present research at a conference, there will be people who will think we are only there because we were given a break somewhere

along the line,' says Post. "But when the president of Harvard University appears to support the theory of innate differences, that pushes the stereotype into the realm of fact and makes it acceptable to think that women are just a little dumber by nature." MIT biology professor Nancy Hopkins, a Harvard alum who attended the Jan. 14 conference, walked out on Summers because, she says, his comments made her "sick." A few hours later, she told a reporter from *The Boston Globe* about Summers's remarks, which were made during a private session on women in science hosted by the National Bureau of Economics. After the *Globe*'s story, Hopkins ended up on the "Today" show. That attention, she says, may be the only good to come out of the media firestorm. "People will realize what these women face," she says. "They must deal with men like Larry Summers. They'll tell you they have no bias, but in their head they are thinking, 'Can women really do math?'"

In his talk, Summers proposed two other possible barriers for women: the conflict between tenure clocks and biological clocks, and outright bias against women (which he seemed to dismiss). Many women scientists blame these problems—not a lack of ability—for the dearth of women professors. Junior faculty need to spend their 20s and 30s on research and publication. Those are the same years when women have children. Time is an enemy for women in other professions, especially law and medicine. But while women doctors and lawyers benefit from lots of successful role models, academic science continues to be dominated by men. Harvard physics professor Melissa Franklin says that even though she has many talented women physics majors whom she tries to encourage, relatively few consider graduate school. "The atmosphere isn't compelling or welcoming to them," she says. "It's a very subtle thing."   4

And sometimes not so subtle. Lillian Pierce was Princeton's valedictorian when she graduated in 2002 and received her master's in math from Oxford as a Rhodes scholar. Now back at Princeton, she's studying for her Ph.D. Even with that sterling resume, she says, "I myself have experienced behavior that is hard to explain in terms of anything but discrimination: senior male mathematicians ignoring my presence when I'm introduced to them or suggesting point-blank that I pursue another career, such as medicine." She says too many of her female friends "drop out of graduate programs simply because they're disillusioned with the environment, not because they can't handle the math."   5

Even against this background, there has been some progress. Kristina Johnson, dean of engineering at Duke, says that more universities are making efforts to assist male and female faculty members with young families. "I've got 18 women on my faculty and the majority are raising children under 12," she says. "Yes, it's a challenge to raise kids and go through the tenure process, but it's one that both men and women face. Men don't want to miss out on raising their kids, either." But ultimately, the best remedy against bias would be more women on top, like Princeton's Tilghman, Susan Hockfield of MIT or Shirley Ann Jackson of Rensselaer Polytechnic Institute. "People need to see a career trajectory of someone who looks like them," says Jackson, "a trajectory that shows them that, with talent, a real career is possible." Although maybe not at Harvard—for now.   6

Vocabulary

Directions: Locate each of the key words in the reading selection. Try to figure out each word's meaning by using the context. Confirm your guess by checking the dictionary or thesaurus. Write the meanings of the words in the margin of the text. Then record the meanings in the chart below.

Key Word	Paragraph	Meaning
1. brouhaha	Introduction	
2. tenure-track	1	
3. elite	1	
4. inadvertently	2	
5. dearth	4	
6. point-blank	5	
7. trajectory	6	

Guide Questions

Directions: These questions will guide your understanding of what you have read. Write your answers in your notebook, or on a separate sheet of paper if your instructor wishes to collect it. Your answers to these questions will be the basis of class discussion.

1. In paragraph 2, we learn that President Lawrence Summers "threw the issue into the national spotlight." Explain what the issue is and how it came under the national spotlight.
2. In the article we learn that at Harvard in 2004, 32 Harvard faulty members were offered tenure. Of these 32, four were women. We also learn that around the country, women earn nearly half the bachelor's degrees in chemistry and math, but make up 10% of the faculty. How are these facts relevant?
3. As you know from reading this article and the previous one, "Women in Science," Summers is not the only person to question women's innate abilities in science. Why did *his* remarks spark so much reaction?
4. Explain the two possible barriers for women mentioned in paragraph 4.
5. How does Lillian Pierce describe her experience as a woman in science?
6. Summarize the last paragraph, ". . . there has been some progress."

Making Connections

1. Return to "Women in Science." K. C. Cole cites several factors that make women in science "oddities." List them. Then do the same for "Sex and

Science." Compare and contrast the lists. What are the similarities? What are the differences?

2. Remember, the article "Women in Science" was written in 1981. Imagine K. C. Cole were to read this 2005 article, "Sex and Science." How do you think she would react? Write a paragraph or two.

Application

Directions: Return to paragraph 2. Compare the number of female graduates from your college with the number of tenured women on the faculty. This information should be on your school's website or through the school's institutional research office. How do the numbers compare to those cited in paragraph 2?

Writing

Directions: Following are a few of the letters that appeared in *The New York Times* reacting to Summers' statements. Choose one of the letters and respond to it in a letter of your own.

To the Editor:

Re "Harvard President Apologizes Again for Remarks on Gender" (news article, Jan. 20):

When Lawrence H. Summers, the president of Harvard University, suggested that women's underrepresentation in science may be attributed to innate factors related to gender, he created a "teachable moment" for greater public awareness of the need to advance women in science.

Considerable research and experience refute the notion that the status quo for women in science is natural, inevitable and unrelated to social factors. Research also shows that expectations heavily influence learning and performance.

If society and individuals anticipate that women will not perform as well as men, there is a good chance that those expectations will be met.

We must continue to address the many ways people are discouraged from pursuing an interest in science and engineering. Society benefits most when we take full advantage of all the talent among us.

It is time to create a broader awareness that enables women and other underrepresented groups to step beyond historical barriers in science and engineering.

Carol B. Muller
Sally K. Ride
Palo Alto, Calif., Jan. 20, 2005

The writers are, respectively, chief executive of MentorNet, the E-Mentoring Network for Women in Engineering and Science; and a professor of space science, University of California, San Diego. The letter was also signed by 98 other academics and scientists.

To the Editor:

I am saddened that the president of Harvard is under attack for suggesting some possible causes for the relative scarcity of senior women in science. As a woman with a talent for science, I have a personal interest in understanding why I have met so few like me.

We have ample evidence that there are differences in the ways men's and women's brains process information and in the ways their bodies process medications. Why shouldn't science question whether some differences, unrelated to social conditioning, might make the genders more or less competent at science?

While the academic community may have faith that scientific talent is gender-neutral, some of us would still like to know the truth of the matter so that we may one day understand, predict and control it.

Elizabeth Bryson
San Diego, Jan. 20, 2005

To the Editor:

I do not understand the public outcry regarding Lawrence H. Summers's suggestion that innate differences between the sexes may explain why fewer women succeed in science and math careers.

Is Harvard, a bastion of excellence in higher education, not allowed to touch that question? I hope not.

For critical and free-thinking ideas to flourish, it needs to be addressed.

There is a procedure in evaluating hypotheses within the scientific method. If Mr. Summers's statement falls on its merits, it will be because it will be thoroughly investigated and then summarily rejected. This, in turn, will attract more women into the various scientific fields and foster a greater understanding.

Isn't that, after all, the point of science?

Tony McGovern
Broomfield, Colo., Jan. 20, 2005

To the Editor:

Women are a rarity in mathematics and engineering. As a female engineering student, I see this every day. That said, the idea that this fact is representative of the different biological programming between men and women is utter nonsense.

In recent years, the number of women entering these fields has increased significantly, as has the range of female understanding. It is thus not inability that limits numbers, but perhaps the stubborn refusal to let go of ignorant hypotheses.

Kelsey Burrell
La Jolla, Calif., Jan. 20, 2005

Think back to your elementary school days. If your experience is like most people's, all of your teachers were women. Why do you think this was so? Why don't men go into this profession? Has this situation changed in recent years? In the essay that follows, a male elementary school teacher describes his work days and some of the problems he faces as a man doing "woman's work."

ONE MAN'S KIDS

Daniel Meier

I teach first graders. I live in a world of skinned knees, double-knotted shoelaces, riddles that I've heard a dozen times, stale birthday cakes, hurt feelings, wandering stories, and one lost shoe ("and if you don't find it my mother'll kill me"). My work is dominated by six-year-olds.   1

It's 10:45, the middle of snack, and I'm helping Emily open her milk carton. She has already tried the other end without success, and now there's so much paint and ink on the carton from her fingers that I'm not sure she should drink it at all. But I open it. Then I turn to help Scott clean up some milk he has just spilled onto Rebecca's whale crossword puzzle.   2

While I wipe my milk- and paint-covered hands, Jenny wants to know if I've seen that funny book about penguins that I read in class. As I hunt for it in a messy pile of books, Jason wants to know if there is a new seating arrangement for lunch tables. I find the book, turn to answer Jason, then face Maya, who is fast approaching with a new knock-knock joke. After what seems like the tenth "Who's there?" I laugh and Maya is pleased.   3

Then Andrew wants to know how to spell "flukes" for his crossword. As I get to "u," I give a hand signal for Sarah to take away the snack. But just as Sarah is almost out the door, two children complain that "we haven't even had ours yet." I stop the snack mid-flight, complying with their request for graham crackers. I then return to Andrew, noticing that he has put "flu" for 9 Down, rather than 9 Across. It's now 10:50.   4

My work is not traditional male work. It's not a singular pursuit. There is not a large pile of paper to get through or one deal to transact. I don't have one area of expertise or knowledge. I don't have the singular power over language of a lawyer, the physical force of a construction worker, the command over fellow workers of a surgeon, the wheeling and dealing transactions of a businessman. My energy is not spent in pursuing, climbing, achieving, conquering, or cornering some goal or object.   5

My energy is spent in encouraging, supporting, consoling, and praising my children. In teaching, the inner rewards come from without. On any given day, quite apart from teaching reading and spelling, I bandage a cut, dry a tear, erase a frown, tape a torn doll, and locate a long-lost boot. The day is really won through matters of the heart. As my students groan, laugh, shudder, cry, exult, and wonder, I do too. I have to be soft around the edges.   6

7   A few years ago, when I was interviewing for an elementary school teaching position, every principal told me with confidence that, as a male, I had an advantage over female applicants because of the lack of male teachers. But in the next breath, they asked with a hint of suspicion why I chose to work with young children. I told them that I wanted to observe and contribute to the intellectual growth of a maturing mind. What I really felt like saying, but didn't, was that I loved helping a child learn to write his name for the first time, finding someone a new friend, or sharing in the hilarity of reading about Winnie the Pooh getting so stuck in a hole that only his head and rear show.

8   I gave that answer to those principals, who were mostly male, because I thought they wanted a "male" response. This meant talking about intellectual matters. If I had taken a different course and talked about my interest in helping children in their emotional development, it would have been seen as closer to a "female" answer. I even altered my language, not once mentioning the word *love* to describe what I do indeed love about teaching. My answer worked; every principal nodded approvingly.

9   Some of the principals also asked what I saw myself doing later in my career. They wanted to know if I eventually wanted to go into educational administration. Becoming a dean of students or a principal has never been one of my goals, but they seemed to expect me, as a male, to want to climb higher on the career stepladder. So I mentioned that, at some point, I would be interested in working with teachers as a curriculum coordinator. Again, they nodded approvingly.

10   If those principals had been female instead of male, I wonder whether their questions, and my answers, would have been different. My guess is that they would have been.

11   At other times, when I'm at a party or a dinner and tell someone that I teach young children, I've found that men and women respond differently. Most men ask about the subjects I teach and the courses I took in my training. Then, unless they bring up an issue such as merit pay, the conversation stops. Most women, on the other hand, begin the conversation on a more immediate and personal level. They say things like "those kids must love having a male teacher" or "that age is just wonderful, you must love it." Then, more often than not, they'll talk about their own kids or ask me specific questions about what I do. We're then off and talking shop.

12   Possibly, men would have more to say to me, and I to them, if my job had more of the trappings and benefits of more traditional male jobs. But my job has no bonuses or promotions. No complimentary box seats at the ball park. No cab fare home. No drinking buddies after work. No briefcase. No suit. (Ties get stuck in paint jars.) No power lunches. (I eat peanut butter and jelly, chips, milk, and cookies with the kids.) No taking clients out for cocktails. The only place I take my kids is to the playground.

13   Although I could have pursued a career in law or business, as several of my friends did, I chose teaching instead. My job has benefits all its own. I'm able to bake cookies without getting them stuck together as they cool, buy cheap sewing

materials, take out splinters, and search just the right trash cans for useful odds and ends. I'm sometimes called "Daddy" and even "Mommy" by my students, and if there's ever a lull in the conversation at a dinner party, I can always ask those assembled if they've heard the latest riddle about why the turkey crossed the road. (He thought he was a chicken.)

Vocabulary

Directions: Locate each of the key words in the reading selection. Try to figure out each word's meaning by using the context. Confirm your guess by checking the dictionary or thesaurus. Write the meanings of the words in the margin of the text. Then record the meanings in the chart below.

Key Word	Paragraph	Meaning
1. exult	6	
2. hilarity	7	
3. trappings	12	
4. lull	13	
Others?		

Guide Questions

Directions: These questions will guide your understanding of what you have read. Write your answers in your notebook or on a separate sheet of paper if your instructor wishes to collect it. Your answers to these questions will be the basis of class discussion.

1. Describe what the author does for a living. Then describe your reaction to his profession when you first read the article.
2. What does Meier mean when he says in paragraph 5 that his work is not a "singular pursuit"?
3. Why did Meier think he could not give truly honest answers to the principals who interviewed him for jobs as a teacher?
4. Contrast the types of conversations Meier has with women and with men at social occasions.
5. If you know someone who has held a job typically performed by the opposite sex, describe their experience. Would they recommend such a job to you?

Application

Directions: Think back to the essay, "Women in Science" (page 220). In small groups, discuss the similarities and differences between Daniel Meier's and K. C. Cole's experiences in careers dominated by the opposite sex.

Writing

Directions: Reflect on what you have read and on the discussion you had in the Application exercise above. Now, think about and answer this question: Would you take a job in a field dominated by the opposite sex? For example, if you are a woman, would you work as a truck driver, construction worker, or firefighter? If you are a man, would you work as a nurse, elementary school teacher, or secretary? Consider the advantages and disadvantages of such a job. Write your response and supporting reasons for your response in two or three paragraphs.

Do you dread placing your order at a fast-food restaurant? Fear the sneers of the super-market clerk? Spend hours looking for what you want at the store rather than risk the hostility of the clerk lounging in the corner? You are not alone. Customers are expressing more and more frustration at the bad attitudes and incompetent service of workers. Bosses are, too, and they're looking for answers. But a shrug is often the only option. This article appeared in the March 6, 2000, issue of Newsweek.

TIRED OF SMILE-FREE SERVICE?

Keith Naughton

Hustling off to work one morning recently, Ann Andraska pulled into her neighborhood gas station in Ann Arbor, Mich., for a fill-up. On her way to the checkout counter, the elementary-school speech therapist grabbed a Coke and a five-pound bag of ice. As she fumbled with the ice while trying to pull money from her purse, the cashier barked, "Would you put that stuff down! I need the money." Andraska did as she was told, and the clerk flung her change across the counter. Shocked by such rudeness, Andraska sighed. "If you want better service," the clerk growled, "go across the street." 1

The problem is, it's not likely to be much better across the street. It's no secret that service is abysmal, a fact confirmed last week by a new University of Michigan survey of customer satisfaction that puts an exclamation point on an unfortunate Econ 101 lesson: as unemployment has fallen to its lowest level in 30 years, it's tough to find good workers. And that's why customer satisfaction at fast-food restaurants, retailers, gas stations and banks has fallen to its lowest level since the consumer survey began in 1994. The real burden, though, falls on the frontline managers who not only have to recruit and train workers who aren't exactly the creamiest of the crop, but also have to tolerate the bad service of their employees or else resume the hunt for new workers. In this overheated business climate, entire staffs can turn over three times in a year, despite $10-an-hour wages. Employees who stick around more than 90 days are often considered old hands. Terry Guth, director of staffing for 7-Eleven convenience stores, has started combing welfare rolls for applicants. Store owners offer new hires up to $12 an hour to serve Slurpees. The war for workers is more fierce than the battle for customers. "We're all fighting it out for people," he says. 2

Recruiters desperately seeking applicants are coming up with new strategies. Target, the big discount chain, installed kiosks in the front of its stores where prospects can fill out a computerized application and be on the job in 24 hours. "Applicants are so scarce, you have to be able to respond quickly," says vice president Betty Kimbrough. "If we don't get to your application for a week, you're probably already working for someone else." In addition to offering fat paychecks that make a mockery of the $5.15 minimum wage, retailers like Wal-Mart are now extending medical benefits and 401(k) savings plans to part-timers. Home Depot is so anxious to recruit workers it spent millions to launch its first national 3 television help-wanted ad. The commercial, filled with smiling employees who promise that "great careers are built" at Home Depot, got the green light after executives calculated that having too few staffers cost them tens of millions in lost sales. "If you don't have enough people, that represents lost revenue," says Cindy Durning, Home Depot's recruitment vice president. The ad seemed to work. Since it debuted, Home Depot says, applications have quadrupled at some stores.

4   The luxury of leisurely classroom training for new recruits has all but vanished. Fresh hires at Wal-Mart and McDonald's no longer spend days locked in the back room watching training videos. Most training comes on the job, and if the rookie needs more he can log on to the computer in the break room. "We used to teach them the history of the potato, but they don't need all that to make fries," says Barry Mehrman, McDonald's director of human resources. Critics say this rush to get inexperienced workers behind the counter explains why service is declining. "You see a lot of trainees these days fumbling at the cash register," says economist Russ Thibeault of Applied Economic Research in New Hampshire. As quality hires grow scarce, bosses find they must teach the most rudimentary manners. "Some people just don't want to smile," says Charles Valluzzo, a McDonald's franchisee in Baton Rouge, La., who is hiring more workers off welfare. "It's a challenge to motivate these people. You've got to sit there and work with them daily."

5   And be awfully forgiving if you want them to stick around. With help-wanted signs papering the windows of stores everywhere, workers hold the power and managers hesitate to reprimand. Arrive late for work or don't show up at all? Don't worry, the boss will give you another chance. "If someone was late three times in a row in the past, I might let them go," says Bill Tarpey, who manages Sunset Foods in Lake Forest, Ill. "Now I think twice. Without bodies, you can't give good serivce." Even dressing down a customer is a forgivable offense. When a cashier at a 7-Eleven in Farmington Hills, Mich., recently snapped at a young woman who balked when asked to show ID to buy alcohol, owner Jim Chatham sent the worker to the back room to cool off. But he never considered firing her. "I'm not going to dump a good employee just because two or three customers had a bad reaction," says Chatham. "I always back my employees."

6   So much for the days when the customer was always right. These days customers had better just bite their tongues. Mary Beltrian discovered that when she complained to the manager of her car wash in Chicago after a worker sprayed bleach on her dashboard. "The manager told me he didn't get paid enough to deal with it," says the 36-year-old nurse. A Detroit couple who filed a $100 million lawsuit against McDonald's last week claim they received even rougher treatment. They allege they were beaten by three Detroit McDonald's employees after they tried to return a watery milkshake. McDonald's Detroit marketing manager Vicky Free responded: "This matter is under investigation and litigation, and it's inappropriate to discuss it further."

7   As workers have grown more frustrated with customers, they've begun to vent their hostility online. The customerssuck.com site gets 1,200 hits a day. In the anonymity of cyberspace, workers rail about customers' dumbest questions ("How much is a 99-cent cheeseburger?") and give their finicky shoppers pet

names ("Return Rita," "Mr. SlowMotion Man"). Quincy, Mass., liquor-store manager George Duncan, 25, started the customerssuck.com site two years ago, giving it the slogan "The customer is never right." Duncan argues that the booming economy has made consumers arrogant and corporate owners even more greedy. Workers, he contends, are caught in the middle. "Companies still want more profits, even though they are relying on fewer people to do the work," says Duncan. "It can be a nightmare for the clerk."

Predictably, not many customers are sympathetic. Los Angeles vending-machine salesman Ruben Nogales fumes about the inept service he's been getting lately from the trainees running the drive-throughs he frequents for lunch. When Nogales pulled up to the window at a taco joint recently, he was handed the wrong order and his debit card was charged $450 for the lunch. The manager had to get involved to unravel the mess. Nogales vows he'll never return to that restaurant. "I don't care how hungry I am," he huffs. "It's not worth the aggravation." With service suffering everywhere, Nogales's chances of having a happy meal are growing slim. But hey, at least the economy is still booming. So have a nice day.

8

Vocabulary

Directions: Locate each of the key words in the reading selection. Try to figure out each word's meaning by using the context. Confirm your guess by checking the dictionary or thesaurus. Write the meanings of the words in the margin of the text. Then record the meanings in the chart below.

Key Word	Paragraph	Meaning
1. abysmal	2	
2. combing	2	
3. kiosks	3	
4. reprimand	5	
5. dressing down	5	
6. allege	6	
7. unravel	8	
Others?		

Guide Questions

Directions: These questions will guide your understanding of what you have read. Write your answers in your notebook or on a separate sheet of paper if your instructor wishes to collect it. Your answers to these questions will be the basis of class discussion.

1. According to the article, why is it difficult to find good workers these days?
2. Why does the author say "the real burden . . . falls on the frontline managers"?
3. Cite some of the statistics from the article regarding pay, other incentives, and worker turnover.
4. According to the article, what is the effect of low unemployment on the following:
   a. training for workers
   b. attitudes of workers
   c. the service that workers provide to customers?
5. Cite one of the examples of poor service mentioned in the article. Does the description of poor/hostile service ring true to you? Have you had similar experiences? Do you think service is worse than it was in the past?
6. According to the article, is the problem all one-sided? Or are some customers at fault, too?
7. If you have ever worked in a service job, did you encounter difficult customers? How did you handle those situations?

Application/Writing

1. Who do you think is more at fault: the customers or the workers? Why? Can you think of any solution to the problem of poor/hostile service? Discuss your ideas with your classmates. Then write a letter to *Newsweek* explaining your solution.
2. Describe an experience you've had as a customer with a surly clerk (or alternatively, your experience trying to serve a hostile customer). Write a paragraph or two.

This article reports on the findings of a survey of the readers of the magazine Working Woman. *Before you read, try your hand at answering some of the questions from the same survey.*

For each of the situations below, state whether you think it is an ethical problem or not an ethical problem.

1. *Unethical or no problem: Your boss treats clients to cocaine.*
2. *Unethical or no problem: A real estate agent showing a house doesn't say that the basement floods.*
3. *Unethical or no problem: An executive learns that his company is about to be sold, which will send its stock price soaring. He leaks this information to two clients as well as to several friends.*
4. *Unethical or no problem: An administrative assistant routinely makes up excuses for her boss when he takes long lunches with his secretary.*
5. *Unethical or no problem: After a year of poor sales, a sales representative convinces her boss to let her give expensive gifts to prospective clients. The tactic works and sales increase.*
6. *Unethical or no problem: A publisher gives his college-age niece a highly sought-after unpaid summer internship at his company.*
7. *Unethical or no problem: Company policy forbids employees to discuss salaries with each other, but two people trade information to negotiate better with their boss.*
8. *Unethical or no problem: A manager has accumulated sick days. She calls in sick even though she isn't and takes a few days off.*
9. *Unethical or no problem: A job applicant finds out the morning before her job interview that she is pregnant. She decides not to say anything rather than jeopardize her chances.*

HOW ETHICAL IS AMERICAN BUSINESS?

Ronni Sandroff

Would you work for a company that was polluting the environment . . . or a boss who lied to customers? Do you think it's unethical to flirt to make a sale? Or to call in sick when you need a "mental health" day? More than fourteen hundred *Working Woman* readers examined their scruples—and those of their colleagues—by responding to "Business Ethics: What Are Your Personal Standards?" published in the February issue. Hundreds went beyond the survey to enclose heartfelt letters. Their conclusion? Fair play is disappearing from the American business scene—and it hurts.

The majority of respondents said they personally have witnessed such foul play as lying to employees; expense-account abuses at the highest levels; and in-office jockeying involving favoritism, nepotism, and taking credit for other people's work. Almost half have seen discrimination based on sex and color, more than a third, sexual harassment; and just under a third, lying to make a sale. And they charge that this apparent erosion of the fair-play ethic is not only disheartening but is also harmful to productivity, job stability, and profits in American business.

3   "I worked for a medical-device manufacturer that released a product for humans without implant studies," wrote one reader. Her protests went unheeded and the product failed in some cases, causing unnecessary surgery in already weakened patients. The same company was sued for sending a maintenance man on an industrial espionage mission to sift through a competitor's garbage and collect information. Are tales like this symptomatic of a decline in American business ethics, or are they just a reflection of business as usual? Fifty-six percent of the respondents in the *Working Woman* ethics survey believe that American business ethics have deteriorated in the past ten years.

4   Contributing to employees' dismay, perhaps, is the fact that bad deeds seem to go unpunished: The companies or institutions that most respondents have worked for have not gotten into trouble over ethical violations. Part of the reason may be that the violations readers have seen most often, such as lying to employees, expense-account abuses, and so on, are difficult to prosecute.

5   And where is this wrongdoing taking place? When asked which industries were hotbeds of unethical behavior, a startlingly high number of readers—66 percent—pointed the finger at the government. We might dismiss this as simply good old American government-bashing if it weren't for the fact that women who work for the government are among those most likely to bash it: 62 percent of government workers feel the government is most unethical. "The government is the most unethical institution I've ever been associated with," wrote one reader. In contrast, other occupation groups think their ethics are better than the popular perception. For example, only 9 percent of lawyers—compared with 40 percent of all respondents—rated law as the most unethical.

6   How will a concern for ethics affect future career patterns? Ethics-wise, most respondents are willing to put their money where their mouths are: A strong majority of those polled said they would not work for a company with a history of environmental accidents, insider trading or worker accidents, or a law firm that defends known racketeers. Women in the helping professions were most scrupulous about where they'd work. However, more lawyers said they would work for any of these companies. "If all attorneys decided that they were too 'ethical' to defend 'known criminals,'" one reader reminded us, "accused persons would have no rights."

Where Do You Draw the Line?

7   Umpiring the ethics of the workplace is not merely a spectator sport. Every worker is a player. What personal decisions do people make—and why do they make them? When it comes to personal scruples, the issues seem less clear-cut. Readers consider stealing time (in the form of phony sick days or personal phone calls) and supplies (computer software, office staples) or sharing company discounts with outsiders only minor violations. And trading competitive information with friends in the same industry is OK with almost half the respondents. More than 60 percent would use a stolen secret report from a competitor's company.

"Unethical behavior is quickly becoming acceptable behavior," wrote an 8
information-systems director from St. Louis. "Some of us do little things like
[putting] an occasional lunch with a friend on the old expense account. Without
proper controls, the occasional lunch becomes the occasional trip or vacation. The
result is still the same: Someone else pays for the ride."

The majority of respondents (53 percent) agreed that most successful busi- 9
ness people occasionally have to compromise their principles. In fact, in a number of areas, women who rated themselves as highly successful (and generally had
the highest incomes and education levels) were more willing to bend and break
rules than less successful women. "Had I taken this survey five years ago while in
middle management, my answers would have been much more black-and-white.
The more exposed to business I become, the more aware I am of the gray areas. Is
this because there are gray areas, or because justification has begun to set in?" one
reader wondered.

The Reasons—and Excuses?

When asked if it's sometimes necessary to break the rules to get ahead, 42 per- 10
cent of the respondents said yes and 44 percent said no. Some readers blamed the
decline in ethics on the atmosphere created in the executive suite. "A fearful,
angry employee will steal to get even for the emotional beating she feels she is
taking," wrote one respondent. Another asked: "How ethical is it for large
corporations to deny workers a pay raise while upper management still receives
ridiculously large bonuses? This type of entrenched corruption at high levels
eventually creates dishonest behaviors at the lower levels."

Unfair treatment of women managers and workers sometimes is used as a 11
justification for not being completely aboveboard with employers. Take the possibility of pregnancy's having a negative impact on a woman's career. Seventy-six
percent of respondents did not have ethical difficulty with a job applicant who
doesn't tell a prospective employer that she's pregnant. Women with high incomes and education levels were more likely than others to think this way.

Standing Your Ground—and Yielding It

Petty thievery and lies aside, what do people do when confronted with a truly 12
grievous wrong, such as the release of a dangerous product, or theft that is
likely to bankrupt a company? About two out of three women over thirty years
of age have had some experience in taking an ethical stand at work (though
fewer than half of those in the eighteen-to-twenty-five-year-old group have yet
been tested).

Did their stand get results? Respondents were split. "My attempts at 'cor- 13
recting' ethical wrongs never engendered lasting change," wrote one discouraged
reader who has worked for years in both the public and private sectors and ended
up with a "great feeling of futility."

Another reader learned the hard way that fighting the good fight is worthwhile. 14
"I had a good job that I quit rather than make the tough decision," she wrote.
Six months later a male co-worker took the risk and informed one owner that the

owner's partner was a cheat. The partner was forced out and the co-worker was rewarded with his job. "I would have been in line for the position if I had stayed and tattled," she wrote. She's since learned to speak out. "I have found that you can usually get the ethical point across and still get the job done."

15   Of women who have taken an ethical stand that has affected their careers, 37 percent said it had a positive effect and 30 percent said it had a negative effect. Some of the women who took a stand with negative results—like getting fired—have learned, with bitterness, to keep their mouths and eyes shut. "In the two years I have worked full-time, I have seen numerous unethical situations. More often than not, I have decided to make it 'someone else's problem' so as not to jeopardize my career or my peace of mind."

16   This sort of detached cynicism can be painful for the individual. "While working on this survey I faced a very unsettling fact about myself," wrote one reader. "I find that I choose the path of least resistance more often than not [even though] I believe in honesty. It is scary to see how easily and subtly unethical behavior has become a pattern in my working life, as though one can be one person at work and a totally different creature at home."

17   What's the answer? Do written codes of ethics help? Should the government step in? Overwhelmingly respondents said the ethical decisions they make on the job were learned at their parents' knees, and those values continue to be the most influential, along with religious teachings and the influences of friends, business colleagues, superiors, and books. Eleven percent had taken a special course in ethics, but only a few of these (1 percent) found that it made a difference.

18   Since many areas of confusion—such as pirating computer software and accepting gifts from suppliers—are not covered in the Ten Commandments, business ethics specific to the contemporary scene are clearly needed. Yet according to our respondents, these issues tend to be discussed only when a problem arises. Of readers whose workplaces do not have a formal code of ethics, almost 60 percent think it would be helpful. However, fewer than a third want government regulation of ethics.

19   The traditional American idea put forth by James Madison that free institutions should not depend on virtue but be fueled by selfish impulses, properly balanced—is echoed by one reader: "There must be a way to teach ethics as self-interest rather than sacrifice: to emphasize that right action is the best way to build community values, trust, and long-term business relationships."

20   Is this possible in the real world? "I work for a corporation in which the company's standards of conduct are an everyday topic of conversation," wrote one reader. Her company insists on honest business dealings with customers and will not allow stealing confidential information from competitors. "My guess is that we are considered too principled for our own good. But when organizations within the company stray from company values, the results are always bad: low profits, high turnover, poor product quality—and hell to pay with the executive committee." This reader is thrilled to be out of the ethical mire of her previous jobs and to find that, at least in some places, fair play can be a winning strategy.

Vocabulary

Directions: Locate each of the key words in the reading selection. Then read and study each word in its context and try to determine its meaning. Use a dictionary or thesaurus to check your guess. Write the meanings of the words in the margin of the text.

Record the new words you've learned in the chart below.

Key Word	Paragraph	Meaning
1. scruples	1	
2. nepotism	2	
3. erosion	2	
4. unheeded	3	
5. deteriorated	3	
6. hotbeds	5	
7. entrenched	10	
8. engendered	13	
9. cynicism	16	
Others?		

Guide Questions

Directions: The purpose of these guide questions is to ensure your understanding of what you have read. They also will help you to analyze and evaluate the author's ideas and apply them to the real world and your own life.

Write answers to the questions in your notebook or on a separate sheet of paper if your instructor wishes to collect them. Your answers will form the basis of class discussion.

1. Describe the survey, its source, and its purpose.
2. The author of the article states her conclusion at the very beginning of the article; paraphrase it here.
3. Summarize some of the most important findings of the survey.

4. The author asks if the personal stories told by respondents to the survey are "symptomatic of a decline in American business ethics, or are they just a reflection of business as usual?" What does she mean by this question? What answer does she give?

5. According to the selection, where is the "hotbed" of unethical behavior? Does the answer surprise you? Why or why not?

6. Which group listed its own profession as the least unethical?

7. How did most people respond when asked if they would work for a company that allowed unethical situations to persist?

8. The author makes it clear that making ethical decisions is something that every worker must do. Give a few examples from your own knowledge and experience of the personal decisions employees have to make.

9. True or false: According to the article, the more successful and highly paid an employee is, the more likely he or she is to bend and break ethical rules.

10. a. Answer this question from your own perspective: Is it sometimes necessary to break the rules to get ahead?
    b. How did the respondents to the survey answer that same question?

11. Paragraph 16 begins, "This sort of detached cynicism can be painful for the individual." What is the author referring to here?

12. According to the respondents to the survey, where did they learn the values they used in making ethical decisions at work?

13. List some possible solutions to the problems of making ethical decisions at work.

Application

Here are some further results of the survey. A list of ethical violations is followed by the percentage of respondents who have personally observed them.

Violations	Percent who have witnessed violation
Fairness violations	
Favoritism or nepotism	70%
Taking credit for others' work	67%
Doing business with sexist clients	52%
Discrimination	47%
Sexual harassment	41%
Dishonesty	
Lying to employees	62%
Violating confidentiality	64%
Lying to make a sale	31%
Stealing	
Expense-account abuses	52%
Bribery	5%
Sexual trading	
Flirting to make a sale	43%
Sexual intimacy with boss	29%
Sex with co-worker on company time	19%
Sex with client to make a sale	10%

Have you personally observed any of these violations? Which ones? What did you do about it? Why? Discuss these questions with your classmates.

Writing

Directions: Return to the answers you gave to the survey questions in the introduction to the selection. Below are the actual results of the survey. Compare your answers to the ones respondents gave.

1. Your boss treats clients to cocaine.
   Unethical   99%
   No problem   1%

2. A real estate agent showing a house doesn't say that the basement floods.
   Unethical   92%
   No problem   8%

3. An executive learns that his company is about to be sold, which will send its stock price soaring. He leaks this information to two clients as well as to several friends.
   Unethical   91%
   No problem   9%

4. An administrative assistant routinely makes up excuses for her boss when he takes long lunches with his secretary.
   Unethical   56%
   No problem   44%

5. After a year of poor sales, a sales representative convinces her boss to let her give expensive gifts to prospective clients. The tactic works and sales increase.
   Unethical   46%
   No problem   54%

6. A publisher gives his college-age niece a highly sought-after unpaid summer internship at his company.
   Unethical   42%
   No problem   58%

7. Company policy forbids employees to discuss salaries with each other, but two people trade information to negotiate better with their boss.
   Unethical   40%
   No problem   60%

8. A manager has accumulated sick days. She calls in sick even though she isn't and takes a few days off.
   Unethical   34%
   No problem   66%

9. A job applicant finds out the morning before her job interview that she is pregnant. She decides not to say anything rather than jeopardize her chances.
   Unethical   24%
   No problem   76%

Choose one of the questions from this list. State your answer and then explain why you answered it the way you did. Write one paragraph.

Harold Krents studied at Harvard and Oxford, was a partner in a Washington, D.C., law firm, was the inspiration for a long-running Broadway show, Butterflies Are Free, *and wrote a popular TV movie,* To Race the Wind. *Throughout his life, Krents worked to ensure equal opportunity for the handicapped. He died in 1987 at the age of 43 of a brain tumor.*

In this selection, Krents describes his frustrating search for work and his rejection by employers—not because he lacked ability but because he had a disability.

DARKNESS AT NOON

Harold Krents

1   Blind from birth, I have never had the opportunity to see myself and have been completely dependent on the image I create in the eye of the observer. To date it has not been narcissistic.

2   There are those who assume that since I can't see, I obviously also cannot hear. Very often people will converse with me at the top of their lungs, enunciating each word very carefully. Conversely, people will also often whisper, assuming that since my eyes don't work, my ears don't either.

3   For example, when I go to the airport and ask the ticket agent for assistance to the plane, he or she will invariably pick up the phone, call a ground hostess and whisper: "Hi, Jane, we've got a seventy here." I have concluded that the word *blind* is not used for one of two reasons: Either they fear that if the dread word is spoken, the ticket agent's retina will immediately detach, or they are reluctant to inform me of my condition of which I may not have been previously aware.

4   On the other hand, others know that, of course, I can hear, but believe that I can't talk. Often, therefore, when my wife and I go out to dinner, a waiter or waitress will ask Kit if "he would like a drink" to which I respond that "indeed he would."

5   This point was graphically driven home to me while we were in England. I had been given a year's leave of absence from my Washington law firm to study for a diploma in law degree at Oxford University. During the year I became ill and was hospitalized. Immediately after admission, I was wheeled down to the X-ray room. Just at the door sat an elderly woman—elderly I would judge from the sound of her voice. "What is his name?" the woman asked the orderly who had been wheeling me.

6   "What's your name?" the orderly repeated to me.

7   "Harold Krents," I replied.

8   "Harold Krents," he repeated.

9   "When was he born?"

10   "When were you born?"

11   "November 5, 1944," I responded.

12   "November 5, 1944," the orderly intoned.

13   This procedure continued for approximately five minutes, at which point even my saint-like disposition deserted me. "Look," I finally blurted out, "this is

absolutely ridiculous. Okay, granted I can't see, but it's got to have become pretty clear to both of you that I don't need an interpreter."

"He says he doesn't need an interpreter," the orderly reported to the woman.   14

The toughest misconception of all is the view that because I can't see, I can't   15
work. I was turned down by over forty law firms because of my blindness, even though my qualifications included a cum laude degree from Harvard College and a good ranking in my Harvard Law School class.

The attempt to find employment, the continuous frustration of being told   16
that it was impossible for a blind person to practice law, the rejection letters, not based on my lack of ability but rather on my disability, will always remain one of the most disillusioning experiences of my life.

Fortunately, this view of limitation and exclusion is beginning to change.   17
On April 16, 1976 the Department of Labor issued regulations that mandate equal-employment opportunities for the handicapped. By and large, the business community's response to offering employment to the disabled has been enthusiastic.

I therefore look forward to the day, with the expectation that it is certain to   18
come, when employers will view their handicapped workers as a little child did me years ago when my family still lived in Scarsdale.

I was playing basketball with my father in our backyard according to proce-   19
dures we had developed. My father would stand beneath the hoop, shout, and I would shoot over his head at the basket attached to our garage. Our next-door neighbor, aged five, wandered over into our yard with a playmate. "He's blind," our neighbor whispered to her friend in a voice that could be heard distinctly by Dad and me. Dad shot and missed; I did the same. Dad hit the rim; I missed entirely; Dad shot and missed the garage entirely. "Which one is blind?" whispered back the little friend.

I would hope that, in the near future, when a plant manager is touring   20
the factory with the foreman and comes upon a handicapped and nonhandi-capped person working together, his comment after watching them work will be, "Which one is disabled?"

Vocabulary

Directions: Locate each of the key words in the reading selection. Then read and study each word in its context and try to determine its meaning. Use a dictionary or thesaurus to check your guess. Write the meanings of the words in the margin of the text.

Record the new words you've learned in the following chart.

Key Word	Paragraph	Meaning
1. narcissistic	1	
2. enunciating	2	
3. retina	3	

Key Word	Paragraph	Meaning
4. disillusioning	16	
Others?		

Guide Questions

Directions: These guide questions will help to ensure your understanding of what you have read. They will also help you to analyze and evaluate the author's ideas and apply them to the real world and your own life.

Write answers to the questions in your notebook or on a separate sheet of paper if your instructor wishes to collect them. Your answers will form the basis of class discussion.

1. Describe Harold Krents: state all the facts and inferences you can draw from the selection.
2. What are some of the problems Krents has encountered because of his blindness?
3. What does Krents say was the most "disillusioning experience" of his life? Why does he feel this way?
4. What is Krents's main purpose in writing this essay?

Application

Directions: Discuss the question of whether a blind person can be an effective lawyer. What are some problems he or she would face? In which areas would blindness make no difference at all?

Writing

Directions: Choose one of the people Krents describes—either the airport ticket agent, the waiter in the restaurant, or the woman at the hospital in England. Write that person a letter, reacting to his or her treatment of Krents.

SHORT TAKE

How to Get the Job You Want: Tips for the Job Hunter

1. *Do your homework.* Check the company's website, stock performance, annual report. Be familiar with its products and/or services. One employer reports that he is turned off by candidates who do not know the most

basic facts about the company. If you can't be bothered to prepare for an interview, it raises serious questions about how well you will perform on the job.

2. *Have your questions ready.* At some point the interviewer will ask if you have any questions. Take advantage of that opening to find out everything you can about the job. You can also use this time to introduce any of your qualifications that haven't come up yet in the interview.

3. *Dress right.* Even if the company is a "casual operation," you can never go wrong if you wear a suit to the interview. Take it easy on the jewelry and makeup.

4. *Use your head.* There are lots of ways to blow an interview. One candidate answered a cell phone call during his interview. Guess whether he got the job.

5. *Be ready for the interviewer's questions.* Here are some frequently asked questions:

> What are your long-range career goals?
>
> Why did you choose the career you are preparing for?
>
> What is your greatest strength?
>
> What is your greatest weakness?
>
> Tell me about yourself.
>
> How has your education prepared you for your career?
>
> In what ways do you think you could make a contribution to our company?
>
> What two or three accomplishments in your life are you the most proud of?
>
> What extracurricular activities have you participated in? What did you learn from them?
>
> Why are you seeking a job with this company?
>
> Describe a mistake you have made and what you learned from it.
>
> Why should we hire you?

Ten percent of college graduates pursue the appealing notion of postponing a "real" job in favor of a year or so of doing something fun, noble, or just plain interesting. As the author points out, the year after graduation may be the only time a person has the flexibility to do something unconventional before the responsibilities of family, mortgage, and the demands of a career kick in. Have you ever thought about doing something completely different?
This article appeared in U.S. News & World Report *in October 1998.*

MY BRILLIANT INTERIM CAREER

Katherine T. Beddingfield

1   Kristen Bergevin is a postponer and proud of it. When she graduated from the University of Southern California in 1996, she didn't want to put on a suit and heels and become a corporate slave. Instead, she purchased a $200 work permit for Britain and a plane ticket, and spent six months toiling abroad, first selling high-tech gadgets at Selfridge's department store in London, then bartending for a bit in an Edinburgh pub. "I was scared at first that I might mess up my career," says Bergevin, "but I learned that I could cope with just about anything—even budgeting in a foreign currency. After that, finding a job here was a piece of cake."

2   Perhaps as many as 1 in 10 freshly minted graduates postpone a "real" job in favor of an interim position. The numbers haven't changed much in recent years, but reasons have. Not so long ago postponers were serving up lattes because of the slumping economy. These days, the vast majority of them deliberately delay the career grind anywhere from several months to a couple of years. Confident that the job market will welcome them when they're ready, they pursue appealing interim jobs. With some 60 percent of college students graduating under the weight of student loans, the six-month window before the 10 years of loan repayments kick in provides many "the last opportunity to do something frivolous," notes Ron Lieber, coauthor of *Taking Time Off.* Here are some opportunities that beckon—and dangers that lurk.

Sorry, Too Late

3   First, the bad news. Postponing a post-college job hunt can have serious repercussions—and not just with your parents. In business and finance, postponers may lose out on prestigious and lucrative jobs, warns Marcia Harris, director of career services at the University of North Carolina–Chapel Hill. Entry-level financial analyst positions at brokerage firms, for example, are typically reserved for new graduates only. Even a six-month lag can knock an applicant out of the running. Or you could leave town when jobs are plentiful and return to a cool employment climate. Playing catch-up is another postponer plight. Interim barkeep Bergevin, now 24 and a Los Angeles public relations associate, figures she is about a year behind her classmates in salary and job responsibilities.

4   The noblest way to postpone is to save the world. On the domestic front, AmeriCorps members work for a year on projects from housing renovation to

child immunization. But many want to combine travel and community service. Barbara Hinsman, who graduated this spring from Notre Dame, is now in Kenya teaching farming techniques during a two-year Peace Corps stint. Her classmate Ryan Murphy has put a job with a big accounting firm on hold to work at the Farm of the Child, an orphanage, Catholic school, and health clinic in Honduras. They're among the 10 percent of Notre Dame students who sign up for volunteer service programs after graduation, having had a taste of community service integrated into undergraduate programs.

You could be disappointed by an organization claiming to steer you to international do-good possibilities. A group that charges thousands of dollars for placement could be a for-profit venture; you may feel more like a drop-in tourist than a member of the community during your time abroad. Organizations like the Council on International Educational Exchange offer hundreds of projects for about a $300 placement fee.   5

As a rule, service opportunities provide room and board, and occasionally help repay student loans. You'll have to cover other expenses from your savings: Many do-gooders do not want to be poor forever but figure right after school is the best time to heed the "call to be of service," says Andrea Shappell, director of senior transition programs at Notre Dame.   6

Teaching English abroad is more lucrative than other do-gooder jobs, and the sense of accomplishment and adventure can be just as great. Applicants need not speak the local language or be a certified teacher. But the heyday of "hopping on a plane and saying, 'Hey, I'm here to teach,'" is over, says William Nolting, head of University of Michigan's overseas opportunities office. Some countries, particularly in Eastern Europe, have upped requirements for teachers, preferring that they arrive, if not certified, at least with some tutoring background. Dozens of programs place would-be teachers in schools throughout Japan (where the rules require that you assist a native teacher rather than run your own classroom), Korea, and Taiwan, as well as in Eastern Europe and, to a lesser degree, Latin America.   7

You won't get rich, but you won't be poor, either. Anthony Hand, who taught English to high schoolers in northern Japan for three years beginning in July 1993, found the annual salary of 3.6 million yen (now about $30,000) quite comfortable. He traveled to Korea, Hong Kong, even New Zealand, and paid for his mother to visit for a month. His counterparts living in the urban sprawl of Tokyo or Kyoto felt more of a financial pinch. Pay is typically in the local coin; if the currency tumbles against the dollar, you might be too broke to travel outside the country.   8

The hardest part of the job can be the isolation. Hand was the first (and only) Westerner in his remote village. But the loneliness was never overwhelming. He studied Japanese sign language on the side and improved his rudimentary Japanese speaking skills by befriending locals. Temporary teachers who feel they can't complete the commitment, usually a year, can opt out, but if the program has paid for their airfare, they may be assessed a penalty of several hundred dollars.   9

On Parole

10   Or maybe you just want to have fun. Some postponers equate the "real world" with jail time. "They're doing the things we'd all like to do," laughs North Carolina's Harris as she ticks off jobs held by recent graduates at ski resorts and dude ranches. Experts suggest devising a plan for re-entry to reality. Set a date (probably no more than a year away) and a savings plan to accrue the bare minimum needed to make the transition—say, a month's rent.

11   That is, if you come back. Shannon McKee graduated in December 1992 from Texas Christian University and decided to sign on for six months with Norwegian Cruise Lines before starting business school in the fall. She worked in the gift shop on a Caribbean-based luxury liner—a plum job since the venue closes while the ship is in port. "I had lots of time off," says McKee. Earning about $1,000 per month, with nearly every need from food to dry cleaning provided, McKee had the cash to earn scuba certification during port calls in Bermuda.

12   Six years, three promotions, and dozens of ports later, McKee is working 16-hour days as cruise director aboard the Norwegian Majesty. She puts out the daily ship newsletter, involves passengers in poolside games, and oversees the captain's cocktail parties. Business school is nowhere on the horizon. "I couldn't give all this up to do a desk job." She may be at sea, but she has launched a career.

Vocabulary

Directions: Locate each of the key words in the reading selection. Try to figure out each word's meaning by using the context. Confirm your guess by checking the dictionary or thesaurus. Write the meanings of the words in the margin of the text. Then record the meanings in the chart below.

Key Word	Paragraph	Meaning
1. frivolous	2	
2. beckon	2	
3. lucrative	7	
4. heyday	7	
5. rudimentary	9	
Others?		

Guide Questions

Directions: These questions will guide your understanding of what you have read. Write your answers in your notebook or on a separate sheet of paper if your instructor wishes to collect it. Your answers to these questions will be the basis of class discussion.

1. What is an "interim career"?
2. According to the article, has there been a change in the numbers of people taking on interim careers, or their reasons for choosing interim careers, in recent years?
3. What are some of the reasons people give for taking on an interim career?
4. Select one of the careers mentioned in the article that appeals to you and describe it.
5. Describe some of the disadvantages of choosing an interim career.

Application/Writing

Do you know anyone who has had an interim career? Does the idea of an interim career appeal to you? If you could choose an interim career, what would you do, and why? Write two paragraphs.

SHORT TAKE

Directory of Business Names

Does a person's name affect the career he or she chooses? Consider this list, collected from business directories around the world, of the names of real people in real jobs.

A dentist in Paris: Docteur Ache

Lawyers in Ireland: Argue and Phibbs

A librarian in Brooklyn: Novella Booker

A disease counselor in California: Mr. Clapp

A pathologist in Florida: Dr. Croaker

An eye doctor in Michigan: Dr. I. Doctor

A judge in Massachusetts: Lawrence J. Felony

A dental technician in Germany: Walburga Floss

A company in Hong Kong: The Genuine Imitation Jewelry Company

A urologist in New Jersey: Dr. Bum Suck Lee

A priest in New York City: Father O'Pray

A gynecologist in New York City: Dr. Zotan Ovary

Plumbers in England: Plummer and Leek

A pathologist in Connecticut: Dr. David P. Stiff

All these names are from John Train's delightful book, *Crazy Quilt* (HarperCollins, 1996).

Feeling a bit hungry? How about a nice snack of seafood-flavored Cheetos? No? Then con-
sider a reindeer sausage pizza with a can of sweet corn for dessert. Or pasta with ketchup
on top? All of these culinary treats are popular items in other countries. This essay, first
published in the Wall Street Journal *in 1996, describes the challenges of marketing to the*
wildly different tastes of people in different countries. While for us it might be a fun sur-
prise to find a mayo and potato-topped pizza in Tokyo, international marketers hate
surprises. That's why they spend time and money studying the preferences of potential cus-
tomers all over the world.

CUSTOM-MADE

Tara Parker-Pope

1   Pity the poor Domino's Pizza Inc. delivery man.

2   In Britain, customers don't like the idea of him knocking on their doors—
they think it's rude. In Japan, houses aren't numbered sequentially—finding an
address means searching among rows of houses numbered willy-nilly. And in
Kuwait, pizza is more likely to be delivered to a waiting limousine than to someone's front door.

3   "We honestly believe we have the best pizza delivery system in the world,"
says Gary McCausland, managing director of Domino's international division.
"But delivering pizza isn't the same all over the world."

4   And neither is making cars, selling soap, or packaging toilet paper. International marketers have found that just because a product plays in Peoria,* that
doesn't mean it will be a hit in Helsinki.

5   To satisfy local tastes, products ranging from Heinz ketchup to Cheetos chips
are tweaked, reformulated, and reflavored. Fast-food companies such as McDonalds's
Corp., popular for the "sameness" they offer all over the world, have discovered that
to succeed, they also need to offer some local appeal—like selling beer in Germany
and adding British Cadbury chocolate sticks to their ice-cream cones in England.

6   The result is a delicate balancing act for international marketers: How does
a company exploit the economies of scale that can be gained by global marketing while at the same time making its products appeal to local tastes?

7   The answer: Be flexible, even when it means changing a tried-and-true
recipe, even when consumer preferences, like Haagen-Dazs green tea ice cream,
sound awful to the Western palate.

8   "It's a dilemma we all live with every day," says Nick Harding, H.J. Heinz Co.'s
managing director for Northern Europe. Heinz varies the recipe of its famous
ketchup in different markets, selling a less-sweet version in Belgium and Holland,
for instance, because consumers there use ketchup as a pasta sauce (and mayonnaise
on french fries). "We're looking for the economies from globalizing our ideas, but
we want to maintain the differences necessary for local markets," says Mr. Harding.

---

* "Plays in Peoria" is a common expression which means something is acceptable to most middle-class
Americans.

For those who don't heed such advice, the costs are high. U.S. auto makers, 9 for instance, have done poorly in Japan, at least in part because they failed to adapt. Until recently, most didn't bother even to put steering wheels on the right, as is the standard in Japan. While some American makers are beginning to conform, European companies such as Volkswagen AG, Daimler-Benz AG, and Bayerische Motoren Werke AG did it much sooner, and have done far better in the Japanese market as a result.

For Domino's, the balancing act has meant maintaining the same basic pizza 10 delivery system world-wide—and then teaming up with local franchisers to tailor the system to each country's needs. In Japan, detailed wall maps, three times larger than those used in its stores elsewhere, help delivery people find the proper address despite the odd street numbering system.

In Iceland, where much of the population doesn't have phone service, 11 Domino's has teamed with a Reykjavik drive-in movie theater to gain access to consumers. Customers craving a reindeer-sausage pizza (a popular flavor there) flash their turn signal, and a theater employee brings them a cellular phone to order a pizza, which is then delivered to the car.

Local Domino's managers have developed new pizza flavors, including *mayo* 12 *jaga* (mayonnaise and potato) in Tokyo and pickled ginger in India. The company, which now has 1,160 stores in 46 countries, is currently trying to develop a nonbeef pepperoni topping for its stores in India.

When Pillsbury Co., a unit of Britain's Grand Metropolitan PLC, wanted to 13 begin marketing its Green Giant brand vegetables outside the United States, it decided to start with canned sweet corn, a basic product unlikely to require any flavor changes across international markets. But to Pillsbury's surprise, the product still was subject to local influences. Instead of being eaten as a hot side dish, the French add it to salad and eat it cold. In Britain, corn is used as a sandwich and pizza topping. In Japan, school children gobble down canned corn as an after-school treat. And in Korea, the sweet corn is sprinkled over ice cream.

So Green Giant tailored its advertising to different markets. Spots show 14 corn kernels falling off a cob into salads and pastas, or topping an ice-cream sundae. "Initially we thought it would be used the same as in the United States," says Stephen Moss, vice president, strategy and development, for Green Giant. "But we've found there are very different uses for corn all over the world."

And Green Giant has faced some cultural hurdles in its race to foreign markets. Although vegetables are a significant part of the Asian diet, Green Giant 15 discovered that Japanese mothers, in particular, take pride in the time they take to prepare a family meal and saw frozen vegetables as an unwelcome shortcut. "Along with the convenience comes a little bit of guilt," says Mr. Moss.

The solution? Convince moms that using frozen vegetables gives them the op- 16 portunity to prepare their families' favorite foods more often. To that end, Green Giant focused on a frozen mixture of julienned carrots and burdock root, a traditional favorite root vegetable that requires several hours of tedious preparation.

The company also has introduced individual seasoned vegetable servings for 17 school lunch boxes, with such flavors as sesame-seasoned lotus root. Although fresh vegetables still dominate the market, Green Giant says its strategy is starting to show results, and frozen varieties now account for half the vegetable company's sales in Japan.

18   The drive for localization has been taken to extremes in some cases: Cheetos, the bright orange and cheesy-tasting chip brand of PepsiCo Inc.'s Frito-Lay unit, are cheeseless in China. The reason? Chinese consumers generally don't like cheese, because many of them are lactose-intolerant. So Cheetos tested such flavors as Peking duck, fried egg, and even dog to tempt the palates of Chinese. Ultimately, says Tom Kuthy, vice president of marketing for PepsiCo Foods International's Asia-Pacific operations, the company picked a butter flavor, called American cream, and an Asianized barbecue flavor called Japanese steak. Last year, Frito rolled out its third flavor, seafood.

19   In addition to changing the taste, the company also packaged Cheetos in a 15-gram size priced at one yuan, about 12 cents, so that even kids with little spending money can afford them. The bottom line: These efforts to adapt to the local market have paid off. Mr. Kuthy estimates that close to 300 million packages of Cheetos have been sold since they were introduced two years ago in Guangzhou. Cheetos are now available in Shanghai and Beijing as well.

20   Frito isn't through trying to adapt. Now the company is introducing a 33-gram pack for two yuan. Mr. Kuthy also is considering more flavors, but dog won't be one of them. "Yes, we tested the concept, but it was never made into a product," he says. "Its performance was mediocre."

21   Other PepsiCo units have followed with their own flavor variations. In Thailand, Pizza Hut has a *tom yam*-flavored pizza based on the spices of the traditional Thai soup. In Singapore, you can get a KFC Zinger chicken burger that is hot and spicy with Asia's ubiquitous chili. The Singaporean pizza at Pizza Hut comes with ground beef, green peppers and chili. Elsewhere in Asia, pizzas come in flavors such as Mongolian, with pork, chili, and garlic; salmon, with a creamy lobster sauce; and Satay, with grilled chicken and beef.

22   Coming up with the right flavor combinations for international consumers isn't easy. Part of the challenge is building relationships with customers in far-flung markets. For years, the founders of Ben & Jerry's Homemade Inc. had relied on friends, co-workers, and their own taste buds to concoct such unusual ice-cream flavors as Chunky Monkey and Cherry Garcia.

23   But introducing their ice cream abroad, by definition, meant losing that close connection with their customers that made them successful. "For Ben and me, since we've grown up in the United States, our customers were people like us, and the flavors we made appealed to us," says co-founder Jerry Greenfield, scooping ice cream at a media event in the Royal Albert Hall in London. "I don't think we have the same seat-of-the-pants feel for places like England. It's a different culture."

24   As a result, one of the company's most popular flavors in the United States, Chocolate Chip Cookie Dough, flopped in Britain. The nostalgia quotient of the ice cream, vanilla-flavored with chunks of raw cookie dough, was simply lost on the Brits, who historically haven't eaten chocolate-chip cookies. "People

didn't grow up in this country sneaking raw cookie-dough batter from Mom," says Mr. Greenfield.

The solution? Hold a contest to concoct a quintessential British ice   25
cream. After reviewing hundreds of entries, including Choc Ness Monster and Cream Victoria, the company in July introduced Cool Britannia, a combination of vanilla ice cream, strawberries, and chocolate-covered Scottish shortbread. (The company plans to sell Cool Britannia in the United States eventually.)

And in a stab at building a quirky relationship with Brits, the duo opted   26
for a publicity stunt when Britain's beef crisis meant farmers were left with herds of cattle that couldn't be sold at market. Ben & Jerry's creative solution: Use the cows to advertise. The company's logo was draped across the backs of grazing cattle, and the stunt made the front page of major London newspapers.

The company has just begun selling ice cream in France but isn't sure   27
whether the company will try contests for a French flavor in that market. One reason: It's unclear whether Ben & Jerry's wry humor, amusing to the Brits, will be understood by the laconic French. "We're going to try to get more in touch, more comfortable with the feel of the French market first," says Mr. Greenfield.

But for every success story, there have been a slew of global marketing mis-   28
takes. In Japan consumer-products marketer Procter & Gamble Co. made several stumbles when it first entered the market in the early 1970s.

The company thought its thicker, more-absorbent Pampers diapers in big   29
packs like those favored in America would be big sellers in Japan. But Japanese women change their babies twice as often as Americans and prefer thin diapers. Moreover, they often have tiny apartments and no room to store huge diaper packs. The company adapted by making thinner diapers packaged in smaller bags. Because the company shifted gears quickly, Procter & Gamble is now one of the largest and most successful consumer-goods companies in Japan, with more than $1 billion in annual sales and market leadership in several categories.

Vocabulary

Directions: Locate each of the key words in the reading selection. Try to figure out each word's meaning by using the context. Confirm your guess by checking the dictionary or thesaurus. Write the meanings of the words in the margin of the text. Then record the meanings in the chart below.

Key Word	Paragraph	Meaning
1. tweaked	5	
2. mediocre	20	

Key Word	Paragraph	Meaning
3. quintessential	25	
4. slew	28	
Others?		

Guide Questions

Directions: These questions will guide your understanding of what you have read. Write your answers in your notebook, or on a separate sheet of paper if your instructor wishes to collect it. Your answers to these questions will be the basis of class discussion.

1. In a sentence, explain why the author says we should "pity the poor Domino's pizza man."
2. Explain the balancing act that international marketers must cope with (paragraph 6). Please use your own words.
3. a. Describe the cultural problem the Green Giant company encountered when it tried to sell frozen vegetables in Japan and how they solved it.
   b. Give one example of how Ben & Jerry's ice cream company solved a similar problem.
4. Describe Proctor & Gamble's marketing mistake in Japan (beginning in paragraph 28). Be sure to use your own words.
5. Write a main idea sentence in your own words that sums up this article.

Writing

Directions: Choose one of the questions below and write a paragraph in response.

1. Have you had a personal experience related to the information in the article? If so, tell the story in a paragraph.
2. Assume that you are the president of a company that makes automobiles. What kind of research should you do before you try to sell your cars in a foreign country?
3. Assume you are the president of a company that makes beer. What information about the foreign country should you have before you try to sell your product in that country?

SHORT TAKE

It Got Lost in the Translation

Even experts in business can fall flat on their faces when they forget the importance of language in human affairs. Here are some examples of language goofs by companies involved in international marketing:

—Several years ago Estée Lauder introduced a new foundation make-up in Germany called Country Mist. In the nick of time, a local manager called U.S. headquarters with a linguistic SOS: *Mist* means "manure" in German. The name was changed to Country Moist.

—An ad for Nitto Koygo Company, a golf course designer in Tokyo, goes like this: "Preparing for you club-life of luxurious relaxation always there. Feel and Taste it at any one of our golf clubs both in Japan and overseas as well, please."

—The slogan "Come Alive with Pepsi" almost appeared in the Chinese version of *Reader's Digest* as "Pepsi Brings Your Ancestors Back from the Grave."

—"Body by Fisher" was translated into "Corpse by Fisher" in Flemish.

—The French government published an English-language catalog promoting local CAD/CAM products. Referring to one software program, it read: "Different versions are available for educational institutes for symbolic prices."

—Tokyo Gas Company's slogan in English reads "My Life, My Gas."

—When Totes Inc. bought the German company Jagra-Haus, it announced the company would be renamed Totes Deutschland. Executives retreated when they learned the new corporate name meant "dead Germany."

COLLABORATIVE LEARNING

Working in Groups to Guide Your Own Reading

All of the reading selections so far in this unit have been accompanied by questions and exercises that are meant to help you understand and use what you've read. However, in much of your college reading (not to mention in your real life), you will be expected to master the material on your own.

Research has shown that one of the most effective ways to learn is in *groups*. In college, working with classmates can help you to master the material of a college course. The give-and-take that comes naturally when working with other people helps us to avoid falling into bad habits like *passive reading*. (We have all had the awful experience of reading a whole chapter, then realizing that we don't remember one single thing we've read.) Working with other students will help you to avoid such problems. For this assignment, form groups of approximately four students. In your group, read and think about the two following reading selections, "Hispanic USA: The Conveyor Belt Ladies" by Rose Del Castillo Guilbault and "Less Is More: A Call for Shorter Work Hours" by Barbara Brandt. Then, create your own vocabulary chart, guide questions, and application and writing assignments.

Follow these steps to complete the assignment:

1. Preview the selection before you read—look at and think about the title, any headings or subheadings, the first paragraph, the last paragraph and the first sentence of each paragraph.
2. Read through the selection one time quickly.
3. Read the selection a second time, more carefully. This time mark the text. Review how to do this by turning to page 421, "Learning Strategy III—Marking Text."
4. Brainstorm with your group. Ask yourselves: What important issues is the author discussing? What new information did you learn? Can the issues discussed in the selection be connected to those you have already studied? Can any of the information here be applied to situations in your own life?
5. Now, create a set of exercises similar to those you have completed in previous chapters of this book:
   a. **Vocabulary.** Make a list of key words from the text. Set them up in chart format as on page 218.
   b. **Guide Questions.** Write questions that will guide understanding of the major ideas in the reading.
   c. **Application.** Prepare an application exercise that takes one or more of the important ideas in the reading and relates it to real life.
   d. **Writing.** Create a writing assignment to conclude the chapter.

Before you begin, it would be a good idea to review the questions and exercises in the previous reading selections in this book for reference.

When you are finished, submit your work to your instructor. Your instructor may review and combine the work of all the groups and return the exercise to the class. You will then have the opportunity to *answer* the questions you and your classmates have developed.

Now, use your skills as an active independent reader to tackle the following reading selections. Good luck!

Most of us have had to suffer through summer jobs—usually low-paying, high-boredom work suitable for a temporary, untrained worker. While we may have dreaded the work, the money was welcome and usually essential. In this article, Rose Del Castillo Guilbault describes her last summer job before college. She sorted tomatoes on a conveyor belt, side by side with migrant workers, women who, at first, embarrassed her, but whom she soon came to like and respect.

HISPANIC USA: THE CONVEYOR-BELT LADIES
Rose Del Castillo Guilbault

1   The conveyor-belt ladies were the migrant women, mostly from Texas, I worked with during the summers of my teenage years. I call them conveyor-belt ladies because our entire relationship took place while sorting tomatoes on a conveyor belt.

2   We were like a cast in a play where all the action occurs on one set. We'd return day after day to perform the same roles, only this stage was a vegetable-packing shed, and at the end of the season there was no applause. The players could look forward only to the same uninspiring parts on a string of grim real-life stages.

3   The women and their families arrived in May for the carrot season, spent the summer in the tomato sheds, and stayed through October for the bean harvest. After that, they emptied the town, some returning to their homes in Texas (cities like McAllen, Douglas, Brownsville), while others continued on the migrant trail, picking cotton in the San Joaquin Valley or grapefruits and oranges in the Imperial Valley.

4   Most of these women had started in the fields. The vegetable-packing sheds were a step up, easier than the back-breaking, grueling work the field demanded. The work was more tedious than strenuous, paid better, provided fairly steady hours and clean bathrooms. Best of all, you weren't subjected to the elements.

5   The summer I was sixteen, my mother got jobs for both of us as tomato sorters. That's how I came to be included in the seasonal sorority of the conveyor belt.

6   The work consisted of standing and picking flawed tomatoes off the conveyor belt before they rolled off into the shipping boxes at the end of the line. These boxes were immediately loaded onto waiting delivery trucks, so it was crucial not to let imperfect tomatoes through.

7   The work could be slow or intense, depending on the quality of the tomatoes and how many there were. Work increased when the company's deliveries got backlogged or after rainy weather had delayed picking.

8   During those times, it was not unusual to work from 7 A.M. to midnight, playing catch-up. I never heard anyone complain about the overtime. Overtime meant desperately needed extra money.

9   I was not happy to be part of the agricultural work force. I would have preferred working in a dress shop or baby-sitting, like my friends. But I had a dream that would cost a lot of money—college. And the fact was, this was the highest-paying work I could do.

But it wasn't so much the work that bothered me. I was embarrassed be- 10
cause only Mexicans worked at packing sheds. I had heard my schoolmates joke
about the "ugly, fat Mexican women" at the sheds. They ridiculed the way they
dressed and laughed at the "funny way" they talked. I feared working with
them would irrevocably stigmatize me, setting me further apart from my Anglo classmates.

At sixteen I was more American than Mexican and, with adolescent arro- 11
gance, felt superior to these "uneducated" women. I might be one of them, I
reasoned, but I was not like them.

But it was difficult not to like the women. They were a gregarious, enter- 12
taining group, easing the long, monotonous hours with bawdy humor, spicy
gossip, and inventive laments. They poked fun at all the male workers and did
hysterical impersonations of a dyspeptic Anglo supervisor. Although he didn't
speak Spanish (other than *"Mujeres, trabajo, trabajo!"* Women, work, work!), he
seemed to sense he was being laughed at. That would account for the sudden
rages when he would stamp his foot and forbid us to talk until break time.

"I bet he understands Spanish and just pretends so he can hear what we say," 13
I whispered to Rosa.

"*Ay, no, hija,* it's all the buzzing in his ears that alerts him that these *viejas* 14
(old women) are bad-mouthing him!" Rosa giggled.

But it would have been easier to tie the women's tongues in a knot than to 15
keep them quiet. Eventually the ladies had their way and their fun, and the men
learned to ignore them.

We were often shifted around, another strategy to keep us quiet. This gave 16
me ample opportunity to get to know everyone, listen to their life stories, and
absorb the gossip.

Pretty Rosa described her romances and her impending wedding to a hand- 17
some field worker. Bertha, a heavy-set, dark-skinned woman, told me that Rosa's
marriage would cause nothing but headaches because the man was younger and
too handsome. Maria, large, moon-faced, and placid, described the births of each
of her nine children, warning me about the horrors of childbirth. Pragmatic
Minnie, a tiny woman who always wore printed cotton dresses, scoffed at Maria's
stupidity, telling me she wouldn't have so many kids if she had ignored that
good-for-nothing priest and gotten her tubes tied!

In unexpected moments, they could turn melancholic: recounting the babies 18
who died because their mothers couldn't afford medical care; the alcoholic, abusive husbands who were their "cross to bear"; the racism they experienced in
Texas, where they were branded "dirty Mexicans" or "Mexican dogs" and not
allowed in certain restaurants.

They spoke with the detached fatalism of people with limited choices and 19
alternatives. Their lives were as raw and brutal as ghetto streets—something
they accepted with an odd grace and resignation.

I was appalled and deeply affected by these confidences. The injustices they 20
endured enraged me; their personal struggles overwhelmed me. I knew I could
do little but sympathize.

21   My mother, no stranger to suffering, suggested I was too impressionable when I emotionally told her the women's stories. "That's nothing," she'd say lightly. "If they were in Mexico, life would be even harder. At least there's opportunities here, you can work."

22   My icy arrogance quickly thawed, that first summer, as my respect for the conveyor-belt ladies grew.

23   I worked in the packing sheds for several summers. The last season also turned out to be the last time I lived at home. It was the end of a chapter in my life, but I didn't know it then. I had just finished junior college and was transferring to the university. I was already over-educated for seasonal work, but if you counted the overtime, no other jobs came close to paying so well, so I went back one last time.

24   The ladies treated me with warmth and respect. I was a college student, deserving of special treatment.

25   Aguedita, the crew chief, moved me to softer and better-paying jobs within the plant. I went from the conveyor belt to shoving boxes down a chute and finally to weighing boxes of tomatoes on a scale—the highest-paying position for a woman.

26   When the union's dues collector showed up, the women hid me in the bathroom. They had decided it was unfair for me to have to join the union and pay dues, since I worked only during the summer.

27   "Where's the student?" the union rep would ask, opening the door to a barrage of complaints about the union's unfairness.

28   Maria (of the nine children) tried to feed me all summer, bringing extra tortillas, which were delicious. I accepted them guiltily, always wondering if I was taking food away from her children. Others would bring rental contracts or other documents for me to explain and translate.

29   The last day of work was splendidly beautiful, warm and sunny. If this had been a movie, these last scenes would have been shot in soft focus, with a crescendo of music in the background.

30   But real life is anti-climactic. As it was, nothing unusual happened. The conveyor belt's loud humming was turned off, silenced for the season. The women sighed as they removed their aprons. Some of them just walked off, calling *Hasta la próxima!* Until next time!

31   But most of the conveyor-belt ladies shook my hand, gave me a blessing or a big hug.

32   "Make us proud!" they said.

33   I hope I have.

Vocabulary

Directions: Mark any important words in the reading selection that you don't know. Then list them in the following chart along with their paragraph numbers. Try to figure out each word's meaning by reading over the context carefully for clues to help you guess the meaning of the unfamiliar word. Check your dictionary or thesaurus to confirm your guess.

After you discuss the words with your group members, write the meanings in the margin of the text, near the word. Then enter them in the chart below.

Key Word	Paragraph	Meaning

Guide Questions

Directions: Develop a list of questions that elicit the important ideas in the reading selection. Start at the beginning and work your way sequentially through the text until you have addressed all of the author's major ideas.

Application

Directions: When you have a list of guide questions, read through the selection again. This time, write one or more questions that require the application of the information in the text to a situation in the real world.

Writing

Directions: Your last task is to prepare a writing assignment. For example, you might ask for a paragraph in which the writer comments on the ideas in the reading selection. You might also ask for a summary of the selection.

Most Americans consider the forty-hour work week to be normal and natural. But many observers think that Americans are working too long and too hard. Here, the author argues that overwork has become a major social problem that has reached crisis proportions. See if you agree with her.

LESS IS MORE: A CALL FOR SHORTER WORK HOURS
Barbara Brandt

1   America is suffering from overwork. Too many of us are too busy, trying to squeeze more into each day while having less to show for it. Although our growing time crunch is often portrayed as a personal dilemma, it is in fact a major social problem that has reached crisis proportions over the past twenty years.

2   The simple fact is that Americans today—both women and men—are spending too much time at work, to the detriment of their homes, their families, their personal lives, and their communities. The American Dream promised that our individual hard work, paired with the advances of modern technology, would bring about the good life for all. Glorious visions of the leisure society were touted throughout the fifties and sixties. But now most people are working more than ever before, while still struggling to meet their economic commitments. Ironically, the many advances in technology, such as computers and fax machines, rather than reducing our work load, seem to have speeded up our lives at work. At the same time, technology has equipped us with "conveniences" like microwave ovens and frozen dinners that merely enable us to adopt a similar frantic pace in our home lives so we can cope with more hours at paid work.

3   A recent spate of articles in the mainstream media has focused on the new problems of overwork and lack of time. Unfortunately, overwork is often portrayed as a special problem of yuppies and professionals on the fast track. In reality, the unequal distribution of work and time in America today reflects the decline in both standard of living and quality of life for most Americans. Families whose members never see each other, women who work a double shift (first on the job, then at home), workers who need more flexible work schedules, and unemployed and underemployed people who need more work are all casualties of the crisis of overwork.

4   Americans often assume that overwork is an inevitable fact of life—like death and taxes. Yet a closer look at other times and other nations offers some startling surprises.

5   Anthropologists have observed that, in pre-industrial (particularly hunting and gathering) societies, people generally spend 3 to 4 hours a day, 15 to 20 hours a week, doing the work necessary to maintain life. The rest of the time is spent in socializing, partying, playing, storytelling, and artistic or religious activities. The ancient Romans celebrated 175 public festivals a year in which everyone participated, and people in the Middle Ages had at least 115.

6   In our era, almost every other industrialized nation (except Japan) has fewer annual working hours and longer vacations than the United States. This includes all

of Western Europe, where many nations enjoy thriving economies and standards of living equal to or higher than ours. Jeremy Brecher and Tim Costello, writing in *Z Magazine* (October 1990), note that "European unions during the 1980s made a powerful and largely successful push to cut working hours. In 1987 German metalworkers struck and won a 37.5-hour week; many are now winning a 35-hour week. In 1990, hundreds of thousands of British workers won a 37-hour week."

In an article about work time in the *Boston Globe,* Suzanne Gordon notes   7
that workers in other industrialized countries "enjoy—as a statutory right— longer vacations [than in the United States] from the moment they enter the work force. In Canada, workers are legally entitled to two weeks off their first year on the job. . . . After two or three years of employment, most get three weeks of vacation. After ten years, it's up to four, and by twenty years, Canadian workers are off for five weeks. In Germany, statutes guarantee eighteen days minimum for everyone, but most workers get five or six weeks. The same is true in Scandinavian countries, and in France."

In contrast to the extreme American emphasis on productivity and commit-   8
ment, which results in many workers, especially in professional-level jobs, not taking the vacations coming to them, Gordon notes that "In countries that are America's most successful competitors in the global marketplace, all working people, whether lawyers or teachers, CEOs or janitors, take the vacations to which they are entitled by law. 'No one in West Germany,' a West German embassy's officer explains, 'no matter how high up they are, would ever say they couldn't afford to take a vacation. Everyone takes their vacation.'"

And in Japan, where dedication to the job is legendary, Gordon notes that   9
the Japanese themselves are beginning to consider their national workaholism a serious social problem, leading to stress-related illnesses and even death. As a result, the Japanese government recently established a commission whose goal is to promote shorter working hours and more leisure time.

Most other industrialized nations also have better family-leave policies than   10
the United States, and in a number of other countries workers benefit from innovative time-scheduling opportunities, such as sabbaticals.

While the idea of a shorter workweek and longer vacations sounds appealing   11
to most people, any movement to enact shorter work time as a public policy will encounter surprising pockets of resistance, not just from business leaders but even from some workers. Perhaps the most formidable barrier to more free time for Americans is the widespread mind-set that the forty-hour workweek, eight hours a day, five days a week, fifty weeks a year, is a natural rhythm of the universe. This view is reinforced by the media's complete silence regarding the shorter work-time and more favorable vacation and family-leave policies of other countries. This lack of information, and our leaders' reluctance to suggest that the United States can learn from any other nation (except workaholic Japan), is one reason why more Americans don't identify overwork as a major problem or clamor for fewer hours and more vacation. Monika Bauerlein, a journalist originally from Germany, now living in Minneapolis, exclaims, "I can't believe that people here aren't rioting in the streets over having only two weeks of vacation a year."

12   A second obstacle to launching a powerful shorter work time movement is America's deeply ingrained work ethic, or its modern incarnation, the workaholic syndrome. The work ethic fosters the widely held belief that people's work is their most important activity and that people who do not work long and hard are lazy, unproductive, and worthless.

13   For many Americans today, paid work is not just a way to make money but is a crucial source of their self-worth. Many of us identify ourselves almost entirely by the kind of work we do. Work still has a powerful psychological and spiritual hold over our lives—and talk of shorter work time may seem somehow morally suspicious.

14   Because we are so deeply a work-oriented society, leisure-time activities—such as play, relaxation, engaging in cultural and artistic pursuits, or just quiet contemplation and "doing nothing"—are not looked on as essential and worthwhile components of life. Of course, for the majority of working women who must work a second shift at home, much of the time spent outside of paid work is not leisure anyway. Also, much of our nonwork time is spent not just in personal renewal, but in building and maintaining essential social ties—with family, friends, and the larger community.

15   Today, as mothers and fathers spend more and more time on the job, we are beginning to recognize the deleterious effects—especially on our young people—of the breakdown of social ties and community in American life. But unfortunately, our nation reacts to these problems by calling for more paid professionals—more police, more psychiatrists, more experts—without recognizing the possibility that shorter work hours and more free time could enable us to do much of the necessary rebuilding and healing, with much more gratifying and longer-lasting results.

16   Of course, the stiffest opposition to cutting work hours comes not from citizens but from business. Employers are reluctant to alter the eight-hour day, forty-hour workweek, fifty weeks a year because it seems easier and more profitable for employers to hire fewer employees for longer hours rather than more employees—each of whom would also require health insurance and other benefits—with flexible schedules and work arrangements.

17   Harvard University economist Juliet B. Schor, who has been studying issues of work and leisure in America, reminds us that we cannot ignore the larger relationship between unemployment and overwork: While many of us work too much, others are unable to find paid work at all. Schor points out that "workers who work longer hours lose more income when they lose their jobs. The threat of job loss is an important determinant of management's power on the shop floor." A system that offers only two options—long work hours or unemployment—serves as both a carrot and a stick. Those lucky enough to get full-time jobs are bribed into docile compliance with the boss, while the spectre of unemployment always looms as the ultimate punishment for the unruly.

18   Some observers suggest that keeping people divided into "the employed" and "the unemployed" creates feelings of resentment and inferiority/superiority between the two groups, thus focusing their discontent and blame on each other rather than on the corporations and political figures who actually dictate our nation's economic policies.

Our role as consumers contributes to keeping the average workweek   19
from falling. In an economic system in which addictive buying is the basis
of corporate profits, working a full forty hours or more each week for fifty
weeks a year gives us just enough time to stumble home and dazedly—almost
automatically—shop; but not enough time to think about deeper issues or to work
effectively for social change. From the point of view of corporations and policymakers, shorter work time may be bad for the economy, because people with
enhanced free time may begin to find other things to do with it besides mindlessly
buying products. It takes more free time to grow vegetables, cook meals from scratch,
sew clothes, or repair broken items than it does to just buy these things at the mall.

Any serious proposal to give employed Americans a break by cutting into   20
the eight-hour work day is certain to be met with anguished cries about international competitiveness. The United States seems gripped by the fear that our
nation has lost its economic dominance, and pundits, policymakers, and business leaders tell us that no sacrifice is too great if it puts America on top again.

As arguments like this are put forward (and we can expect them to increase in   21
the years to come), we need to remember two things. First, even if America maintained its dominance (whatever that means) and the economy were booming again,
this would be no guarantee that the gains—be they in wages, in employment
opportunities, or in leisure—would be distributed equitably between upper management and everyone else. Second, the entire issue of competitiveness is suspect
when it pits poorly treated workers in one country against poorly treated workers in
another, and when the vast majority of economic power, anyway, is in the control of
enormous multinational corporations that have no loyalty to the people of any land.

Vocabulary

Directions: Mark any important words in the reading selection that you don't know. Then
list them in the following chart along with their paragraph numbers. Try to figure out
each word's meaning by reading its context carefully for clues to help you guess the
meaning of the unfamiliar word. Check your dictionary or thesaurus to confirm your
guess. After you discuss the words with your group members, write the meanings in the
margin of the text, near the word. Then enter them in the chart.

Key Word	Paragraph	Meaning

Guide Questions

Directions: Develop a list of questions that elicit the important ideas in the reading selection. Start at the beginning and work your way sequentially through the text until you have addressed all of the author's major ideas.

Application

Directions: When you have a list of guide questions, read through the selection again. This time, write one or more questions that require the application of the information in the text to a situation in the real world.

Writing

Directions: Your last task is to prepare a writing assignment. For example, you might ask for a paragraph in which the writer comments on the ideas in the reading selection. You might also ask for a summary of the selection.

SPECIAL PROJECT

WORK

Career Exploration

For this project you will do research on the career you hope to have when you finish school. The report should answer the questions below:

1. What is the nature of the work? What does the worker do all day? Describe a typical day.
2. Where does the work take place? Is it in an office, a clinic, a lab, outdoors? Describe the working conditions.
3. What is the typical annual starting salary? What is the typical salary for someone with ten years' experience?
4. What is the employment outlook for this particular career at the present time? Are there jobs available?
5. List some of the major employers in this field in your area.
6. What about this job will make you happy and satisfied? Do you think there will be any negative aspects to the job? If so, how will you cope with them?

Many resources are available to help you complete this project. Your school library and your local public library have many magazines and publications related to every job imaginable. Find a magazine or journal that is read by workers in that field and become familiar with it.

The Internet offers a wealth of resources for job seekers. A few suggestions follow:

www.careerbuilder.com
www.collegegrad.com
www.collegenet.com
www.interbiznet.com

Government agencies provide websites with general information about jobs and employment:

U.S. Department of Labor	www.dol.gov
U.S. Equal Employment Opportunity Commission	www.eeoc.gov
U.S. Small Business Administration	www.sba.gov

Nonprofit organizations and labor unions also provide information on websites:

AFL-CIO	www.aflcio.org
Better Business Bureau	www.bbb.com
Communication Workers of America	www.cwa-union.org

Most companies have a website where you can find information about products, services, working conditions, and even available jobs. Think of a company or institution that interests you and try an address or a keyword search. Following are a few examples and their addresses:

American Express Small Business Services	www.americanexpress.com/smallbusiness/resources
ElderCare	www.eldercare.com
Gap Stores	www.gapinc.com/careers
Gateway	www.gateway.com
Hewlett-Packard	www.hp.com
Kinko's	www.fedexkinkos.com
Liz Claiborne	www.lizclaiborne.com
McDonald's	www.mcdonalds.com
Nantucket Nectars	www.juiceguys.com
Procter & Gamble	www.pg.com
Samuel Adams Brewery	www.samadams.com
Target	www.target.com

UNIT FIVE

CRITICAL READING AND THINKING ABOUT CONTROVERSIAL ISSUES

It is better to debate a question without settling it than to settle it without debate.

—Joseph Joubert

Thinking about Critical Reading and Thinking

Have you ever expressed a strong opinion about a controversial subject, say the death penalty, a political candidate, or gun control? Have you ever been challenged to support your view but been unable to explain your position? How did you feel? Embarrassed? Foolish? Many of us go through life with "unexamined" ideas. We accept views of our parents, teachers, and friends without analyzing them, and only discover our ignorance when we are questioned. Socrates,* perhaps the greatest philosopher who ever lived, tells us "the unexamined life is not worth living." An important part of our college experience should be the examination of ourselves—taking a look at our values, our opinions and beliefs about our world, and why we hold them. In the story below, we see one way of "examining" something. Read the story and decide if you think the blind men's way of looking at the issue of the elephant is a good way to learn about something.

The Blind Men and the Elephant

Once upon a time in a land far away, there was a kingdom of the blind. All of the people were blind, including the king. The king of the land was a very inquisitive man who always wanted to know more about the world. Having heard wondrous tales of an amazing animal called the elephant, he called the three wisest men of the kingdom and ordered them to go and find the elephant so they could come back and tell him what

---

*Socrates (469–399 BC) was a Greek philosopher and mentor to Plato. He spent most of his life in profound philosophical discussions. He believed that the highest meaning of life could be attained through self-knowledge.

the elephant was like. The three wise men went off and did, indeed, find the elephant. The first blind man went up to the elephant, felt its tail, and said, "The elephant is very like a rope!" The second man touched the elephant's trunk and said, "The elephant is very like a snake!" The third man touched the elephant's ear and said, "The elephant is very like a fan!"

Now, answer these questions about the story.

1. Which, if any, of the blind men now knows what an elephant is like?
2. When the wise men return and report to the king, will he know what the elephant is like? Why or why not?
3. How could the king find out what the elephant is really like?

Remember that this story is a *fable*. A fable is a story that teaches us a moral or lesson. The characters in such stories are not real, but are symbols of someone or something in real life. Keep the fable in mind as you read the next selection, "Critical Reading — Critical Thinking." You will see that the elephant is a symbol of any important or controversial issue, while the blind men represent the different single perspectives on the issue. We cannot find out what an elephant is really like — or what an issue is really about — unless we actively seek out and then combine all the different perspectives on it.

CRITICAL READING—CRITICAL THINKING
Mary Fjeldstad

One of our greatest challenges as adults is developing a clear understanding   1
about the way things are in the complex, ever-changing world around us. In our
lives, many issues arise that demand our attention, our analysis, and our decision.
Unfortunately, most of us have not been well trained in thinking critically. We
tend to accept the guidance of people whom we respect or who are better informed than we are. Thus, we often reach adulthood still clinging to the attitudes
taught us by our parents and other authority figures from our youth. Educated
persons, however, are not satisfied with "borrowing" the opinions and ideas of
others—they insist on forming their own. To do so, they must carefully analyze
their beliefs. This is the first step in developing a responsible opinion. Before we
can develop a complete understanding of an issue, we must consider other viewpoints that may be equally valid. For example, imagine you are looking at a
sculpture from one spot, trying to understand the artist's message. While your
view of the sculpture may be *accurate,* it is not *complete.* It is not until you walk
around the sculpture and see it from different *perspectives* that you can get a full
sense of what it really looks like.

It is the same with most of the important issues and problems in life—one   2
perspective is not enough to give us the whole picture. It is essential to seek
other perspectives on the issues we are trying to understand. What are some
ways we can get information on other perspectives? One way is to use our imaginations. Take, for example, the emotional issue of abortion. To develop an understanding of the issue, we must examine it from all possible points of view.
What are the possible perspectives on this issue? One perspective is that of the
pregnant woman, another is that of the prospective father, others are those of
the family of each prospective parent, doctors, religious groups, the fetus itself,
and, of course, society as a whole. We can use our imaginations to inform ourselves by mentally putting ourselves in the shoes of each of these persons or
groups. How would I feel if I were the husband of a pregnant woman who
wished to have an abortion? How would I feel as the doctor? Or the minister?
What if the pregnant woman was the victim of a rape? Or a drug addict who
had already given birth to several addicted children or children who were sub-
sequently abused? What is the impact on society of the decision that will be
made?

Other ways of learning about additional perspectives include reading about   3
them in books, magazines, and newspapers, listening to television and radio
broadcasts, and, of course, discussing them with other people.

Learning about each of the perspectives on an issue helps us to see the arguments.   4
An *argument* in this context means a *reason*—something that supports the way a person feels about an issue. For example, when you were considering the issue of

whether to go to college, you probably thought of several different arguments supporting a decision to go to school; for example:

1. It will help prepare me for a better job.
2. I will earn more money in the long run.
3. I am bored with my life as it is now.
4. It will help me grow as a person.
5. It will help me develop my mind.
6. I will meet new people with similar interests.
7. I will make new friends.

Although some of these arguments may be more important to you than others, all of them are *reasons* to support the decision to go to college. On the other hand, despite all these good arguments, going to school may still not be the right thing for you. You must examine other sides of the issue: what are some arguments *against* attending college?

5   When you learn about developing and analyzing arguments, you will be learning a skill that is important beyond the world of the classroom. You will need to argue many questions in your life. You will, no doubt, argue about political and moral issues. Someone you love may be considering an abortion, or the school in your neighborhood may decide to hand out condoms to students. You may discover a large industry is dumping toxic wastes in the water near your home. You may apply for financial aid or for a scholarship and be turned down unfairly. You may receive a grade in a course that you feel is lower than you deserve. In each of these situations you will need to consider all of the available information and all of the different perspectives before coming to a decision of your own. Once you have developed an opinion, you will then be able to present your view to others in a reasonable and effective way. Thus, stating arguments is not limited to the sort of issues reported in newspapers and magazines. When you apply for a job, decide to get married, or give advice to a friend, you need to know how to argue effectively.

6   In order to consider all the perspectives of an issue, we must be open to the viewpoints of other people and be willing to listen and exchange ideas with them. This process is called a discussion, or *dialogue.* If you felt strongly about the abortion issue, for example, it might make you feel uncomfortable to listen to someone who disagrees with you. But that is the only way you can be sure your own position is supported and strong. Listening to others' points of view should always make us re-examine our own; we may not change our minds, but we will have a more valuable opinion because it has been examined.

7   The selections in this unit will help you clarify your ideas on some of the important issues of the day. By reading, thinking, and writing about them, you will learn to formulate good arguments of your own—and to hold opinions that are mature and valuable. As you read, keep in mind the words of the great French philosopher René Descartes:

It is now some years since I detected how many were the false beliefs that
I had believed to be true since my earliest youth. And since that time,

I have been convinced that I must once and for all seriously try to rid myself of all the opinions which I had formerly accepted, and begin to build anew, if I wanted to establish any firm and permanent structure for my beliefs.

Vocabulary

Directions: Locate each of the key words in the reading selection. Try to figure out each word's meaning by using the context. Confirm your guess by checking the dictionary or thesaurus. Write the meanings of the words in the margin of the text. Then record the meanings in the chart below.

Key Word	Paragraph	Meaning
1. perspective	1	
2. prospective	2	
3. argument	4	
4. dialogue	6	
Others?		

Marking Text

Turn to page 421, "Learning Strategy III—Marking Text." Read and study the information on how to mark your text. Then mark the selection you just read, "Critical Reading— Critical Thinking."

Application

Directions: We experience argumentation all the time in our daily lives—listening to a political candidate trying to persuade us to vote for him or her, a friend trying to convince us to lend him money, classmates trying to convince a teacher to postpone a test, a daughter begging to get a tattoo, a son to buy the latest fashion.

An important skill in school and in life is to be able to understand the arguments people are making in order to persuade us of something. In the following, the writer makes several arguments in favor of polygamy. Read the essay carefully, then in small groups analyze the arguments made by the author. Pull out the arguments the author makes in favor of polygamy—in this case, of allowing men to take two or more wives. Compare your group's list of arguments with the lists of your classmates.

IN DEFENSE OF POLYGAMY

B. Aisha Lemu

1   Perhaps the aspect of Islam (with respect to women) that is most prominent in the Western mind is that of polygamy. Firstly let me clarify that Islam does not impose polygamy as a universal practice. The Prophet himself was a monogamist for the greater part of his married life, from the age of twenty-five when he married Khadija until he was fifty when she died.

2   One should therefore regard monogamy as the norm and polygamy as the exception.

3   One may observe that, although it has been abused in some times and some places, polygamy has, under certain circumstances, a valuable function. In some situations it may be considered as the lesser of two evils and in other situations it may even be a positively beneficial arrangement.

4   The most obvious example of this occurs in times of war when there are inevitably large numbers of widows and girls whose fiancés and husbands have been killed in the fighting. One has only to recall the figures of the dead in the first and second world wars to be aware that literally millions of women and girls lost their husbands and fiancés and were left alone without any income or care or protection for themselves or their children. If it is still maintained that, under these circumstances, a man may marry only one wife, what options are left to the millions of other women who have no hope of getting a husband? Their choice, bluntly stated, is between a chaste and childless old maidenhood, or becoming somebody's mistress—that is, an unofficial second wife with no legal rights for herself or her children. Most women would not welcome either of these since most women have always wanted and still do want the security of a legal husband and family.

5   The compromise, therefore, is for women under these circumstances to face the fact that, if given the alternative, many of them would rather share a husband than have none at all. And there is no doubt that it is easier to share a husband when it is an established and publicly recognized practice than when it is carried on secretly along with attempts to deceive the first wife.

6   And it is no secret that polygamy of a sort is widely carried on in Europe and America. The difference is that, while the Western man has no legal obligations to his second, third, or fourth mistresses and their children, the Muslim husband has complete legal obligations toward his second, third, or fourth wife and their children.

7   There may be other circumstances unrelated to war—individual circumstances where marriage to more than one wife may be preferable to other available alternatives—for example, where the first wife is chronically sick or disabled. There are, of course, some husbands who can manage this situation, but no one would deny its potential hazards. A second marriage, in some cases, could be a solution acceptable to all three parties.

Again, there are cases in which a wife is unable to have children while the   8
husband very much wants them. Under Western laws, a man must either accept
his wife's childlessness if he can, or, if he cannot, he must find a means of divorce
in order to marry again. This could be avoided in some cases if the parties agreed
on a second marriage.

There are other cases where a marriage has not been very successful and the   9
husband loves another woman. This situation is so familiar that it is known as
the Eternal Triangle. Under Western laws the husband cannot marry the second
woman without divorcing the first one, but the first wife may not wish to be divorced. She may no longer love her husband, but she may still respect him and
wish to stay with him for the security of marriage, for herself and their children.
Similarly, the second woman may not wish to break up the man's first family.
There are certain cases such as this where both women could accept a polygamous
marriage rather than face divorce on the one hand or an extramarital affair on the
other.

I have mentioned some of these examples because, to the majority of West-   10
erners, polygamy is only thought of in the context of a harem of glamorous young
girls, not as a possible solution to some of the problems of Western society itself.

SHORT TAKE

Argumentation

The word *argumentation* can be confusing. Our first reaction may be to think of
the everyday word *argument*—a disagreement, a quarrel. But writing an argumentation paper has nothing to do with anger or unpleasantness. While we may
throw dishes and slam doors in an argument with our family, *argumentation* requires that we think and express ourselves clearly, without letting our feelings in-
terfere. An argumentation paper is an articulate, well-organized statement of our
ideas. It attempts to convince others to consider our point of view, and, perhaps,
to persuade them to agree with us.

The most important aspect of argumentation, though, is not winning. It is
gaining the respect of others, convincing them we are worthy of their attention
and consideration. If we can win this, we have won something more valuable than
the vote on the issue at hand. It is essential, then, to treat our opponents with respect. No one will listen to us if we treat them as if they were fools. Do not be
contemptuous of those who disagree with you. Try not to be narrow-minded. Do
not assume you have a monopoly on the truth. And remember, you cannot expect
others to listen to you if you do not listen to them.

In this consumer age, people demand a perfect product and don't hesitate to sue when they feel they've been saddled with "damaged goods." Does an implied warranty cover children as well? If an adopted child turns out to be different from what the parents expected, should they be allowed to return the goods? The following article from Time *magazine discusses this growing problem in an age of demand for designer cars, houses, clothes, and even children.*

WHEN THE LULLABY ENDS

Andrea Sachs

1   Most eleven-year-olds don't have a lawyer, but Tony is a special case. His adoptive parents decided, five years after his adoption, that Tony had not properly "bonded" with them, and returned him to the state in March. They kept Sam, Tony's natural younger brother. Patrick Murphy, the Chicago public guardian who was appointed to serve as Tony's attorney, says the youngster is an "absolute joy to be around." But there have been scars. Says Murphy: "One of the tragic things is that Tony blames himself."

2   Tony is one of at least one thousand children adopted in the United States each year who will be returned to agencies by their new parents. Some are sent back because of unmet expectations, others because they have severe emotional problems the parents cannot handle. In a risk-averse age when consumer standards have become more exacting and family commitments seem less binding, there is a danger that adopted children could be viewed as commodities that come with an implied warranty. The problem presents a major challenge for the legal system. "This is not a question of damaged goods; it's a matter of what's in the best interest of the child," says Neil Cogan of Southern Methodist Law School.

3   Social workers used to believe that all an adopted child needed was a loving home. But now many admit that even the most committed parents may be overwhelmed by unexpected problems. In 1986 Dan and Rhonda Stanton adopted a blond baby girl they named Stacey René. "We thought we had a perfect baby because she didn't cry," says Dan, an insurance agent in suburban Dallas. Their contentment faded as the months passed and Stacey did not develop properly. She didn't babble and laugh like their friends' babies and couldn't pinch with her individual fingers. The tentative diagnosis: Rett's syndrome, a rare genetic disorder in which the brain stops growing. Devastated, the Stantons took Stacey back to the agency and have not seen her since. "We made a commitment to her, but we were not able to live up to that commitment," says Rhonda. "She turned out to be totally different from what we thought we had adopted."

4   If adoptive parents are saddled with an unforeseen defect, who should shoulder the load? Most experts put the onus on the adoptive parents. "Families, having decided to do an adoption, assume a certain risk," says Professor William Winslade of the University of Texas Medical School in Galveston.

"If it is an incredibly difficult burden, it seems unfair not to give parents, who have provided the benefit to society by making the adoption, some special help. But I don't think the burden should be totally given back to the state either. Parents adopt because they want the joys—and the sorrows—of having children."

About 2 percent of all adoptions in the United States fail. But for older children and children with special needs, the numbers are far higher. For children older than two, 10 percent of the adoptions are dissolved. For ages twelve to seventeen, the rate shoots up to around 24 percent. This poses a special problem, since healthy adoptable babies are increasingly scarce due to the fact that more single women now opt to have abortions or to keep their infants. More families are therefore adopting older or handicapped children. This seems to be a main cause of the growing return-to-sender phenomenon. 5

As the problem of disrupted adoptions spreads, specialists are looking more closely at agency methods. One cause for failure is a practice that Berkeley professor Richard Barth describes as "stretching." In essence, it is a bait-and-switch game: would-be parents are encouraged to adopt a child different from the one they wanted by the withholding of some negative information. For example, a couple who want a baby are persuaded to take an older child and are never told that several earlier placements have not worked out because of emotional problems. Though the motive is benevolent—finding a home for a hard-to-place child—Barth regards the tactic as unethical. 6

Some disappointed parents have begun to fight back in the courts. The notion of "wrongful adoption"—which claims that agencies are liable for damages if they place children without fully disclosing their health backgrounds—is gaining legal recognition. Frank and Jayne Gibbs of Philadelphia are suing two agencies for $6 million, following their adoption of a seven-year-old boy who turned out to be violently disturbed. After the adoption, says the couple, they discovered that he had been horribly abused, including an attempt by his natural mother to cut off his genitals. 7

Many states have passed medical disclosure laws, which make it easier to obtain accurate information about a child. Agencies themselves are attempting to gather more data. The Golden Cradle adoption agency, in Cherry Hill, New Jersey, requires natural mothers to fill out ten-page medical histories that ask about everything from hay fever and heavy drinking to Down's syndrome and blood transfusions. Genetic counselors are often called in as consultants. "We believe an ounce of prevention is worth a pound of cure," says agency supervisor Mary Anne Giello. 8

Still, there are no warranties on adoptions. Those who set out looking for perfect "designer" children are likely to be disappointed. Nor is it possible—or even necessary—to know everything about a child. "People shouldn't get the idea that they can't be parents unless they have a DNA portrait of a kid," says Professor Joan Hollinger of the University of Detroit Law School. Instead, adoptive parents, armed with as much information as possible, should face the inevitable mysteries—just as all parents do. 9

Vocabulary

Directions: Locate each of the key words in the reading selection. Try to figure out each word's meaning by using the context. Confirm your guess by checking the dictionary or thesaurus. Write the meanings of the words in the margin of the text. Then record the meanings in the chart below.

Key Word	Paragraph	Meaning
1. risk-averse	2	
2. implied	2	
3. babble	3	
4. onus	4	
5. opt	5	
6. benevolent	6	
7. inevitable	9	
Others?		

Guide Questions

Directions: These questions will guide your understanding of what you have read. Write your answers in your notebook or on a separate sheet of paper if your instructor wishes to collect it. Your answers to these questions will be the basis of class discussion.

1. Eleven-year-old Tony is used as an example in this selection to illustrate a new problem in our society. Explain the problem.
2. Note the use of the word *commodities* in paragraph 2.
   a. Define the word *commodity*.
   b. Look through the selection: what other terms can you find that seem to categorize children as products rather than as persons?
   c. Why is this view of children as products creating a problem with adopted children?
3. How have social workers' views of the needs of adopted children changed?
4. React to the comment by Ms. Stanton in paragraph 3, "We made a commitment to [the baby], but we were not able to live up to that commitment." If Ms. Stanton had said this to you, how would you have answered her?

5. What is the main cause of the new "return to sender" phenomenon, according to the selection?

6. How have some adoption agencies contributed to the problem of failed adoptions?

7. Explain how other adoption agencies have worked to prevent problems.

8. Put yourself in the place of an adoptive parent who discovers that his or her new child has a serious physical or mental disability, and that the adoption agency knew about the problem but never informed you. How would you react? What would you do?

9. What is Professor Hollinger's opinion on adoptive parents returning a child because the child is not exactly what they expected?

Marking Text

Mark the text of "When the Lullaby Ends." (Remember, marking text is explained in the section titled "Learning Strategy III—Marking Text" on page 421.)

Application/Writing

Directions: Discuss *all* of the questions below with your classmates. Then write a response to any *one* of the four questions.

1. Remember that to be able to evaluate an issue it is necessary to view it from all possible perspectives. First, take a look at the "return to sender" situation from the viewpoint of adoptive parents. Read the story below:

   After several years of unsuccessfully trying to have a baby, Carol and Jim Field adopt a little girl. At first they are thrilled and happy—she is a beautiful child. Soon, however, it becomes clear that there is something terribly wrong. The baby smiles happily, but never coos or babbles as babies do. She does not respond to colorful toys or to her parents' voices. Fearfully, Carol and Jim consult a doctor who determines that the baby is deaf and blind. Horrified, the Fields seek every kind of treatment that might make their baby hear and see. Finally, they accept that she cannot be helped. Unable to cope with a handicapped child, the Fields decide to return the baby to the adoption agency.

   Imagine that you are Jim or Carol. Write a letter to the agency. In the letter explain, first, that you have decided to return the child. Second, explain your reasons for doing so.

2. Now look at Jim and Carol's situation from the perspective of the agency. Write an answering letter in which you explain to the Fields all the reasons they should not return the baby.

3. Write your own letter to Carol and Jim, explaining to them what you think they should do and why.

4. Imagine that it is twenty years in the future. Look at this situation from the perspective of the baby. Pretend you are the child, who is now grown up. Write a letter from her to Carol and Jim reacting to their decision.

As science rushes forward, ethics must hurry to catch up. This article describes recent advances in genetics and the confusing choices they force on us. It appeared in Time *magazine in September 1999.*

IF WE HAVE IT, DO WE USE IT?

Nancy Gibbs

1 We've seen these visions glinting in the distance for some time—the prospect that one day parents will be able to browse through gene catalogs to special-order a hazel-eyed, redheaded extrovert with perfect pitch. Leave aside for the moment whether there really is an "IQ gene" . . . or the argument over what really constitutes intelligence. Every new discovery gives shape and bracing focus to a debate we have barely begun. Even skeptics admit it's only a matter of time before these issues become real. If you could make your kids smarter, would you? If everyone else did, would it be fair not to?

2 It's an ethical quandary and an economic one, about fairness and fate, about vanity and values. Which side effects would we tolerate? What if making kids smarter also made them meaner? What if only the rich could afford the advantage? Does God give us both the power to re-create ourselves and the moral muscles to resist? "The time to talk about it in schools and churches and magazines and debate societies is now," says bioethicist Arthur Caplan of the University of Pennsylvania. "If you wait, five years from now the gene doctor will be hanging out the MAKE A SMARTER BABY sign down the street."

3 What makes the conversation tricky is that we're already on the slippery slope. Doctors can screen fetuses for genetic diseases like cystic fibrosis and Duchenne muscular dystrophy; one day they may be able to treat them in utero. But correcting is one thing, perfecting is another. If doctors can someday tinker with a gene to help children with autism, what's to prevent them from tinkering with other genes to make "normal" children smarter? Technology always adapts to demand; prenatal sex-selection tests designed to weed out inherited diseases that strike one gender or the other—hemophilia, for instance—are being used to help families have the son or daughter they always wanted. Human-growth hormone was intended for children with a proven severe deficiency, but it came to be used on self-conscious short kids—if their parents could afford as much as $30,000 for a year's injections.

4 Self-improvement has forever been an American religion, but the norms about what is normal keep changing. Many parents don't think twice about straightening their kids' crooked teeth but stop short of fixing a crooked nose, and yet, in just the past seven years, plastic surgery performed on teens has doubled. As for intellectual advantages, parents soak their babies in Mozart with dubious effect, put a toy computer in the crib, elbow their way into the best preschools to speed them on their path to Harvard. Infertile couples advertise for an egg donor in the *Yale Daily News*, while entrepreneurs sold the sperm of Nobel laureates.

"What, if anything, is the difference between getting one's child a better   5
school and getting one's child a better gene?" asks Erik Parens of the Hastings
Center, a bioethics think tank. "I think the answer has to do with the difference
between cultivating and purchasing capacities." Buying a Harvard education
may enhance a child's natural gifts, he argues, but it's not the same as buying
the gifts.

Every novel, every movie that updates Frankenstein provides a cautionary   6
tale: these experiments may not turn out as we expect. Genetic engineering is
more permanent than a pill or a summer-school class. Parents would be making
decisions over which their children had no control and whose long-term impact
would be uncertain. "Human organisms are not things you hang ornaments on
like a Christmas tree," says Thomas Murray, Hastings' director. "If you make
a change in one area, it may cause very subtle changes in some other area. Will
there be an imbalance that the scientists are not looking for, not testing for, and
might not even show up in mice?"

What if it turned out that by enhancing intellectual ability, some other   7
personality trait changed as well? "Everything comes at a price," argues UCLA
neurobiologist Alcino Silva. "Very often when there's a genetic change where we
improve something, something else gets hit by it, so it's never a clean thing." The
alarmists, like longtime biotech critic Jeremy Rifkin, go further. "How do you
know you're not going to create a mental monster?" he asks. "We may be on the
road to programming our own extinction."

The broader concern is one of fairness. Will such enhancement be available to   8
everyone or only to those who can afford it? "Every parent in the world is going to
want this," says Rifkin. "But who will have access to it? It will create a new form
of discrimination. How will we look at those who are not enhanced, the child
with the low IQ?" Who would have the right to know whether your smarts were
natural or turbo-charged? How would it affect whom we choose to marry—those
with altered genes or those without? If, as a parent, you haven't mortgaged the
house to enhance your children, what sort of parent does that make you? Will a
child one day be able to sue her parents for failing to do everything they could
for her?

But just for the sake of argument, suppose raising IQ didn't require any   9
permanent, expensive genetic engineering at all. Scientists are studying brain-
boosting compounds. Suppose they found something as cheap and easy as aspirin;
one pill and you wake up the next morning a little bit brighter. Who could argue
with that?

Some people are worried about the trend toward making people more   10
alike—taller, thinner, smarter. Maybe it's best for society as a whole to include
those with a range of needs and talents and predispositions, warts and all. "As
someone who morally values diversity," says ethicist Elizabeth Bounds of Emory
University's Candler School of Theology, "I find this frightening. We run the risk
of shaping a much more homogeneous community around certain dominant values, a far more engineered community." What sort of lottery would decide who
is to leap ahead, who is to be held back for an overall balance? At the moment,

nature orchestrates our diversity. But human nature resists leaving so much to chance, if there is actually a choice.

11   The debate raises an even more basic question: Why would we want to enhance memory in the first place? We may imagine that it would make us happier, except that we all know smart, sad people; or richer, except that there are wildly successful people who can't remember their phone number. Perhaps it would help us get better grades, land a better job, but it might also take us down a road we'd prefer not to travel. "You might say yes, it would be wonderful if we could all have better memories," muses Stanford University neuropsychiatrist Dr. Robert Malenka. "But there's a great adaptive value to being able to forget things. If your memory improves too much, you might not be a happier person. I'm thinking of rape victims and soldiers coming back from war. There's a reason the brain has evolved to forget certain things."

12   In the end it is the scientists who both offer the vision and raise the alarms. People with exceptional, photographic memories, they note, sometimes complain of mental overload. "Such people," says University of Iowa neurologist Dr. Antonio Damasio, "have enormous difficulty making decisions, because every time they can think of 20 different options to choose from." There is luxury and peace in forgetting, sometimes; it literally clears the mind, allows us to focus on the general rather than the specific and immediate evidence in front of us. Maybe it even makes room for reflection on questions like when better is not necessarily good.

Vocabulary

Directions: Locate each of the key words in the article. Try to figure out each word's meaning by using the context. Confirm your guess by checking the dictionary or thesaurus. Write the meanings of the words in the margin of the text. Then record the meanings in the following chart.

Key Word	Paragraph	Meaning
1. prospect	1	
2. extrovert	1	
3. skeptics	1	
4. quandary	2	
5. tinker	3	
6. dubious	4	
7. alarmists	7	

Key Word	Paragraph	Meaning
Others?		

Guide Questions

Directions: These questions will guide your understanding of what you have read. Write your answers in your notebook or on a separate sheet of paper if your instructor wishes to collect it. Your answers to these questions will be the basis of class discussion.

1. The author begins her examination of this issue with two probing questions: If you could make your kids smarter, would you? If everyone else did, would it be fair not to? At first glance, the answers to these questions seem obvious, but as we read and learn more about the consequences of such decisions, the answer becomes more difficult. Arthur Caplan says, "The time to talk about it in schools and churches and magazines and debate societies is now." Why is it so important to discuss these issues *now?*

2. What does the author mean when she says "we're already on the slippery slope"?

3. Give an example of how "technology always adapts to demand."

4. In paragraph 4, the author says the "norms about what is normal keep changing." Give an example of this from the article. Can you think of an example of your own?

5. Explain the "cautionary tale" of stories like *Frankenstein.*

6. Explain why the issue of fairness is an important part of this discussion.

7. Some people see a threat to diversity in the great advances in technology. Explain what they are worried about.

8. How could anyone argue with the notion of enhancing memory? Is there a downside to the idea of improving memory?

Marking Text

Mark the text of "If We Have It, Do We Use It?" (If you need to review how to mark the text, turn to page 421, "Learning Strategy III—Marking Text.")

Application

The article concludes with the statement, "Maybe it even makes room for reflection on questions like when better is not necessarily good." In your groups discuss the following issues:

Until just a few years ago, making a baby girl or baby boy was pretty much a hit-or-miss affair. Not anymore. Parents who have access to the latest genetic testing techniques can now predetermine their baby's sex with great accuracy. Before too long, it may be possible to screen kids right after conception for such things as height, body type, hair and eye color, what kind of diseases they may be subject to (and resistant to), and perhaps even their IQ.

Sounds great? But, for the sake of argument, what if lots more couples decided they wanted a boy baby than a girl. Would we face a future population of young men with no women to marry? What would a society overrepresented by males be like?

What if you could choose your baby's hair color and body type? Would you? Should you? Would most people choose to have babies with blonde hair? Blue eyes? Six feet tall males? Who could play both basketball and the piano? Do we want a society of people who all look the same and have similar talents?

Should insurance cover the genetic tests? Should the government pay for them? If not, then would only wealthy people have access to these choices? What impact would this have on society?

What would happen if these types of genetic tinkering led to unforeseen problems? What if, say, adjusting the gene that determines height also turned out to produce a deadly heart condition? Who would be responsible? Who would bear the cost of caring for the child?

Writing

Directions: Choose one of the assignments that follows.

1. Write an essay titled "If We Have It, Do We Use It?" Write at least four paragraphs answering the question by summarizing the concerns raised in the article.

2. Write an essay reacting to one of the issues raised in the article and in your group discussion. For example, you may want to discuss the issue of fairness or of diversity. Or you may want to discuss the dangers of tinkering with genes when we don't yet know what unforeseen consequences there may be. Or you may want to speculate on what you would do if you had the opportunity to alter your own child-to-be's genetic makeup. Write at least four paragraphs.

Not so long ago, very premature babies were certain to die. The lungs of the tiniest pree-
mies lack a surface lubricant that allows the tissue to stretch as the air goes in and out.
Without it, the lung tissue rips, and the baby dies. Now, science has developed techniques
to save these babies, even those weighing less than two pounds. But what happens after the
medical miracles are performed? The children, their parents, and society as a whole are left
to face the sometimes grim consequences. This story appeared in The New York Times *in*
May 2000.

AS THE TINIEST BABIES GROW,
SO CAN THEIR PROBLEMS

Sheryl Gay Stolberg

It has been 11 years since Alex Martin was born, a 1-pound 2-ounce bundle of
miniature bones and bright red skin, with fingers no bigger than matchsticks
and legs so thin they might have fit inside his father's wedding band. His parents, Rick and Allison, waited four months to send birth announcements. "The
doctors kept telling us we had to plan for his funeral," Mrs. Martin explained.

Today, Alex is a blond-haired, fair-skinned fifth grader, with clear brown
eyes, gold-rimmed glasses and a collection of what his mother calls labels: mild
cerebral palsy, asthma, hyperactivity and Asperger's syndrome, a form of autism.
At an age when most children have conquered fractions, Alex wrestles with addition. He learned to read about a year ago and is racing through the Hardy Boys
series. But speaking is a challenge; words roll around like marbles in his mouth.

Alex cannot ride a bike. He still wears sneakers that fasten with Velcro, because his fingers cannot master the intricacies of laces. Often, he retreats into a
private fantasy world. A recent weekday afternoon found Alex sitting cross-
legged in the backyard of his family's home in Raleigh, N.C., spinning stories to
an audience of no one as he smashed rocks against the dirt. "Life," Mrs. Martin
says, "is overwhelming for him."

It is also overwhelming, at times, for his parents, who are discovering first-
hand what scientists are beginning to document about babies born as tiny as
Alex: their lives often grow more complicated over time. Long after their worries
about simply keeping Alex alive have faded, the Martins are faced with new and
no less daunting concerns, from whether their son will ever be able to make
change at the grocery store, or drive a car or maintain a job, to who will care for
him after they die.

It has been more than 20 years since doctors began saving extremely premature infants, and about a decade since advances in neonatology vastly improved
the survival of babies of very low birth weight—those weighing less than 1,500
grams, or 3 pounds 4 ounces. The tiniest of these babies—micropreemies, they
are called—are born as much as 14 weeks early and weigh less than 750 grams,
or 1 pound 10 ounces.

For the first time, thousands of such children are now well into their school
years. The conventional medical wisdom, based on previous studies, had been

that those like Alex, who are not seriously physically disabled, would catch up to other youngsters by age 5. And many do just fine. But as the first large group of tiny babies grows up, new research is showing that academic and behavioral problems often surface in the school years.

7   Researchers had previously had no way of knowing for sure what the long-range effects of complications like bleeding in the brain might be. And they are only now beginning to get a clear picture.

8   "We used to say if they got to 2 or 3 and they were doing fine, they'd be O.K.," said Dr. Deborah E. Campbell, director of the division of neonatology at Montefiore Medical Center in the Bronx. "Now we know that is not necessarily true."

9   In one recent study of 150 teenagers who weighed 2 pounds or less at birth, nearly one-third had significant physical disorders, including cerebral palsy, blindness and deafness. Nearly half were receiving special education assistance, compared with 10 percent in a control group. But the study, which appeared in February in the journal *Pediatrics,* also found that even those children with minor physical problems scored significantly lower on achievement tests than those in the control group.

10   "We can save tiny babies now, which we weren't able to save before, but with the technology there is a price," said the study's author, Dr. Saroj Saigal, a neonatologist at McMaster University in Hamilton, Ontario. Dr. Saigal said she had been flooded with letters, many with the same message: "Behind the success, as this child is called by the medical profession, there are lots of problems."

11   The vast leaps in survival of extremely premature infants came with the widespread use of a synthetic form of surfactant, a chemical that helps babies' lungs absorb oxygen. Before surfactant, about one-quarter of the smallest babies survived; today, about one-half will live.

12   Babies of very low birth weight make up only a tiny fraction of all newborns. According to the National Center for Health Statistics, of the 3.9 million infants born in the United States in 1998, 1.4 percent, or about 56,000, were considered in this category. Of these, 16,647 were micro-preemies.

13   It is difficult for doctors to know if low-birth-weight babies born today will fare any better than those born a decade ago. But Dr. Maureen Hack, a neonatologist at Rainbow Babies and Children's Hospital in Cleveland, who has followed premature infants as they grow, says she suspects the outcomes will be much the same.

14   Dr. Hack said a recent study of infants born weighing less than 1,000 grams found slightly higher rates of cerebral palsy and slightly lower intelligence quotients than in those of the same weight born in earlier decades. "Even though survival has improved, how the children are doing later has at best stayed the same," she said. "You are replacing death with impairment."

15   There is no thornier decision in medicine than the decision to rescue a tiny baby. It is expensive, costing as much as $2,000 a day, and wrenching for doctors and parents. Studies like Dr. Hack's and Dr. Saigal's are intensifying the long-running debate about the ethics of using sophisticated technology to save children with uncertain futures.

For parents, the questions are hardly academic. They feel lucky that their   16
children are alive, although in quiet moments some will confess that they wonder if they made the right choice.

"Every day I count my blessings," said Raquel Bolden of Cleveland, whose   17
8-year-old daughter, Mischa, was one of Dr. Hack's patients. Mischa, who weighed
a little more than 2 pounds at birth, has mild cerebral palsy and severe hearing loss.

Like most hospitals with neonatal intensive care units, Rainbow Babies and   18
Children's has a follow-up clinic for premature babies, and Mischa was seen there.
But as is typical, the tracking at Rainbow stops at age 3. After that, medical and
educational professionals lump disabled premature children with the estimated
six million disabled youngsters in the United States.

When Mischa was younger, Mrs. Bolden said, she worried about her daugh-   19
ter's physical condition. Hoping to improve Mischa's strength, she signed her up
for gymnastics and ice skating. "Now," she said, "I'm more worried mentally."

In the first grade, Mischa is having trouble with math. Mrs. Bolden, who un-   20
til recently was a single mother, working and going to school full time, is considering a tutor, though she is not certain how to pay for one. Mischa has trouble
filtering out background noise, and Mrs. Bolden said she had fought with school
officials to pay for hearing-aid amplifiers.

"I read a few preemie books when she was little," Mrs. Bolden said, "but   21
there is no manual when they get older."

Decisions about rescuing children like Mischa at birth play out every day in   22
neonatal intensive care units. The one at Montefiore Medical Center, like all such
wards, is a place of dreams and heartache.

Everything is in miniature. Tiny creatures, their eyes protected by dark   23
patches, their fragile bodies connected to a maze of tubes, sleep in plastic cases,
many under the glow of violet lights to cure jaundice. Diapers and pacifiers look
as though they were made for dolls. Feedings are measured in half teaspoons.

As director of this unit, Dr. Campbell faces the delicate task of answering   24
the questions of new parents who inevitably want to know what the future will
bring.

"You want to give hope, you want to encourage them," Dr. Campbell said,   25
"but you've got to keep everybody reasoned."

Some advocates for parents of premature children say that if doctors were   26
more forthright, parents might make different choices about whether to rescue
their babies.

"Parents are very rarely told about the long-term, so-called minor disabili-   27
ties," said Helen Harrison, author of "The Premature Baby Book," a guidebook
for parents. "These minor disabilities, of course, can keep children from living independently, or ever having a social life or being able to function in society."

Doctors say they do routinely hold discussions with parents on whether to   28
withhold care. But they also say that making predictions is difficult. How well
premature infants fare depends on their birth weight—every extra ounce improves their chances—and on whether they suffer any serious complications. It
also depends on socioeconomics.

29   The Reyes family is a case in point. Jacqueline Reyes is a single mother of two boys who lives in the Soundview section of the Bronx. Her 8-year-old son, Duron, is healthy. But her 5-year-old, Dominic, born weighing a little more than a pound, has severe cerebral palsy. He still wears diapers and cannot sit by himself.

30   On a recent morning, Ms. Reyes took Dominic to the Children's Evaluation and Rehabilitation Center at the Albert Einstein College of Medicine in the Bronx, where doctors are evaluating the boy to get him into kindergarten. As a child with disabilities, Dominic was entitled by federal law to attend preschool at taxpayer expense. But his mother was unaware of the law, and so he never went.

31   Dominic is also entitled to occupational and physical therapy, and Ms. Reyes said therapists did visit him at home for a time, but stopped coming a couple of years ago. Now the doctors at Einstein are considering referring Dominic for surgery to correct a hip problem that the center's director, Dr. Herbert J. Cohen, said might not have developed had the boy's therapy continued.

32   For Ms. Reyes, however, therapy and school are pushed to the back burner by the tasks of daily living like grocery shopping and doing the laundry. Until December, when she showed up at the Einstein center, she did not have a wheelchair for Dominic and simply carried him wherever she went. She lives on the second floor of an apartment building with no elevator and no ramp. When she goes out, she said, she takes her children to the bottom of the stair-well and sits Dominic in his older brother's lap while she runs back up for the chair.

33   Dr. Cohen says the Reyes family is not unusual. Parents of disabled children, particularly the poor, often miss out on services for their children. Once, he said, his center had a program for following infants at high risk of disabilities. But it was disbanded two years ago after cuts in federal and state reimbursements. For children like Dominic, Dr. Cohen said, the future often depends "on how good an advocate the parent is."

34   And even knowledgeable advocates face challenges, as the Martins can attest. Mr. Martin runs the National Computer Center for the federal Environmental Protection Agency and his wife is a former E.P.A. biologist. They have begun an Internet site to provide support for families like theirs.

35   When the Martins moved to North Carolina from the Washington area nearly two years ago, Alex scored below normal on an I.Q. test. Convinced the low score was the result of overmedication for his hyperactivity, the Martins hired a psychologist to repeat the exam; this time, the test scores were normal. Alex's special education teacher, Jan Valletta, said that without the Martins' backing, Alex would have been labeled mentally retarded.

36   "People misjudge Alex," Mrs. Valletta said. "They think from seeing him in the hall that he's retarded, or there's not much there. But Alex is really very intelligent; what makes him different is that he is intelligent, but he cannot communicate."

37   In the time that she has been teaching Alex, Mrs. Valletta says, she has seen vast improvement. She is trying to draw him out of his fantasy world and kindle

his interest in science instead. Alex likes to write, but holding a pen is difficult, so he is getting instruction in typing on the computer. Learning to read has given him confidence, and his social skills are improving.

In the school gym one recent morning, two girls from the regular fifth-grade class took pains to pick Alex when the physical education teacher told them to split up into teams. "The girls," Mrs. Valletta said, "are crazy about Alex."   38

To the Martins, these are encouraging signs. But if the past is any predictor of the future, they know there is uncertainty ahead.   39

"What prematurity is about," Mrs. Martin said, "is risk. And that risk never goes away."   40

Vocabulary

Directions: Locate each of the key words in the reading selection. Try to figure out each word's meaning by using the context. Confirm your guess by checking the dictionary or thesaurus. Write the meanings of the words in the margin of the text. Then record the meanings in the chart below.

Key Word	Paragraph	Meaning
1. intricacies	3	
2. daunting	4	
3. neonatology	5	
4. fare	13	
5. academic	16	
Others?		

Guide Questions

Directions: These questions will guide your understanding of what you have read. Write your answers in your notebook or on a separate sheet of paper if your instructor wishes to collect it. Your answers to these questions will be the basis of class discussion.

1. The story begins with the description of one child, Alex, who was born weighing one pound, two ounces. His mother comments that "life is overwhelming for him." Explain why life is overwhelming, for both Alex and his parents.

2. How has the ability to save the lives of very tiny babies progressed over the past twenty years?

3. What was the "conventional wisdom" about the future of preemies who were not seriously physically disabled?

4. Now that many of these very premature babies are reaching their teens, what are scientists discovering about their physical and mental conditions?

5. Cite Dr. Maureen Hack's conclusion in paragraph 14 on the outcomes of saving very low-birth-weight babies.

6. Explain why "there is no thornier decision in medicine" than that of saving a tiny baby.

7. Explain the point made by some advocates for parents of premature children that "if doctors were more forthright, parents might make different choices about whether to rescue their babies."

8. Why do doctors say it is difficult to make predictions about the children's future?

Application/Writing

Can you imagine yourself in the unimaginable position of the parent of a micropreemie? Of course you would want to be as informed as possible about the risks and benefits of the possible medical procedures. Go back and reread the article carefully. Identify all the arguments you can find that are in favor of rescuing a baby weighing, say, under two pounds. Then identify all the arguments against saving the baby. If you have information from your own knowledge or experience, include it in your discussion.

In a small group, discuss the arguments you have identified with your classmates. Prepare a master list of arguments for your group.

Which set of arguments seems the more persuasive to you? Why? Once you have chosen a position, write an essay arguing the OPPOSITE of what you chose, either pro or con, regarding the rescue of this imaginary micropreemie.

SHORT TAKE

Controversial Cases

Modern medicine has spawned record numbers of twins, triplets and even septuplets in recent years, and fertility advances have opened the door to childbirth for much older mothers than ever before.

But along with the miracles have come troubling questions.

Should doctors take into account a woman's age before allowing her to undergo costly fertility treatments?

Does selective abortion of some fetuses save the lives of others or set up an ungodly game of Russian roulette in the womb?

Here's a look at some recent cases that raised troubling questions:

- The nation celebrated with Bobbi and Kenny McCaughey of Iowa when they gave birth to a record seven babies. Doctors cautioned, however, that multiple-birth children often have developmental problems and are more susceptible to problems such as cerebral palsy, blindness, mental retardation, and seizure disorders.
- A Saudi couple—who already had six kids—nearly went broke trying to care for their septuplets. Although the Saudi royal family wound up footing the hospital bill, the stressed-out couple's marriage broke up amid the publicity.
- Arceli Kew, 63, of California became the world's oldest mom after she lied about her age to be admitted to a fertility program. People question whether it was proper to impregnate a woman who may not live long enough to bring up the child.

A child shoots a child, stirring debate on gun control, social safety nets, and good and evil. This article appeared in Time *in March 2000.*

THE KILLING OF KAYLA

Julie Grace, Jay Branegan, and Victoria Rainert

1 At the end of the movie *The Manchurian Candidate,* Frank Sinatra, unable to fathom the depth and extent of the evil that had been done to the mind of a man programmed to become a killer, cries, "Hell, hell!" People may say the same thing after last week's school shooting of a six-year-old girl by a six-year-old boy. On Tuesday the boy brought a pistol to an elementary school in Mount Morris Township, near Flint, Mich., and shot a classmate, Kayla Rolland, to death. He is too young to be charged with anything, but the county prosecutor has charged the man who left the loaded gun lying around with involuntary manslaughter, contributing to the delinquency of a minor and gross neglect—each of which has a wider application. The story may be too unusual for the drawing of larger lessons, but one reason it is so troubling is that it touches the worst of America's social ills, including the shaping of a boy who became a loaded gun himself.

2 Who killed Kayla Rolland? A six-year-old classmate did it. On Tuesday morning he went to the Theo J. Buell Elementary School carrying both a concealed Davis .32 semiautomatic handgun, advertised as "the original pocket pistol," and a knife. Another kid reported the knife to a teacher, and it was taken away. The boy held on to the gun. Shortly before 10 A.M., Chris Boaz, a seven-year-old, witnessed the following scene:

3 The children were changing classrooms, from a small reading group to a computer-training class. This is contrary to the police report that the crime occurred inside a classroom. The kids were on the first level heading to the second when the boy pulled out his pistol. Kayla was walking ahead of him, up the school stairs. He called out, "I don't like you." She had her back to him, then turned and asked, as a challenge, "So?" The boy, who had first pointed the gun at another classmate, swung around and fired a single bullet that entered Kayla's right arm and traveled through her vital organs. Boaz says he saw blood on both sides of Kayla's stomach. She grabbed her stomach, then her neck, gasping for air.

4 The shooter ran to the bathroom to hide and tossed the gun into the trash. Kayla was treated by paramedics at the school and was taken to Hurley Medical Center, where she was pronounced dead at 10:29 A.M.

5 Immediately after the shooting, the principal made an announcement over the public-address system ordering teachers to lock all classroom doors. The school was closed at 11 A.M., and police were called for crowd control when distraught parents rushed to pick up their children. The boy, who did not attempt to run away, was taken to the principal's office, where he was questioned, and later to a police station.

6 The boy's father, Dedric Owens, is in jail for violating parole after serving time for possession of cocaine "with intent to deliver." The boy and his eight-year-old

brother had been living with their mother Tamarla until recently, when she was evicted. The two boys then moved into a crack house, where guns were traded for drugs, with their uncle and the 19-year-old man who left the murder weapon, evidently loaded, under some blankets. A search of the house produced a loaded pump-action shotgun and a rock of crack cocaine. The boy and his brother had been sharing a single sofa as a bed.

Outside the white clapboard house, dented hubcaps and other discarded auto parts lay strewn among candy wrappers, soda bottles and wires. Broken windows were covered with a blue tarp. A light so dim it might have been a continuation of the dark showed from inside. Of the boy, Genesee County Sheriff Robert Pickerell said, "He was basically living in hell." 7

Who killed Kayla Rolland? The hell in which the boy lived has to be partly responsible, because it helped produce a child full of rage and confusion. The boy was said to have played normal street games. He was also known to have started fights. Boaz said the boy once punched him because he wouldn't give him a pickle. He said the boy was made to stay after school nearly every day for saying "the F word," flipping people off, pinching and hitting. Some weeks before, he had stabbed a girl with a pencil. He had attacked Kayla before and, on the day prior to the killing, tried to kiss her and was rebuffed. 8

Early on the morning of the shooting, he and his brother got into a fight with Boaz's 10-year-old uncle. Boaz's uncle punched the boy, who said, according to Boaz's grandmother, "Do you want me to take my gap [sic] out and shoot you?" The boy's father once asked his son, "Why do you fight?" The boy replied, "I hate them." 9

With a record of behavior like this, one might ask why no one was paying more helpful attention to him. The teacher to whom the knife was reported did not take him to the principal's office, where he could have been searched. There is no sign that any social-service organization was watching, or even that one was in the vicinity. His parents were worse than useless to him. Tamarla, a drug addict, admitted that she exposed her children to marijuana regularly. Boaz's mother tried to comfort her son, who is growing increasingly agitated about the killing he saw and does not want to return to school. She explained that the boy who did the shooting "cried out for help, and nobody helped him." 10

Not family. Not school officials. Not any social-service agency. Not the police. The people who lived next door to the crack house reported conditions there many times, but the police did not respond. One neighbor said, "It took a killing to get these people out of here." 11

The last thing that the opponents of gun control wish to hear is that guns too are partly responsible for killing Kayla, but of course they are. In response to the child's death, President Clinton challenged Congress to break the logjam on gun legislation. Senator Orrin Hatch and Representative Henry Hyde, chairmen of the Senate and House Judiciary committees, which have failed since last summer to get through a compromise bill with modest strictures on the sale and possession of weapons and a requirement that guns be sold with trigger locks, agreed last week to meet with the President at the White House. On the "Today" show, 12

Clinton said that while the bill has stalled, "every single day there are 13 children who die from guns."

13   Among the compromise bill's more contentious items are the regulation of gun shows and background checks for gun sales. Polls indicate that more people favor stronger gun control and that more are willing to make it a voting issue in the coming elections. But the atmosphere in the Republican Congress remains inhospitable to any effective bill. A proposal to have background checks for a mere three business days barely passed the Senate last year after the killings at Columbine. The day after the President appeared on Today, a representative of the National Rifle Association repeated the equally true and irrelevant argument that what happened in Michigan was the fault of parents, not guns.

14   The boy did the shooting, but how responsible is he for the act? The law in most states contends that under the age of seven, a child cannot understand the consequences of a criminal act, and indeed, the police said the boy—in spite of his history of violent behavior—did not seem to comprehend the gravity of what he had done. The Genesee County prosecutor said the boy could not have formed criminal intent.

15   The legal matter here is easier to deal with than the question of his awareness of good and evil. The influences on the boy at home could have armed him with the urge for revenge. But how aware was he of a wrong act? And did he understand that death is irreversible? If he did, how can he be absolved of knowing the consequences?

16   Ron Avi Astor, of the School of Social Work and Education at the University of Michigan, says that "just because a child understands that a gun could cause serious harm and death doesn't mean that society needs to treat the six-year-old in the same way it would a 20-year-old. We understand that children are more vulnerable." He also notes that with more aggressive kids, provocation becomes paramount. The boy who killed Kayla may have felt humiliated—by her, by everything—which became a justification for any act. Astor cautions, though, that culpability is just one piece of the problem. If we do not create a place and a structure for children as a whole, he says, "we'll see groups of children who should have been treated earlier committing horrible acts."

17   Whatever one concludes about responsibility, this incident will end as too many child killings have ended in recent years—with mournful speeches and eulogies and civic burial mounds made up of heart-shaped balloons, poems, and stuffed animals staring blankly into space. At least that is how it will end for Kayla. For the boy, who can tell? The state will probably take custody of him, his brother and five-year-old sister. It is possible that an enlightened environment somewhere will produce a wholly different child, and just as possible that the wounds go too deep and that he will emerge into adulthood knowing perfectly the meaning and consequences of criminal acts as he blithely commits them.

18   Last week the nation went through the sort of moment that is growing too familiar not only in content but also in the emotions it engenders. On the same day, one could feel heartbroken and fearful that one's children were in danger in their schools, and yet, also, that this is the way life goes these days, and who,

after all, can do anything about it? If that attitude of inevitability prevails, some would say it answers the question "Who killed Kayla Rolland?"

Vocabulary

Directions: Locate each of the key words in the article. Try to figure out each word's meaning by using the context. Confirm your guess by checking the dictionary or the-saurus. Write the meanings of the words in the margin of the text. Then record the meanings in the chart below.

Key Word	Paragraph	Meaning
1. fathom	1	
2. distraught	5	
3. rebuffed	8	
4. logjam	12	
5. strictures	12	
6. contentious	13	
7. gravity	14	
8. culpability	16	
Others?		

Guide Questions

Directions: These questions will guide your understanding of what you have read. Write your answers in your notebook or on a separate sheet of paper if your instructor wishes to collect it. Your answers to these questions will be the basis of class discussion.

1. Throughout the article the authors repeat the question, "Who killed Kayla?" List and explain each of the possible answers they give.
2. Explain the comment by Chris Boaz's mother in paragraph 10, "[the boy] cried out for help, and nobody helped him."
3. Explain the first sentence in paragraph 12, "The last thing that the opponents of gun control wish to hear is that guns too are partly responsible for killing Kayla. . . ."

4. a. According to the article, what are some of the laws that have been proposed to control guns?

   b. Have any of these attempts at gun control legislation succeeded?

5. According to the laws in most states, are children under the age of seven responsible for their actions? Do you think they should be?

6. What do you think the authors' answer to the question "Who killed Kayla?" might be? Can you infer their opinion from evidence in the article? Pay special attention to paragraph 18.

Application

Has there been any change in gun control legislation since this article was written in March 2000? Do some research in the library or on the Internet. Two sites worth looking at are the following:

www.handguncontrol.org
The website of the largest pro gun control organization in the country. Contains much useful information on legislation and links to articles advocating gun control.

www.nra.org
The site of the powerful (anti-gun control) National Rifle Association.

Writing

In one or two paragraphs, summarize the answers to the question, "Who killed Kayla?" that are in the article. Then, in a concluding paragraph, state your own opinion and why you feel the way you do. Remember to support your opinion with arguments, not with emotions or unsupported opinion.

If your teacher threatened to give you an F, would it motivate you to work harder? Or would you give up in despair? Would it lower your self-esteem or make you want to prove the teacher wrong? In this essay from Newsweek, *Mary Sherry, a teacher of adult literacy, argues that passing students who have not mastered the work cheats them—of their education—and that it sets them up to fail in the future. Do you think students who don't work hard should be passed anyway? Do you think that the threat of failure is a positive educational tool?*

IN PRAISE OF THE F WORD

Mary Sherry

Tens of thousands of eighteen-year-olds will graduate this year and be handed 1
meaningless diplomas. These diplomas won't look any different from those awarded their luckier classmates. Their validity will be questioned only when their employers discover that these graduates are semiliterate.

Eventually a fortunate few will find their way into educational-repair 2
shops—adult-literacy programs, such as the one where I teach basic grammar and writing. There, high-school graduates and high-school dropouts pursuing graduate-equivalency certificates will learn the skills they should have learned in school. They will also discover they have been cheated by our educational system.

As I teach, I learn a lot about our schools. Early in each session I ask my stu- 3
dents to write about an unpleasant experience they had in school. No writers' block here! "I wish someone would have had made me stop doing drugs and made me study." "I liked to party and no one seemed to care." "I was a good kid and didn't cause any trouble, so they just passed me along even though I didn't read well and couldn't write." And so on.

I am your basic do-gooder, and prior to teaching this class I blamed the poor 4
academic skills our kids have today on drugs, divorce and other impediments to concentration necessary for doing well in school. But, as I rediscover each time I walk into the classroom, before a teacher can expect students to concentrate, he has to get their attention, no matter what distractions may be at hand. There are many ways to do this, and they have much to do with teaching style. However, if style alone won't do it, there is another way to show who holds the winning hand in the classroom. That is to reveal the trump card of failure.

I will never forget a teacher who played that card to get the attention of one 5
of my children. Our youngest, a world-class charmer, did little to develop his intellectual talents but always got by. Until Mrs. Stifter.

Our son was a high-school senior when he had her for English. "He sits in 6
the back of the room talking to his friends," she told me. "Why don't you move him to the front row?" I urged, believing the embarrassment would get him to settle down. Mrs. Stifter looked at me steely-eyed over her glasses. "I don't move seniors," she said. "I flunk them." I was flustered. Our son's academic life flashed before my eyes. No teacher had ever threatened him with that before. I regained

my composure and managed to say that I thought she was right. By the time I got home I was feeling pretty good about this. It was a radical approach for these times, but, well, why not? "She's going to flunk you," I told my son. I did not discuss it any further. Suddenly English became a priority in his life. He finished out the semester with an A.

7   I know one example doesn't make a case, but at night I see a parade of students who are angry and resentful for having been passed along until they could no longer even pretend to keep up. Of average intelligence or better, they eventually quit school, concluding they were too dumb to finish. "I should have been held back," is a comment I hear frequently. Even sadder are those students who are high-school graduates who say to me after a few weeks of class, "I don't know how I ever got a high-school diploma."

8   Passing students who have not mastered the work cheats them and the employers who expect graduates to have basic skills. We excuse this dishonest behavior by saying kids can't learn if they come from terrible environments. No one seems to stop to think that—no matter what environments they come from—most kids don't put school first on their list unless they perceive something is at stake. They'd rather be sailing.

9   Many students I see at night could give expert testimony on unemployment, chemical dependency, abusive relationships. In spite of these difficulties, they have decided to make education a priority. They are motivated by the desire for a better job or the need to hang on to the one they've got. They have a healthy fear of failure.

10   People of all ages can rise above their problems, but they need to have a reason to do so. Young people generally don't have the maturity to value education in the same way my adult students value it. But fear of failure, whether economic or academic, can motivate both.

11   Flunking as a regular policy has just as much merit today as it did two generations ago. We must review the threat of flunking and see it as it really is—a positive teaching tool. It is an expression of confidence by both teachers and parents that the students have the ability to learn the material presented to them. However, making it work again would take a dedicated, caring conspiracy between teachers and parents. It would mean facing the tough reality that passing kids who haven't learned the material—while it might save them grief for the short term—dooms them to long-term illiteracy. It would mean that teachers would have to follow through on their threats, and parents would have to stand behind them, knowing their children's best interests are indeed at stake. This means no more doing Scott's assignments for him because he might fail. No more passing Jodi because she's such a nice kid.

12   This is a policy that worked in the past and can work today. A wise teacher . . . gave our son the opportunity to succeed—or fail. It's time we return this choice to all students.

Vocabulary

Directions: Locate each of the key words in the reading selection. Try to figure out each word's meaning by using the context. Confirm your guess by checking the dictionary or thesaurus. Write the meanings of the words in the margin of the text. Then record the meanings in the chart below.

Key Word	Paragraph	Meaning
1. validity	1	
2. impediments	4	
3. trump card	4	
4. flustered	6	
Others?		

Guide Questions

Directions: These questions will guide your understanding of what you have read. Write your answers in your notebook or on a separate sheet of paper if your instructor wishes to collect it. Your answers to these questions will be the basis of class discussion.

1. Explain why Sherry says students in classes like hers will eventually discover that "they have been cheated by our educational system."
2. Sherry uses her own son as an example. How does his experience support her argument in favor of failing students?
3. Explain Sherry's description of the threat of flunking as a "positive teaching tool."
4. In your opinion, what are the pros of passing students who have not mastered the work? What are the cons?

Writing

1. Sherry concludes that failure (or the threat of failure) can be a useful motivational tool. Do you agree? Write one paragraph agreeing or disagreeing with Sherry's conclusion.
2. Sherry says that individual students need to take responsibility for their own learning. How can a student take responsibility for his education? What motivates you to do your best in school? How can you help yourself when you don't feel motivated? Write two or three paragraphs.

Making Connections

To learn more about the issue of grades, read the next selection, "Ivy League Grade Inflation."

Reports of grade inflation appear periodically in newspapers and journals, prompting outrage among the public and embarrassment among educators. Is this an issue to be worried about? In 1972, 42% of students entering private colleges and 25% of those entering public colleges had A averages. Today, the figures are 70% and 53%, respectively. In the year 2000 it was reported that half of all grades at Harvard University were A's, up one-third since 1985. One expert predicted that by mid-century, all grades at all colleges will be A's. This editorial, which appeared in USA Today, *discusses the causes of grade inflation and its effects on students and on society as a whole.*

IVY LEAGUE GRADE INFLATION

USA Today

1   When a report found recently that eight out of every 10 Harvard students graduate with honors and nearly half receive A's in their courses, the news prompted plenty of discussion and more than a few jokes. But is grade inflation worth worrying about?

2   Really smart students probably deserve really high grades. Moreover, tough graders could alienate their students. Plus, tough grading makes a student less likely to get into graduate school, which could make Harvard look bad in college rankings.

Evidence of Grade Inflation at Ivy League Schools

- In 1966, 22% of Harvard undergraduate students earned A's. By 1996, that figure rose to 46%. That same year, 82% of Harvard seniors graduated with honors.
- In 1973, 31% of all grades at Princeton were A's. By 1997 that rose to 43%. In 1997, only 12% of all grades given at Princeton were below the B range.

Source: American Academy of Arts & Sciences.

3   All are among reasons cited by professors in explaining why grade inflation is nothing to worry about. And all are insufficient justification for the practice. College-grade inflation—which is probably an extension of the well-documented grade inflation in high schools—is a problem. And it extends well beyond Harvard.

4   Fewer than 20% of all college students receive grades below a B-minus, according to a study released this week by the American Academy of Arts & Sciences. That hardly seems justified at a time when a third of all college students arrive on campus so unprepared that they need to take at least one remedial course.

5   The report sifts through several possible causes for the inflated grades. Among them:

A holdover practice from the 1960s, when professors knew that F's triggered a draft notice and a trip to Vietnam.

An influx of more students, including some minorities, who are less prepared for college work. Grading leniency is believed to encourage their continued academic participation and promote self-esteem.

Evaluation systems in which students grade professors, thereby providing an incentive for teachers to go easy on their future evaluators.

An explosion in the number of overburdened adjunct professors who lack the time to evaluate each student more accurately.

The authors of the report cast doubt on several of those explanations, including the influx of minorities. They barely touch on an obvious explanation offered by several professors: Families paying more than $30,000 a year for a college education expect something more for their money than a report card full of gentleman's C's. 6

More important than the reasons for inflated grades is the impact they have. 7

When all students receive high marks, graduate schools and business recruiters simply start ignoring the grades. That leads the graduate schools to rely more on entrance tests. It prompts corporate recruiters to depend on a "good old boy/girl" network in an effort to unearth the difference between who looks good on paper and who is actually good. 8

Put to disadvantage in that system are students who traditionally don't test as well or lack connections. In many cases, those are the poor and minority students who are the first in their families to graduate from college. No matter how hard they work, their A's look ordinary. 9

Viewed in that light, the fact that 50% of all Harvard students now get A's is a troubling problem. 10

Vocabulary

Directions: Locate each of the key words in the reading selection. Try to figure out each word's meaning by using the context. Confirm your guess by checking the dictionary or thesaurus. Write the meanings of the words in the margin of the text. Then record the meanings in the chart below.

Key Word	Paragraph	Meaning
1. prompted	1	
2. holdover	5	
3. leniency	5	
4. incentive	5	
Others?		

Guide Questions

Directions: These questions will guide your understanding of what you have read. Write your answers in your notebook or on a separate sheet of paper if your instructor wishes to collect it. Your answers to these questions will be the basis of class discussion.

1. In the first paragraph, the writer asks if grade inflation is worth worrying about. What answer do you find by reading the rest of the essay?
2. Paraphrase the information the author gives in paragraph 4.
3. The author gives some reasons for high grades. List them here.
4. According to the essay, what is the impact of inflated grades?
5. a. This article is titled "Ivy League Grade Inflation." Which colleges are considered "Ivy League"? Use your library or check on the Internet to learn the names of the Ivy League colleges.
   b. Is it your impression that grade inflation exists in your school as well? What evidence do you have to support your answer?
6. Do you have any personal experience that relates to this issue? What is your opinion—is grade inflation a problem? Or is it being overblown?

Writing

Think about your answer to guide question 6. Discuss the issue with your classmates to get their perspective. Then write a paragraph or two expressing your opinion on the issue of grade inflation.

Making Connections

Imagine a conversation between the author of "Ivy League Grade Inflation" and "In Praise of the F Word." Would they agree with each other? What might they say to one another?

SHORT TAKE

Gimme an A—Or Else!

Grade inflation is reaching record levels at American high schools, according to a new survey of incoming freshmen at more than 400 colleges and universities across the country. Almost half of the entering college students had an A average in high school. This number is 18% higher than it was in 1968. Linda Sax of the Higher Education Research Institute of the University of California at Los Angeles says, "Something is amiss." Dr. Sax believes that parents and students are pressuring teachers for higher grades because of the intense competition to get into desirable colleges. Teachers feel pressure to not damage students' self-esteem. They are pressured to not ruin students' chances to attend the schools of their choice. A study by the College Board supports the findings of the study. According to its statistics, high school seniors' grades have climbed, but SAT scores have remained the same. The Board's spokesman said the trend began to intensify in the early 1990s when more and more families began to take an interest in their children's choice of schools and at the same time there was an economic boom, allowing parents to choose more expensive schools. He predicted a "correction" soon, saying not all students deserve A's.

One of the most controversial and painful issues of our time is that of euthanasia—helping or allowing someone to die by either active or passive methods. As our society ages, and medical science is able to keep people alive who would have died "naturally" in the past, most of us will be confronted with this decision at some point in our lives. As with all important topics, perhaps more so, we must carefully consider the different perspectives and examine the arguments on all sides of the subject of euthanasia before we can form a good opinion.

In any discussion about euthanasia, one argument is inevitable: We do not have the right to "play God." But what does it mean to "play God"? The answer "to let nature take its course" is not very helpful. After all, if we let nature take its sometimes cruel course, we would not attach the patient to a life-support machine in the first place. If we let nature take its course, we would not rush to resuscitate a person who is dying. Aren't we facing these painful life-and-death decisions because we are, indeed, "playing God" by using medical technology? What, then, is "playing God"? Is it removing life-sustaining equipment (or never using it)? Or is it artificially prolonging a tormented life? This story appeared in Newsweek *in 1983.*

A CRIME OF COMPASSION

Barbara Huttmann

"Murderer," a man shouted. "God help patients who get *you* for a nurse."   1

"What gives you the right to play God?" another one asked.   2

It was *The Phil Donahue Show* where the guest is a fatted calf and the audience a two hundred-strong flock of vultures hungering to pick at the bones. I had told them about Mac, one of my favorite cancer patients. "We resuscitated him fifty-two times in just one month. I refused to resuscitate him again. I simply sat there and held his hand while he died."   3

There wasn't time to explain that Mac was a young, witty, macho cop who walked into the hospital with thirty-two pounds of attack equipment, looking as if he could single-handedly protect the whole city, if not the entire state. "Can't get rid of this cough," he said. Otherwise, he felt great.   4

Before the day was over, tests confirmed that he had lung cancer. And before the year was over, I loved him, his wife, Maura, and their three kids as if they were my own. All the nurses loved him. And we all battled his disease for six months without ever giving death a thought. Six months isn't such a long time in the whole scheme of things, but it was long enough to see him lose his youth, his wit, his macho, his hair, his bowel and bladder control, his sense of taste and smell, and his ability to do the slightest thing for himself. It was also long enough to watch Maura's transformation from a young woman into a haggard, beaten old lady.   5

When Mac had wasted away to a sixty-pound skeleton kept alive by liquid food we poured down a tube, i.v. solutions we dripped into his veins, and oxygen we piped to a mask on his face, he begged us: "Mercy . . . for God's sake, please just let me go."   6

7   The first time he stopped breathing, the nurse pushed the button that calls a "code blue" throughout the hospital and sends a team rushing to resuscitate the patient. Each time he stopped breathing, sometimes two or three times in one day, the code team came again. The doctors and technicians worked their miracles and walked away. The nurses stayed to wipe the saliva that drooled from his mouth, irrigate the big craters of bedsores that covered his hips, suction the lung fluids that threatened to drown him, clean the feces that burned his skin like lye, pour the liquid food down the tube attached to his stomach, put pillows between his knees to ease the bone-on-bone pain, turn him every hour to keep the bedsores from getting worse, and change his gown and linen every two hours to keep him from being soaked in perspiration.

8   At night I went home and tried to scrub away the smell of decaying flesh that seemed woven into the fabric of my uniform. It was in my hair, the upholstery of my car—there was no washing it away. And every night I prayed that Mac would die, that his agonized eyes would never again plead with me to let him die.

9   Every morning I asked his doctor for a "no-code" order. Without that order, we had to resuscitate every patient who stopped breathing. His doctor was one of several who believe we must extend life as long as we have the means and knowledge to do it. To not do it is to be liable for negligence, at least in the eyes of many people, including some nurses. I thought about what it would be like to stand before a judge, accused of murder, if Mac stopped breathing and I didn't call a code.

10   And after the fifty-second code, when Mac was still lucid enough to beg for death again, and Maura was crumbled in my arms again, and when no amount of pain medication stilled his moaning and agony, I wondered about a spiritual judge. Was all this misery and suffering supposed to be building character or infusing us all with the sense of humility that comes from impotence?

11   Had we, the whole medical community, become so arrogant that we believed in the illusion of salvation through science? Had we become so self-righteous that we thought meddling in God's work was our duty, our moral imperative, and our legal obligation? Did we really believe that we had the right to force "life" on a suffering man who had begged for the right to die?

12   Such questions haunted me more than ever early one morning when Maura went home to change her clothes and I was bathing Mac. He had been still for so long, I thought he at last had the blessed relief of coma. Then he opened his eyes and moaned, "Pain . . . no more . . . Barbara . . . do something . . . God, let me go."

13   The desperation in his eyes and voice riddled me with guilt. "I'll stop," I told him as I injected the pain medication.

14   I sat on the bed and held Mac's hands in mine. He pressed his bony fingers against my hand and muttered, "Thanks." Then there was one soft sigh and I felt his hands go cold in mine. "Mac?" I whispered, as I waited for his chest to rise and fall again.

15   A clutch of panic banded my chest, drew my finger to the code button, urged me to do something, anything . . . but sit there alone with death. I kept one finger on the button, without pressing it, as a waxen pallor slowly transformed his face

from person to empty shell. Nothing I've ever done in my forty-seven years has taken so much effort as it took *not* to press that code button.

Eventually, when I was as sure as I could be that the code team would fail to bring him back, I entered the legal twilight zone and pushed the button. The team tried. And while they were trying, Maura walked into the room and shrieked, "No . . . don't let them do this to him . . . for God's sake . . . please, no more."   16

Cradling her in my arms was like cradling myself, Mac, and all those patients and nurses who had been in this place before, who do the best they can in a death-denying society.   17

So a TV audience accused me of murder. Perhaps I am guilty. If a doctor had written a no-code order, which is the only *legal* alternative, would he have felt any less guilty? Until there is legislation making it a criminal act to code a patient who has requested the right to die, we will all of us risk the same fate as Mac. For whatever reason, we developed the means to prolong life, and now we are forced to use it. We do not have the right to die.   18

Vocabulary

Directions: Locate each of the key words in the reading selection. Try to figure out each word's meaning by using the context. Confirm your guess by checking the dictionary or thesaurus. Write the meanings of the words in the margin of the text. Then record the meanings in the following chart.

Key Word	Paragraph	Meaning
1. resuscitated	3	
2. haggard	5	
3. craters	7	
4. negligence	9	
5. lucid	10	
6. impotence	10	
7. meddling	11	
Others?		

Guide Questions

Directions: These questions will guide your understanding of what you have read. Write your answers in your notebook or on a separate sheet of paper if your instructor wishes to collect it. Your answers to these questions will be the basis of class discussion.

1. Although Huttmann has a larger story to tell, she focuses on one man's story. She describes Mac, a young, healthy cop transformed by lung cancer into a sixty-pound skeleton, barely alive. Why do you think Huttmann describes Mac's physical condition and his suffering in such gruesome detail that it is painful to read?

2. In paragraph 11, Huttmann asks some wrenching questions about the attitude and behavior of the medical community. Why do you think she uses the words *arrogant* and *self-righteous* in her questions? What basic question is she really asking?

3. When Huttmann appears on *The Phil Donahue Show,* she is accused by members of the audience of being a "murderer." In your opinion, is she a murderer? Why?

4. Explain Huttmann's final statement, "We do not have the right to die."

Application

Directions: Imagine you are the doctor Huttmann describes in paragraph 9. Write a letter from him to Huttmann explaining your reasons for continuing to resuscitate Mac.

Writing

Directions: Write a response to Barbara Huttmann, agreeing or disagreeing with her actions in allowing Mac to die. Be sure to give good, clear reasons to support your opinion. Write at least 250 words.

This story first appeared in The Boston Globe *in July 1989.*

DREAMING OF DISCONNECTING A RESPIRATOR

Elissa Ely

Late one night in the Intensive Care Unit, one eye on the cardiac monitor and one on the Sunday paper, I read this story: 1

An infant lies in a hospital, hooked to life by a respirator. He exists in a "persistent vegetative state" after swallowing a balloon that blocked the oxygen to his brain. This "vegetative state," I've always thought, is a metaphor inaccurately borrowed from nature, since it implies that with only the proper watering and fertilizer, a comatose patient will bloom again. 2

One day his father comes to visit. He disconnects the respirator and, with a gun in hand, cradles his son until the infant dies. The father is arrested and charged with murder. 3

In the ICU where I read this, many patients are bound to respirators. I look to my left and see them lined up, like potted plants. Some will eventually be "weaned" back to their own lung power. Others will never draw an independent breath again. 4

In Bed No. 2, there is a woman who has been on the respirator for almost two months. When she was admitted with a simple pneumonia, there were no clues she would come apart so terribly. On her third day, she had a sudden and enigmatic seizure. She rolled rapidly downhill. Her pneumonia is now gone, but her lungs refuse independence: she can't come off the machine. 5

I know little about this patient except that she is elderly and European. (It is the peculiar loss of hospital life that patients often exist here with a medical history, but not a personal one.) I sometimes try to picture her as she might have been: busy in a chintz kitchen smelling of pastries. She might have hummed, rolling dough. Now there is a portable radio by the bed, playing Top Ten, while the respirator hisses and clicks 12 times a minute. 6

The family no longer visits. They have already signed the autopsy request, which is clipped to the front of her thick chart. Yet in their pain, they cannot take the final step and allow us to discontinue her respirator. Instead, they have retired her here, where they hope she is well cared for, and where she exists in a state of perpetual mechanical life. 7

I have dreamed of disconnecting my patient's respirator. Every day I make her death impossible and her life unbearable. Each decision—the blood draws, the rectal temperatures, the oxygen concentration—is one for or against life. No action in the ICU is neutral. Yet many of these decisions are made with an eye toward legal neutrality—and this has little to do with medical truth. The medical truth is that this patient exists without being alive. The legal neutrality is that existence is all that is required. 8

9   Late at night, reading in the ICU, the story of that father—so dangerous and impassioned—puts me to shame. I would never disconnect my patient from her respirator; it is unthinkable. But this is not because I am a doctor. It is because I feel differently toward her than the father toward his son.

10   I do not love her enough.

Vocabulary

Directions: Locate each of the key words in the story. Try to figure out each word's meaning by using the context. Confirm your guess by checking the dictionary or thesaurus. Write the meanings of the words in the margin of the text. Then record the meanings in the chart below.

Key Word	Paragraph	Meaning
1. enigmatic	5	
2. perpetual	7	
Others?		

Guide Questions

Directions: These questions will guide your understanding of what you have read. Write your answers in your notebook or on a separate sheet of paper if your instructor wishes to collect it. Your answers to these questions will be the basis of class discussion.

1. Who is the author of this essay? Where did the author write it?
2. The author provides two examples of persons in a "vegetative state." Briefly describe each person.
3. The author contrasts "medical truth" with "legal neutrality." What point is she making?
4. React to the author's last sentence, "I do not love her enough."

Application

1. Use the Internet or your library to investigate the current laws on passive euthanasia in your state. For example, would the father who disconnected the respirator in this story be charged with murder in your state? What are the laws in your state on actions such as Barbara Huttmann's?
2. Here is an opportunity to use your thinking skills in real-life situations. Below are some cases in which life-or-death decisions had to be made by patients, doctors, and family members. Read about each case and ask yourself what your decision would have been. Before you answer, remember to

think about the issue from all perspectives. Then, try to imagine all the pro and con arguments. Finally, develop your personal opinion. Write your opinion, then write the supporting arguments that back it up.

Remember: Your goal is to develop a *valid opinion.*

Case 1

Doctors at a university hospital examined a seventeen-year-old boy whose bone cancer of the upper arm had recurred in spite of radiation treatments. The physicians advised amputation of the limb and warned that, without the operation, the boy would probably die. But the boy, a star baseball player who had been scouted by several major league teams, begged his parents and the doctors to let him keep his arm so that he could continue to play baseball.

If you were the parents, what instructions would you give the doctors? Remember to state good, solid reasons for your decision.

Case 2

After the age of eighteen, when she suffered kidney failure, Marilyn Duke had to go to a hospital three times a week for dialysis treatments. (This is a painful procedure in which the patient is hooked up to a machine for several hours while the machine purifies the patient's blood, eliminating wastes. This purification is the normal function of a healthy kidney.)

When she was thirty-three, Marilyn decided she could no longer endure life under these conditions. She told her doctor that she wanted to discontinue the dialysis but, knowing that without medical help she would die in agony, she asked him to ease her pain in her final days. Her doctor said he could only treat her if she was in a hospital. When she returned to the hospital, doctors tried to put Marilyn on the dialysis machine again. She refused to go on the machine and the hospital discharged her. Marilyn died nine days after her last dialysis treatment.

If you were Marilyn, would you have made the same choice? Give arguments to support your choice.

Case 3

A forty-four-year-old man, a single parent of three children, was hospitalized with brain cancer. Doctors agreed his case was terminal. One night he suddenly suffered cardiac arrest, but an alert intern got the man's heart beating again and the patient lived one more month.

Did the doctor do the right thing in resuscitating the man? Why or why not?

Writing

Directions: Refer to the reading selection, "A Crime of Compassion" by Barbara Huttmann. Write two paragraphs. In the first paragraph, write what you think would be Elissa Ely's reaction to Barbara Huttmann's actions in "A Crime of Compassion." In the second paragraph, write what you think Barbara Huttmann would say to Elissa Ely about her decision to not disconnect the respirator.

SPECIAL PROJECT

Research and Write an Essay on a Controversial Topic

Throughout this unit, you have been reading and thinking about many different topics and the viewpoints of various writers, and no doubt you considered all this information as it supports (or fails to support) your opinions. In this project, you will have the chance to investigate and write about a topic of your own choice.

You may do this project collaboratively, in a group of two to four persons, or you may work on your own.

Choose a Topic

Select a topic that interests you. You may choose from the list of possible topics provided at the end of this section, or your instructor will suggest a topic.

Research

Look in the library for books, magazines, and newspapers that contain information on your topic. Because you are investigating a current issue, books will probably be less useful to you than magazines and newspapers, but if you find one that is helpful, by all means use it.

Search the Internet for information on your topic. Some suggestions for sources on the Web follow.

Be sure to look for and take notes on information on BOTH SIDES of the issue you are investigating. Only by examining the subject from all perspectives can we hope to develop a worthwhile opinion.

Decide

When you have gathered sufficient information to understand the topic, decide what your position will be. Choose either pro or con. It is not necessary that you truly support this position. In fact, it is probably more valuable to write about the position you do NOT support. In either case, be sure you have sufficient arguments to support your position.

Write

In the first paragraph, state the topic and your position on the topic.

In the body of the essay, include all the arguments (including facts, explanations, and examples) that you discovered when doing your research.

In your final paragraph, restate your main idea and the arguments that you find most persuasive.

References

The last page of the paper should be a list of the references (Works Cited) that you used to write your paper. Include every book, magazine, newspaper, and Internet source.

World Wide Web Sources

For general information:

CNN	www.cnn.com
The New York Times	www.nytimes.com
Time	www.time.com
Newsweek	www.newsweek.com
U.S. News & World Report	www.usnews.com
National Public Radio	www.npr.org
The *Los Angeles Times*	www.latimes.com
The *Boston Herald*	www.bostonherald.com

For specific information, look for the websites of organizations directly concerned with the issue. For example, the issue of animal rights will be examined at the sites run by PETA (People for the Ethical Treatment of Animals; www.peta-online. org) and Critiques of Animal Rights (www.animalrights.net).

Any listing of specific Web resources is out of date almost as soon as it is published, so consult your instructor and your friendly school or public librarian for assistance.

Evaluating Sources on the Web

As with books, newspapers, and magazines, it is crucial to evaluate the reliability and accuracy of your source. For example, you would probably be safe in assuming a news article from *The Washington Post* is credible. On the other hand, information found in the *National Enquirer* is not. Information on the Internet can be tricky to evaluate. Remember that the Net is a very democratic institution—anyone can put up a site and spout his or her opinion, whether they know anything or not.

Here is a list of questions you can ask about your source to decide if it is reliable:

Is the site run by a known agency or organization?

Is there an author listed for the site or the document?

Does the author have credentials? Does the author seem credible?

Is the document written in good clear English? If there are grammar or spelling errors, you can assume the article has not been edited and may not be reliable.

Does the article contain real substance, or is it mostly bells and whistles?

Know your source! If you want objective information, that is, just the facts, do not rely on information in sources that have a known bias: For example, you could not expect to find unbiased information on the Democratic party's candidates by reading the Republican party's website. Similarly, do not expect a balanced view of the gun control debate on the website of the National Rifle Association.

List of Possible Topics for Research

Immigration—Should there be limits? What should they be? Should there be amnesty for illegal immigrants?

Welfare/workfare—Should people who receive welfare be made to work for their benefits?

Gun control

Abortion rights

Capital punishment

Legalization of marijuana

Tuition-free higher education

Vivisection—Should animals be used for experimentation of such things as drugs, cosmetics, and household products?

Affirmative action—Should preferences be given to members of groups that have been discriminated against historically?

Should the customs and traditions of other countries be allowed to be practiced by immigrants when they come to this country if the custom violates American laws and/or ethics (examples: polygamy, female circumcision)?

Cloning—of animals, of humans

Grade inflation

Gay marriage

UNIT SIX

READING AND THINKING ABOUT TEXTBOOKS

He that loves reading has everything within his reach.

—William Godwin

Textbook reading is probably the most challenging type of reading you will do in your life. It poses difficulties for a number of reasons. First, you are usually reading about things that are new to you; there is often a great deal of new information to be learned. Second, the typical chapter in a college textbook is longer than what you normally read in, say, the newspaper or a magazine. Third, there are often many new words and concepts you must learn and remember. So, it is important to use all your study skills when attacking your textbooks.

In this unit you will find chapters from textbooks used in colleges around the country. Each chapter is accompanied by suggestions on previewing, annotating, and learning important terminology. Following each chapter you will find examples of the actual test questions that students who take the course see on their exams. Working with these sample chapters will give you valuable experience with real college materials.

Steps for Studying Textbook Chapters

Begin by reviewing how to preview: previewing is discussed on page 415, "Learning Strategy I—Previewing." Review the four steps for previewing a chapter on page 416.

Next, read, reread, and mark the chapter. Review the steps for marking text on page 421, "Learning Strategy III—Marking Text." Remember, the important first step is to read through the entire chapter one time quickly to get a feel for the information it contains. If the chapter seems very long, divide it up into manageable chunks and attack one chunk at a time. After the first "get-acquainted" reading, go back and read the chapter again. This time, read carefully, underlining and annotating as you go along.

Finally, reflect for a moment on what you have learned. What do you think are the key ideas that you are expected to learn from this chapter? What concepts will you need to remember for the next exam? For the next course in your major? Are there ideas and terms that you will need to know in order to have a successful career? Are there things you would like to remember for the rest of your life?

Remember, *active reading* will help you with the challenging assignments you face in college. *Be active with your textbooks.* While you are underlining and annotating, be sure to mark words you need to look up. Put a question mark next to things you don't understand or want to discuss with a classmate or the instructor. Ask yourself questions as you read along and try to find the answers to your questions.

At the end of each of the chapters in this unit, you will see exam questions actually used by the instructors who teach the course in which the text is used. Answering these questions will help you to test the effectiveness of your reading and studying.

Now, use your skills as an active independent reader to tackle the following textbook chapters. Good luck!

EDUCATION

A Chapter from the Textbook
Sociology in Our Time, Fifth Edition

Diana Kendall

PREVIEWING

Your first step in studying a textbook chapter is previewing. Review the benefits of previewing and how to do it well by reading the section in this book titled "Learning Strategy I—Previewing" on page 415.

The questions here will help you to preview the chapter "Education."

1. Note that the chapter begins with an anecdote. Skim to find the topic of the little story. Then read the last part of the story beginning with the words "Consider this question…" to get an idea of what the chapter will cover.
2. You will find that the chapter is clearly and logically organized. Read the headings and subheadings to see what you will be expected to learn.
3. How does the author indicate key terms she thinks are important to learn?
4. How long is the chapter? Can you read it in one sitting or do you need to divide it into sections?

Education

QUESTIONS AND ISSUES

Chapter Focus Question: How do race, class, and gender affect people's access to and opportunities in education?

How do educational goals differ in various nations?

During my first semester at Santa Barbara City College . . . my classes included aerobics, typing and remedial math. Who would have guessed that after spending three years there, I would be attending Harvard University?

Without the opportunity to study at my local community college, I probably wouldn't have gone to college at all. My high school grades would have sufficed to get me into a decent university, but I didn't consider myself college material. After all, none of my six brothers and sisters had attended college; most didn't even finish high school. My parents have the equivalent of a second-grade education. Mexican immigrants who do not speak English, my mother worked as a maid and my father as a dishwasher. Considering my resources, I thought the convenience and limited cost of a community college made it my most viable option.

But enrolling in a community college was also one of the smartest decisions I ever made. Despite my slow start, I learned the skills I needed to move ahead academically. . . . I also began to explore educational alternatives. And transferring to a reputable four-year university became my most important goal. I specifically wanted to transfer to an Ivy League university because I thought that would open more doors for me.

—Cynthia G. Inda (1997: 31) describing how a community college gave her the opportunity to pursue her educational and career goals

AP Photo/Lawrence Journal-World, Mike Yoder

ynthia is one of hundreds of thousands of people who have attended community colleges to gain knowledge and skills that will benefit them and enhance their opportunities in the future. In fact, a substantial proportion of college students start their higher education at community colleges.

From pre-kindergarten through postgraduate studies, education is one of the most significant social institutions in the United States and other high-income nations. Although most social scientists agree that schools are supposed to be places where people acquire knowledge and skills, not all of them agree on how a large number of factors—including class, race, gender, age, religion, and family background—affect individuals' access to educational opportunities or to the differential rewards that accrue at various leve ls of academic achievement. Consider this question, for example: Is higher education (at the college and university level) stratified by social class? According to the sociologist Dennis Gilbert (2003: 168), the answer is both yes and no:

> (1) The American system of higher education is so big and so open that it provides major opportunities for talented youths from lower and middle-class families to prepare themselves for successful careers that raise them above the level of their parents, and (2) the American system of higher

■ Community colleges, especially those located on reservations, have increased access to higher education for some Native Americans. However, Native Americans as a category remain far below median levels of educational attainment in the United States.

education is sufficiently stratified that its main function is to reproduce for each generation of children the status positions held by their parents. Does the American system of higher education promote mobility or reproduction? The answer appears to be both.

In this chapter, we will look further into this issue as we discuss education as a key social institution and analyze some of the problems that affect contemporary elementary, secondary, and higher education. Before reading further, take the quiz in Box 16.1 to see what you know about education.

AN OVERVIEW OF EDUCATION

Education is the social institution responsible for the systematic transmission of knowledge, skills, and cultural values within a formally organized structure. Education is a powerful and influential force in contemporary societies. As a social institution, education imparts values, beliefs, and knowledge considered essential to the social reproduction of individual personalities and entire cultures (Bourdieu and Passeron, 1990). Education grapples with issues of societal stability and social change, reflecting society even as it attempts to shape it. Early socialization is primarily informal and takes place within our families and friendship networks; socialization then passes to the schools and other, more-formalized organizations created for the specific purpose of educating people. Today, education is such a significant social institution that an entire subfield of sociology—the *sociology of education*—is devoted to its study.

How did education emerge as such an important social institution in contemporary industrialized nations? To answer this question, we begin with a brief examination of education in historical–global perspective.

EDUCATION IN HISTORICAL– GLOBAL PERSPECTIVE

Education serves an important purpose in all societies. At the microlevel, people must acquire the basic knowledge and skills they need to survive in society. At the macrolevel, the social institution of education is an essential component in maintaining and perpetuating the culture of a society across generations. *Cultural transmission*—the process by which children and recent immigrants become acquainted with the dominant cultural beliefs, values, norms, and accumulated knowledge of a society—occurs through informal and formal education. However, the process of cultural transmission differs in preliterate, preindustrial, and industrial nations.

Informal Education in Preliterate Societies

Preliterate societies existed before the invention of reading and writing. These societies have no written language and are characterized by very basic technology and a simple division of labor. Daily activity often centers around the struggle to survive against natural forces, and the earliest forms of education are survival oriented. People in these societies acquire knowledge and skills through *informal education*—learning that occurs in a spontaneous, unplanned way. Through direct informal education, parents and other members of the group provide information about how to gather food, find shelter, make weapons and tools, and get along with others. For example, a boy might learn skills such as hunting, gathering, fishing, and farming from his father, whereas a girl might learn from her mother how to plant, gather, and prepare food or how to take care of her younger sisters and brothers. Such informal education often occurs through storytelling or ritual ceremonies that convey cultural messages and provide behavioral norms. Over time, the knowledge shared through information education may become the moral code of the group.

Formal Education in Preindustrial, Industrial, and Postindustrial Societies

Although *preindustrial societies* have a written language, few people know how to read and write, and formal education is often reserved for the privileged. Education becomes more formalized in preindustrial and industrial societies. *Formal education* is learning that takes place within an academic setting such as a school, which has a planned instructional process and teachers who convey specific knowledge, skills, and thinking processes to students.

Box 16.1 SOCIOLOGY AND EVERYDAY LIFE

How Much Do You Know About U.S. Education?

True	False	
T	F	1. The United States has the highest ratio of university students per 100,000 population of any developed nation.
T	F	2. Women and men earn about the same number of doctoral degrees in the United States each year.
T	F	3. Public education in the United States dates back more than 150 years.
T	F	4. Equality of opportunity is a vital belief in the U.S. educational system.
T	F	5. The United States has never established nationwide educational goals.
T	F	6. Gender differences in science achievement are decreasing in U.S. public schools.
T	F	7. Core classes such as history and mathematics were never conducted in languages other than English in public schools in the United States before the 1960s civil rights movement.
T	F	8. The federal government has limited control over how funds are spent by school districts because most of the money comes from the state and local levels.

Answers on page 323.

Perhaps the earliest formal education occurred in ancient Greece and Rome, where philosophers such as Socrates, Plato, and Aristotle taught elite males the skills required to become thinkers and orators who could engage in the art of persuasion (Ballantine, 2001). During the Middle Ages, the first colleges and universities were developed under the auspices of the Catholic church.

The Renaissance and the Industrial Revolution had a profound effect on education. During the Renaissance, the focus of education shifted to the importance of developing well-rounded and liberally educated people. With the rapid growth of industrial capitalism and factories during the Industrial Revolution, it became necessary for workers to have basic skills in reading, writing, and arithmetic. However, from the Middle Ages until the end of World War I, only the sons of the privileged classes were able to attend European universities. Agriculture was the economic base of society, and literacy for people in the lower classes was not deemed important.

As societies industrialize, the need for formal education of the masses increases significantly. In the United States, the free public school movement was started in 1848 by Horace Mann, who stated that education should be the "great equalizer." By the mid-1850s, the process of mass education had begun in the United States as all states established free, tax-supported elementary schools that were readily available to children throughout the country. *Mass education* refers to providing free, public schooling for wide segments of a nation's population.

Some early forms of mass education took place in one-room schoolhouses such as the one shown here, where children in various grades were all taught by the same teacher. How do changes in the larger society bring about changes in education?

© Gabe Palmer/Corbis

As industrialization and bureaucratization intensified, managers and business owners demanded that schools educate students beyond the third or fourth grade so that well-qualified workers would be available for rapidly emerging "white-collar" jobs in management and clerical work (Bailyn, 1960). By the middle of the nineteenth century, the idea of universal free public schooling was fairly well established in the United States. In addition to educating the next generation of children for the workplace, public schools were also supposed to serve as the primary agents of socialization for millions of European immigrants arriving in the United States seeking economic opportunities and a better life. By the 1920s, educators had introduced the "core" curriculum: courses such as mathematics, social sciences, natural sciences, and English. This core is reflected in the contemporary "back to basics" movement, which calls for teaching the "three R's" (reading, 'riting, and 'rithmetic) and enforcing stricter discipline in schools.

Contemporary U.S. education attempts to meet the needs of the industrial and postindustrial society by teaching a wide diversity of students a myriad of topics, including history and science, computer skills, how to balance a checkbook, and how to avoid contracting AIDS. According to sociologists, many functions performed by other social institutions in the past are now under the auspices of the public schools. For example, full-day kindergartens and extended-day programs for school-age children are provided by many U.S. school districts because of the growing number of working parents who need high-quality, affordable care for their children. Within the regular classroom setting, many teachers feel that their job description encompasses too many divergent tasks. According to Ruth Prale, an elementary reading specialist,

> A teacher today is a social worker, surrogate parent, a bit of disciplinarian, a counselor, and someone who has to see to it that they eat. Many teachers are mandated to teach sex education, drug awareness, gang awareness. And we're supposed to be benevolent. And we haven't come to teaching yet! (qtd. in Collins and Frantz, 1993: 83)

Box 16.1 SOCIOLOGY AND EVERYDAY LIFE

Answers to the Sociology Quiz on U.S. Education

1. **False.** Canada has the most university students (7,197) per 100,000 population. The United States is second, with 5,653 students per 100,000 population, followed by New Zealand (4,232) and South Korea (4,208) (Ash, 1997).

2. **False.** Men earn 58 percent of the doctorates, whereas women earn 42 percent. In the physical sciences, however, men earn 76 percent of the degrees, as compared to 24 percent for women (*Chronicle of Higher Education*, 2001).

3. **True.** As far back as 1848, free public education was believed to be important in the United States because of the high rates of immigration and the demand for literacy so that the country would have an informed citizenry that could function in a democracy (J. Wright, 1997).

4. **True.** Despite the fact that equality of educational opportunity has not been achieved, many people still subscribe to the belief that this country's educational system provides equality of opportunity to the masses, who can make of it what they will (J. Wright, 1997).

5. **False.** In 1994, Congress passed the Goals 2000: Educate America Act, which established eight major goals for education. Among these goals were a high school graduation rate of 90 percent and having U.S. students become first in the world in science and mathematics achievement (AAUW, 1995).

6. **False.** Gender differences in science achievement are not decreasing and may actually be increasing. According to the National Assessment of Educational Progress, gender differences in science achievement for nine- and thirteen-year-olds increased from the late 1970s to the 1990s due to a significant increase in the performance of male students and a lag in performance for female students (AAUW, 1995).

7. **False.** Late in the nineteenth and early in the twentieth century, some classes were conducted in the language of recent immigrants, such as the Italians, the Polish, and the Germans.

8. **True.** Most funding for public education comes from state and local property taxes, and similar sources of revenue.

At all levels of U.S. education, from kindergarten through graduate school, controversy exists over what should be taught, how it should be taught, and who should teach it. Do other nations have similar questions regarding their educational systems? Let's take a brief look at how educational systems are organized in Japan and Bosnia.

Contemporary Education in Other Nations

In this section, we will examine schools in two nations that frequently show up in the U.S. media. Because the United States and Japan are often compared to each other in the global marketplace, social analysts frequently compare the educational systems of these high-income countries. Similarly, since Bosnia is known for racial–ethnic factions and problems with racism, social analysts often examine how Bosnian schools handle ethnic and religious discord.

Education in Japan Like other countries, Japan did not make public education mandatory for children until the country underwent industrialization. During the Meiji period (1868–1912), feudalism was eliminated, and Japan embarked on a new focus on youth and "bureaucratic" universal education (White, 1994). In hopes of catching up with the West, Japanese officials created an educational system and national educational goals. Education was viewed as a form of economic and national development and as a means of identifying talent for a new technological elite (White, 1994).

Today, Japanese educators, parents, students, and employers all view education as a crucial link in Japan's economic success. Japanese schools not only emphasize conformity and nationalism, but also highlight the importance of obligation to one's family and of learning the skills necessary for employment. Beginning at about three years of age, many Japanese toddlers are sent to cram schools (*jukus*) to help them qualify for good preschools.

In both cram schools and public schools, students learn discipline and thinking skills, along with physical activities such as karate and gymnastics to improve agility. By the time children reach elementary school, they are expected to engage in cooperative activities with their classmates. In some schools, children are responsible for preparing, serving, and cleaning up after the midday meal. At the end of the day, children may be seen cleaning the chalkboards and even mopping the floors, all as a part of the spirit of cooperation they are being taught.

In Japan, the middle-school years are especially crucial: Students' futures are based on the academic status track on which they are placed while in middle school. Moreover, the kind of jobs they will hold in the future depends on the university or vocational–technical school they attend, which in turn

depends on the high school they attend. By the third year of middle school, most students are acutely aware of their academic future and of how their lives and friendships change as they go through the educational process, as one former student recalled:

> Middle school was fun; I was with my friends and I could throw myself into sports and I didn't have to study very hard. I couldn't be sure which of my friends would be with me in high school. Now that I am in high school, I know these will be my friends for life—they've been with me through very tough times. (qtd. in White, 1994: 77)

Up until high school, the student population of a school typically reflects the neighborhoods in which children live. However, at the high school level, entrance to a particular school is based on ability: Some Japanese students enter vocational schools that teach them skills for the workplace; others enter schools that are exclusively for the college-bound. Many analysts have noted the extent to which most Japanese vocational schools provide state-of-the-art equipment and instruction in fields with wide employment opportunities. Consequently, graduates of most vocational high schools do not have problems finding relatively well-paid employment upon graduation.

Typically, the instruction in Japanese high schools for the college-bound is highly structured, and all students are expected to respond in unison to questions posed by the teacher. Students are expected to be fluent in more than one language; many Japanese high schools teach English, particularly vocabulary and sentence construction. Science and math courses are challenging, and Japanese students often take courses such as algebra and calculus several years before their U.S. counterparts. Students must be prepared for a variety of college entrance examinations because each college and university gives its own test, and all tests occur within a few weeks of one another.

Girls and young women in the United States would likely feel stifled by the lack of educational opportunities experienced by their counterparts in Japan.

Although there have been some changes, many parents and educators still believe that a good junior college education is all that young women need in order to be employable and marriageable (White, 1994). At the college and university level, the absence of women as students and professors is especially profound. Although a woman recently became the first-ever female president of a state-run university (Nara Women's University) in Japan, women account for fewer than 5 percent of all presidents of colleges and universities (Findlay-Kaneko, 1997). Moreover, the lack of child-care facilities within the universities remains a pressing problem for women students and faculty in Japanese higher education.

Young men also experience extreme pressures in the Japanese system. In fact, high rates of school truancy occur as tens of thousands of students balk at going to school, and still others experience school-related health problems such as stomach ulcers, allergy disorders, and high blood pressure (White, 1994).

Education in Bosnia

To understand education in contemporary Bosnia, it is important to consider the country's history. Located in eastern Europe and frequently subject to ethnic strife, the nation of Bosnia-Herzegovina has sought to maintain schools throughout violent clashes among its three principal ethnic groups: Muslims, Eastern Orthodox Serbs, and Roman Catholic Croats. Despite the existence of a formal peace agreement in 1995 between these groups, animosities remain strong.

Journalists and social scientists have found that each of the principal ethnic groups has taken control over how its children are educated and how cultural ideas are presented to them by teachers and in textbooks. Many schools identify and educate students by their ethnic background. For example, in history classes, students are segregated into ethnically distinct classrooms and taught different versions of history, language, and art, depending on their ethnic and religious identity (Hedges, 1997). The fact that schools with integrated classrooms have seen an increase in conflicts between students from different ethnic groups undoubtedly contributes to this situation. According to one Serbian sociologist, his teenage daughter came home in tears because of comments made in her class about the Serbian "aggressors": "She would not return to school for 10 days. Many of her friends now cross the line at the edge of the city to take classes in schools run by the Bosnian Serbs to avoid ridicule and harassment" (qtd. in Hedges, 1997: A4).

What will happen in the future is unknown. There is some cause for optimism that educational opportunities for children in Bosnia and Herzegovina will improve as organizations such as the United Nations Children's Fund (UNICEF) and some universities in the United States seek to help Bosnia with educational reform (University of Utah, 2003). Even with efforts at greater inclusion in Bosnian schools, many problems of discrimination and exclusion remain unresolved. According to recent reports, "Apartheid is a word still used to describe education in Bosnia" (Bosnia Action Coalition, 2001). Three issues continue to be central points of contention in Bosnian education: language, religion, and control of the schools (McCreight, 2001). The case of Bosnian education illustrates how difficult it is for teaching and learning to take place in an environment where there is little consensus about a shared sense of values, history, and what is important for the future. How much consensus exists in the United States regarding education?

What Did I Learn from Previewing?

Take a minute to think about what you learned when you previewed the chapter. The headings told you the chapter would focus on broad issues (e.g., phrases like "global perspective," "informal education," and "formal education"). These headings very clearly guide you to the structure of the chapter. You saw how key terms are indicated by the use of boldface and italic type.

☞ Now that you have spent a few minutes previewing the chapter, you are ready to read and understand the text easily and thoroughly. Return now to the beginning of the chapter and read it carefully.

Mark the Text

Now that you've previewed and read it once, mark the text—underline important ideas, write notes in the margin, circle key words, write question marks next to anything you don't understand. (To review how to mark the text, turn to page 421, "Learning Strategy III—Marking Text.") If you have any questions, be sure to bring them up with your classmates or ask your instructor. Remember, when it's time for an exam, you only need to review the marks and comments you've made on the text.

Vocabulary

You've seen that the author kindly calls your attention to key terms and concepts by writing them in boldface and italic type. If you find a term that you don't fully understand be sure to mark it so you can ask a classmate or your instructor about it. If there are any words in the definitions you don't understand, be sure to look them up. For example, do you understand the difference between *preliterate* and *literate societies?* Is the term *mass education* clear to you? What does *mass* mean in this context?

Exam Questions

This textbook is used in many introduction to sociology courses around the country. Following are some examples of exam questions given by instructors who actually teach the course. Test your understanding of the chapter by answering the questions.

Multiple Choice Questions

1. Education serves an important purpose in all societies. At the _____, people must acquire the basic knowledge and skills they need to survive in society.

   a. mesolevel
   b. macrolevel
   c. tertiary level
   d. microlevel

2. Education serves an important purpose in all societies. At the _____, the social institution of education is an essential component in maintaining and perpetuating the culture of a society across generations.

   a. macrolevel
   b. tertiary level
   c. microlevel
   d. mesolevel

3. _____ is the process by which children and recent immigrants become acquainted with the dominant cultural beliefs, values, norms, and accumulated knowledge of a society.

   a. Cultural discovery
   b. Cultural transmission
   c. Cultural diffusion
   d. Cultural absorption

4. _____ societies existed before the invention of reading and writing. These societies have no written language and are characterized by very basic technology and a simple division of labor. The earliest forms of education are survival oriented.

   a. Preindustrial
   b. Industrial
   c. Postindustrial
   d. Preliterate

5. _____ is learning that occurs in a spontaneous, unplanned way.

   a. Formal education
   b. Manifest education
   c. Informal education
   d. Latent education

6. In preliterate societies, parents and other members of the group provide information about how to gather food, find shelter, make weapons and tools, and get along with others. This is accomplished through direct _____ education.

   a. informal
   b. manifest
   c. formal
   d. latent

7. A boy might learn skills such as hunting, gathering, fishing, and farming from his father, whereas a girl might learn from her mother how to plant, gather, and prepare food or how to take care of her younger sisters and brothers. Such _____ often occurs through storytelling or ritual ceremonies that convey cultural messages and provide behavioral norms.

    a. formal education
    b. latent education
    c. informal education
    d. manifest education

8. Although _____ societies have a written language, few people know how to read and write, and formal education is often reserved for the privileged.

    a. preliterate
    b. preindustrial
    c. industrial
    d. postindustrial

9. _____ is learning that takes place within an academic setting such as school, which has a planned instructional process and teachers who convey specific knowledge, skills, and thinking processes to students.

    a. Institutional education
    b. Primary education
    c. Formal education
    d. Manifest education

10. Perhaps the earliest _____ occurred in ancient Greece and Rome, where philosophers such as Socrates, Plato, and Aristotle taught elite males the skills required to become thinkers and orators who could engage in the art of persuasion.

    a. manifest education
    b. institutional education
    c. primary education
    d. formal education

11. During the _____, the focus of education shifted to the importance of developing well-rounded and liberally educated people.

    a. Middle Ages
    b. Renaissance
    c. Industrial Revolution
    d. Great Depression

12. With the rapid growth of capitalism and factories during the
    _____, it became necessary for workers to have basic skills in
    reading, writing, and arithmetic.

    a. Great Depression
    b. Middle Ages
    c. Renaissance
    d. Industrial Revolution

13. _____ refers to providing free, public schooling for wide
    segments of a nation's population.

    a. Mass education
    b. Formal education
    c. State education
    d. National education

14. By the 1920s, educators had introduced the core curriculum, which
    consisted of all the following courses, EXCEPT

    a. mathematics.
    b. natural sciences.
    c. music education.
    d. social sciences.

15. Japanese schools not only emphasize _____ and nationalism, but
    also highlight the importance of _____ to one's family.

    a. individualism; commitment
    b. individualism; obligation
    c. conformity; commitment
    d. conformity; obligation

16. Concerning the instruction in Japanese high schools for the college-
    bound, all of the following are true, EXCEPT

    a. students are expected to be fluent in more than one language.
    b. students often take challenging math and science courses several
       years before their U.S. counterparts.
    c. students only focus on their native language, focusing on vocabulary
       and sentence construction.
    d. students must be prepared for a variety of college entrance
       examinations.

17. In Bosnia many schools identify and educate students by:

    a. their chronological age.
    b. their racial identity.
    c. their economic status
    d. their ethnic background.

18. Even with efforts at greater inclusion in Bosnian schools, many problems of discrimination and exclusion remain unresolved. All of the following continue to be central points of contention in Bosnian education, EXCEPT

    a. language.
    b. funding.
    c. religion.
    d. control of the schools.

Short Response Questions

1. Provide a brief overview of education: define education and describe cultural transmission.
2. From a global perspective, describe the informal education in preliterate societies.
3. From a global perspective, trace the formal education in preindustrial, industrial, and postindustrial societies.
4. Summarize contemporary education in other nations, using education in Japan as a model.
5. Compare contemporary education in other nations, citing education in Bosnia as the model.

Essay Questions

1. Provide a personal perspective on how good of a job overall you think the U.S. "mass education" system is doing in educating its students.
2. Imagine that you had the authority to change five things about the education system in the United States. Identify what you would change, and discuss how these changes would improve the education system.

LANGUAGE AND CULTURE

A Chapter from the Textbook
Looking Out/Looking In, Eighth Edition

Ronald B. Adler and Neil Towne

PREVIEWING

The first step in studying a textbook chapter should be previewing. First, to review the benefits and methods of previewing, read and study "Learning Strategy I—Previewing" on page 415. The following questions will guide your preview of "Language and Culture."

1. Read the title. What do you think the chapter will be about?
2. Read the first four paragraphs quickly. They will introduce you to the tone and content of the chapter. (If you enjoy the examples of "bungled translations" in the first paragraph, you'll also like reading "It Got Lost in the Translation" in *The Thoughtful Reader* on page 257).
3. Read the subtitles of the chapter. Are there any words or phrases that you don't understand? If so, be sure to mark them so you can ask about them in class.
4. Are any tables or charts included in the chapter? What do they contain?
5. How do the authors indicate the words or terms they feel are important?
6. List the other helpful features (such as a glossary, a summary, margin notes, etc.) that the chapter contains.

LANGUAGE AND CULTURE

INTRODUCTION

Anyone who has tried to translate ideas from one language to another knows that conveying the same meaning isn't always easy. Sometimes the results of a bungled translation can be amusing. For example, the American manufacturers of Pet milk unknowingly introduced their product in French-speaking markets without realizing that the word *pet* in French means "to break wind." Likewise, the English-speaking representative of a U.S. soft-drink manufacturer naively drew laughs from Mexican customers when she offered free samples of Fresca soda pop. In Mexican slang the word *fresca* means "lesbian."

Even choosing the right words during translation won't guarantee that non-native speakers will use an unfamiliar language correctly. For example, Japanese insurance companies warn their policyholders who are visiting the United States to avoid their cultural tendency to say "excuse me" or "I'm sorry" if they are involved in a traffic accident. In Japan, apologizing is a traditional way to express goodwill and maintain social harmony, even if the person offering the apology is not at fault. But in the United States an apology can be taken as an admission of guilt and result in Japanese tourists being held accountable for accidents in which they may not be responsible.

Difficult as it may be, translation is only a small part of the differences in communication between members of different cultures. Differences in the way language is used and the very world view that a language creates make communicating across cultures a challenging task.

VERBAL COMMUNICATION STYLES

Using language is more than just choosing a particular group of words to convey an idea. Each language has its own unique style that distinguishes it from others. Matters like the amount of formality or informality, precision or vagueness, and brevity or detail are major ingredients in speaking competently. And when a communicator tries to use the verbal style from one culture in a different one, problems are likely to arise.

One way in which verbal styles vary is in their *directness*. Anthropologist Edward Hall identified two distinct cultural ways of using language. **Low-context cultures** use language primarily to express thoughts, feelings, and ideas as clearly and logically as possible. Low-context communicators look for the meaning of a statement in the words spoken. By contrast, **high-context cultures** value language as a way to maintain social harmony. Rather than upset others by speaking clearly, communicators in these societies learn to discover meaning from the context in which a message is delivered: the nonverbal behaviors of the speaker, the history of the relationship, and the general social rules that govern interaction

TABLE 1   Low- and High-Context Communication Styles

Low Context	High Context
Majority of information carried in explicit verbal messages, with less focus on the situational context	Important information carried in contextual cues (time, place, relationship, situation); less reliance on explicit verbal messages
Self-expression valued; communicators state opinions and desires directly and strive to persuade others to accept their own viewpoint	Relational harmony valued and maintained by indirect expression of opinions; communicators abstain from saying "no" directly
Clear, eloquent speech considered praiseworthy; verbal fluency admired	Communicators talk "around" the point, allowing the other to fill in the missing pieces; ambiguity and use of silence admired

between people. Table 1 summarizes some key differences between the ways low- and high-context cultures use language.

North American culture falls toward the low-context end of the scale. Residents of the United States and Canada value straight talk and grow impatient with "beating around the bush." By contrast, most Asian and Middle-Eastern cultures fit the high-context pattern. In many Asian cultures, for example, maintaining harmony is important, and so communicators will avoid speaking clearly if that would threaten another person's face. For this reason, Japanese or Koreans are less likely than Americans to offer a clear "no" to an undesirable request. Instead they would probably use roundabout expressions like "I agree with you in principle, but . . ." or "I sympathize with you. . . ."

The same sort of clash between directness and indirectness can aggravate problems between straight-talking, low-context Israelis who value speaking clearly and Arabs, whose high-context culture stresses smooth interaction. It's easy to imagine how the clash of cultural styles could lead to misunderstandings and conflicts between Israelis and their Palestinian neighbors. Israelis could view their Arab counterparts as evasive, while the Palestinians could perceive the Israelis as insensitive and blunt.

Even within a single country, subcultures can have different notions about the value of direct speech. For example, Puerto Rican language style resembles high-context Japanese or Korean more than low-context English. As a group, Puerto Ricans value social harmony and avoid confrontation, which leads them to systematically speak in an indirect way to avoid giving offense.

Another way in which language styles can vary across cultures is whether they are *elaborate* or *succinct*. Speakers of Arabic, for instance, commonly use language that is much more rich and expressive than most communicators who use English. Strong assertions and exaggerations that would sound ridiculous in English are a common feature of Arabic. This contrast in linguistic style can lead to misunderstandings between people from different backgrounds. As one observer put it,

> First, an Arab feels compelled to overassert in almost all types of communication because others expect him to. If an Arab says exactly what he means without the expected assertion, other Arabs may still think that he means the opposite. For example, a simple "no," by a guest to the host's requests to eat more or drink more will not suffice. To convey the meaning that he is actually full, the guest must keep repeating "no" several times, coupling it with an oath such as "By God" or "I swear to God." Second, an Arab often fails to realize that others, particularly foreigners, may mean exactly what they say even though their language is simple. To the Arabs, a simple "no" may mean the indirectly expressed consent and encouragement of a coquettish woman. On the other hand, a simple consent may mean the rejection of a hypocritical politician.

Succinctness is most extreme in cultures where silence is valued. In many Native American cultures, for example, the favored way to handle ambiguous social situations is to remain quiet. When you contrast this silent style to the talkativeness that is common in mainstream American cultures when people first meet, it's easy to imagine how the first encounter between an Apache or Navajo and an Anglo might feel uncomfortable to both people.

Along with differences such as directness and indirectness and elaborate and succinct styles, a third way languages differ from one culture to another involves *formality* and *informality.* The informal approach that characterizes relationships in countries like the United States, Canada, and Australia, and the Scandinavian countries is quite different from the great concern for using proper speech in many parts of Asia and Africa. Formality isn't so much a matter of using correct grammar as of defining social position. In Korea, for example, the language reflects the Confucian system of relational hierarchies. It has special vocabularies for different sexes, for different levels of social status, for different degrees of intimacy, and for different types of social occasions. For example, there are different degrees of formality for speaking with old friends, nonacquaintances whose background one knows, and complete strangers. One sign of being a learned person in Korea is the ability to use language that recognizes these relational distinctions. When you contrast these sorts of distinctions with the casual friendliness many North Americans use even when talking with complete strangers, it's easy to see how a Korean might view communicators in the United States as boorish, and how an American might see Koreans as stiff and unfriendly.

LANGUAGE AND WORLD VIEW

Different linguistic styles are important, but there may be even more fundamental differences that separate speakers of various languages. For almost 150 years, some theorists have put forth the notion of **linguistic determinism**: that the world view of a culture is unavoidably shaped and reflected by the language its members speak. The best-known example of linguistic determinism is the notion that Eskimos have a large number of words (estimated at everything from seventeen to one hundred) for what we simply call "snow." Different terms are used to describe conditions like a driving blizzard, crusty ice, and light powder. This example suggests how linguistic determinism operates. The need to survive in an Arctic environment led Eskimos to make distinctions that would be unimportant to residents of warmer environments, and once the language makes these distinctions, speakers are more likely to see the world in ways that match the broader vocabulary.

Even though there is some doubt that Eskimos really have so many words for snow, other examples do seem to support the principle of linguistic determinism. For instance, bilingual speakers seem to think differently when they change languages. In one study, French-Americans were asked to interpret a series of pictures. When they spoke in French, their descriptions were far more romantic and emotional than when they used English to describe the same kinds of images. Likewise, when students in Hong Kong were asked to complete a values test, they expressed more traditional Chinese values when they answered in Cantonese than when they spoke English. In Israel, both Arab and Jewish students saw bigger distinctions between their group and "outsiders" when using their native language than when they spoke in English, a neutral tongue. Examples like these show the power of language to shape cultural identity . . . sometimes for better, and sometimes for worse.

Linguistic influences start early in life. English-speaking parents often label the mischievous pranks of their children as "bad," implying that there is something immoral about acting wild. "Be good!" they are inclined to say. On the other hand, French adults are more likely to say *Sois sage!*—"Be wise." The linguistic implication is that misbehaving is an act of foolishness. Swedes would correct the same action with the words *Var snäll!*—"Be friendly," "Be kind." By contrast, German adults use the command *Sei artig!*—literally "Be of your own kind"—in other words, get back in step, conform to your role as a child.

The best-known declaration of linguistic determinism is the **Sapir–Whorf hypothesis,** formulated by Edward Sapir and Benjamin Whorf. Following Sapir's theory, Whorf observed that the language spoken by Hopi Native Americans represents a view of reality that is dramatically different from more familiar tongues. For example, the Hopi language makes no distinction between nouns and verbs. Therefore the people who speak it describe the entire world as being constantly in process. Whereas we use nouns to characterize people or objects as being fixed or constant, Hopi view them more as verbs, constantly changing.

In this sense our language represents much of the world rather like a snapshot camera, whereas Hopi reflects a world view more like a motion picture.

Although there is little support for the extreme linguistically deterministic viewpoint that it is *impossible* for speakers of different languages to view the world identically, the more moderate notion of **linguistic relativism**—that language exerts a strong influence on perceptions—does seem valid. As one scholar put it, "The differences between languages are not so much in what *can* be said, but in what it is *relatively easy* to say." Some languages contain terms that have no English equivalents. For example, consider a few words in other languages that have no English equivalents:

Nemawashi (Japanese): The process of informally feeling out all the people involved with an issue before making a decision

Lagniappe (French/Creole): An extra gift given in a transaction that wasn't expected by the terms of a contract

Lao (Mandarin): A respectful term used for older people, showing their importance in the family and in society

Dharma (Sanskrit): Each person's unique, ideal path in life, and knowledge of how to find it

Koyaanisquatsi (Hopi): Nature out of balance; a way of life so crazy it calls for a new way of living

Once words like these exist and become a part of everyday life, the ideas that they represent are easier to recognize. But even without such terms, each of the concepts above is still possible to imagine. Thus, speakers of a language that includes the notion of *lao* would probably treat its older members respectfully and those who are familiar with *lagniappe* might be more generous. Despite these differences, the words aren't essential to follow these principles. Although language may shape thoughts and behavior, it doesn't dominate them absolutely.

The importance of language as a reflection of world view isn't just a matter of interest for anthropologists and linguists. The labels we use in everyday conversation both reflect and shape the way we view ourselves and others. This explains why businesses often give employees impressive titles, and why a woman's choice of the label "Ms." or "Mrs." can be a statement about her identity.

Relational titles aren't the only linguistic elements that may shape attitudes about men and women. Language reforms like avoiding "he" as a gender-neutral pronoun can lead to less discriminatory thinking. A recent study examined precisely this question. Students were corrected every time they used "he" as a generic pronoun in their writing. At the end of a semester, results showed that the corrections did reduce the use of gender-biased language. However, students did not change their mental images or their attitudes toward language reforms.

Along with **gender labeling, ethnic group labeling** can both affect and reflect the way members of an ethnic group define themselves. Over the years, labels of racial identification have gone through cycles of popularity. In North America, the first freed slaves preferred to be called *Africans.* In the late

LOOKING AT DIVERSITY

The Bilingual World of the Deaf

Larry Littleton lost his hearing at age seven after contracting spinal meningitis. He spent the next eight years relying exclusively on lip reading to understand others' speech and using his own voice to express ideas. At age fifteen he learned American Sign Language and finger spelling. Larry has worked for Southern California Edison conducting energy audits, and he volunteers his time speaking to students and community groups.

Most people don't realize that American Sign Language (ASL) is a complete language with its own vocabulary. Some of the symbols we use even have different meanings in ASL than they do in other sign languages. For example, I just came back from Australia, where the sign that we use to mean "sex" means "fun," and the one that means "socks" to us means "learn" to them. You can imagine how confused I was when an Australian used his sign language to ask me, "Are you having fun learning while you're here?" and I thought he was asking, "Are you having sex in socks while you're here?"

Being a bilingual speaker who understands both ASL and English helps me appreciate how different the two languages are. For one thing, I think ASL is a more expressive language. English speakers depend on words to get ideas across. In ASL, a lot more of the meaning comes from how you act out a sign. For example, in ASL the difference between "I'm a little sorry," "I'm sorry" and "I'm terribly sorry" come from your facial expression, your posture, and the way you gesture as you make the sign. I guess you could say that being expressive may be *useful* in spoken language, but it's *essential* in ASL.

Besides being more expressive than English, ASL is more concise. I just read about a study of one elementary-school classroom with a hearing teacher and an ASL interpreter. In one week the speaking teacher used almost eighty-six thousand words; but the interpreter only used forty-three thousand words to get across the same message to the deaf students. Maybe the interpreter missed some ideas, but I also think the difference came because sign language is so concise and expressive. Let me show you an example. In speaking I could

tell you "Sorry, I've lost my train of thought." In ASL, the whole idea gets communicated almost instantly, in one sign [he demonstrates]. Here's another example: I can make one sign [he gestures] that means the same as the seven words: "Don't worry: It's not a big deal."

ASL is good at communicating concepts, but it doesn't work as well when the message contains specific details. When people who are deaf need to get across a precise message—a phone number or somebody's name, for example, they usually fingerspell. Fingerspelling has its own set of symbols for each letter of the alphabet, and you communicate by spelling the word out one letter at a time. Fingerspelling isn't really a different language from English: it's just a different way of "writing."

I think ASL and spoken languages both have strengths. Because they're precise, spoken languages are useful when you need to get across specific details. But when you want to be expressive, I think ASL works much better. I know one ASL interpreter whose translations are beautiful: Almost everything she says comes across like poetry or music. I also think sign languages are more universal. A while ago I was traveling in Europe with a bunch of hearing people. When we got to countries where nobody could speak the local language, my signing got us through a lot of tough situations. I think that's because using sign language develops a communicator's creativity and expressiveness. The same thing happened when I was in Thailand last year. Almost nobody spoke English in the village where I lived, but I got along pretty well because I have had so much practice expressing my ideas with my face and gestures, and also because I spend so much time and energy observing how others act.

I think everybody can benefit from being bilingual, and ASL is a wonderful second language to learn. Besides developing your expressiveness, it can help you appreciate that people who are deaf have the same ideas and feelings that hearing people do.

nineteenth and early twentieth centuries *colored* was the term of choice, but later *Negro* became the respectable word. Then, in the sixties, the term *Black* grew increasingly popular—first as a label for militants, and later as a term preferred by more moderate citizens of all colors. More recently *African American* has gained popularity. Recent surveys have found that between 60 and 72 percent of Blacks surveyed prefer the term *Black,* while between 15 and 25 percent prefer *African American.* (The rest either had no opinion or chose other labels.)

Decisions about which name to use reflect a person's attitude. For example, one recent survey revealed that individuals who prefer the label *Black* choose it because it is "acceptable" and "based on consensus" of the larger culture. They describe themselves as patriotic, accepting of the status quo, and attempting to assimilate into the larger culture. By contrast, people who choose the term *Afro-American* derive their identity from their ethnicity and do not want to assimilate into the larger culture, only succeed in it.

SUMMARY

Different languages often shape and reflect the view of a culture. Low-context cultures, like the United States, use language primarily to express feelings and ideas as clearly and unambiguously as possible. High-context cultures, such as Japan and Saudi Arabia, however, avoid specificity in order to promote social harmony. Some cultures value brevity and the succinct use of language, while others have high regard for elaborate forms of speech. In some societies, formality is important, while others value informality. Beyond these differences, there is evidence to support linguistic relativism—the notion that language exerts a strong influence on the world view of the people who speak it.

KEY TERMS

ethnic group labeling

high-context cultures

gender labeling

linguistic determinism

linguistic relativism

low-context cultures

Sapir–Whorf hypothesis

What Did I Learn from Previewing?

Reflect for a moment on what you learned by previewing this chapter. First, the title, "Language and Culture" should have triggered many associations in your mind. For example, if you have read any of the selections in Unit 2 or Unit 3 of *The Thoughtful Reader*, try to make connections between them and the information in this textbook excerpt. The subtitles, "Verbal Communication Styles" and "Language and World View," serve as an outline to the content of the chapter. The key terms the authors think you should know are written in boldface type. Two of the key terms, low-context and high-context communication styles, are presented in a table. Finally, a summary repeats the highlights of the chapter.

☞ Now that you have spent a few moments previewing the chapter, you are ready to read and understand the text more easily and thoroughly. Return now to the chapter and read it through.

Mark the Text

Now that you have previewed and read the chapter, you are ready to master the ideas that it contains. As you read through a second time, mark the text—underline important ideas, write notes in the margin, circle key words, write question marks next to anything you don't understand. (To review how to mark the text, turn to page 421, "Learning Strategy III—Marking Text") When you have finished marking the text, discuss any questions you have with your classmates. And remember—when exam time comes along, you only need to review the marks and comments you have written.

Vocabulary

Note that, in this textbook chapter, the authors give you a list of the *key terms*—important words they think you should know and remember. Be sure to find and mark each term in the text. Mark any term you don't understand so you'll remember to ask a classmate or the instructor for an explanation. It would be a good idea to keep a special section of your notebook where you write the terms and their meanings.

Exam Questions

Each instructor will have his or her own style of testing. Following are several examples of exam questions used by instructors who actually teach the course in which this text is used. Test your understanding of the chapter by answering these questions.

Short Essay Questions

1. Contrast low-context cultures with high-context cultures. Write two to four sentences.
2. Define and explain the concept of linguistic relativism.
3. In *The Thoughtful Reader*, read "Speaking Different Languages," on page 199. Using the information in this chapter, "Language and Culture," explain the problem the American woman had in Turkey. Write one paragraph.

Matching

Match the terms in column 1 with their definitions in column 2.

1

_____ 1. high-context cultures

_____ 2. low-context cultures

_____ 3. linguistic determinism

_____ 4. linguistic relativism

_____ 5. Sapir–Whorf hypothesis

2

a. theory of linguistic determinism in which language is determined by a culture's perceived reality

b. cultures that avoid direct use of language, relying on the context of a message to convey meaning

c. the theory that a culture's world view is unavoidably shaped and reflected by the language its members speak

d. cultures that use language primarily to express thoughts, feelings, and ideas as clearly and logically as possible

e. a moderate theory that argues that language exerts a strong influence on the perceptions of the people who speak it

True/False

Mark the statements below as true or false.

_____ 1. According to research, the name you use to describe your ethnic group can reflect your attitude about many aspects of life.

_____ 2. The United States would fall into the category of low-context cultures.

_____ 3. Ambiguity and vagueness are forms of language that are to be avoided at all costs.

_____ 4. A person from the United States is more likely to value direct language than is someone from Japan.

THE FAMILY

A Chapter from the Textbook
Sociology in a Changing World, Third Edition

William Kornblum

PREVIEWING

Your first step in studying a textbook should always be a preview of the chapter. Turn to page 415, "Learning Strategy I," to review previewing. The following questions will help you preview "The Family."

1. List the subtitles of the chapter "The Family."
2. Does the author use boldface type, italics, or some other special print to indicate key terms? List a few of the key terms.
3. List the titles of any important charts, tables, or other figures the author uses in the chapter.
4. What other helpful features did you find in the text?

THE FAMILY

DEFINING THE FAMILY

Introduction

The family is a central institution in all human societies, although it may take many different forms. A **family** is a group of people related by blood, marriage, or adoption. Blood relations are often called *consanguineous attachments* (from the Latin *sanguis,* "blood"). Relations between adult persons living together according to the norms of marriage or other intimate relationships are called conjugal relations. The role relations among people who consider themselves to be related in these ways are termed **kinship**.

The familiar kinship terms—*father, mother, brother, sister, grandfather, grandmother, uncle, aunt, niece, nephew, cousin*—refer to specific sets of role relations that may vary greatly from one culture to another. In many African societies, for example, "mother's brother" is someone to whom the male child becomes closer than he does to his father and from whom he receives more of his day-to-day socialization than he may from his father. Note that biological or "blood" ties are not necessarily stronger than ties of adoption. Adopted children are usually loved with the same intensity as children raised by their biological parents. And many family units in the United States and other societies include "fictive kin"—people who are so close to members of the family that they are considered kin despite the absence of blood ties. Finally, neither blood ties nor marriage nor adoption adequately describes the increasingly common relationship between unmarried people who consider themselves a couple or a family.

The smallest units of family structure are usually called **nuclear families**. This term is usually used to refer to a wife and husband and their children, if any. Nowadays one frequently hears the phrase "the traditional nuclear family" used to refer to a married mother and father and their children living together. But as we will see throughout this chapter, there is no longer a "typical" nuclear family structure. Increasingly, therefore, sociologists use the term *nuclear family* to refer to two or more people related by consanguineous or conjugal ties or by adoption who share a household; it does not require that both husband and wife be present in the household or that there be any specific set of role relations among the members of the household.

The nuclear family in which one is born and socialized is termed one's **family of orientation**. The nuclear family one forms through marriage or cohabitation is known as one's **family of procreation**. The relationship between the two is shown in the figure on the next page.

Kinship terms are often confusing because families, especially large ones, can be rather complex social structures. It may help to devote a little time to

NUCLEAR AND EXTENDED FAMILY RELATIONSHIPS

Ego's Grandparents

Paternal Aunt   Father   Mother   Maternal Uncle

Ego's Spouse   Ego   Ego's Sister   Ego's Brother   Ego's Cousins

Daughter   Daughter   Son

■ Ego's Family of Orientation
■ Ego's Family of Procreation
■ Ego's Extended Family—Maternal

△ **Male**
○ **Female**

This diagram shows the family relationships of a hypothetical individual, Ego. Ego was born and socialized into what sociologists call the family of orientation. Ego formed a family of procreation through marriage or cohabitation.

working through the figure above. "Ego" is the person who is taken as the point of reference. You can readily see that Ego has both a family of orientation and a family of procreation. So does Ego's spouse. Ego's parents become the in-laws of the spouse, and the spouse's parents are Ego's in-laws. But like the vast majority of people, Ego also has an **extended family** that includes all the nuclear families of Ego's blood relatives—that is, all of Ego's uncles, aunts, cousins, and grandparents. Ego's spouse also has an extended family, which is not indicated in the figure, nor is it defined as part of Ego's extended family. But relationships with the spouse's extended family are likely to occupy plenty of Ego's time. Indeed, as the figure shows, the marriage bond brings far more than two individuals together. Most married couples have extensive networks of kin to which they must relate in many, varied ways throughout life.

VARIATIONS IN FAMILY STRUCTURE

For the past several years sociologists have been demonstrating that the traditional household consisting of two parents and their children is no longer the typical American family. In the 1940s an American household was about eight times more likely to be headed by a married couple than by unrelated individuals. By 1980 the ratio had declined to about 2.5. Data from Donald Bogue's analysis of trends in family composition reveal that the proportion of married-couple families declined from 78.2 percent of all households in 1950 to slightly less than 60 percent in 1983. In 1990 the proportion stood at 48 percent.

This trend points to a far greater diversity of family types, including far more people living alone and far more women raising children alone, than ever before. There are also more households composed of unrelated single people who live together not just because they are friends but because only by doing so can they afford to live away from their families of orientation. Thus, when they discuss family norms and roles, sociologists must be careful not to represent the traditional nuclear family, or even the married couple, as typical. These considerations become especially important when they discuss low-income and minority families.

THE CHANGING FAMILY

In his pioneering study of changes in the family, William J. Goode argued that the structure of family units becomes simpler as societies undergo industrialization. Goode was not the first social scientist to make this observation; however, his study was the first to be based on extensive historical and comparative data. After reviewing changes in family structure in Europe and North America during the preceding seventy-five years, Goode concluded that the smaller family unit composed of a married couple and their children (i.e., the conjugal family) was increasingly dominant in industrial societies. For Goode, the change from the larger extended family to the smaller and more geographically mobile nuclear family was part of an even larger worldwide revolution in which people are demanding greater control over the conditions that shape their lives.

From the standpoint of the family, this "revolution" translates into demands for freedom to select one's mate, to decide where to live after marriage, to decide whether to have children and how many to have, and even to terminate the marital relationship. Such choices were often impossible in earlier family systems, in which marriages were arranged, the married couple was expected to live within a larger extended family, and couples were expected to have numerous children.

According to Goode, the driving forces behind the large-scale changes in family structure in this century were economic and technological. The more families had to adapt to an economy in which income was earned outside the family, the more the family had to be mobile and flexible. Families must be willing to move from one place to another in search of employment. Geographic mobility, in turn, meant that children would not be able to maintain households in which their parents could live, that is, extended families consisting of "three generations under one roof." And because children no longer worked in the home or on the farm, they became less important in economic terms than they had been in earlier epochs; families therefore had fewer children.

In the three decades since Goode's study appeared, there has been a wealth of new research that has further developed the idea of a transition from extended to nuclear family systems as a result of industrialization. More recent studies often focus on issues related to defining the family, studying family history, and distinguishing between ideal and actual family patterns.

PROBLEMS OF DEFINITION   If one studies who lives in households (i.e., who lives together and eats together more or less regularly), the traditional or "Dick and Jane" family (Mom, Dad, Dick, Jane, and their dog, Spot) appears to be the most prevalent family form. However, if one also considers patterns of interaction with others, the family unit might include, say, a grandmother living in a nearby apartment with an unmarried aunt, as well as a divorced uncle in a nearby community. This approach is illustrated in a volume titled *Beyond the Nuclear Family Model*, which compares patterns of family structure and interaction in several industrialized societies and finds a wide range of possible patterns. For example, although families may not live with "three generations under one roof," they may live in nuclear family units in close proximity to one another, a pattern that continues to sustain large extended families. Technologies like the telephone and jet travel allow family members to see one another fairly frequently when they are separated by geographic distance. And when divorce breaks apart a nuclear family and the parents remarry, the reconstituted family may be embedded in a larger set of extended-family relations that may occupy even more of the members' time. None of these patterns was predicted in the theories of Goode and others who studied the revolution in family structure.

STUDIES OF FAMILY HISTORY   Studies of family form and patterns of family interaction over time have found a good deal of evidence that challenges the conclusions of Goode's research. For example, demographer Peter Laslett found that in some parts of England the emergence of the nuclear family seems to have preceded industrialization by many decades. When people migrated to new agricultural regions, they often left behind extended kin groups and became more dependent on the smaller nuclear-family group. Laslett and other researchers have found that modern technologies like the telephone or the automobile enable members of smaller family units, who formerly might have lost touch with their extended families, to maintain their kinship ties.

Similarly, in her research on industrialization in the mill towns of Massachusetts, Tamara Hareven found evidence that extended families often sent family members whom the land could not support, especially young women, to the towns. There they might marry and form urban families, but often they returned home and married into farm families. In most cases the urban workers managed to maintain close ties with their rural kin, especially through letters and visits to friends.

In the case of the black family, research by social historian Herbert Gutman on the effects of slavery and industrialization has shown that slaves often formed extended families that included strong nuclear units. During the Reconstruction period after the Civil War, many families that had been torn apart by slavery were reunited. Toward the end of the nineteenth century, however, migration caused by the industrialization of agriculture in the South and the demand for unskilled labor in large northern cities created instability in many black families, a pattern that would become prevalent in later decades of the twentieth century. In sum, therefore, the theory that industrialization creates a single dominant family form and predictable patterns of family interaction is no longer widely accepted in the social sciences.

IDEAL VERSUS ACTUAL FAMILY PATTERNS   When politicians and government officials talk about "preserving family values," they often have in mind the traditional two-parent nuclear family. To many people this remains the ideal family form. In reality, however, as Table 1 shows, such families are less prevalent today than they were in earlier decades. Increasing numbers of families are headed by a single parent, usually the mother but sometimes the father. Moreover, two-parent families may actually be reconstituted, that is, created by remarriage after divorce or the death of a spouse. Thus what appears to be a conventional nuclear family is really a far more complicated family form with extended ties among parents and siblings in different nuclear families.

Among lower-income people these patterns are especially prevalent—so much so that some researchers have concluded that families without fathers are a direct consequence of poverty. Although they tend to share the same norms of family life as other members of society, poor people bear added burdens that make it difficult, if not impossible, for them to actually meet those norms. In particular, men in such families may not be able to provide their expected share of family income and hence may become demoralized and unable to maintain family relationships. This is especially true when teenagers father children before they are adequately prepared to take economic responsibility for them. Thus, in poor families the father often is not a central figure, and female-headed families are the dominant family form.

Contemporary social–scientific research on family structure and interaction increasingly focuses on issues like those just described. At the same time, there is growing recognition that the actual form the family takes may vary greatly at different stages of the life course. For example, as the proportion of elderly people in

TABLE 1   FAMILY COMPOSITION IN THE UNITED STATES, 1970–2000

Type of Family	1970	1990	1995	2000
All families (in millions)	51.2	64.5	68.0	71.7
Total	100.0%	100.0%	100.0%	100.0%
Married couple with children	49.6	36.9	36.2	34.5
Married couple without children	37.1	41.7	41.8	42.8
Female head with children	5.7	10.2	10.0	9.7
Male head with children	0.7	1.8	2.2	2.7
Other families	6.9	9.4	9.8	10.3

Source: Ahlburg and DeVita, 1992.

the population increases, more families must decide whether to care for an aging parent at home. Let us therefore take a closer look at how families change throughout the "family life cycle."

THE FAMILY LIFE CYCLE

Sociologist Paul Glick, an innovator in the field of family demography and ecology, first developed the concept of the *family life cycle,* the idea that families pass through a sequence of five stages:

- Family formation: first marriage
- Start of childbearing: birth of first child
- End of childbearing: birth of last child
- "Empty nest": marriage of last child
- "Family dissolution": death of one spouse

These are "typical" stages in the life cycle of conventional families. Although there are other stages that could be identified within each of these—such as retirement (the years between the time of retirement and the death of one spouse) or the "baby stage" (during which the couple is rearing preschool-age children)—the ones that Glick listed are most useful for comparative purposes.

As the "typical" family structure becomes ever more difficult to identify owing to changes in family norms, the stages of family development also vary. In fact, the stages of the family life cycle have become increasingly useful as indicators of change rather than as stages that all or most families can be expected to experience. The Census Bureau estimates, for example, that there are at least three million heterosexual couples in the United States who are cohabiting. This number represents a sixfold increase since 1970, when an estimated 500,000 cohabiting couples were counted. (Note also that the census figures include only heterosexual couples and therefore vastly underestimate the total number of cohabiting couples.) Although the majority of cohabiting couples will eventually marry, many others will break up or continue to live together without marrying. Fifty-five percent of white women and 42 percent of black women in their first cohabiting union will marry their male partner.

When sociologists look at the median age at which people experience the various stages of the family life cycle, significant trends emerge. Consider age at first marriage. In 1890 the median age of Americans at first marriage was 26.1 years for men and 22 years for women; by 1965 it had reached the historic low of 22.8 and 20.6. Then it began rising again slowly, until by 1986 it was 25.5 for men and 23.3 for women, approaching the pattern of a century ago (see Table 2). Age at first marriage tends to be somewhat higher for males than for females and is associated with educational attainment; more highly educated people are more likely to delay marriage. There is also a tendency for members of minority groups to marry later, owing to the proportionately lower income levels of these populations. People with lower incomes tend to delay marriage or not to marry because they lack the material means to sustain a marital relationship.

TABLE 2   ESTIMATED MEDIAN AGE AT FIRST MARRIAGE: UNITED STATES, 1890–1990

Year	Median Age at First Marriage	
	Men	Women
1890	26.1	22.0
1900	25.9	21.9
1910	25.1	21.6
1920	24.6	21.2
1930	24.3	21.3
1940	24.3	21.5
1950	22.8	20.3
1960	22.8	20.3
1970	23.6	21.8
1980	24.7	22.0
1990	26.3	24.1

Source: Census Bureau, 1992.

As it passes through the family life cycle, every family experiences changes in its system of role relations. In analyzing these changes, social scientists often modify Glick's stages so as to focus more sharply on interactions within the family. An example is the set of "developmental" stages shown in Table 3. There are major emotional challenges at each of these stages. For example, families with adolescent children must adapt to the children's growing independence. This may involve going through a stage of negotiation over such issues as money, cars, and dating. But researchers who study family life note that parents are often confused about how to interact with their adolescent children. They may assume that it is normal for adolescents to leave the family circle and to become enmeshed in their own peer groups, which often get into trouble. However, as Carol Gilligan has pointed out, adolescents also want the continuing guidance and involvement of adults.

Earlier research by Erikson and Bettelheim also found that too much emphasis on adolescence as a time of separation from the family can be a form of social cop-out in which adults fail to provide meaningful goals and activities for adolescents. Many social scientists feel that adolescence is a time for building interdependence as well as independence. By this they mean that adolescents need to become involved in prosocial interactions such as assistance in caring for elderly or younger family members, or involvement in community agencies or social movements.

The severe economic recession of the early 1990s had a major impact on the transition from dependence to independence for many young American adults. The Population Reference Bureau reports that "compared with the 1970s, more young adults (ages eighteen to twenty-four) are living at home with their parents. . . . Over half (54 percent) of all eighteen–twenty-four year olds lived with their parents in 1991." This trend will change as the economy improves, but

TABLE 3   STAGES OF THE FAMILY LIFE CYCLE

Stage	Emotional Process	Required Changes in Family Status
1. Between families: The unattached young adult	Accepting parent–offspring separation	a. Differentiation of self in relation to family of origin b. Development of intimate peer relationships c. Establishment of self in work
2. The joining of families through marriage: The newly married couple	Commitment to new system	a. Formation of marital system b. Realignment of relationships with extended families and friends to include spouse
3. The family with young children	Accepting new generation of members into the system	a. Adjusting marital system to make space for child(ren) b. Taking on parenting roles c. Realignment of relationships with extended family to include parenting and grandparenting roles
4. The family with adolescents	Increasing flexibility of family boundaries to include children's independence	a. Shifting of parent–child relationships to permit adolescents to move in and out of system b. Refocus on midlife marital and career issues c. Beginning shift toward concerns for older generation
5. Launching children and moving on	Accepting a multitude of exits from and entries into the family system	a. Renegotiation of marital system as a dyad b. Development of adult-to-adult relationships between grown children and their parents c. Realignment of relationships to include in-laws and grandchildren d. Dealing with disabilities and death of parents (grandparents)
6. The family in later life	Accepting the shifting of generational roles	a. Maintaining own and/or couple functioning and interests in face of physiological decline; exploration of new familial and social role options b. Support for a more central role for middle generation c. Making room in the system for the wisdom and experience of the elderly; supporting the older generation without overfunctioning for them d. Dealing with loss of spouse, siblings, and other peers, and preparation for own death; life review and integration

Source: McGoldrick and Carter, 1982.

many young adults will continue to live with their family of orientation and be frustrated in their desire to become independent and form their own families.

In later stages of family life the parents must be willing to watch their grown children take on the challenges of family formation while they themselves worry about maintaining their marital roles or caring for their own parents. The latter issue is taking on increasing importance in aging societies like the United States. And since women are still expected to be more nurturing and emotionally caring than men, it often falls to women to worry about the question of "where can Mom live?" According to Elaine Brody, a leading researcher on this issue, "It's going to be primarily women for a long time. Women can go to work as much as they want, but they still see nurturing as their job." Moreover, "with many more very old people, and fewer children per family, almost every woman is going to have to take care of an aging parent or parent-in-law."

As if these stages were not stressful enough, consider the complications resulting from divorce, remarriage, and the combining of children of different marriages in a new family. It is increasingly common, for example, for teenagers and young adults to have parents who are dating and marrying, and for children to have four parental figures in their lives instead of two. These more complex family systems also pass through the stages of the family life cycle. On television, a wholesome family like the "Brady Bunch" accomplishes this with modest resources and lots of love. In reality, however, such families may experience severe stress. Children in such families often learn to maintain a cheerful demeanor so that adults will not worry about them, but inside they generally experience far more emotional turmoil than children who have not been through the experience of family breakup. The difficulties such children experience—for example, in trying to feel at home in more than one place and having to carry their belongings back and forth—are only now beginning to be understood.

The difficulties faced by children in "intact" as well as troubled families raise the age-old questions of how people decide whom to marry and what makes marriages last. Couples normally do not think they will split up when they marry, nor can they understand the emotional and social consequences of divorce before they have children, but the more people understand some of the reasons for selecting particular individuals as mates and the reasons that some relationships are more lasting than others, the more insight they gain into their own relationships. In the next section, therefore, we examine the sociology of mate selection and marriage.

Dynamics of Mate Selection and Marriage

In the animal kingdom, mating involves only the two partners. For mankind, it is the joining of two enormously complex systems. We may think of mate selection and marriage as matters that affect only the partners themselves, but in reality the concerns of parents and other family members are never very far from either person's consciousness. And, as we will see shortly, the values of each partner's extended family often have a significant impact on the mate-selection process.

MARRIAGE AS EXCHANGE   People in Western cultures like to think that interpersonal attraction and love are the primary factors in explaining why a couple forms a "serious" relationship and eventually marries. But while attraction and love are clearly important factors in many marriages, social scientists point out that in all cultures the process of mate selection is carried out according to basic rules of bargaining and exchange. Sociologists and economists who study mate selection and marriage from this exchange perspective ask who controls the marriage contract, what values each family is attempting to maximize in the contract, and how the exchange process is shaped by the society's stratification system.

Among the upper classes of China and Japan before the twentieth century, marriage transactions were controlled by the male elders of the community—with the older women often making the real decisions behind the scenes. In many societies in the Middle East, Asia, and preindustrial Europe, the man's family negotiated a "bride price" with the woman's family. This price usually consisted of valuable goods like jewelry and clothes, but in some cultures it took the form of land and cattle. Throughout much of Hindu India, in contrast, an upper-class bride's family paid a "groom price" to the man's family. Although such norms appear to be weakening throughout the world, "arranged marriages" remain the customary pattern of mate selection in many societies. The following account describes factors that are often considered in arranging a marriage in modern India:

> Every Sunday one can peruse the wedding ads in the classifieds. Many people still arrange an alliance in the traditional manner—through family and friend connections. Caste is becoming less important a factor in the selection of a spouse. Replacing caste are income and type of job. The educational level of the bride-to-be is also a consideration, an asset always worth mentioning in the ad. A faculty member at a college for girls has estimated that 80 to 90 percent of the students there will enter an arranged marriage upon receiving the B.A. Perhaps 10 percent will continue their studies. In this way, educating a daughter is parental investment toward securing an attractive, prosperous groom.

In all of these transactions the families base their bargaining on considerations of family prestige within the community, the wealth of the two families and their ability to afford or command a given price, the beauty of the bride and the attractiveness of the groom, and so on. Different cultures may evaluate these qualities differently, but in each case the parties involved think of the coming marriage as an exchange between the two families. But do not get the idea that only selfish motives are involved in such marriages. Both families are also committing themselves to a long-standing relationship because they are exchanging their most precious products, their beloved young people. Naturally, they want the best for their children (as this is defined in their culture), and they also want a climate of mutual respect and cooperation in their future interfamily relationships.

NORMS OF MATE SELECTION

ENDOGAMY/EXOGAMY   All cultures have norms that specify whether a person brought up in that culture may marry within or outside the cultural group. Marriage within the group is termed **endogamy**; marriage outside the group is termed **exogamy**. In the United States, ethnic and religious groups normally put pressure on their members to remain endogamous—that is, to choose mates from their own group. These rules tend to be especially strong for women. Among Orthodox Jews, for example, an infant is considered to have been born into the religion only if the mother is Jewish. Children of mixed marriages in which the mother is not Jewish are not considered Jewish by birth. The conflict between Orthodox and Reformed Jews over the status of children born to non-Jewish mothers who have converted to Judaism is an example of conflict over endogamy/exogamy norms. Many African tribes have developed norms of exogamy that encourage young men to find brides in specific villages outside the village of their birth. Such marriage systems tend to promote strong bonds of kinship among villages and serve to strengthen the social cohesion of the tribe while breaking down the animosity that sometimes arises between villages within a tribe.

HOMOGAMY   Another norm of mate selection is **homogamy,** or the tendency to marry a person from a similar social background. The parents of a young woman from a wealthy family, for example, attempt to increase the chances that she will associate with young men of the same or higher social-class standing. She is encouraged to date boys from "good" families. After graduating from high school she will be sent to an elite college or university, where the pool of eligible men is likely to include many who share her social-class background. She may surprise her parents, however, and fall in love with someone whose social-class, religious, or ethnic background is considerably different from hers. But when this happens she will invariably have based her choice on other values that are considered important in the dating and marriage market, values like outstanding talent, good looks, popularity, or sense of humor. She will argue that these values outweigh social class, especially if it seems apparent that the young man will gain upward mobility through his career. Often the couple will marry and not worry about his lower social-class background. On the other hand, the untalented, homely, poor man may aspire to a bride with highly desirable qualities, but he cannot offer enough to induce either her or her family to choose him, for they can find a groom with more highly valued qualities.

Numerous sociologists have studied the phenomenon of homogamy. In a post–World War II study entitled *Elmtown's Youth,* for example, August Hollingshead found that 61 percent of the adolescents in a small midwestern city dated within their social class and 35 percent dated members of adjacent classes. In two out of three cases in which a boy crossed class lines, he dated a girl from a lower social-class background. And in two out of three cases in which a girl crossed class lines, she went out with a boy from a higher social class. Those who dated members of a higher class were found to have special qualities in terms of looks, popularity, leadership skills, or athletic ability. Many other studies of dating and mate selection have demonstrated the same patterns of social-class homogamy and the same kinds of departures from that norm. It is reasonable to conclude, therefore, that cultural norms that stress homogamy in dating and marriage also tend to reproduce the society's system of social-class stratification in the next generation.

Homogamy in mate selection generally serves to maintain the separateness of religious groups. Because the Census Bureau does not collect systematic data on religious preferences, it is extremely difficult to obtain accurate data on religious intermarriage. Yet sociologists and religious leaders agree that, although parents continue to encourage their children to marry within their religion, there is a trend away from religious homogamy, particularly for Protestants and Catholics.

The norm of homogamy also applies to interracial marriage. Before 1967, when the United States Supreme Court struck them down as unconstitutional, many states had laws prohibiting such marriages. After that decision, marriages between blacks and whites increased by about 26 percent, from about 51,000 in 1960 to about 65,000 in 1970, and their number continues to increase. Yet as a proportion of all marriages, black–white marriages remain only 4 percent of the total and are less common than other types of interracial marriages. Thus the norm of racial homogamy remains relatively strong in the United States.

ROMANTIC LOVE

Although exchange criteria and homogamy continue to play a significant role in mate selection, for the past century romantic attraction and love have been growing in importance in North American and other Western cultures. Indeed, the conflict between romantic love and the parental requirement of homogamy is one of the great themes of Western civilization. "Let me not to the marriage of true minds / Admit impediments," wrote Shakespeare in a famous sonnet. The "star-crossed lovers" from feuding families in *Romeo and Juliet,* and the lovers who have forsaken family fortunes to be together in innumerable stories and plays written since Shakespeare's time, attest to the strong value we place on romantic love as an aspect of intimate relationships between men and women.

In his review of worldwide marriage and family patterns, William J. Goode found that compared with the mate-selection systems of other cultures, that of the United States "has given love greater prominence. Here, as in all Western societies to some lesser degree, the child is socialized to fall in love." Yet although it may be taken for granted that people will form couples on the basis of romantic attachment, important changes in the structure of Western societies had to occur before love as we know it could become such an important value in our lives. In particular, changes in economic institutions as a result of industrialization required workers with more education and greater maturity. These changes, in turn, lengthened the period of socialization, especially in educational institutions. This made it possible for single men and women to remain unattached long enough to gain the emotional maturity they needed if they were to experience love and make more independent decisions in selecting their mates.

However familiar it may seem to us, love remains a mysterious aspect of human relationships. We do not know very much—from a verifiable, scientific standpoint—about this complex emotional state. We do not know fully what it means to "fall in love" or what couples can do to make their love last. But two promising avenues of research on this subject can be found in Winch's theory of complementarity and Blau's theory of emotional reciprocity.

COMPLEMENTARY NEEDS AND MUTUAL ATTRACTION   Robert F. Winch's theory of complementary needs, based on work by the psychologist Henry A. Murray, holds that people who fall in love tend to be alike in social characteristics such as family prestige, education, and income but different in their psychological needs. Thus, according to Winch, an outgoing person often falls in love with a quiet, shy person. The one gains an appreciative audience, the other an entertaining spokesperson. A person who needs direction is attracted to one who needs to exercise authority; one who is nurturant is attracted to one who needs nurturance; and so on.

Winch and others have found evidence to support this theory, but there are some problems with this research. It is difficult to measure personal needs and the extent to which they are satisfied. Moreover, people also show a variety of patterns in their choices of mates. Some people, in fact, seem to be attracted to each other because of their similarities in looks and behavior rather than because of their differences.

ATTRACTION AND EMOTIONAL RECIPROCITY   Blau's theory of emotional reciprocity as a source of love is based on his general theory that relationships usually flourish when people feel satisfied with the exchanges between them. When people feel that they are loved, they are more likely to give love in return. When they feel that they love too much or are not loved enough, they will eventually come to feel exploited or trapped and will seek to end the relationship. In research on 231 dating couples, Zick Rubin found that among those who felt this equality of love, 77 percent were still together two years later, but only 45 percent of the unequally involved couples were still seeing each other. As Blau explained it, "Only when two lovers' affection for and commitment to one another expand at roughly the same pace do they mutually tend to reinforce their love."

Blau's exchange approach confirms some popular notions about love—particularly the ideas that we can love someone who loves us and that inequalities in love can lead to separation. And yet we still know little about the complexities of this emotion and how it translates into the formation of the most basic of all social groups, the married couple. This is ironic, because books, movies, and popular songs probably pay more attention to love than to just about any other subject.

Francesca M. Cancian, a leading researcher on love in a changing society, notes that a price of the high value men and women place on individuality is "a weakening of close relationships." As people spend time enhancing their own lives they may become more self-centered and feel less responsible for providing love and nurturance. Cancian's research on loving relations among couples of all kinds has convinced her that people are increasingly seeking a form of love that "combines enduring love with self-development." She regards this kind of relationship as based on "interdependencies" in which each member of the couple attempts to assist the other in realizing his or her potential and at the same time seeks to strengthen the bond between them. But she finds that, in order to foster a loving interdependent relationship, couples often need to sacrifice a certain amount of independence and career advancement—not a simple matter in a culture that places a high value on individual achievement.

The nature of loving relationships is likely to be a subject of highly creative sociological research in coming years. Since capacity to love and be loved depends on individual characteristics as well as on social conditions, much of the research in this area will be done by social psychologists (see Box 1 on page 356).

MARRIAGE AND DIVORCE   More than any other ritual signifying a major change in status, a wedding is a joyous occasion. Two people are legally and symbolically joined before their kin and friends. It is expected that their honeymoon will be pleasant and that they will live happily ever after. But 20 percent of first marriages end in annulment or divorce within the first three years. Of course, divorce can occur at any time in the family life cycle, but the early years of family formation are the most difficult for the couple because each partner experiences new stresses that arise from the need to adjust to a complex set of new relationships. As Monica McGoldrick and Elizabeth A. Carter point out, "Marriage requires that a couple renegotiate a myriad of personal issues that they have previously defined for themselves or that were defined by their parents, from when to sleep, have sex, or fight, to how to celebrate holidays, and where and how to live, work, and spend vacations." For people who were married before, these negotiations can involve former spouses and shared children, resulting in added stress for the new couple.

In the United States and other Western societies, the rate of divorce rose sharply after World War II, accelerated even more dramatically during the 1960s and 1970s, and has decreased only slightly since then (see Table 4). These statistics often lead sociologists to proclaim that there is an "epidemic of divorce" in the United States. But demographer Donald Bogue has concluded that "the divorce epidemic is not being created by today's younger generation. It has been created by today's population aged thirty or more, who married in the 1960s and before." This generation was noted for its search for self-realization, often at the expense of intimate family relationships. It is not yet clear whether subsequent generations, who appear to be somewhat more pragmatic, will continue this trend. If they do, we can expect high divorce rates to continue.

Most states in the United States now have some form of no-fault divorce that reduces the stigma of divorce by making moral issues like infidelity less relevant than issues of child custody and division of property. While the growing acceptance of divorce helps account for why divorce rates are so much higher in the United States than in other nations with highly educated populations, Americans today also place a higher value on successful marriage than their parents may have. This means that they often divorce in the expectation of forming another, more satisfying and mutually sustaining relationship.

TRIAL MARRIAGE   In the 1980s it was widely believed that the practice of "trial marriage," or cohabitation before marriage, would result in greater marital stability: Couples who lived together before marriage would gain greater mutual understanding and a realistic view of marital commitment, and this would result in a lower divorce rate among such couples after they actually married. However, as the 1990s approached, it became evident that these expectations were unfounded;

BOX 1   LOVE OF A LIFETIME?

USING THE SOCIOLOGICAL IMAGINATION

It takes a lot of imagination to sustain love. Insight into both oneself and one's mate is vital, but so is a sociological imagination. It is not hard to know how social conditions affect a person's feelings in the long and short term, but it is surprising how few people develop the capacity to see the world the way those close to them see it. When caught up in the early passion of love this may not be a problem. But as the relationship develops they need as much imagination and understanding as possible. An awareness of the various dimensions of intimate love may help.

Social psychologists who study love in married and unmarried couples are finding new evidence that confirms what many people have long known intuitively: It is in fact quite difficult for couples to maintain the level of passion they experienced in the early stages of their marriage. "People don't know what they are in for when they fall in love," asserts Yale's Robert Sternberg. "The divorce rate is so high, not because people make foolish choices, but because they are drawn together for reasons that matter less as time goes on."

Sternberg believes that love has three components: intimacy, passion, and commitment. The first is a shared sense that the couple can reveal their innermost feelings to each other even as those feelings change. Passion is largely a matter of physical attraction and sexuality. Commitment is a shared sense that each member of the couple is permanently devoted to the other. Research shows that the fullest love demands all three of these qualities, but that over a long relationship passion is the first to fade; intimacy develops slowly and steadily as a result of shared experiences and values; and commitment develops more gradually still (see graphs).

In the early stages of a love relationship, the couple may become so caught up in their passion that they do not help each other develop as autonomous individuals. This can produce serious problems in later stages of the relationship. At the same time, commitment alone cannot substitute for the other two qualities of love. "You have to work constantly at rejuvenating a relationship," Sternberg explains, "You can't just count on its being OK, or it will tend toward a hollow commitment, devoid of passion and intimacy. People need to put the kind of energy into it that they put into their children or career." Studies by Sternberg and many others find that children who have been deprived of parental love, especially by the parent of the opposite sex, often have trouble developing commitment and sharing intimacy. Often they avoid feeling vulnerable and dependent on another person by avoiding strong emotional ties altogether.

TABLE 4   DIVORCE RATES FOR SELECTED COUNTRIES, 1960–1988

Country	Divorces per 1,000 Married Women			
	1960	1970	1980	1988
United States	9.2	14.9	22.6	20.7
Canada	1.8	6.3	10.8	12.6
France	2.9	3.3	6.3	8.4
Germany (western)	3.6	5.1	6.1	8.8
Japan	3.6	3.9	4.8	4.9
Sweden	5.0	6.8	11.4	11.4
United Kingdom	2.0	4.7	12.0	12.3

Source: *Statistical Abstract, 1991.*

in fact, the divorce rate among couples who had lived together before marriage was actually higher than the rate for couples who had not done so. Within ten years of the wedding, 38 percent of those who had lived together before marriage had divorced, compared to 27 percent of those who had married without cohabiting beforehand.

On the basis of an analysis of data from a federal government survey of over 13,000 individuals, Larry Bumpass and James Sweet concluded that couples who cohabit before marriage are generally more willing to accept divorce as a solution to marital problems. They also found that such couples are less likely to be subject to family pressure to continue a marriage that is unhappy or unsatisfactory. In addition, cohabitation has become a predictable part of the family life cycle, not only before marriage but in the interval between divorce and remarriage. Among individuals who remarried between 1980 and 1987, 60 percent lived with a person of the opposite sex beforehand.

THINK ABOUT IT CRITICALLY

Summary

During the 1992 presidential election campaign family policies and "family values" were used as "wedge issues" to create divisions in the electorate. These issues were raised by some candidates to suggest that people in single-parent or gay families are deviant or otherwise threatening to the nation's values. From what you have learned in this chapter, why did the appeal to "family values" seem to fail so badly?

A *family* is a group of people related by blood, marriage, or adoption, and the role relations among family members are known as *kinship* relations. The smallest unit of family structure is the *nuclear family*, consisting of two or more people, related by consanguineous ties or by adoption, who share a household. The nuclear family in which one is born and socialized is one's *family of orientation*, and the nuclear family one forms through marriage or cohabitation is one's *family of procreation*. An *extended family* includes an individual's nuclear family plus all the nuclear families of his or her blood relatives.

The traditional household consisting of two parents and their children is no longer the typical American family. Since the 1940s there has been a dramatic increase in female-headed single-parent families and in nonfamily households, as well as in the numbers of women and men living alone and in the numbers of unmarried same-sex couples.

Studies of changes in family structure have shown that family units become simpler as societies undergo industrialization. Economic and technological changes require the family to adapt to an economy in which income is earned outside the family; this means that families must become smaller, more mobile, and more flexible. More recent research has found that nuclear families have not entirely replaced extended families, although extended families do not always live under one roof. Modern technologies like the telephone and the automobile enable members of smaller family units to maintain kinship ties with their extended families.

The typical stages of the family life cycle are family formation, start of childbearing, end of childbearing, "empty nest," and family dissolution (i.e., the death of one spouse). As it passes through this cycle, every family experiences changes in its system of role relations. These changes present major emotional challenges, which are often complicated by divorce, remarriage, and the combining of children of different marriages in a single family.

In all cultures the process of mate selection is carried out according to basic rules of bargaining and exchange. In many societies the customary pattern of mate selection is the "arranged" marriage, in which the families of the bride and groom negotiate the marriage contract. All cultures also have norms that specify whether a person brought up in that culture may marry within or outside the cultural group. Marriage within the group is termed *endogamy;* marriage outside the group is termed *exogamy*. In societies in which marriages are based on attraction and love, individuals tend to marry people similar to themselves in social background, a tendency that is referred to as *homogamy*. Homogamy generally serves to reproduce the society's system of social-class stratification in the next generation and to maintain the separateness of religious and racial groups.

Compared with the mate selection systems of other cultures, that of the United States gives love greater prominence. Yet, from a scientific standpoint, little is known about this complex emotional state. It appears that people who fall in love tend to be alike in social characteristics but different in their psychological needs; however, this is not always the case. There is also considerable evidence that love relationships are more lasting when the partners' affection for each other is roughly equal.

In the United States and other Western societies, the rate of divorce has risen sharply since World War II. In the 1980s it was widely believed that the practice of cohabitation before marriage would result in greater marital stability, but in fact the divorce rate among couples who had lived together before marriage was actually higher than the rate for couples who had not done so.

Glossary

Endogamy   a norm specifying that a person brought up in a particular culture may marry within the cultural group

Exogamy   a norm specifying that a person brought up in a particular culture may marry outside the cultural group

Extended Family   an individual's nuclear family plus the nuclear families of his or her blood relatives

Family   a group of people related by blood, marriage, or adoption

Family of Orientation   the nuclear family in which a person is born and raised

Family of Procreation   the nuclear family a person forms through marriage or cohabitation

Homogamy   the tendency to marry a person who is similar to oneself in social background

Kinship   the role relations among people who consider themselves to be related by blood, marriage, or adoption

Nuclear Family   two or more people related by blood, marriage, or adoption who share a household

What Did I Learn from Previewing?

Now reflect for a moment on what you learned by previewing this chapter. For example, the title, "The Family," certainly brought to your mind many associations. All of the examples of family types, structures, and cycles are quite familiar to us. Our task, then, is to learn and apply the technical terms of sociology to the real-life situations we already know. Only by doing this can we make and understand statements and predictions about the family in general. Subtitles such as "Defining the Family" and "The Family Life Cycle" gave you a good idea as to the content of the chapter. The key terms the author thinks you should know are written in boldface type. Many of the key terms are elaborated in tables. A summary paraphrases the highlights of the chapter. The key terms are repeated for you in a glossary at the end of the chapter.

☞   Now that you have previewed the text, return to the chapter and give it a close reading.

Mark the Text

Now that you have previewed and read the chapter, you are ready to master the ideas that it contains. As you read through a second time, mark the text–underline important ideas, write notes in the margin, circle key words, write question marks next to anything you don't understand. (To review how to mark the text, turn to page 421, "Learning Strategy III—Marking Text.") When you have finished marking the text, discuss any questions you have with your classmates. And remember—when exam time comes along, you only need to review the marks and comments you have written.

Vocabulary

In this textbook, the author indicates the *key terms*—important words he thinks you should know and remember—both by using boldface type in the text itself and in a glossary at the end of the chapter. Be sure to find and mark each term in the text. Remember to mark any term you don't understand so you'll remember to ask a classmate or the instructor for an explanation. It is also a good idea to keep a special section of your notebook where you write the terms and their meanings.

Exam Questions

Test your understanding of the many ideas in this chapter by answering the questions that follow. This chapter, "The Family," was taken from a textbook that is used in introduction to sociology courses. These exam questions are the actual ones given by instructors who teach the course.

Short Essay Questions

1. Distinguish between the family of orientation and the family of procreation.
2. List the stages of the family life cycle as developed by Glick.
3. Explain the exchange factor in mate selection.
4. Explain the relationship between endogamy and homogamy.

Multiple Choice Questions

Directions: Choose the letter of the best answer for each question.

_____ 1. The network of role relations among people who consider themselves to be related by blood, marriage, or adoption is referred to as

    a. consanguinity.
    b. family.
    c. kinship.
    d. siblings.

_____ 2. Fictive kin are

    a. blood relatives within the nuclear family.
    b. people who are considered to be kin despite the lack of blood ties.
    c. people who become relatives as a result of adoption.
    d. relatives that one acquires through marriage.

_____ 3. Two or more people related by blood, marriage, or adoption who share a household are

    a. a conjoint family.
    b. a conjugal family.
    c. an extended family.
    d. a nuclear family.

_____ 4. The nuclear family in which one is born and socialized is one's family of

    a. indoctrination.
    b. initiation.
    c. orientation.
    d. procreation.

_____ 5. The nuclear family that one forms through marriage or cohabitation is one's family of

    a. indoctrination.
    b. initiation.
    c. orientation.
    d. procreation.

_____ 6. The practice of marrying someone from one's own cultural group is termed

    a. endogamy.
    b. exogamy.
    c. monogamy.
    d. polygamy.

_____ 7. Mark and Katherine are very much in love and plan to marry. He is the son of devout Presbyterians; Katherine is the daughter of practicing Catholics. In sociological terms, their marriage would be

    a. ambiguous.
    b. endogamous.
    c. exogamous.
    d. homogamous.

_____ 8. In recent years the median age of Americans at first marriage has

    a. decreased.
    b. fallen dramatically.
    c. remained the same.
    d. risen slowly.

_____ 9. Which of the following statements about marriage is *always* true?

    a. Interpersonal attraction and love are the primary factors in explaining why people marry.
    b. Marriage affects only the partners themselves.
    c. Marriage is primarily an economic relationship.
    d. Mate selection is carried out according to basic rules of bargaining and exchange.

_____ 10. The tendency to marry a person similar to oneself is termed

    a. heterogamy.
    b. hexogamy.
    c. homogamy.
    d. hyperogamy.

_____ 11. Which of the following theories argues that people who fall in love tend to be alike in social characteristics, like family prestige, education, and income but different in their psychological needs?

    a. complementary needs
    b. emotional reciprocity
    c. mutual attraction
    d. social determinism

_____ 12. What proportion of all first marriages end in annulment or divorce within the first three years?

    a. 20 percent
    b. 40 percent
    c. 50 percent
    d. 75 percent

HUMAN RESOURCE MANAGEMENT

A Chapter from the Textbook
Contemporary Business, Eleventh Edition

Louis E. Boone and David L. Kurtz

PREVIEWING

Remember, your first step in studying a textbook chapter should always be to preview. If you need to review how to preview, turn to "Learning Strategy I—Previewing" on page 415. The questions and suggestions below will help you preview this chapter well.

1. Note the many helpful features in this chapter, beginning with a snapshot of the military reserves. Skim the story about the reserves; what does the story have to do with motivating employees?
2. Now read the brief Chapter Overview.
3. List the headings and subheadings in the chapter.
4. Are there any special features, such as margin notes, quotes, graphs, or charts?
5. How do the authors indicate key terms they think are important?

Motivating the Reserves

For several years, America has been fighting a war against terrorism. Unlike other wars, this one has involved an elusive enemy composed of fragmented groups from many countries. Fighting this war requires the involvement of tens of thousands of American military reservists and National Guard personnel.

Reservists serve in the Army, Navy, Air Force, Marines, and Coast Guard; they are average working men and women whose *other* job is in the military. These individuals were called on to assist in military operations in Afghanistan, where U.S. forces toppled the maverick Taliban regime and began rebuilding the country. A year later, they were sent to various posts in the Middle East to disarm Iraq. These reservists and National Guard personnel are human resources to two employers: the U.S. military and the many businesses left short-staffed back home.

Army materials courtesy of the U.S. Government

When they enlist, reservists and members of National Guard units understand that they may be called to serve at any time. They train for the possibility, and their employers are aware of the situation. But when the call comes, invariably people's lives are thrown into chaos. They got their affairs in order and said good-bye to loved ones before reporting for tours of duty that could last for months, and their employers

dealt with potential losses in productivity from a temporary loss of personnel. A total of 100,000 to 250,000 employees absent for several months or a year adds up to a sizable loss of labor hours and expertise. Since many of these workers are members of police or fire-fighting departments back home—or health-care workers at hospitals—these institutions were hard-pressed to make up for the loss. "Any time anyone on the force is missing, it's an issue," said David Gerdes, police chief in Joliet, Illinois. "With a medium-sized department, it's not going to kill us. I feel sorry for the smaller departments."

But employers everywhere rose to the occasion. Instead of merely complying with the law that protects military reservists from dismissal while they are deployed on assignment, many companies went a step farther, increasing benefits to cover their employees' additional expenses and to support the sacrifices they were making. Because the U.S. government pays the reservist's private-sector salary for only 22 days and military pay is typically lower than what employees are making before call-up, many employers either continued to pay full salaries for periods ranging from three months to one year or paid the difference between their salary and military pay for a similar period. Large firms were better equipped to meet the challenge than smaller ones. "Reservists who work for large companies may find their employer more than willing to make up the difference between their civilian pay and military pay," observed John Challenger, CEO of outplacement firm Challenger, Gray & Christmas. Boeing's plan pays the salary differential for an extraordinary five years, and software giant Sun Microsystems in Palo Alto, California, which has about 40 employees in the reserves or National Guard, pledged to provide 60 percent of employees' salaries for up to 12 months and health coverage for two years. But a smaller company probably wouldn't be able to do this.

UPS, employer of 5,000 reservists, not only provides continuing health care and salaries to those who are called up, but each week, UPS employees contact local reservists' families to find out whether they have any special needs while their loved ones are away. "That's the family atmosphere of UPS," explained spokesman Steve Holmes. "They call to check on them, to see if they need their yards mowed or kids watched, to see if they can help them out."

Although federal law protects military reservists in a number of ways, by offering temporary caps on mortgage interest rates and credit card loans, protection from eviction, and protection from dismissal with the right to return to their former employment for up to five years, UPS and many other companies go beyond legal requirements to support their employees. In the long run, this type of support benefits not only the employees but also the companies and society as a whole. Says Lea Soupata, senior vice president of human resources at UPS, "We have great people who have been with us from anywhere from one to 20 years. They are well trained and professional—and at some point [they] are going to be coming back."

Chapter Overview

The importance of people to the success of any organization is the very definition of **management:** the use of people and other resources to accomplish organizational objectives. In this chapter, we address the critical issues of human resource management and motivation. We begin with a discussion of the ways organizations attract, develop, and retain employees. Then we describe the concepts behind motivation and the way human resource managers apply them to increase employee satisfaction and organizational effectiveness.

We also explore the reasons for labor unions and focus on legislation that affects labor–management relations. The process of collective bargaining is then discussed, along with tools used by unions and management in seeking their objectives.

Human Resource Management Is Vital to All Organizations

human resource management function of attracting, developing, and retaining enough qualified employees to perform the activities necessary to accomplish organizational objectives.

Most organizations devote considerable attention to **human resource management,** the function of attracting, developing, and retaining enough qualified employees to perform the activities necessary to accomplish organizational objectives. Human resource managers are responsible for developing specific programs and activities as well as creating a work environment that generates employee satisfaction and efficiency.

Relationships between employers and employees changed enormously during the past century. One hundred years ago, firms hired employees by posting notices at their sites stating that workers were needed and would be hired the following day. Such a notice might list required skills, such as carpentry or welding, or simply list the number of employees the firm required. People looking for work would line up at the employer's shop or factory the next day—a small number in prosperous times and a larger number in leaner times. Someone in authority made hiring decisions, often based on arbitrary criteria, after reviewing the candidates. Sometimes the first people in line were hired; sometimes the healthiest and strongest were hired. After being hired, the new employees were expected to work under a precise set of rules, such as the humorous list shown in Figure 9.1.

Today, flexibility and complexity characterize the relationship between employers and employees. Earlier, you learned that developing and sustaining a world-class workforce are essential for a firm to compete effectively. Human resource managers face challenges created by profound changes in the makeup of the labor force, a shortage of qualified job candidates, changes in the structure of the workplace, and employees' desires to balance their work and personal lives. These managers must also develop programs and policies that satisfy an increasingly diverse employee population while monitoring a growing number of employment-related laws that influence how they implement their firms' practices.

> ### They Said It
>
> The best way to get what you want is to help other people get what they want.
>
> —*Zig Ziglar (b. 1927)*
> *American motivational speaker*

Midsize and larger organizations create human resource departments that systematically handle the tasks of attracting, training, and retaining employees. They often have people who specialize in individual areas of human resource management such as diversity training or employee benefits. In smaller companies, most human resource managers are generalists because they are responsible for several tasks.

Entrepreneurs and small-business managers usually assume most of the responsibility for human resource management. However, a growing number of small firms are outsourcing this function to **professional employer organizations (PEOs).** A PEO is a company that helps firms with a wide range of human resource services, including hiring and training employees, administering payroll and benefits programs, handling workers' compensation and unemployment insurance, and ensuring compliance with labor laws. These PEOs work in partnership with employers in these key decisions. Because the PEO typically negotiates benefits for a large number of business clients, it can shop for better deals. And by handling a firm's human resource activities, a PEO enables a small firm to focus on production, marketing, and finance, as well as on motivating and leading employees. One such PEO, ADP TotalSource, helped Dogwood Golf and Country Club in Georgia find and keep the right staff. In such an organization, a skilled staff is needed to meet the

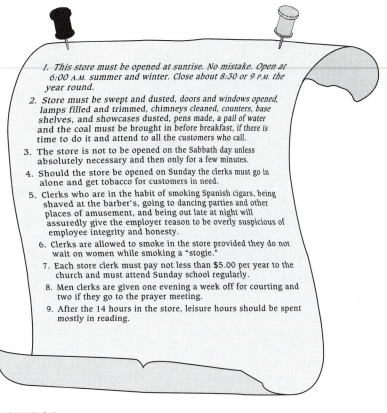

1. *This store must be opened at sunrise. No mistake. Open at 6:00 A.M. summer and winter. Close about 8:30 or 9 P.M. the year round.*

2. *Store must be swept and dusted, doors and windows opened, lamps filled and trimmed, chimneys cleaned, counters, base shelves, and showcases dusted, pens made, a pail of water and the coal must be brought in before breakfast, if there is time to do it and attend to all the customers who call.*

3. The store is not to be opened on the Sabbath day unless absolutely necessary and then only for a few minutes.

4. Should the store be opened on Sunday the clerks must go in alone and get tobacco for customers in need.

5. Clerks who are in the habit of smoking Spanish cigars, being shaved at the barber's, going to dancing parties and other places of amusement, and being out late at night will assuredly give the employer reason to be overly suspicious of employee integrity and honesty.

6. Clerks are allowed to smoke in the store provided they do not wait on women while smoking a "stogie."

7. Each store clerk must pay not less than $5.00 per year to the church and must attend Sunday school regularly.

8. Men clerks are given one evening a week off for courting and two if they go to the prayer meeting.

9. After the 14 hours in the store, leisure hours should be spent mostly in reading.

FIGURE 9.1
Rules for Clerks, 1905

needs of members and guests. However, turnover in the resort and country club business is very high, with competitors always ready to lure away key employees. ADP TotalSource designed an attractive benefits package that allowed Dogwood to recruit and retain skilled employees. In addition, the PEO handles every detail of the administrative responsibilities related to human resources. According to Dogwood's general manager, "ADP TotalSource is the human resources expert. When you run your business alone as I do, you want reassurance that your people are taken care of."

Human resource management can be viewed in two ways. In a narrow sense, it includes the functions performed by human resource professionals. But in a broader sense, it involves the entire organization, even when a staff department assumes those responsibilities or a firm outsources the functions. Supervisors and general managers also participate in hiring, training, evaluating performance, and motivating employees. Since a company's success depends largely on the commitment and talents of its people, a growing number of firms are measuring and rewarding managers' performance in retaining employees and attracting qualified job candidates. Similarly, many companies consider workforce diversity to be a

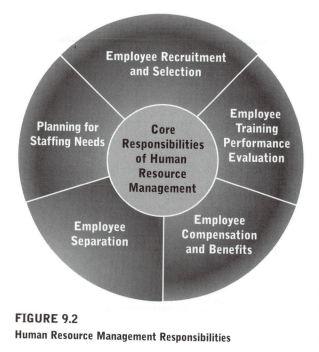

FIGURE 9.2
Human Resource Management Responsibilities

source of competitive advantage in serving various customer groups and thinking creatively. At these organizations, management goals may also include measures of employee diversity. In addition, some firms ask nonmanagement employees to participate in hiring decisions and evaluating their coworkers' performance.

The core responsibilities of human resource management include planning for staffing needs, recruitment and selection, training and evaluating performance, compensation and benefits, and employee separation. In accomplishing these five tasks shown in Figure 9.2, human resource managers achieve their objectives of (1) providing qualified, well-trained employees for the organization, (2) maximizing employee effectiveness in the organization, and (3) satisfying individual employee needs through monetary compensation, benefits, opportunities to advance, and job satisfaction.

Human Resource Planning

Concept Check

1. Why are flexibility and complexity part of today's relationship between employers and employees?
2. What is a professional employer organization (PEO)?

Human resource managers develop staffing plans based on their organization's competitive strategies. They forecast the number of employees their firm will need and determine the types of skills necessary to implement its plans. Human resource managers are responsible for adjusting their company's workforce to meet the requirements of expanding in new markets; reducing costs, which may require laying off employees; or adapting to new technology. They formulate both long- and short-term plans to provide the right number of qualified employees.

Human resource managers also must plan how to attract and keep good employees with the right combination of pay, benefits, and working conditions. At Trilogy Software, this aspect of human resource planning is at the core of the company's strategy. Trilogy develops software that handles information processing related to sales and marketing, an industry in which only fast-moving, highly sophisticated companies can succeed. So the company has a strategy to continually expand its staff of software developers. Knowing that it is competing for talent with software giants like Microsoft and Cisco, Trilogy targets college campuses, recruiting the brightest, most energetic students it can find. As a substitute for work experience, the company sends these young recruits to an intense three-month orientation program called Trilogy University, where they work on the firm's products as they learn about the software industry and the company culture. Trilogy appeals to recruits by emphasizing that their contribution to the company matters. "By hiring great people and giving them mission-critical responsibilities from the first day on the job, Trilogy ensures our ability to respond to competitive challenges, and to achieve the goal of building a high-impact company," states the company Web site.

> **Concept Check**
> 1. Why do human resource managers need to develop staffing plans?
> 2. How do human resource managers attract and keep good employees?

Recruitment and Selection

In recruiting and selecting employees, human resource managers strive to match applicants' skills with those the organization needs. To ensure that potential employees bring the necessary skills or have the capacity to learn them, most firms implement the recruitment and selection process shown in Figure 9.3.

Finding Qualified Candidates

Finding the right candidate for a job isn't as simple as it sounds, despite the number of layoffs in many industries in recent years. According to one estimate, the number of workers between the ages of 25 and 54 will dramatically decrease over the next 20 years, and the percentage of the labor force with a college degree who are age 25 and over will barely reach 32 percent. So human resource managers must be creative in their search for qualified employees. Businesses access both internal and external sources to find the best candidates for specific jobs. Policies of hiring from within emphasize internal sources, so many employers consider their own employees first for job openings. Internal recruiting is less expensive than external methods, and it helps boost employee morale. But if recruiters can find no qualified internal candidate, they must look for people outside the organization. Recruitment from external sources involves advertising in newspapers and trade magazines, placing radio and television ads, and working through state and private employment agencies, college recruiting and internship offices, retiree job banks, and job fairs. One of the most effective external sources is employee referrals, in which employers ask current employees to recommend applicants, rewarding them with bonuses or prizes for new hires.

Many firms are using the Internet as a recruiting tool. They have career sections on their Web sites, providing general employment information and listing

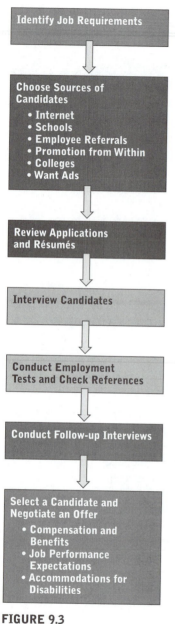

FIGURE 9.3

Steps in the Recruitment and Selection Process

open positions. Applicants may even be able to submit a résumé and apply for an open position online. As the Careers Prologue pointed out, some firms also post job openings at employment Web sites, such as Monster.com. Internet recruiting is a quick, efficient, inexpensive way to reach a large pool of job seekers. According to employers and career counselors, online recruiting has become a common method of finding qualified job candidates.

Another recent trend for some businesses is to review the welfare rolls of people looking for work. Bank of America has been doing this for several years. The firm has a partnership with Goodwill Industries International, which trains welfare recipients for jobs such as cashiers and tax processors. Bank of America hired about 5,000 workers through the program during a recent five-year period and continues to recruit 150 per month. "We're mindful of the labor-shortage projections and see these populations as continuing to provide us with a wonderful source of labor and higher retention rates," says Karen B. Shawcross, a senior vice president at Bank of America.

Selecting and Hiring Employees

In selecting and hiring employees, human resource managers must follow the requirements set out by federal and state laws. Title VII of the Civil Rights Act of 1964 prohibits employers from discriminating against applicants based on their race, religion, color, sex, or national origin. The Americans with Disabilities Act of 1990 prohibits employers from discriminating against disabled applicants. The Civil Rights Act created the Equal Employment Opportunity Commission (EEOC) to investigate discrimination complaints. The EEOC also assists employers in setting up affirmative-action programs to increase job opportunities for women, minorities, disabled people, and other protected groups. The Civil Rights Act of 1991 expanded the remedies available to victims of employment discrimination by including the right to a jury trial, punitive damages, and damages for emotional distress.

Failure to comply with equal employment opportunity legislation can expose an employer to fines and other penalties, negative publicity, and poor employee morale. The EEOC files hundreds of cases each year, with damages paid by businesses in the tens of millions annually. At the same time, opponents to such laws have launched initiatives to restrict affirmative-action standards and protect employers against unnecessary litigation. In one instance, California voters passed a proposition that prohibits the state from granting hiring preferences to minorities.

BUSINESS TOOL KIT

Interview Inquiries

Whether you end up on the management side of an organization or not, you need to know what questions can and cannot be asked of you during a job interview. Companies may ask you questions directly pertaining to the job itself and the skill set needed to perform the job. They cannot ask you about your gender, family, religion, national origin, or disabilities. Listen carefully for illegal questions during your interview and politely decline to respond to them. Here is a list of Do's and Don'ts pertaining to interview questions:

DO'S:

- What is your preferred management style?
- Describe what you think this job entails and what you might like and dislike about the work.
- Describe a conflict you've had with other staff members and how you resolved it.
- You have two bosses asking you to do conflicting tasks. How would you handle this dilemma?
- What database systems, spreadsheets, and software do you have experience with?

DON'TS:

- Do you have (or are you planning to have) a family?
- Where are you from or what is your ethnic origin?
- How many sick days did you take last year?
- What year were you born?
- What are your political views?
- What is your religion or which holidays do you observe/not observe?
- What is your sexual orientation/preference?
- What are your child care arrangements?
- Do you have any particular physical/mental traits or disabilities?
- Have you ever been arrested?

Sources: Peter Cardinal, "Questions You Should Ask When Hiring: Choosing the Best Candidate for Your Staff Depends a Lot on Selecting the Right Interview Questions," *Family Practice Management,* June 2003, p. 46; William J. Lynott, "How to Hire the Right Person and Stay Out of Trouble While You're Doing It: It's Important to Know What Questions to Ask and Not to," *Podiatry Management,* April–May 2003, p. 91; "Ask the Right Questions," *The Practical Accountant,* November 2002, p. 22; Deborah J. Myers, "Five Steps to Successful Hiring: Employers Have to Be Careful What They Ask Job Candidates During the Interview Process," *Alaska Business Monthly,* October 2002, p. 86.

Increases in protected employees and discrimination lawsuits have elevated the importance of human resource managers in the hiring process. To prevent violations, human resource personnel must train managers involved in interviewing to make them knowledgeable about employment law. For example, the law prohibits asking an applicant any questions relating to marital status, number of children, race, nationality, religion, or age. Interviewers also may not ask questions about applicants' criminal records, mental illness histories, or alcohol-related problems. In addition, human resource managers can help organizations establish systems to promote fair employment practices. Several CBS-owned television stations were sued by the Equal Employment Opportunity Commission for sex discrimination. The EEOC alleged that these stations practiced discrimination against female technicians in regard to salary, training, and promotions. CBS and the EEOC settled the lawsuit, with CBS agreeing to pay $8 million to approximately 200 female employees. CBS also agreed to put in place extensive mechanisms to help prevent future discrimination. For more information about employment-litigation issues, visit the Web sites of the Society for Human Resource Management (**http://www.shrm.org**) and the EEOC (**http://www.eeoc.gov**).

Employers must also observe various other legal restrictions governing hiring practices. Some firms try to screen out high-risk employees by requiring drug testing for job applicants, particularly in industries where employees are responsible for public safety, such as airlines and other public transportation. But drug testing is controversial because of concerns about privacy. Also, positive test results may not accurately indicate drug use, and traces of legal drugs, such as prescribed medications, may chemically resemble traces of illegal substances.

Recruitment and selection are expensive processes because a firm incurs costs for advertising job openings, interviewing applicants, and conducting background checks, employment tests, and medical exams. A bad hiring decision is even more expensive, though. A hiring mistake causes a firm to spend money to train and motivate a less than optimal employee, as well as risk the potential costs of poor decisions by that employee. Other costs resulting from a bad hiring decision may include lawsuits, unemployment compensation claims, recruiting and training a replacement, and reductions in productivity and employee morale.

To avoid the costly results of a bad hiring decision, many employers require applicants to complete employment tests. These tests help verify the skills that candidates list on their application forms or résumés to ensure that they meet the performance expectations of the job. A variety of tests are available to gauge applicants' knowledge of mechanical, technical, language, and computer skills. One example is the Wonderlic Basic Skills Test, which measures candidates' basic math and verbal skills. This test is intended to be a more objective and accurate way to measure qualifications than simply asking candidates about their educational background.

Following a hiring decision, a growing number of firms protect themselves from discrimination lawsuits by including explicit employment-at-will policies in their employee manuals. **Employment at will** means that the employment relationship can be terminated at any time by either the employee or the employer for any reason. Many people believe that the equal opportunity law prohibits employers from firing employees, but successful lawsuits must cite specific illegal practices such as discrimination in hiring based on sex, race, age, or disability. Although most state laws recognize the principle of employment at will, court decisions in firing disputes sometimes favor

Concept Check
1. What are some of the costs associated with recruitment and selection?
2. What is employment at will?

employees when their employers have failed to provide written proof of at-will policies and employees' acceptance of the policies. For further protection, some employers also publish policies that call for mandatory arbitration of employment disputes and waivers of the right to jury trials in such disputes.

Orientation, Training, and Evaluation

Once hired, employees need information about what is expected of them and how well they are performing. Companies provide this information through orientation, training, and evaluation. A newly hired employee often completes an orientation program administered jointly by the human resource department and the department in which the employee will work. During orientation, employer representatives inform employees about company policies regarding their rights and benefits. Many organizations give new hires copies of employee manuals that describe benefits programs and working conditions and expectations. They also provide different types of training to ensure that employees get a good start at the company.

Training Programs

Employees are increasing their requests for training so they can build skills and knowledge that will prepare them for new job opportunities. Training is also a good investment from the employer's perspective. A firm should view employee training as an ongoing process throughout each employee's tenure with the company. Companies like Trilogy and Bank of America, both of which were mentioned earlier, make training a vital part of selecting and hiring employees, as well as developing their careers. Investment firm Edward Jones, rated the nation's top company to work for by *Fortune,* provides an average of 146 hours of training per year to its employees. Why so much time? "In order to grow you have to be trained," says managing partner John Bachmann, "or you get trapped in the present."

On-the-Job Training　One popular instructional method is **on-the-job training,** which prepares employees for job duties by allowing them to perform tasks under the guidance of experienced employees. A variation of on-the-job training is apprenticeship training, in which an employee learns a job by serving for a time as an assistant to a trained worker. Patio Enclosures, a construction firm based in Ohio, made its employees more productive and more committed to the company by setting up an apprenticeship program. Apprenticeship programs are much more common in Europe than in the U.S. While American apprenticeships usually focus on blue-collar trades—such as lawn care, plumbing and heating services, and blacksmithing—in Europe many new entrants to white-collar professions complete apprenticeships.

Classroom and Computer-Based Training   Off-the-job training involves some form of classroom instruction such as lectures, conferences, audiovisual aids, computer instruction, and special machines to teach employees everything from basic math and language skills to complex, highly skilled tasks. Pharmaceutical giant Pfizer offers training at just about every level of the company, including self-paced courses through Harvard University and an on-site master's degree program.

Many firms are replacing classroom training with computer-based training programs. These programs can save an employer money by reducing travel costs and employee time away from work. In addition, computer-based training offers consistent presentations, since the training content won't vary with the quality of the instructor. Audio and visual capabilities help these systems to simulate the work environment better than some classroom training could, and employees also benefit from greater control over the learning process. They can learn at their own pace and convenience, and they generally do not have to wait for the company to schedule a class before they can begin adding to their knowledge. Despite these advantages, firms also offer traditional classroom training because it usually provides more opportunities for employees to interact with the instructor and with one another. Some people learn better through human interaction, and some have difficulty disciplining themselves to complete a computer-based learning program on their own.

Off-the-job training frequently involves use of the Internet. The Web provides a convenient means of delivering text, audio, and video training materials to employees wherever they are located. Online training programs also can offer interactive learning, such as simulations in which employees see the results of their decisions.

When a firm decides to enter a foreign market, human resource managers must prepare employees who will work in overseas assignments by providing training in language skills, cultural practices, and adapting to the everyday living requirements abroad. Employees may begin an international assignment with the professional skills and job qualifications they need, but most benefit from additional cultural and language training to help them make successful transitions.

Management Development   A **management development program** provides training designed to improve the skills and broaden the knowledge of current and potential executives. The share of the workforce in their mid-20s to mid-30s, who traditionally have been the group developing management skills, is shrinking, and many members of the workforce are approaching retirement age. Without the luxury of developing executive talent slowly over the years, organizations instead provide programs that help managers quickly learn how to lead a fast-moving company through turbulent times.

The content of management development programs may involve reviews of issues facing the company, as well as **benchmarking,** or learning the best practices of the best companies so they can serve as performance standards to strive for. The teachers may be the company's own executives. At other times, managers may be encouraged to receive counseling from an outside management coach, who helps them improve their skills. Bob Nardelli, CEO of Home Depot, is trying to create a "coaching environment" throughout his company. "I absolutely believe that people, unless coached properly, never reach their maximum capabilities," he says. Nardelli also created a leadership institute at Home Depot's Atlanta headquarters. Here high-potential managers meet with Nardelli and other senior executives to complete courses in leadership, merchandising, store planning, and financial operations.

Performance Appraisals

Organizations also help employees improve their performance by providing feedback about their past performance. A **performance appraisal** is an evaluation of an employee's job performance by comparing actual results with desired outcomes. Based on this evaluation, managers make objective decisions about compensation, promotions, additional training needs, transfers, or terminations. Rating employees' performance and communicating perceptions of their strengths and weaknesses are important elements in improving a firm's productivity and profits. Performance appraisals are not confined to business. Government agencies, not-for-profit organizations, and academic institutions also conduct them.

performance appraisal evaluation of an employee's job performance by comparing actual results with desired outcomes.

Some firms conduct peer reviews, in which employees assess the performance of coworkers, while other firms allow employees to review their supervisors and managers. One type of performance appraisal is the **360-degree performance review,** a process that gathers feedback from a review panel of 8 to 12 people, including coworkers, supervisors, team members, subordinates, and sometimes customers. The idea is to get as much frank feedback from as many perspectives as possible. However, this approach to performance appraisal tends to generate considerable work for both employees and managers—each of whom may have to review 20 or more people—and volumes of paperwork. Also, since the evaluations are anonymous, staff members with an ax to grind might try to use the system to their advantage in personal disputes.

Still, the 360-degree system appears to be gaining in popularity. A survey of large U.S. firms found that a majority of them are using the multirater system, up from around 40 percent in 1995. At United Parcel Service (UPS), managers receive 360-degree reviews every six months. The managers' peers, employees, and supervisors rate them in such areas of performance as leadership,

Concept Check

1. Describe some aids in off-the-job training.
2. What is a management development program?
3. What is the main way an organization provides employees with feedback about their performance?

customer focus, people skills, and knowledge of business and financial issues. To ensure that the feedback is used constructively, the UPS human resource department first provides employees with training on the purpose and uses of performance reviews. Also, to simplify the process and reduce the amount of time devoted to performance reviews, the UPS system is automated.

Compensation

Human resource managers work to develop an equitable compensation system spanning wages and salaries plus benefits. Because human resource costs represent a sizable percentage of any firm's total product costs, excessive wage rates may make its goods and services too expensive to compete effectively in the marketplace. Inadequate wages, however, lead to difficulty in attracting qualified people, high turnover rates, poor morale, and inefficient production.

wage compensation based on an hourly pay rate or the amount of output produced.

salary compensation calculated on a periodic basis, such as weekly or monthly.

The terms *wages* and *salary* are often used interchangeably, but they refer to different types of pay systems. **Wages** represent compensation based on an hourly pay rate or the amount of output produced. Firms pay wages to production employees, maintenance workers, and sometimes retail salespeople. **Salaries** represent compensation calculated periodically, such as weekly or monthly. Office personnel, executives, and professional employees usually receive salaries.

An effective compensation system should attract well-qualified workers, keep them satisfied in their jobs, and inspire them to succeed. Most firms base their compensation policies on the following five factors:

1. Salaries and wages paid by other companies that compete for the same people
2. Government legislation, including the federal, state, or local minimum wage
3. The cost of living
4. The firm's ability to pay
5. Worker productivity

Several cities have required businesses to pay a so-called living wage of as much as $11.75 per hour. A **living wage** is generally defined as one that allows a worker to support a family of four without having to receive any form of public assistance, such as food stamps. In some cities, living wage laws apply only to businesses with city contracts, but in other cities, the laws apply to all businesses. When Baltimore became the first city to adopt a living wage law, critics argued that the law would actually reduce employment and hobble businesses forced to pay higher wages. However, more than 60 municipalities have since passed living wage laws. From a human resource perspective, one study found that the slight job losses caused by these laws were more than offset by the decrease in family poverty.

Many employers balance rewarding workers with maintaining profits by linking more of their pay to superior performance. They try to motivate employees to excel by offering some type of incentive compensation in addition to salaries or wages. Today, almost one-tenth of the compensation of salaried workers is some form of variable pay. These programs include:

- Profit sharing, which awards bonuses based on company profits
- Gain sharing, which awards bonuses based on surpassing predetermined performance goals
- Lump-sum bonuses and stock options, which reward one-time cash payments and the right to purchase stock in the company based on performance
- Pay for knowledge, which distributes wage or salary increases as employees learn new job tasks

Figure 9.4 summarizes the four types of incentive compensation programs.

Some companies, such as Altria, Schering-Plough, and Anheuser-Busch, offer these programs to top and middle managers, as well as to employees with professional degrees. However, other companies believe that everyone should get a slice of the profit pie. Procter & Gamble, Freddie Mac, and Pfizer are some examples. Of course, during slow economic times, benefits such as stock options are less desirable—and even disastrous—in certain cases. Also, controversy rages over top executives who continue to receive bonuses while lower-level employees are forced to accept pay cuts or reduced benefits. But at semiconductor manufacturer Xilinx, workers took a 6 percent pay cut—while the CEO's salary was slashed 20 percent.

FIGURE 9.4
Four Forms of Incentive Compensation

Employee Benefits

In addition to wages and salaries, firms provide many benefits to employees and their families as part of the compensation they pay. **Employee benefits** are rewards such as retirement plans, health and disability insurance, sick leave, child care and elder care, and tuition reimbursement, provided entirely or in part at the company's expense. Benefits represent a large component of an employee's total compensation. Although wages and salaries account for around 72 percent of the typical employee's earnings, the other 28 percent takes the form of employee benefits.

The share of total compensation provided as benefits has grown over the years. General Motors spent $4.2 billion for health care recently; prescription drugs alone cost the company $1.3 billion. And employees at UPS, Anheuser-Busch, and Pfizer pay relatively little for their health-care

They Said It

High motivation is as precious as talent. Barriers which must be hurdled bring highly motivated people to the top.

—*John W. Gardner (1912–2002)*
American writer and public official

employee benefits
rewards such as retirement plans, health insurance, vacation, and tuition reimbursement provided for employees either entirely or in part at the company's expense.

coverage, while retirees receive free coverage. But the increasing costs of health-care benefits have left some employers looking for ways to hold the line. One increasingly used, but highly controversial, technique involves collecting data about employees' weight, smoking and alcohol consumption rates, exercise habits, and medical test results to use as inputs in creating employee wellness programs. The companies use the information to predict which workers may become ill. At Logan Aluminum in Russellville, Kentucky, employees receive an additional $200 a year for voluntarily filling out the health risk assessment forms. Such programs raise privacy issues, however.

Some benefits are required by law. U.S. firms are required to make Social Security and Medicare contributions as well as payments to state unemployment insurance and workers' compensation programs, which protect workers in case of job-related injuries or illnesses. The Family and Medical Leave Act of 1993 requires covered employers to offer up to 12 weeks of unpaid, job-protected leave to eligible employees. Firms voluntarily provide other employee benefits, such as child care and health insurance, to help them attract and retain employees. In 2003, California became the first state to sign *paid* family leave into law.

In spite of the share of benefits that U.S. companies offer, they pale in comparison with European firms. Europeans, on average, get six weeks of paid vacation—double or triple what their American counterparts receive. And the length of the workweek has steadily dropped across Europe in the past two decades. A 35-hour workweek is commonplace in Germany, Italy, and France. In fact, the French government has mandated a 35-hour workweek for all companies. Such generosity has a cost, though. Multinational companies have moved work abroad because the cost of hiring a European worker for a shorter workweek is too expensive. Also, the European Union's goal of becoming the most competitive economy in the world by the end of the first decade of the 21st century is not likely to be met if trends continue. Growth per capita—a measure of a country's standard of living—is approximately 1 percent in Europe compared with the United States's 3 percent. As one professor of labor economics at Humboldt University in Berlin put it, "You have to work to grow."

Pensions and other retirement plans have been another area of concern for U.S. companies. Some companies have reduced the amount of matching contributions they will make to workers' **401(k) plans,** retirement savings plans for which employees can make pretax contributions to retirement accounts. Some companies have been cutting back on cash contributions to their employees' plans and are contributing company stock instead. However, many companies and employees are uncomfortable with this practice in the wake of the collapse of Enron and other firms, which took employees' savings with them. Still, plenty of firms—such as mortgage financer Freddie Mac and Anadarko Petroleum—continue to contribute to their employees' savings as generously as allowed by law.

Many companies now recognize the importance of fulfilling employee requests for "family-friendly" benefits that help them care for children, aging parents, or other dependents. Such benefits—ranging from child-care facilities to paid time off and flexible work hours—help employees juggle responsibilities. Almost nine of ten large U.S. companies offer dependent-care spending accounts to help pay for child care, and almost half offer some form of elder-care program. SAS Institute offers employees a superlative on-site child-care facility for a monthly fee of only $300, a cafeteria with pianist, an on-site health clinic, and a huge fitness center. Adobe Systems offers workers three-week paid sabbaticals every five years, while the Container Store provides domestic partner benefits.

What Did I Learn from Previewing?

Take a minute to think about what you learned by previewing the chapter. First, consider the title. Were you familiar with the term *human resources?* Whenever you encounter a word or phrase in a title that you do not understand, it is essential that you find its meaning before you continue. In this case, your first step would be to check the glossary at the end of the textbook. There you would find this definition: *human resources*—an organization's employees. If the book did not contain a glossary, you could go immediately to the dictionary. In the *Merriam Webster Collegiate Dictionary* you will find *human resources* defined as *personnel.*

The headings in the chapter gave you a clear idea of its content and organization. The key terms are written in boldface type and reviewed in the margins. Concept checks help make sure you are understanding as you read along. Charts illustrate key points. Spending just a few minutes previewing this chapter will save you time in the long run: reading the full text is now much easier because you know what to expect and you are ready to understand and remember.

☞ Return now to the beginning of the chapter and read it carefully.

Mark the Text

Now that you've previewed and read it once, mark the text—underline important ideas, write notes in the margin, circle key words, write question marks next to anything you don't understand. (To review how to mark the text, turn to page 421, "Learning Strategy III—Marking Text.") If you have any questions, be sure to bring them up with your classmates or ask your instructor. Remember, when it's time for an exam, you only need to review the marks and comments you've made on the text.

Vocabulary

You've seen that the authors call your attention to key terms and concepts by writing them in boldface type and, in some cases, repeating them in the margins. If you find a term that you don't fully understand, be sure to mark it so you can ask a classmate or your instructor about it. If there are any words in the definitions you don't understand, be sure to look them up.

Exam Questions

This chapter is excerpted from a very popular textbook used in many colleges around the country. Following are some examples of exam questions given by instructors who actually teach the course. Test your understanding of the chapter by answering the questions.

Review Questions

1. What are the core responsibilities of human resource managers?
2. What are the three main objectives of human resource managers?
3. What methods do companies use to recruit and select employees?
4. What types of training programs are popular today?
5. On what five factors are compensation policies usually based?

6. Name at least three employee benefits that are required by law and three more that are provided voluntarily by many firms.

Application

Would you accept a job you didn't particularly like because the firm offered an attractive benefits package? Why or why not? Do you think your answer will change as you grow older? Why?

Fill-In Questions

Directions: Complete the following questions using the terms in the list.

A. Performance appraisal
B. Employment at will
C. Wage
D. Human resource management
E. Salary
F. Downsizing

1. The function of recruiting, developing, and retaining sufficient numbers of qualified employees is called _____.

2. _____ means the employment relationship can be started or terminated at any time by either the employee or the employer.

3. Evaluation of an employee's job performance is _____.

4. A(n) _____ is a compensation based on the hours worked or products produced.

5. A worker paid a(n) _____ receives a set amount periodically, such as once a week or once a month.

Multiple Choice Questions

1. The process of attracting, training, developing, motivating, and appraising a sufficient quantity of qualified employees to perform the activities necessary to accomplish organizational objectives is part of _____

   a. human resource management.
   b. human asset accounting.
   c. an assessment center.
   d. management development.

2. Today the relationship between employees and employers is characterized by _____ and _____.

   a. rigidity; simplicity
   b. rigidity; complexity
   c. flexibility; simplicity
   d. flexibility; complexity

3. All of the following pose challenges to human resource managers today EXCEPT _____

    a. an increasingly diverse workforce.
    b. employee desires to balance work and personal lives.
    c. fewer government regulations and employment-related laws.
    d. a shortage of qualified job candidates.

4. All of the following are core responsibilities of human resource managers EXCEPT _____

    a. employee recruitment.
    b. sales forecasts.
    c. employee compensation and benefits.
    d. employee training and performance evaluation.

5. In a broad sense, human resource management involves _____

    a. top managers only.
    b. top and middle managers only.
    c. specialists from the matrix organization only.
    d. trained specialists from the human resource department as well as general managers throughout the organization.

6. With the exception of _____, all of the following will have an impact on staffing needs.

    a. expansion into a new market
    b. an increase in the number of suppliers in the industry
    c. the need to lower operating expenses
    d. adaptation of new technology

7. _____ is the first step in the recruitment and selection of employees.

    a. Identifying job requirements
    b. Choosing sources of candidates
    c. Conducting employment tests
    d. Reviewing applications

8. The human resource manager at Futursim Products needs to fill five clerical positions. What common sources might the manager use to locate qualified people?

    a. Temporary help agencies and corporate headhunters
    b. Executive search firms and private employment agencies
    c. Newspaper advertisements and vocational/technical institutes
    d. Vocational/technical institutes and unions

9. A bad hiring decision may cost a firm all of the following EXCEPT
   _____.

   a. reductions in productivity
   b. reductions in employee morale
   c. costs involved in lawsuits and unemployment claims
   d. reductions in the sex-step recruitment approach

10. Which of the following is an example of on-the-job training?

    a. Online training programs
    b. Conferences
    c. Apprenticeship programs
    d. Instructional training with special machines

11. Learning the best practices of the best companies is an approach
    referred to as _____

    a. benchmarking.
    b. performance appraisal.
    c. orientation.
    d. management development.

Essay Questions

1. What is human resource management? How does the human resource
   function differ in small and large firms?
2. Identify and briefly explain some of the challenges facing today's human
   resource managers.
3. Explain the core responsibilities of human resource management.
4. Give three examples of a organization's competitive strategies that would
   require human resource managers to develop staffing plans.
5. List and briefly explain the benefits and drawbacks to the various sources
   of new recruits.
6. What does *employment at will* mean? Why have so many companies
   adopted this practice?
7. Identify the five factors upon which most firms base their compensation
   systems.
8. Identify and briefly describe each of the four most popular methods of incentive compensation.

THE INTERNET AND THE WORLD WIDE WEB

A Chapter from the Textbook
Understanding Computers Today and Tomorrow, Tenth Edition

Deborah Morley and Charles S. Parker

PREVIEWING

Remember to always preview the chapters of your textbook—it will help you better understand and remember what you read. (Review how to preview on page 415, "Learning Strategy I—Previewing.")

For this chapter, read (don't skim) the *Overview*. Do you know the answers to the questions in paragraph 3? Keep the questions in mind as you read along.

Quickly skim the remainder of the chapter. Use the questions below to help you get the most out of your previewing.

1. List the headings and subheadings in the section titled "Evolution of the Internet."
2. How do the authors indicate important terms you need to learn?
3. Skim the section "The Internet Community Today." List the seven groups that make up the Internet community.
4. How many "myths" about the Internet are listed?
5. Skim the section called "Searching the Internet." You may already know a great deal about searching. List the heading of at least one section that might contain information that will be new to you.
6. What will you learn about in "Beyond Browsing and E-Mail"?
7. Does the chapter contain any graphics? What kind of information do they contain?

It's hard to believe that before 1990 few people outside the computer industry and academia had ever heard of the Internet, and even fewer had used it. Why? Because the hardware, software, and communications tools needed to unleash the power of the Internet as we know it today were not available then. In fact, it is only in the last few years that technology has evolved enough to allow multimedia applications, such as downloading audio and video files and viewing animated presentations, to become an everyday activity.

What a difference a few years can make. Today, the Internet and the World Wide Web are household words, and in many ways they have redefined how people think about computers and communications.

Despite the popularity of the Internet, however, many users cannot answer some important basic questions about it. What makes up the Internet? Is it the same thing as the World Wide Web? How did the Internet begin and where is it heading? What types of tools are available to help people make optimum use of the Internet? How can the Internet be used to find specific information? This chapter addresses questions such as these.

This chapter begins with a discussion of the evolution of the Internet, from the late 1960s to the present. Then it looks into the many individuals, companies, and organizations that make up the Internet community. Next, the chapter covers the different options for connecting to the Internet, including the types of Internet access devices, Internet connections, and ISPs available. Then, it's on to one of the most important Internet skills you should acquire—efficient Internet searching. To help you appreciate the wide spectrum of resources and activities available through the Internet, we also take a brief look at some of the most common applications available via the Internet. The final sections of the chapter discuss a few of the important societal issues that apply to Internet use and take a look at the Internet's future.

EVOLUTION OF THE INTERNET

The **Internet** is a worldwide collection of interconnected networks that support personal and commercial communications and information exchange. It consists of thousands of separate, but interconnected, networks that are accessed daily by millions of people. Just as the shipping industry has simplified transportation by providing standard containers for carrying all sorts of merchandise via air, rail, highway, and sea, the Internet furnishes a standard way of sending messages and information across virtually any type of computer platform and transmission media. While *Internet* has become a household word only during the past few years, it has actually operated in one form or another for decades.

> **TIP**
>
> It is estimated that over 615 million people worldwide use the Internet.

> **Internet.** The largest and most well-known computer network, linking millions of computers all over the world.

From ARPANET to Internet2

The roots of the Internet began with an experimental project called *ARPANET*. Since then, the evolution of ARPANET plus the creation of the *World Wide Web* has resulted in the Internet with which we are familiar today.

ARPANET

The Internet began as an experimental network called **ARPANET**, which was created in 1969 by the U.S. Department of Defense's *Advanced Research Projects Agency* (*ARPA*). One objective of the ARPANET project was to create a computer network that would allow researchers located in different places to communicate with each other. Another objective was to build a computer network capable of sending data over a variety of paths to ensure that network communications could continue even if part of the network was destroyed, such as in a nuclear attack or by a natural disaster.

Initially, ARPANET connected four supercomputers. As it grew during its first few years, ARPANET enabled researchers at a few dozen academic institutions to communicate with each other and with government agencies on topics of mutual interest. However, the Department of Defense got much more than it bargained for. With the highly controversial Vietnam War in full swing, ARPANET's e-mail facility began to handle not only legitimate research discussions but also heated debates about U.S. involvement in Southeast Asia. As students began to access ARPANET, other unintended uses, such as playing computer games, began.

As the experiment grew during the next decade, hundreds of college and university networks were connected to ARPANET. These local area networks consisted of a mixture of DOS- and Windows-based computers, Apple Macintoshes, UNIX workstations, and so on. Over the years, *protocols* (standards) were developed for tying this mix of computers and networks together, for transferring data over the network, and for ensuring that data is transferred intact. Other networks soon connected to ARPANET, which eventually evolved into the present day Internet. The Internet infrastructure today can be used for a variety of purposes, such as exchanging e-mail and instant messages; participating in discussion groups, chat sessions, and videoconferences; downloading software and music; purchasing goods and services; and transferring files between Internet users. One of the most widely used Internet resources is the *World Wide Web*.

The World Wide Web

In its early years, the Internet was used primarily by the government, scientists, and educational institutions. Despite its popularity in academia and with government researchers, the Internet went virtually unnoticed by the general public and the business community for over two decades, primarily for two basic reasons—it was hard to use, and it was slow. Early Internet users had to type cryptic commands (see the first image in Figure 9-1), because the easy-to-use, attractive graphical user interfaces (GUIs) so commonplace today were still largely unknown.

>ARPANET. The predecessor of the Internet, named after the Advanced Research Projects Agency (ARPA), which sponsored its development.

EARLY 1990s
Even at the beginning of the 1990s, using the Internet for most people meant learning how to work with a cryptic sequence of commands. Virtually all information was text-based.

TODAY
Today's Web pages organize much of the Internet's content into easy-to-read pages; instead of typing cryptic command sequences, users click hyperlinks to access the information they want. Web pages today can contain a wide variety of multimedia elements, such as the text, graphics, and animation used on the Web page shown above.

FIGURE 9-1
Using the Internet: Back in the "old days" versus now.

As always, however, technology improved and new applications quickly evolved. First, communications hardware improved and computers gained speed and better graphics capabilities. Then, in 1989, a researcher named Tim Berners-Lee working at *CERN* (a physics laboratory in Europe), proposed the idea of the **World Wide Web**. He envisioned the World Wide Web as a way to organize information in the form of pages linked together through selectable text or images (today's hyperlinks) on the screen. Although the introduction of Web pages didn't replace other Internet resources (such as e-mail and collections of downloadable files), it became a popular way for researchers to provide written information to others.

Things really got rolling with the arrival of the graphical user interface. In 1993, a group of professors and students at the University of Illinois *National Center for Super-computing Applications* (*NCSA*) released *Mosaic*, the first graphically based Web browser. Mosaic used a graphical user interface and allowed Web pages to include graphical images in addition to text. Soon after, use of the World Wide Web began to increase dramatically because the graphical interface and graphical Web pages made using the World Wide Web both easier and more fun than in the past. Today's Web pages are a true multimedia experience. They can contain text, graphics, animation, sound, video, and three-dimensional virtual reality objects (refer to the second image in Figure 9-1).

Although the Web is only part of the Internet, it is by far one of the most popular and one of the fastest-growing parts. As interest in the Internet snowballed, companies

>World Wide Web. The collection of Web pages available through the Internet.

began looking for ways to make it more accessible to customers, to make the user interface more functional, and to make more services available over it. Today, most companies regard their use of the Internet and World Wide Web as an indispensable competitive business tool and many individuals view the Internet as a vital research and communications medium.

One remarkable characteristic of both the Internet and World Wide Web is that they are not owned by any person or business, and no single person, business, or organization is in charge. Web pages are developed by individuals and organizations and hosted on Web servers owned by an individual; a school, business, or other organization; or a service provider. PCs and other devices used to access the Internet typically belong to individuals, organizations, or public facilities. Each network connected to the Internet is owned and managed individually by that network's network administrator, and the main communications media used as the *Internet backbone* are typically owned by telecommunications companies, such as telephone and cable companies. As a whole, the Internet has no owner or network administrator. The closest thing to an Internet governing body is a variety of organizations, such as the *Internet Society* (*ISOC*) and the *World Wide Web Consortium* (*W3C*). These organizations are involved with such issues as establishing the protocols used on the Internet, making recommendations for changes, and encouraging cooperation between and coordinating communication among the networks connected to the Internet.

Internet2

The next significant improvements to the Internet infrastructure may be a result of *Internet2*, a consortium of over 200 universities working together with industry and the government. Internet2 was created to develop and implement advanced Internet applications and technologies in hope of leading to improvements for tomorrow's Internet. One of the primary goals of the Internet2 project is to ensure that new network services and applications are quickly applied to the broader Internet community, not just to the Internet2 participants. It is important to realize that Internet2 does not refer to a new physical Internet that will eventually replace the Internet—it is simply a research and development project geared to ensuring that the Internet in the future can handle tomorrow's applications.

A complementary project is the *Next Generation Internet* (*NGI*). While Internet2 is university sponsored, NGI is a federal government-sponsored, multi-agency research and development program working to develop advanced networking technologies and revolutionary applications that require advanced networking capabilities. Internet2 is working in cooperation with the NGI project, as well as forming partnerships with similar projects in other countries, to ensure a cohesive and interoperable advanced networking infrastructure for the Internet of the future.

The Internet Community Today

The Internet community today consists of individuals, businesses, and a variety of organizations located throughout the world. Virtually anyone with a computer that has communications capabilities can be part of the Internet, either as a user or as a supplier of information or services. Most members of the Internet community fall into one or more of the following groups.

Users

Users are people who avail themselves of the vast amount of resources available through the Internet at work or in their personal lives. There are nearly 200 million Internet users in the United States alone and they come from all walks of life. The U.S. *digital divide*—the disproportionate higher level of Internet use for certain groups of individuals (typically the more affluent and more educated)—is beginning to lessen as free Internet access is becoming more commonplace in libraries, schools, and other public locations. That, combined with the availability of cheap PCs and Internet access in many areas today, has helped Internet use begin to approach the popularity and widespread use of phones and TVs.

Internet Service Providers

Internet service providers (ISPs)—often called *service providers* or *access providers*—are businesses or other organizations that provide Internet access to others, typically for a fee. Communications and media companies—such as conventional and wireless telephone companies and cable and satellite TV providers—typically offer Internet service over their respective media. In addition, a variety of other ISPs provide services over existing communications media. Some, such as America Online and Earthlink, provide service nationwide; others have a more limited geographical area. ISPs act as an onramp to the Internet, providing their subscribers with access to the World Wide Web, e-mail, and other Internet resources. In addition to Internet access, some ISPs provide special online services available only to their subscribers. These ISPs are sometimes referred to as *online service providers.*

Internet Content Providers

Internet content providers supply the information that is available through the Internet. Internet content providers can be commercial businesses, non-profit organizations, educational institutions, individuals, and more. Some examples of content providers are listed next.

▼ A photographer who posts samples of her best work on a Web page.

▼ A political-action group that sponsors an online forum for discussions about topics that interest its members.

▼ A software company that creates a Web site to provide product information and software downloads.

▼ A national newspaper that maintains an online site to provide up-to-the-minute news, feature stories, and video clips.

>**Internet service provider (ISP).** A business or other organization that provides Internet access to others, typically for a fee.
>**Internet content provider.** A person or an organization that provides Internet content.

▼ A television network that develops a site for its newest reality TV show, including statistics, photographs, and live video feeds.

▼ A music publisher that creates a site to provide song demos and to sell downloads of its artists' songs and albums.

▼ A film student who releases his original short movie to be viewed on the Web.

Application Service Providers and Web Services

Application service providers (**ASPs**) are companies that manage and distribute software-based services to customers over the Internet. Instead of providing access to the Internet like ISPs do, ASPs provide access to software applications via the Internet. In essence, ASPs rent software access to companies or individuals—typically, customers pay a monthly or yearly fee to use the applications. One advantage to customers over buying software outright is less up-front money, which means small businesses may be able to afford the same state-of-the-art applications that larger companies use. Another advantage is that using ASP software may result in a reduction of computer support staffing, since the ASP can provide regular, automatic upgrades that all users see the next time they use the application; free or low-cost technical support and training may also be available from the ASP. Leasing applications in this manner also gives customers the flexibility of trying a different application whenever desired, without potentially wasting money purchasing software that may not fit the company's needs. Common ASP applications are office suites, collaboration and communications software, accounting programs, and e-commerce software. Some industry experts—such as the CEOs of Sun Microsystems and Microsoft—predict that within a relatively short period of time, software purchasing as we know it today will not exist. Instead, they believe software will be delivered as a service and the option to purchase software outright may not exist.

One type of special self-contained business application designed to work over the Internet or a company network is a **Web service**. Web services are programs written to strict specifications so that they can work together with other Web services and be used with many different computer systems. Unlike most other applications, Web services themselves don't have a user interface—they are simply a standardized way of allowing different applications and computers to share data and processes via a network. However, a Web service can be added to a Web page or application program to provide specific functionality to end users. For example, Web services can be used to facilitate communications between suppliers and customers, to provide a service via a Web site that was otherwise not feasible (such as the inclusion of mapping information on a Web site or Web application using

---

>Application service provider (ASP). A company that manages and distributes software-based services over the Internet.

>Web service. A self-contained business application that operates over the Internet.

Microsoft's MapPoint .NET Web service), or to add additional functionality to the end user via the Internet (such as a new Web service for Microsoft Office users expected to be available in the near future that allows them to print to any Kinko's locations from their program's File menu). A company that provides Web services is sometimes referred to as a *Web services provider*.

Infrastructure Companies

Infrastructure companies are the enterprises that own or operate the paths or "roadways" along which Internet data travel. Examples of infrastructure companies include telephone, satellite, and cable companies.

Hardware and Software Companies

A wide variety of hardware and software companies make and distribute the necessary products used with the Internet and Internet activities. The firms that supply Web browser, e-mail, Web server, and Web development software fall into this category. So, too, do the companies that make modems, cables, routers, servers, PCs, and other types of hardware used in conjunction with the Internet. The customers of software and hardware companies are users, service and content providers, and infrastructure companies.

The Government and Other Organizations

Many other organizations influence the Internet and its uses. Governments have among the most visible impact; their laws limit both information content and access in the Internet community. In the United States, rulings such as the 1968 *Carterfone Decision* (that allowed companies other than AT&T to utilize the AT&T infrastructure) and the 1996 *Telecommunications Act* (that deregulated the entire communications industry so that telephone companies, cable-TV and satellite operators, and firms in other segments of the industry were free to enter each other's markets), had a large impact on the communications industry in general. In addition, the ability of the government to block potential mergers between communications companies and to break apart companies based on antitrust law to prevent new monopolies also impacts the Internet and communications industry.

Key Internet organizations are responsible for many aspects of the Internet. For example, the Internet Society (ISOC) provides leadership in addressing issues that confront the future of the Internet and oversees the groups responsible for Internet infrastructure standards, such as which protocols can be used and how Internet addresses are constructed. *ICANN (Internet Corporation for Assigned Names and Numbers)* is charged with such responsibilities as IP address allocation and domain name management. The World Wide Web Consortium (W3C) is a group of over 450 organizations dedicated to developing new protocols and specifications to promote the evolution of the Web and to ensure its interoperability. In addition, many colleges and universities support Internet research and manage blocks of the Internet's resources.

Myths About the Internet

Because the Internet is unique in the history of the world—and its content and applications keep evolving—several widespread myths about it have surfaced.

Myth 1: The Internet Is Free

This myth has been perpetuated largely by the fact that people can access Web pages from anywhere in the world and freely engage in long-distance e-mail or chat exchanges without paying additional fees, other than what they pay their ISPs for access to the Internet in general. It is also true that many people—such as students, employees, and consumers who opt for free Internet service or use free access available at public libraries or other public locations—pay nothing to use the Internet. Yet it should also be obvious that someone, somewhere, has to pay to keep the Internet up and running.

Businesses, schools, public libraries, and most home users pay Internet service providers flat monthly fees to connect to the Internet; businesses, schools, libraries, and other larger organizations may also have to lease high-capacity communications lines (such as from a telephone company) to support their high level of Internet traffic. ISPs, phone companies, cable companies, and other organizations who own part of the Internet infrastructure pay to keep their respective physical parts of the Internet running smoothly. ISPs also pay software and hardware companies for the resources they need to support their users. Eventually, most of these costs are passed along to end users through their ISP fees. Usually, free Internet access is supported by advertising revenue gained from onscreen ads (either ads displayed within the browser interface whenever Web pages or e-mail messages are being viewed, or *pop-up* ads that display in new browser windows), similar to regular TV broadcasting, or by selling personal or demographic data obtained from subscribers.

Another reason that this is a myth is the growing trend of subscription or per-use fees to access resources—such as journal or newspaper articles, music, games, and more—via the Internet. Typically, these fees are relatively small and many companies are working on ways to make the processing of small fees (sometimes called *micropayments*) practical. In lieu of a mandatory fee, some sites request donations for use of the site. Many experts expect the use of fee-based Internet content to continue to grow at a rapid pace. In 2002 alone, subscriptions for Web site content surpassed $1 billion.

Myth 2: Someone Controls the Internet

The popularity of conspiracy theories in recent years has contributed to the spread of this myth. In fact, as already discussed, no single group or organization controls the Internet. Governments in each country have the power to regulate the content and use of the Internet within their borders, as allowed by their laws. However, legislators often face serious obstacles getting legislation passed into law—let alone getting it enforced. Making governmental control even harder is the bombproof design of the Internet itself. If a government tries to block access to or from a specific country, for example, users can establish links between the two countries through a third country.

Guidelines by watchdog groups such as the Internet Society (ISOC) have sometimes folded under pressure from the tidal wave of people and organizations that have flocked to the Internet. For example, ISOC's policies that discouraged commercial use of the Internet fell by the wayside many years ago.

Myth 3: The Internet and World Wide Web Are Identical

Since you can now use a Web browser to access most of the Internet's resources, many people think the Internet and the Web are the same thing. Although in everyday use many people use the terms *Internet* and *Web* interchangeably, they're not the same thing. Technically, the Internet is the physical network and the Web is the collection of Web pages accessible over the Internet. The majority of Internet activities today take place via Web pages, but there are Internet resources other than the Web, such as non-Web-based e-mail and collections of files accessed via *FTP (File Transfer Protocol)* programs.

SEARCHING THE INTERNET

While casual surfing is a popular Web pastime, people often turn to the Internet to find specific information. For instance, you might want to find out the price of the latest Tom Cruise DVD at a few online retailers, the flights available from Los Angeles to New York on a particular day, a recipe for clam chowder, the text of Martin Luther King's "I Had a Dream" speech, a map of hiking trails in the Grand Tetons, or Babe Ruth's home run average. The Internet is a storehouse of interesting and useful information, but that vast amount of information is useless if you can't find it when you need it. Consequently, one of the most important skills an Internet user can acquire today is how to successfully search for and locate information on the Internet. To perform more successful Internet searches, you should also be familiar with the various types of search sites available and how they work, as well as some key searching strategies. These topics are discussed next.

Search Sites

There are many different **search sites**—Web sites that enable users to search for and find information on the Internet—available. Many of the most popular search sites, such as Yahoo!, Google, AltaVista, HotBot, Excite, and so on, offer search services using both *keywords* and a *directory*; they may also include other search possibilities, such as searching for music files, image files, newsgroups, or news articles (see Figure 9-2). Since most search sites use some type of *search database* to locate appropriate Web pages as you search, it is important to understand a little about how such a database works.

>**Search site.** A Web site designed to help users search for Web pages that match specified keywords or selected categories.

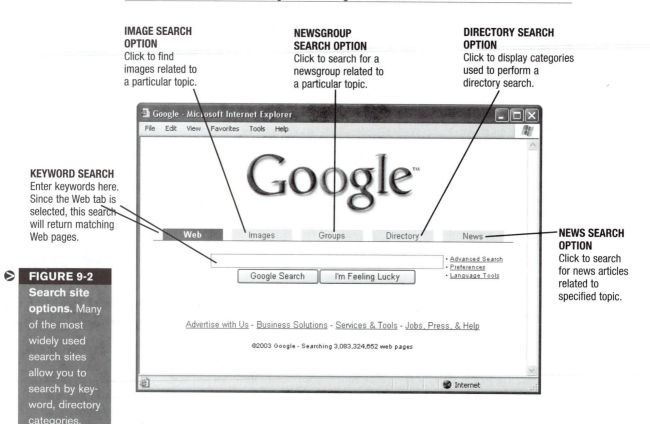

IMAGE SEARCH OPTION
Click to find images related to a particular topic.

NEWSGROUP SEARCH OPTION
Click to search for a newsgroup related to a particular topic.

DIRECTORY SEARCH OPTION
Click to display categories used to perform a directory search.

KEYWORD SEARCH
Enter keywords here. Since the Web tab is selected, this search will return matching Web pages.

NEWS SEARCH OPTION
Click to search for news articles related to specified topic.

FIGURE 9-2
Search site options. Many of the most widely used search sites allow you to search by key-word, directory categories, or more.

Search Databases

While it may appear that a search site actually searches the Internet for you at the time you make a search request, in fact such a search would be entirely too time-consuming to perform in real time. Instead, virtually all search sites use a search database previously filled with millions or billions of URLs classified by various types of keywords or categories and a **search engine** program to retrieve a list of matching Web pages from the database. Since there isn't a single central database of all the Web pages located on the World Wide Web, each search site either creates and maintains its own database or has access to a search database created and maintained by another site. To maintain such a database, typically small, automated programs (often called *spiders* or *webcrawlers*) use the hyperlinks located on Web pages to jump continually from page to page on the Web. At each page, the program records important data about the page—such as its URL, page title, frequently used keywords, and descriptive information added to the page's code

>**Search engine.** A software program used by a search site to retrieve matching Web pages from a search database.

by the Web page author when the page was created—into the database. This information is used to find matching Web pages when the search site receives a search request. Spider programs can be tremendously fast, visiting more than 1 million pages per day. Search databases also obtain information when people who create Web sites submit URLs and keywords to them through an option on the search site.

The size of the search database varies with each particular search site. For example, Google—one of the most popular search sites—has data on over 3 billion Web pages. Search sites also differ in how close a match has to be between the specified search criteria and a Web page before a link to that page (called a *hit*) is displayed. This can be good or bad, depending on the length of the list of matches the search returns and how much time you want to spend looking through the list of hits for something interesting enough to pursue further. To reduce the number of hits displayed, good search strategies (discussed shortly) can be used. Sites also differ regarding the order in which the hits are displayed. Some sites list the most popular sites (usually judged by the number of Web pages linked to it); others list Web pages belonging to organizations that pay a fee to receive a higher rank (sometimes called *sponsored links*) first.

Searching with Keywords

When you know generally what information you want to find but don't know the appropriate URL, one of your best options is to perform a *keyword search*. Many different types of search sites allow the use of keyword searches. With a keyword search, you supply **keywords** (one or more key terms), and then the search engine uses those keywords to pull matching pages from its search database. Once one or more keywords are typed in the appropriate location on the search site's Web page and the Enter key is pressed, the search engine will retrieve and display a list of matching Web pages.

Searching with Directories

Directories are usually a good choice if you want information about a particular category, but don't have a very specific subject in mind. A directory also uses a database, but one that is typically screened by a human editor so it is much smaller, although often more accurate. For example, a spider program may classify a Web page about "computer chips" under the keyword "chips" together with information about potato chips, but a human editor wouldn't. One of the largest directories—the *Open Directory Project*, located at dmoz.org—has classified nearly 4 million Web pages using over 58,000 volunteer editors.

To use a directory located on a search site, categories are selected instead of typing keywords. After selecting a main category, a list of more specific subcategories for the selected main category is displayed. Eventually, after selecting one or more subcategories, a list of appropriate Web pages is displayed.

>**Keyword.** A word typed in a search box on a search site to locate information on the Internet.
>**Directory.** A collection of categories that are used to locate appropriate Web pages from a search database.

Metasearch Sites

Some search sites are *metasearch sites*—that is, they search multiple search sites. Typically the metasearch site doesn't have its own search database. Instead, it acts as a middleman, passing on the specified keywords to a variety of search sites and then summarizing the results.

Natural Language Search Sites

A *natural language search site,* such as the Ask Jeeves search site, allows users to enter search criteria in full sentence form, instead of simply entering keywords. Some natural language sites include directory search capabilities or other search and reference tools, as well.

Search Strategies

There are a variety of strategies that can be employed to help whittle down a list of hits to a more manageable number (some searches can return millions of Web pages). Some search strategies can be employed regardless of the search site being used; others are available only on certain sites. Some of the most useful search strategies are discussed next.

Using Phrases

One of the most straightforward ways to improve the quality of the hits returned is to use *phrase searching*—essentially typing more than one keyword in a keyword search. Most search engines automatically return the hits that include all the keywords typed first, followed by the hits matching most of the keywords, continuing down to the hits that fit only one of the keywords. To force this type of sorting, virtually all search engines allow some type of character—such as quotation marks—to be used to indicate that you want to search for all the keywords. On some sites, quotation marks can also be used to indicate that the keywords need to appear in the exact order they were typed. Because search options vary from site to site, it is best to look for a search tips link on the search site you are using; the search tips should explain the options available for that particular site. Examples of the results from using various search phrases at different sites to find Web pages about hand signals used with dogs are listed in Figure 9-3.

TIP

When searching, be efficient–if an appropriate Web page isn't included among the first page or two of hits, redo the search using more specific criteria or a different search strategy.

Using Boolean Operators

To further specify exactly what you want a search engine to find, *Boolean operators*—most commonly AND, OR, and NOT—can often be used in keyword searches. For example, if you want a search engine to find all documents that cover *both* the Intel and AMD microprocessor manufacturers, you can use the search phrase *Intel AND AMD,* if the search engine supports Boolean operators. If, instead, you want documents that discuss *either* (or both) of these

SEARCH PHRASE USED	SEARCH SITE	NUMBER OF PAGES FOUND	TITLE OF FIRST TWO PAGES FOUND (HIGHLIGHTED ENTRIES INDICATE RELEVANT WEB PAGES)
dogs	AltaVista	4,619,341	I-Love-Dogs.com AKC - American Kennel Club for Purebred Dogs
	Google	9,120,000	I-Love-Dogs.com Guide Dogs for the Blind
	HotBot	5,145,352	I-Love-Dogs.com American Kennel Club
hand signals	AltaVista	627,659	Old Soccer Hand Signals Cree Hand Signals
	Google	1,470,000	Cree Hand Signals Soccer Officials' Hand Signals
	HotBot	539,617	Soccer Officials' Hand Signals Ann Arbor American H.O.G. Hand Signals
dog hand signals	AltaVista	52,341	Cree Hand Signals Why the Deaf Dog Barks
	Google	130,000	Dog Behavior Training, Teach Your Dog Hand Signals! PetsMart.com - Talking with hand signals
	HotBot	77,358	Training a Deaf Dog PetsMart.com - Talking with hand signals
"dog hand signals"	AltaVista	22	Pets with Disabilities - Dog Training Bunker Kennels
	Google	43	Dog Behavior Training, Teach Your Dog Hand Signals! PetsMart.com - Talking with hand signals
	HotBot	21	Training a Deaf Dog PetsMart.com - Talking with hand signals

> **FIGURE 9-3**
> **Examples of phrase searching.** Using different search phrases and different search sites can dramatically change the search results.

companies, the Boolean phrase *Intel OR AMD* can be used. On the other hand, if you want documents about microprocessors that are cataloged with no mention of Intel, *microprocessors NOT Intel* can be used. Just as with other operators, the rules for using Boolean operators may vary from search site to search site—check the search tips for the search site that you are using to see if that site supports Boolean operators. Some sites include an Advanced Search option using a fill-in form to walk you through using Boolean operators and other advanced search techniques; other sites use the characters + for AND and – for NOT.

Using Multiple Search Sites

As illustrated in Figure 9-3, different search sites can return surprisingly different results. Most users have a favorite search site that they are comfortable using. However, it's important to realize that sometimes a different search site may perform better. If you are searching for something and aren't making any progress with one search site, then try another search site.

Using Appropriate Keywords, Synonyms, Variant Word Forms, and Wildcards

When choosing the keywords to be used with a search site, it is important to select words that represent the key concept you are searching for. Unless you are using a natural language site, leave off any extraneous words, such as "the," "a," "in," and so forth. For example, if you want to find out about bed and breakfasts located in the town of Leavenworth, Washington, a keyword phrase such as *Leavenworth Washington bed and breakfast* should return appropriate results.

Another good strategy if your initial search didn't produce the results you were hoping for is to try the synonym approach. *Synonyms*—words that have meanings similar to other words—can be typed as keywords in addition to, or instead of, the original keywords. For example, you could replace *bed and breakfast* with *hotel* or *lodging.* To use synonyms in addition to the original keywords, Boolean operators can be used, such as the search phrase *"bed and breakfast" OR "hotel" OR "lodging" AND Leavenworth AND Washington.*

Variant—or alternate—word forms are another possibility. Try to think of a different spelling or form of your keywords, if your search still doesn't work as desired. For example, *bed and breakfast* could be replaced or supplemented with the variants *bed & breakfast* and *B&B,* and *hand signal* and *hand signaling* are variant word forms for the *hand signals* keywords used in Figure 9-3. Alternative spellings is a form of this strategy, as well.

Another strategy that is sometimes used with keywords is the *wildcard* approach. A wildcard is a special symbol that is used in conjunction with a part of a word to specify the pattern of the terms you want to search for. For instance, the asterisk wildcard (*) is used to represent any number of letters at the asterisk location, so on many sites searching for *hand sign** would search for *hand sign, hand signal, hand signals, hand signaling,* and any other keywords that fit this specific pattern.

Using Field Searches

A more advanced search strategy that can be used when basic searching isn't producing the desired results is *field searching*—a search limited to a particular search characteristic (or *field*), such as the page title, URL, page text, or domain. When a field search is performed, the specific text is searched for only in the specified field (see Figure 9-4 for some examples of field searching along with the results from performing those searches using the AltaVista search site). Many, but not all, search engines support some type of field searches. Check the search tips for the particular search site you are using to see if it has that option.

SEARCH PHRASE USED	NUMBER OF PAGES FOUND	TITLE OF FIRST TWO PAGES FOUND	PAGE URL
title:"tax tips" (searches for Web pages containing "tax tips" in the page title)	7,014	UK Tax Tips Roger Kahan Tax Tips and Facts	www.letaxguard.co.uk/uk-tax-tips.htm www.tak-1.com
url:"taxtips" (searches for Web pages containing "taxtips" in the page URL)	3,848	JA McNichol & Co. Tax Tips Table of Contents	www.mcnichol.netpages/ taxtips .htm www.firstlocation/ Taxtips .htm
text:"tax tips" (searches for Web pages containing "tax tips" in the text of the page)	53,802	Yahoo Tax Center IRS.gov Home	taxes.yahoo.com www.irs.gov
domain.gov (searches for Web pages located on government Web servers-domain ends in ".gov"	6,81,2302	FirstGov "The U.S. Government's Official Web Page National Science Foundation (NSF)" Home Page	www.firstgov. gov www.nsf. gov
title:"tax tips" domain:gov (searches for Web pages containing "tax tips" in the page title located on government Web servers–domain ends in ".gov")	5	OBA Consumer Tax Tips California Department Of Consumer Affairs TAX TIPS	www.dca.ca. gov /press_releases/ 2003/taxtips.htm www.yorkcountry.gov /revenue/ taxtips.htm

Evaluating Search Results

Once a list of potentially matching Web sites is returned as a result of a search, it is time to evaluate the sites to determine their quality and potential for meeting your needs. Two things to look for before clicking on a link for a matching page are:

▼ Does the title and listed description sound appropriate for the information you are seeking?

▼ Is the URL from an appropriate company or organization? For example, if you want technical specifications about a particular product, you may want to start with information on the manufacturer's Web site. If you are looking for government publications, stick with government Web sites.

After an appropriate Web page is found, the evaluation process is still not complete. If you are using the information on the page for something other than idle curiosity, you want to be sure the information can be trusted. Some general guidelines are listed in Figure 9-5 on page 400.

Citing Internet Resources

According to the online version of the Merriam-Webster dictionary, the term *plagiarize* means "to steal and pass off the ideas or words of another as one's own"

FIGURE 9-4 ·
Field searching.
Field searches limit search results to just those pages with a specific Web page title, URL, text, or top-level domain.

Evaluate the source.	Information from the company or organization in question is generally more reliable than information found on an individual's Web site. Government and educational Institutions are usually good sources for historical or research data. If you clicked a link on a Web page to open a document, double-check the URL to make sure you still know what organization the page is from-it may be located on a completely different Web site than the page from which it was accessed.
Evaluate the author.	Does the author have the appropriate qualification for the information in question? Does he or she have a bias or is the information supposed to be objective?
Check the timeliness of the Information.	Web page content may be updated regularly or posted once and forgotten. Always look for the publication date on online newspaper and magazine articles; check for a last updated date on pages containing other types of information you'd like to use.
Verify the Information.	When you will be using Web-based information in a report paper, Web page or other document where accuracy is important try to locate the same information from other reputable Web sources to verify the accuracy of the information you plan to use.

> **FIGURE 9-5**
Evaluating search results. Before using information obtained from a Web page, use the following criteria to evaluate its accuracy and appropriateness.

or to "use another's production without crediting the source." To avoid plagiarizing Web page content, Web pages—as well as any other Internet resources—need to be credited appropriately.

The citation guidelines for Web page content are similar to those for written material. Guidelines for crediting some Internet-based resources are listed next. Different style manuals may have different rules for citing Internet references—the following guidelines were obtained from the American Psychological Association Web site and some examples are listed in Figure 9-6. If in doubt when preparing a research paper, check with your instructor as to the style manual he or she prefers you follow and refer to that guide accordingly.

▼ *Web page article (journal, magazine, etc.)*. List the author, date of publication, article title, and periodical information, similar to a print source, and then add a "Retrieved" statement and date with the appropriate URL of the Web page used.

▼ *Web page content (not an article)*. List the author (if there is one), date of publication (if available; if not, use *n.d.*), and Web page title, followed by a "Retrieved" statement and date with the appropriate URL of the Web page used.

▼ *E-mail correspondence*. List the sender's name followed by a "personal communication" statement and the date received next to the reference in the text. This reference isn't included in the references section.

BEYOND BROWSING AND E-MAIL

While some of the most common Internet activities are Web browsing and e-mail exchange, as well as searching for specific information (as previously discussed in this chapter), there are a host of other activities that can take place via the Internet. Some additional Web-based applications are discussed next.

TYPE OF RESOURCE	CITATION EXAMPLE
Web page article (magazine)	Naughton, Keith. (2003, September 29). Chrysler Shifts Gears. *Newsweek*. Retrieved March 13, 2004 from http://www.msnbc.com/news/969677.asp?0dm=s118k.
Web page article (journal)	Mion, L. (2003, May 31). Care Provision for Older Adults: Who Will Provide? *Online Journal of Issues in Nursing*, 8 no. 2. Retrieved March 1, 2004, from http://www.nursingworld.org/ojin/topic21/tpc21_3.htm.
Web page article (not appearing in a periodical)	Sullivan, Bob (2003, September 26). New Arrest in Internet Attacks Case. MSNBC. Retrieved February 11, 2004, from http://msnbc.com/news/972467.asp?0dm=C14OT.
Web page content (not an article)	*Biography of Ronald Reagan*. (n.d). Retrieved March 5, 2003 from http://www.whitehouse.gov/history/presidents/rr40.html.
E-mail (cited in text, not reference list)	L.A. Chafez (personal communication, March 28, 2003).

Online Financial Transactions

Online financial transactions—a type of *e-commerce*—are fast-growing Web activities. As more and more people have access to the Web from home and discover the convenience of shopping, banking, stock trading, and so forth on their home PCs, the popularity of performing these types of transactions online is likely to continue to grow. One of the major obstacles to online financial transactions is consumer concern for *online security;* some precautions a user can take are discussed next, followed by a look at some of the most common types of online financial transactions.

Online Security Considerations

Since *online fraud, credit card fraud,* and *identity theft* (in which someone gains enough personal information to order products or otherwise pose as another person) are growing problems, it is important to be cautious when participating in online financial activities. To protect yourself, use a credit card whenever possible when purchasing goods or services online so that any fraudulent activities can be disputed, and be sure only to enter your credit card number on a *secure Web page*. To identify a secure Web page, look for a locked padlock or a complete—non-broken—key at the bottom of your Web browser screen, a URL that begins with *https* instead of *http,* or some other indication that a secure server is being used. Secure Web pages should also be used to enter any other type of sensitive information (such as a bank account number or any information that you wouldn't want anyone else to see) and online access to financial accounts should be protected with good user passwords that are changed frequently.

Online Shopping

Online shopping is becoming very popular. With online shopping, products can be purchased directly from large companies—such as L.L. Bean, Dell Computer, Wal-Mart,

> **FIGURE 9-6**
> **Citing Web sources.** It is important to properly credit your Web sources. These examples follow the American Psychological Association citation guidelines.

>**Online shopping.** Buying products or services over the Internet.

Amazon.com, and Macy's—via their Web sites, as well as from a growing number of small retailers. Typically, shoppers locate the items they'd like to purchase by searching online retailer sites or browsing through online catalogs, and then adding the items to their online *shopping carts* or *shopping bags*. When a shopper is finished shopping, he or she follows the checkout procedures—such as supplying the appropriate billing and shipping information—to complete the sale. After the payment is processed, the item is either shipped to the customer (if it is a physical product) or the customer is given instructions on how to download it (if it is a software program, electronic book or article, music, or some other product in electronic form).

Today, you can buy items online using any of several different payment methods. The method you use depends on where you shop. While most online stores accept credit cards, other options may or may not be allowed. Some possible payment methods are listed next.

▼ *Credit card.* You can usually pay for online purchases with a credit card just as you can when buying goods or services in person or over the phone. For online purchases, the credit card number is validated and the charge approved during the checkout process. On secure sites, your credit card data is encrypted (electronically scrambled) when it is sent, so it can't be intercepted by a third party. It is becoming increasingly common for credit card companies to also offer their customers one-time use *virtual credit card numbers* that can be used one time to charge an item to the customer's credit card, but are unusable for additional purchases. Typically, the customer obtains a virtual number online immediately prior to the online purchase.

▼ *Payment services.* Payment services, such as *PayPal,* enable individuals to exchange money via the Internet using their e-mail addresses. To send money, the individual needs to set up an account with an online payment service (such as PayPal), supplying the online payment service with the necessary information (such as a credit card or checking account number) and obtaining a user name and password. Typically, the individual either transfers money into the account before a purchase or sets up the account to automatically use a specified credit card or checking account when money is needed for transfers. The individual can then authorize the payment service to pay a participating merchant or individual a specific amount whenever needed. The recipient is typically notified by e-mail that a payment has been received and then can retrieve the money via the payment services Web site. Some services require both parties to have payment services accounts; others require only the sender to have an account.

▼ *Smart card.* Smart cards containing a prepaid amount of money can be used like a debit card for online purchases. Many individuals feel more secure using a smart card instead of a credit card over the Internet because of the limited amount of spending power available on it, as opposed to a credit card. Smart cards are inserted into a smart card reader to be used. Because of the proliferation of online shopping, some new keyboards and cell phones include a built-in smart card reader; external smart card readers are also available.

▼ *Conventional payment.* Some online merchants realize that consumers are wary of conducting business over the Internet and allow buyers to pay by conventional means. If this option is available on a site, it will usually appear on a checkout page, in the form of an option to request a representative to phone you to arrange payment by check or credit card, or there may be a toll-free phone number that can be used to place your order instead of using the online order form.

Online Auctions

Online auctions are the most common way to buy items online from other individuals. Sellers list items for sale on an auction site (such as eBay or Yahoo! Auctions) by paying a small listing fee and entering a description of the item and a length of time that the auction should run. They can specify a starting bid amount (that bidders see), as well as a minimum selling price (that bidders don't see—they just are told if there is a minimum selling price and if their bid has met or exceeded that price) that must be met in order for there to be a winning bidder. Individuals can enter bids on auction items until the end of the auction. At the time the auction closes, the person with the highest bid is declared the successful bidder (provided the minimum selling price was met, if one was established) and arranges payment and delivery for the item directly with the seller. The seller also pays a percentage of the sale price as a commission to the auction site.

Online Banking

A relatively new online financial application that is becoming extremely popular is **online banking.** Although it used to be available separately for a fee, now many conventional banks—such as Bank of America and Wells Fargo—offer free online banking services to their customers. Online banking services typically include reviewing account activity, sending electronic payments, transferring funds between accounts, and checking your credit card balances (see Figure 9-7).

Online Investing

Buying and selling stocks, bonds, and other types of securities is referred to as **online investing.** Although it is common to see stock quote capabilities on many search and news sites, trading stocks and other securities usually requires an *online broker.* The biggest advantage for using an online broker is the low transaction fee—often just $7 to $15 per trade, generally much less expensive than comparable offline services. It is also much more convenient for those investors who do a lot of trading.

Once an online brokerage account is set up, you can place stock buy and sell orders just as you would with an offline broker. Usually the history of your orders

>**Online auction.** An online activity for which bids are placed on items and the highest bidder purchases the item.
>**Online banking.** Performing banking activities over the Internet.
>**Online investing.** Buying and selling stocks or other types of investments over the Internet.

ONLINE BANKING
Typically allows you to check your account balances, make electronic payments, view your transaction history, and more.

Click to switch to the Bill Pay or Transfer Funds options.

Click to change account or type of information displayed.

Checking account summary information is displayed here.

Enter buy or sell information here to make a trade.

This portfolio uses a Java applet to continually update the quotes in real time.

ONLINE INVESTING
Typically allows you to buy and sell stocks, view your portfolio, get real-time quotes, and more.

FIGURE 9-7
Online banking and investing.

can be viewed online and open orders can be cancelled before they are executed, if desired. Many brokerage and financial sites also have convenient access to a variety of performance history, corporate news, and other useful information for investors. In addition, most online brokers allow you to set up an *online portfolio* that displays the status of the stocks you specify. On some sites, stock price data is delayed 20 minutes; on other sites, real-time quotes are available. Unless the quote or page is automatically refreshed for you on a regular basis, such as with a *Java applet* like the one shown in Figure 9-7, you must reload the Web page (using your browser's Refresh or Reload toolbar button) whenever you want to see updated quotes.

Online Entertainment

There are an ever-growing number of ways to use the Web for entertainment purposes, such as listening to music, watching videos, and playing online games. Some online entertainment options—such as listening to music and watching online videos—require a special media player program. Some common media players are *Windows Media Player, RealOne Player, WinAmp,* and *MusicMatch Jukebox* for Windows PCs; *RealOne Player* and *iTunes* are commonly used with Apple computers. All of these players are available as free downloads, although many have an optional fee-based service for premium Internet radio broadcasts. Some multimedia applications can be accessed with virtually any type of Internet connection; others require a broadband connection.

Online Music

Online music is perhaps one of the hottest Web-based entertainment activities today. Some of the most widely used possibilities are listening to online radio broadcasts and downloading songs to be played later on your PC or portable digital music player (such as an MP3 player). Online radio is broadcast from *online radio stations,* also called *Internet radio stations.* To listen to an Internet radio station, you typically open that Web page in your browser and click an appropriate hyperlink. You will then begin to hear the broadcast via a media player program installed on your PC or a proprietary player that will open automatically. Many media players also have a tool to help you save your favorite radio stations in a list, so you can choose your desired radio station using the player's interface.

Although other formats are possible, most downloaded music is compressed using MP3 file compression to reduce its file size from about 10 MB per minute to less than 1 MB per minute, without a noticeable reduction in quality. To avoid copyright violations, all downloaded music should either be specified as free downloads (sometimes found on sites featuring new artists, for example) or the site should charge an appropriate fee (for royalties owed to the artist or record studio) for the download. Once downloaded, music files can be played from your PC's hard drive using a media player program installed on your PC. Provided the download agreement didn't preclude it,

---

>Online music. Music played or obtained via the Internet.

music files can also be copied to a CD to create a custom music CD or transferred to an MP3 player. For instance, the *iTunes Music Store* allows both Mac and PC users to browse through over 200,000 songs, preview songs for free, and then download the ones they like for 99 cents each. Once downloaded, the songs can legally be played on up to three computers, transferred to a digital music player, and burned on an unlimited number of personal music CDs. Other sites, such as RealOne Rhapsody and MusicMatch Jukebox, offer similar services.

E-Mail Privacy

Many people mistakenly believe that the e-mail they send and receive is private and won't ever be read by anyone other than the intended recipient. Since it is transmitted over public media, however, only *encrypted* (electronically scrambled) e-mail can be transmitted safely. Although it is unlikely this will happen to your personal e-mail, *non-encrypted* e-mail can be intercepted and read by someone else. Consequently, it is wise to view non-encrypted e-mail correspondence as similar to a postcard rather than a letter, from a privacy standpoint. It is also important to realize that your employer and your ISP have access to the e-mail you send through those organizations and they will often *archive* (keep copies of) it. There have been many cases in which e-mail sent by criminal suspects, such as computer hackers and stalkers, has been retrieved by law enforcement from the suspects' ISPs and used to prosecute them. One such e-mail interception system is *Carnivore*.

THE FUTURE OF THE INTERNET

The Internet has changed a great deal since its inception in 1969. From only four supercomputers, it has evolved into a vast network connecting virtually every type of computer. The use of the Internet has changed dramatically, as well. As the structure of the Internet evolves and improves, it can support new types of activities. New types of applications also drive the technological improvements necessary to support them.

The exact composition of the Internet of the future is anyone's guess. It will likely be a very high-speed optical network with virtually unlimited bandwidth. It will be accessed by the PC of the day, which will probably be much smaller and less obtrusive than the standard PC today—possibly built directly into desks, refrigerators, and other objects, or carried around on your body or as some type of portable device. The primary interface will likely be the voice and most network connections will be wireless.

Chances are the Internet will continue to be used for an ever-growing number of day-to-day activities, such as shopping, making voice or video phone calls, controlling home appliances, ordering and downloading TV shows or movies, ordering groceries, paying bills, telecommuting, and so forth. It will also continue to be widely used for business purposes, and high bandwidth will allow a much higher level of real-time video communications facilitating even more use of telecommuting, videoconferencing, and home-based offices. A universal payment system for micropayments is likely to facilitate paying small fees for Web content. Ideally, all of an individual's micropayments would be combined into a single monthly bill.

This is an exciting time for the Internet. It is already firmly embedded in our society, and it will be exciting to see what becomes of all the breathtaking new applications and technological improvements on the horizon and how the Internet will continue to evolve.

What Did I Learn from Previewing?

Depending on your prior knowledge and experience, this chapter may be totally new or just "old hat" (though even computer "experts" often don't know much about the history of the Internet).

The headings and subheadings in the chapter are clear and straightforward. It is obvious that there are many terms to learn (if you didn't know them already). So pay special attention to the words that are written in boldface and italic type, and that are defined at the bottom of the page.

Return to the first page now and read the chapter carefully.

Mark the Text

Now that you have previewed and read the chapter, you are ready to master the ideas that it contains. As you read through a second time, mark the text—underline important ideas, write notes in the margin, circle key words, write question marks next to anything you don't understand. (To review how to mark the text, turn to page 421, "Learning Strategy III—Marking Text.") When you have finished marking the text, discuss any questions you have with your classmates. And remember—when exam time comes along, you only need to review the marks and comments you have written.

Vocabulary

In this textbook, all the key terms are written in boldface or italic type and some are then repeated at the bottom of the page. Note each word you didn't already know. It is a good idea to keep a section of your notebook for those words and meanings that you need to learn.

Test Questions

This chapter comes from a popular textbook used in many colleges around the country. Following are exam questions and projects actually given to students in Introduction to Computer courses. Test your understanding of what you read by answering the questions and completing one or more of the projects.

Key Terms

Directions: Match each key term on the left with the definition on the right that best describes it.

a. application service provider (ASP)

b. ARPANET

c. directory

d. Internet

1. A business or other organization that provides Internet access to others, typically for a fee.

2. A collection of categories that are used to locate appropriate Web pages from a search database.

3. A company that manages and distributes software-based services over the Internet.

4. An online activity for which bids are placed on items and the highest bidder purchases the item.

e. Internet content provider

f. Internet service provider (ISP)

g. keyword

h. online auction

i. online investing

j. online shopping

k. search engine

l. search site

m. World Wide Web

5. A person or an organization that provides Internet content.

6. A Web site designed to help users search for Web pages that match specified keywords or selected categories.

7. A word typed in a search box on a search site to locate information on the Internet.

8. Buying and selling stocks or other types of investments over the Internet.

9. Buying products or services over the Internet.

10. The collection of Web pages available through the Internet.

11. The largest and most well-known computer network linking millions of computers all over the world.

12. The predecessor of the Internet, named after the Advanced Research Projects Agency (ARPA), which sponsored its development.

13. A software program used by a search site to retrieve matching Web pages from a search database.

Quizzes and Exercises

1. True or False? When the Internet was first developed, it was called Mosaic.
2. True or False? On the Internet, an *access provider* and a *content provider* are essentially the same thing.
3. True or False? All search sites allow you to type keywords.
4. Fill in the blank: A(n) _____ is a software program used by a search site to retrieve matching Web pages from a search database.
5. Fill in the blank: With a(n) _____, people bid on products and the highest bidder is allowed to purchase the item.
6. List three different sets of keywords that could be used to search for information on how to maintain a trumpet.
7. What would each of the following searches look for?

   a. hot AND dogs _____
   b. snorkel* _____
   c. text: "Internet privacy" domain: gov _____

8. Select the Internet tool or application from the numbered list below that best matches each of the following situations and write the corresponding number in the blank to the left of each situation. (There is one extra tool or application.)

a. _____ To communicate with a friend in a different state.

b. _____ To pay a bill without writing a check.

c. _____ To play cards with a friend in a different state.

d. _____ To pay only as much as you specify for an item purchased through the Internet.

e. _____ To find Web pages containing information about growing your own Bonsai trees.

1. Online banking
2. E-mail
3. Online shopping
4. Online auction
5. Searching
6. Online gaming

PROJECTS

Hot Topics

1. **Internet Addiction**   Computer and Internet addiction can happen to computer users of all ages, races, income levels, and occupations. As with other addictions, computer or Internet use is said to be a problem when it adversely affects your life, such as causing problems with your health, your family, or your job. According to experts, Internet addiction is growing at a very fast pace and it is a global problem—one study in North Korea found that about 40% of the nation's middle and high school students are addicted to the Internet to some extent.

   For this project, research Internet addiction. Locate two organizations that have information about Internet addiction, including its causes, symptoms, and treatment. Do the organizations agree? Contact either your local mental health organization or school health center and see if Internet addiction is considered an actual mental health condition and, if so, what types of treatment are available in your area. Have you ever noticed behavior exhibited by a friend or relative that might suggest the beginnings of an addiction to any type of technology? Are there precautions individuals can take to avoid becoming addicted to the Internet? Do you think Internet addiction will increase or decrease in the future? At the conclusion of your research, prepare a one-page summary of your findings and submit it to your instructor.

2. **Online Travel Planning**   Planning and booking travel arrangements online is a very popular Internet activity today. There are a number of sites that claim to give discount rates on airplane tickets, hotel rooms, rental cars, and more. Some sites also offer information about weather, sites of interest, and more to help you plan your vacation.

   For this project, review two popular travel sites, such as Expedia.com and Travelocity.com, to see what services they offer and how easy, or difficult, it is to locate the information needed to plan and book a vacation via those sites. Select a destination and use the search facility located on one of the travel sites to obtain a quote for a particular flight on a particular day. Next, go to the Web site for the airline of the flight you were just quoted and use the site to obtain a quote for the same flight. Is there a difference in price or flight availability? Could you make a reservation online through both sites? Would you feel comfortable booking a vacation yourself online or are there other services that a travel agent could provide that you feel would be beneficial? Do you think these sites are most appropriate for making business travel plans or vacation plans, or are they suited to either? At the conclusion of your research, prepare a one-page summary of your findings and submit it to your instructor.

3. **Web Searching**   As discussed in the chapter, search sites can be used to find Web pages containing specific information and there are strategies that can be used to make Web searching an efficient and useful experience.

For this project, perform the following search tasks, answering the questions or printing the information as instructed below. After you have completed all four tasks, submit your results and printouts to your instructor. (Note: Some of the answers will vary from student to student.)

a. Go to the Google search site located at www.google.com and search for *rules*. How many pages were found? What is the name of the first page in the list of hits?

b. Next, search for *backgammon rules*. How many pages were found? Click on the first page and look for a picture of how a backgammon board is initially set up. When you find one, print the page. If you can't find one on that site, select different pages in the hit list or perform another search until you find the proper illustration and then print the page.

c. Perform a new search by clicking the link at the top of the Google page to go to the Advanced Search option. Use the form fields to perform a search for pages that contain all the words *hiking trails Sierra*, don't contain the word *horse,* and have the domain *gov.* After the list of Web pages matching your search criteria is displayed, record the actual search phrase that is now listed in the search box along with the name and URL of the first page displayed in the list of hits.

d. Use Google to search for a Web site that includes a telephone directory. Go to that site and supply the necessary information to search for yourself in the telephone directory. (If you are not currently listed in the phone book, search for a family member or friend that you know has a listed number.) Print the page displaying the requested information.

4. **Online Job Hunting** There are a number of Web sites dedicated to online career planning, posting and reviewing résumés and job announcements, listing average salary information for various positions, and other useful job-hunting tools.

For this project, visit at least two career-oriented Web sites (such as Monster.com or CareerBuilder.com) and review the types of information and services available from the perspective of both a job seeker and an employer. Are there fees for any of the services? If you post a résumé, is it available for anyone to see or are there restrictions on access? When it comes time for you to look for a new job, would you want to use one of these sites? Are the sites useful from an employer's perspective? List any advantages and disadvantages you can think of for using one of these sites to find a new job. Submit your findings and opinions to your instructor in the form of a short paper, not more than two pages in length.

5. **Online Term Papers** There are a large number of Web sites from which term papers on a variety of subjects can be purchased and downloaded. Although many of these sites state that they provide the papers for research purposes only and do not support plagiarism, it is not surprising that some dishonest students turn in purchased online term papers as their own work.

For this project, form a group to discuss the availability and ethical use of online term papers. Has anyone in the group ever visited one of these sites? If so, what services were offered through the site? Was it clear to the student that there was a way of utilizing the site's services without encountering plagiarism problems? Do the members of your group believe it is ethical to use online term papers for research? Can your group think of any other valuable (and legal) reasons for using these types of sites? If a term paper is purchased, instead of copying information without permission from a Web site, does turning it in as an original term paper still constitute plagiarism? Why or why not? What responsibility, if any, does your group feel the Web site has if its papers are used in an illegal or unethical manner? By referring to your course syllabus, student handbook, or school code of ethics, determine the penalties at your school for submitting a plagiarized term paper. Share your findings with the class in the form of a short presentation. The presentation should not exceed 10 minutes and should make use of one or more presentation aids such as the chalkboard, handouts, overhead transparencies, or a computer-based slide presentation (your instructor may provide additional requirements). Your group may also be asked to submit a summary of the presentation to your instructor.

LEARNING STRATEGIES

Strategies to help you get the most out of your reading.

LEARNING STRATEGY I—PREVIEWING

So many of us are frequent television viewers; we have become accustomed to letting information and entertainment come to us, without any effort on our part. But if we read the same way we watch TV, we will miss a lot. Reading well requires us to become partners with the author, to be active participants in the creation of meaning. There are many strategies we can use to be better readers. One of them, previewing, helps us get ready to read actively.

Does this sound familiar? It's your first week of a new semester. You've just spent a wheelbarrow-full of money on your new books. You are full of enthusiasm and have promised yourself you are really going to study hard this term. You open a book to do your first reading assignment and begin to study and what happens? Your mind begins to wander. You come to the end of a page, and even though you know your eyes have passed over every single word on the page, you have no idea what you've read.

Of course, this has happened to everyone: don't panic! There are ways to help yourself, but be prepared: reading for school is different from reading for pleasure. It requires more effort, more concentration—and a plan.

One reason we sometimes find it hard to absorb what we read is that we are reading materials totally new to us. This is especially true in college introductory courses where we are beginning a subject we may never have studied before. Have you noticed that it's easier to read a difficult, perhaps very technical, article about a subject you know well (say baseball, or computers, or fashion), than it is to read a very simple article on an unfamiliar topic (like ecology, perhaps, or astronomy)? The reason is simple: the more you know about a topic, the easier it is to read about that topic. In other words, the more background information you possess, the easier it is to read.

How is this going to help you when you're confronted with a college textbook on a subject you're not familiar with? Previewing the material before reading it is a first step toward acquiring background knowledge. Previewing will introduce you to the goals of the book, its structure, and helpful tools for learning that are contained in the book. Previewing will also "turn on the engine" of your brain, get you thinking, help you remember anything you *do* know about the topic, and, in general, get you ready to study.

Previewing the Textbook

These are the steps to follow to get ready to read your textbook:

First, read and think about the book's title. Are there any words in it you don't know? Look them up. Try to remember what you already know about the subject.

Second, quickly skim the preface or introduction. The author may give some helpful information about the goals and structure of the book.

Third, skim through the table of contents. This will show you the organization of the book and the topics that will be covered.

Fourth, check the table of contents for a glossary. It can appear either at the end of the book or after each chapter. A glossary can be very helpful; it contains definitions of important words used in the book. Using the glossary saves you the time of looking up words in the dictionary and the confusion that often results when a dictionary lists more than one definition; the glossary will list only one—the one used in the textbook.

Fifth, check the table of contents for an index. An index lists all the topics mentioned in the book in alphabetical order, plus their page numbers. Using an index can save lots of time when you are looking for information on one specific subject.

Sixth, check to see if there is an appendix. What does it contain? Sometimes the information in an appendix can be very helpful. For example, a history text's appendix may contain maps to help orient you; an accounting text's appendix may include sample financial statements.

Finally, look quickly through the book. Check to see if there are helpful features, such as summaries at the ends of chapters, or headings and subheadings.

Now spend a moment thinking about what you've just done. Are any of the topics in the title or table of contents familiar to you? Try to remember anything you can about them. Ask yourself what you expect to learn from this book.

You've probably spent four or five minutes previewing the textbook—a small investment of time that will speed up your studying in the long run.

Previewing Each Chapter

When you are ready to study a chapter in a textbook, you'll find previewing a very helpful strategy to "turn on" your brain, help you remember what you already know about the subject, and get ready to absorb new information. These are the steps to follow to prepare yourself to read a chapter:

First, read the title. Think about what it means. If you know anything about the subject, spend a moment to recapture from your memory as much information as you can. If there are any words you don't understand, look them up in the glossary or dictionary.

Second, read the headings and subheadings. This will show you the organization of the chapter and introduce you to the topics to be covered.

Third, see if there is a summary. If there is, read it carefully. It should provide you with a good overview of the chapter and will probably be the most useful part of the chapter later, when it comes time to review.

Fourth, check any questions or exercises before or after the chapter. These questions generally are meant to highlight the most important ideas in the chapter, so it is helpful to keep them in mind as you read.

Previewing the chapter will probably take you three or four minutes. Sometimes, students are impatient and say they'd rather spend these few minutes "really reading" rather than previewing. Studies have shown, however, that students who preview first will read faster, with better comprehension, and remember more. Not a bad return on a few minutes' investment!

Guide Questions

Directions: Write answers to the questions in your notebook or on a separate sheet of paper if your instructor wishes to collect them.

    1. a. Describe the problem many students have when they study a textbook.
      b. Do you ever have this problem?
    2. a. Which topic would you find it easier to read about: television or U.S. geography? Why?
      b. Which topic would be easier to read about, baseball or the Bible? Why?
    3. Explain why previewing can help you read better.
    4. List the steps in previewing a textbook.
    5. List the steps in previewing a chapter.

Application

Directions: Now that you have read and understood the ideas in "Previewing," it's important to use them at once. The following exercises, "Previewing a Textbook" and "Previewing a Chapter," will help you apply the methods you have just read about.

Previewing a Textbook

Directions: Choose one of the textbooks you will be using this term and answer the following questions about it.

    1. a. State the title of the textbook.
      b. Are there any words in the title you don't understand?
      c. Is the title clear? For example, why do you think *this* textbook is called *The Thoughtful Reader?*
    2. Name the author or authors.
    3. Name the course in which you will use this book.
    4. Who is the instructor of the course?
    5. Identify the company that published the book.
    6. Cite the publication date.
    7. Quickly skim the Preface (which may also be called Introduction, Foreword, or To the Student). What does the author say is his or her goal in writing the book?
    8. Turn to the table of contents. List three topics from the table of contents.

9. Are there any words in the table of contents that you don't understand? List them.
10. Does the book have a glossary?
11. Does the book have an index?
12. Does the book have an appendix? What does it contain?
13. Flip through the book. Do the chapters have any helpful features, such as boldface type, headings, summaries, questions, or illustrations? State which features the book has.
14. How much of the book are you expected to read this term? All of it? (Ask your instructor if you don't know.)

Previewing a Chapter

Directions: Preview a chapter of this book or a chapter from one of the other textbooks you are using this semester by answering the following questions. Your instructor will tell you which chapter to preview.

1. Read the title and subheadings (if any).
    a. Are there any words you don't know?
    b. What are they? Look them up and write their meanings.
    c. What topic will be discussed?
    d. What do you already know about the topic?
2. Does the chapter contain a summary?
3. Does the chapter include comprehension questions or other exercises? What are they?
4. List helpful features that the chapter contains, such as boldface type, illustrations, a glossary, margin notes, and so on.

LEARNING STRATEGY II—NARRATIVE AND EXPOSITION

Narrative

Much of the reading we do is the reading of NARRATIVES. To *narrate* is to tell a story. The fairy tales and bedtime stories parents read to their children are narratives. They have characters; things happen to these characters; usually a tone or feeling emerges in the story. Often there is a lesson for the reader to learn.

When you read a narrative, think about:

Who are the characters?

What happens to them?

What is the setting?

Does any special mood (e.g., happiness, sadness, anger, frustration, etc.) or tone emerge?

Is the author making a point? Is there something he/she wants us to remember from the story?

Is there a crisis? A turning point? What happens?

How relevant is the story to the world today? To you personally?

What are some examples of narrative that you have read?

Exposition

EXPOSITION is a type of writing that presents information and teaches ideas. Most textbooks use exposition: they present facts, theories, processes, etc.

Exposition is different from narrative. Narrative tends to be easier to read; we are all familiar with stories—we have heard them all our lives. The familiar form of narrative is simply a beginning, middle, and end. Generally it is easy to follow along, enjoying the ride, without too much worry about understanding and remembering the facts.

Exposition, on the other hand, can take many different forms. Also, your goal in reading exposition is usually different: you are reading to learn.

Different forms of exposition include:

a list of reasons

causes and effects

comparison and contrast

a process or method of doing something

analysis—WHY does something exist or happen

definition

example

When you are reading exposition think about:

What are the major ideas the author is presenting?

What kind of support does the author offer for these major ideas?

What form does the author use (e.g., list, cause and effect, etc.)?

What are you expected to learn and remember?

Most of the textbooks you will read in college are examples of exposition. What other exposition have you read recently?

LEARNING STRATEGY III—MARKING TEXT

Marking text is an excellent way to stay active and involved while studying. It's easy to fool ourselves into thinking that we're studying when all we are really doing is passing our eyes over print. This helps explain why sometimes we can read a whole chapter and realize at the end that we can't remember a single thing we've read! By being *physically* involved, by underlining, marking, and making notes, we are forced to be involved with the text and really pay attention to what we're reading. The more involved we are, the better chance we have of *remembering* what we read.

Why Mark the Text?

1. It forces us to be active, not passive, readers.
2. It gives us a chance to note any questions we have as we read along.
3. It is a real plus when it comes time to study for an exam.

How to Mark a Text

1. <u>Underlining</u> is the most common and popular way of marking. Underline ideas that are important. Ask yourself: Is this new information? Do I need to know and remember this? Will it possibly appear on an exam? Will it be needed for a writing assignment?
2. **But Don't Just Underline:** If you find a particularly important idea, indicate that by double underlining or put an asterisk (*) next to it. You want to distinguish really important points from all the other ideas you've underlined.   *
3. **Label your Underlining.** Next to your underlining, in the margin of the page, write a note explaining why you underlined it: this could be just a label or a few words summarizing it.   *Explain <u>why</u> you underlined*
4. (Circle) words you don't understand. Later, you can go back and look them up or ask the teacher or a classmate about them.
5. Write a **question mark (?)** next to ideas you don't understand. As with circled words, the mark will remind you to ask about them later.   ?

HELP! How Do I Decide What to Underline and Mark?

Here are some tips to help you mark your textbooks:

1. Read the whole chapter very quickly first without marking anything. If the chapter is long, divide it up into sections, and attack one section at a time. Don't try to mark the text on the first read-through—you will almost certainly make mistakes. It is impossible to know what is important (and thus what should be marked) if you don't first have a good feel for the author's message. If there are any "Objectives" or "Focus Questions" at the beginning of the chapter, be sure to read them.
2. On the second reading, underline and mark the information you think you'll need to understand and remember. Don't forget to circle unfamiliar words and put question marks next to confusing ideas.

3. Keep the title and any sub-headings in mind as you read along.
4. Pay special attention to the first sentences of paragraph as you read. Major points are often stated in the first sentence.
5. Note any words in **boldface,** *italics,* or <u>underlined</u>. If the author gives special attention to these words, you should, too.
6. Look for "signal words" that often introduce major ideas, for example: *first, second, third,* and so on; *next; furthermore; another; finally; in addition; therefore; to summarize.*
7. As you underline new ideas, new terminology, important concepts, write notes in the margin to explain why you've underlined.

    Warning:
Be careful not to mark too much! If you underline too much, it is just as useless as not marking anything at all.

Practice
Try out all you've learned by marking the text on the next page.

GESTURES

Gestures are an important form of nonverbal communication. Gestures are usually defined as movements of the arms and hands, but can include whole body movements and posture, too. People who study language and communication say that humans communicated through gestures for many thousands of years before spoken language developed. In fact, they are so basic to our nature that people who have been blind from birth use them.

There are three main types of gestures. The first is called **illustrators**. Illustrators accompany speech and add meaning to the spoken word, but do not have meaning all by themselves. The next time you ask someone for directions, try to notice all the gestures they use—pointing, waving, stepping forward and backward. Or watch people on the phone, waving their hands and moving their heads and body, raising their eyebrows, smiling or frowning, even though obviously no one can see the movements. Without the spoken words, the gestures by themselves are meaningless.

Certain cultures are known to be more expressive with their hands than others. People from the Mediterranean, such as Italians, French and Spanish use their hands more than do Americans or English. Americans, do, however, use illustrators often when they are excited or angry. Most of us use illustrators and people can often be identified just by their gestures. Thus, impersonators use gestures when they imitate famous people. Students usually identify the gestures of their teachers and can imitate them easily.

A second type of gestures is called **emblems**. These are movements that have a direct meaning and can function as replacements for words. Nodding the head means "yes," shaking the head means "no," a flat palm aimed at the listener means "stop" and of course everybody knows the meaning of a raised middle finger.

A third category is the **adaptors**. This is a quite different type of gestures; they are unconscious body movements made in response to something in the environment. For example, we might fiddle with our hair or tap a foot when something makes us feel nervous. We shiver or fold our arms around our body when it's cold. These movements are not consciously intended to convey meaning to others, though sometimes the same gestures can be used on purpose. We might cross our arms around our body to show we feel "cold" toward another person or that we feel the need to protect ourselves from him or her. We might tap our foot to signal impatience or examine our fingernails to show ennui.

It is interesting to note that *too few* gestures can be as significant as *too many*. Limited gesturing may signal a lack of interest, sadness, boredom, or low enthusiasm.

It is important to remember that gestures, while they may not signal a direct, concrete meaning, are important to understanding in interpersonal communication.

How Well Did You Do?
Compare your text marking with this model.

GESTURES

* Main idea → Gestures are an important form of nonverbal communication. Gestures are usu- ** definition*
ally defined as movements of the arms and hands, but can include whole body
movements and posture, too. People who study language and communication say   *blind people*
that humans communicated through gestures for many thousands of years before   *use gestures*
spoken language developed. In fact, they are so basic to our nature that people
who have been blind from birth use them.

There are three main types of gestures. The first is called **illustrators.** Illus- ** 3 Types:*
trators accompany speech and add meaning to the spoken word, but do not have
meaning all by themselves. The next time you ask someone for directions, try to   *(1) illustrators*
notice all the gestures they use—pointing, waving, stepping forward and backward. Or watch people on the phone, waving their hands and moving their heads
and body, raising their eyebrows, smiling or frowning, even though obviously no
one can see the movements. Without the spoken words, the gestures by themselves
are meaningless.

Some cultures   Certain cultures are known to be more expressive with their hands than oth-
more expressive ers. People from the Mediterranean, such as Italians, French and Spanish use their
with hands   hands more than do Americans or English. Americans, do, however, use illustrators often when they are excited or angry. Most of us use illustrators and people
can often be identified just by their gestures. Thus, impersonators use gestures
when they imitate famous people. Students usually identify the gestures of their
teachers and can imitate them easily.

A second type of gestures is called **emblems.** These are movements that have *(2) emblems*
a direct meaning and can function as replacements for words. Nodding the head
means "yes," shaking the head means "no," a flat palm aimed at the listener means
"stop" and of course everybody knows the meaning of a raised middle finger.

A third category is the **adaptors.** This is a quite different type of gestures;   *(3) adaptors*
they are unconscious body movements made in response to something in the environment. For example, we might fiddle with our hair or tap a foot when something makes us feel nervous. We shiver or fold our arms around our body when
it's cold. These movements are not consciously intended to convey meaning to
others, though sometimes the same gestures can be used on purpose. We might
cross our arms around our body to show we feel "cold" toward another person or
that we feel the need to protect ourselves from him or her. We might tap our foot
to signal impatience or examine our fingernails to show (ennui)   *?*
Too few
It is interesting to note that *too few* gestures can be as significant as *too many.*   *vs*
Limited gesturing may signal a lack of interest, sadness, boredom, or low   *Too many*
enthusiasm.

It is important to remember that gestures, while they may not signal a
conclusion → direct, concrete meaning, are important to understanding in interpersonal
communication.

LEARNING STRATEGY IV—WRITING A SUMMARY

What Is a Summary?

A summary is a brief, concise statement, in your own words, of the most important points of a passage (a chapter, an article, an essay, a paragraph, etc.).

Did you know that you are already an expert summarizer? You summarize in your day-to-day life all the time. For example, if a friend asks you about the two-hour movie you saw last night, you don't spend two hours telling her—you summarize. (You'd lose your friend pretty quickly if you didn't.) If you e-mail or write a letter to a relative telling him what you did last week, you summarize. Another example of summarizing is when you write down a telephone message. Can you think of some other examples?

As an expert summarizer, all you need to do now is learn to apply the skill you already have to your college reading and writing.

Why Summarize?

Summary writing offers college students many advantages. The first is that it forces you to truly understand what you have read. If you don't understand, you will not be able to put the text into your own words. Second, writing a summary will help you to remember what you have read. Third, the summaries you write of your textbook chapters or articles are excellent tools for studying when exam time comes along. Wouldn't it be easier to reread your own summaries than to plow through the entire chapter again? Finally, writing summaries will help you to improve your writing skills, because a good summary must be clear and coherent, just as we would like all of our writing to be.

When you write a summary, begin by previewing, reading, and marking your text:

1. Preview and then read the chapter very quickly first without marking anything. If the chapter is long, divide it up into sections, and attack one section at a time. Don't try to mark the text on the first read-through—you will almost certainly make mistakes. It is impossible to know what is important (and thus what should be marked) if you don't first have a good feel for the author's message.

2. On the second reading, underline and mark the information you think you'll need to understand and remember. Don't forget to circle unfamiliar words and put question marks next to confusing ideas. As you underline new ideas, new terminology, important concepts, write notes in the margin to explain why you've underlined.

When you have finished marking the text, follow these steps and write the summary:

3. Determine what is the main idea. Is it directly stated in the selection? Or do you have to compose a main idea yourself? In either case, write the main idea.

> What is a main idea? A main idea (also called the thesis, the central idea, the main point) is an umbrella sentence. We call it an umbrella sentence because, just like a real umbrella, it "covers" everything beneath it. The main idea is large enough to "cover" all the other ideas in the reading selection.

4. Follow the main idea with the important ideas you have underlined or marked. Use your own words as much as possible. This is your first draft.
5. Now proofread your draft: check to make sure you have included all the major ideas, that you have not included unnecessary details (small examples, lengthy explanation, repetitions, etc.) Check your grammar and spelling.
6. Write the final draft.

Below is an example of how you would write a summary of the article "Human Relations in Business."

Step 1—Preview, then read the article quickly.

HUMAN RELATIONS IN BUSINESS

Lorence Long

LaGuardia Community College

Think of the human relations challenges in business! Here are just a few:

Telling the boss she is wrong, without getting her angry;

Encouraging a subordinate to tell you what you need to know to solve a problem that involves your own behavior;

Helping a customer to make a purchase, without overdoing it;

Expressing your criticism of a peer who is not carrying his share of the work, without turning the rest of the office against you (or him);

Handling your supervisor's overtures, which the supervisor says will improve your position in the office, but which might cost you some self-respect.

Some students (and some instructors) may focus so intently on the skill and knowledge of preparing for the business world that they neglect the human relations dimensions of the work situation.

Recent research indicates that human relations are very important in business. Last October, the *Wall Street Journal* asked 782 company chief executives to identify the most important personal traits linked to success. The executives specified "integrity" and "ability to get along with others" as by far the most important success-related characteristics.

Further, when these same people were asked to identify the failings of weak managers in their firms, they cited "inability to understand others" and "inability to work with others" as two of three most common failings. (The most common fault was described as "limited point of view.")

Many people think that they are constitutionally unable to learn how to relate to people more effectively. "I'm just a numbers person," they say in explaining their uncomfortable dealings with others. But human relations skills are like any others: they can be learned, and practice helps to improve performance.

One skill that is helpful in working with people is being able to observe accurately. Most of the time, we see events around us from a very personal viewpoint. Our observations are usually laced with assumptions and inferences that distort our ability to see what is happening. Practice in accurate observation helps us to respond more appropriately to the people around us.

A second skill is that of listening. A major corporation—Sperry—has been spreading across the advertising pages its conviction that listening to each other is the most important skill we can learn. We can learn to hear what the other person is saying without defensiveness or judgmental attitudes. We can learn ways to respond, so that the other person knows that we have heard what he or she was trying to say.

A third area for learning in human relations is that of assertiveness: expressing our needs, feelings, and ideas clearly, but without stifling others or putting them down. Many interpersonal problems arise from our inability to say what is on our minds in a way that other people—bosses, subordinates, peers—can accept.

A fourth area is related to our ability to recognize the culturally conditioned values of people we work with, and to be able to take them into account. Especially when these values clash with our own, we need to be sensitive to the implications of this conflict for our work.

Research indicates that human relations skills are as important as any other to business success and are worthy of serious study.

Step 2—Reread the article, and mark the text.

HUMAN RELATIONS IN BUSINESS

Think of the human relations challenges in business! Here are just a few:

Telling the boss she is wrong, without getting her angry;

Encouraging a subordinate to tell you what you need to know to solve a problem that involves your own behavior;

Helping a customer to make a purchase, without overdoing it;

Expressing your criticism of a peer who is not carrying his share of the work, without turning the rest of the office against you (or him);

Handling your supervisor's overtures, which the supervisor says will improve your position in the office, but which might cost you some self-respect.

Intro

Some students (and some instructors) may focus so intently on the skill and knowledge of preparing for the business world that they neglect the human relations *dimensions* of the work situation.

aspects?

Recent research indicates that human relations are very important in business. Last October, the *Wall Street Journal* asked 782 company chief executives to identify the most important personal *traits* linked to success. The executives specified "integrity" and "ability to get along with others" as by far the most important success-related characteristics.

characte-ristics?

Further, when these same people were asked to identify the failings of weak managers in their firms, they cited "inability to understand others" and "inability to work with others" as two of three most common failings. (The most common fault was described as "limited point of view.")

Many people think that they are constitutionally unable to learn how to relate to people more effectively. "I'm just a numbers person," they say in explaining their uncomfortable dealings with others. But human relations skills are like any others: they can be learned, and practice helps to improve performance.

main idea

One skill that is helpful in working with people is being able to observe accurately. Most of the time, we see events around us from a very personal viewpoint. Our observations are usually laced with assumptions and inferences that distort our ability to see what is happening. Practice in accurate observation helps us to respond more appropriately to the people around us.

1st skill: observing

A second skill is that of listening. A major corporation—Sperry—has been spreading across the advertising pages its conviction that listening to each other is the most important skill we can learn. We can learn to hear what the other person is saying without defensiveness or judgmental attitudes. We can learn ways to respond, so that the other person knows that we have heard what he or she was trying to say.

2nd skill: listening

A third area for learning in human relations is that of assertiveness: expressing our needs, feelings, and ideas clearly, but without stifling others or putting them down. Many interpersonal problems arise from our inability to say what is on our minds in a way that other people—bosses, subordinates, peers—can accept.

3rd skill: assertiveness

A fourth area is related to our ability to recognize the culturally conditioned values of people we work with, and to be able to take them into account. Especially when these values clash with our own, we need to be sensitive to the implications of this conflict for our work.

4th skill: be sensitive to others' values

Research indicates that human relations skills are as important as any other to business success and are worthy of serious study.

Step 3—Write the main idea.

In this case the author has kindly written a main idea statement for us. The first sentence of the third paragraph is an "umbrella" sentence that "covers" all the information in the article:

> *. . . human relations are very important in business*

Changing it to our own words, we can write our own main idea:

> *Human relation skills are important to success in the business world.*

> Remember—a main idea is an umbrella sentence. Like a real umbrella, it should be large enough to "cover" all the other ideas in the reading selection.

Step 4—Follow the main idea with the important points you noted when you marked the text. Paraphrase them.

These skills can be learned and improved with practice. The first important human relations skill is the ability to observe accurately. The second important skill is listening well. A third skill is assertiveness—expressing ourselves without hurting or offending others. A fourth skill is the ability to recognize and appreciate the values of other people, especially if they differ from our own.

Steps 5 and 6—Proofread and then write the final draft. This is how your summary would look:

Human relation skills are important to success in the business world. These skills can be learned and improved with practice. The first important human relations skill is the ability to observe accurately. The second important skill is listening well. A third skill is assertiveness—expressing ourselves without hurting or offending others. A fourth skill is the ability to recognize and appreciate the values of other people, especially if they differ from our own.

LEARNING STRATEGY V—DIRECTION WORDS

When your instructor asks you to *paraphrase* information or to *define* a term or to *analyze* a problem, do you know exactly what to do? Words like *paraphrase, define,* and *analyze* are called **direction words.** These words are used frequently in college. You will see them on exams and homework assignments and hear them in class lectures. Knowing their meanings and how to use them will help you to answer questions correctly. The following is a list of the most common direction words and their meanings. An example of how each word is used is given. Study the examples to make sure you understand each word.

Analyze—To break down into parts in order to better understand the whole

> Q: Analyze the decision to increase property taxes in the town of East Liniment.

> A: The population of East Liniment has increased 20% over the past five years. The majority of residents are young families. This has necessitated building a new elementary school and a new high school. In addition, a two million dollar expansion has been proposed for the town library. Increasing the currently modest property tax rate was felt by the local officials to be the best source of revenue to meet these needs.

Cite—To name or to quote (as a fact, authority, or example)

> Q: Cite the author of the "Law of Effect."

> A: Edward L. Thorndike is the author of the "Law of Effect."

Classify—To arrange according to some stated category

> Q: Classify the patient's stage of development according to Erikson's stages of development.

> A: According to Erikson's stages of development, this patient is an infant, and thus is dependent on others for care.

Compare—To state the similarities between two things; **contrast**—to state differences between two things

> Q: Compare and contrast your role as a parent with your role as a student.

> A: Both roles require a sense of responsibility and commitment. Guiding, advising, and supporting your children in every way requires constant vigilance and attentiveness, which at times is difficult when you feel tired and burdened with other responsibilities.

> As a parent, you cannot always foresee and plan for unexpected events. Your son's soccer game or an unexpected illness can arise which require that you change previous plans. As a student, once you become

familiar with the course requirements at the start of the semester, you can work out a fairly consistent schedule, which includes class times, study times, and other school associated activities. However, despite the differences, both roles require self-discipline and the ability to be flexible.

Define—To give a concise, clear meaning as briefly as possible (as in a dictionary)

Q: Define microbiology.

A: Microbiology is the study of life too small to be seen with the naked eye.

Describe—To paint a picture using words

Q: Describe the plants on the street where you live.

A: The street has an abundance of trees and flowering plants. The trees are deciduous that is, they shed their leaves in the fall. However, the change in leaf color is not as dramatic as one sees farther north. At the base of each tree is a simple fence enclosing a variety of different types of flowering plants—tulips, pansies. Several of the tenants living on the first floor of the apartment houses have placed window boxes containing mostly geraniums, pansies, and ivy.

Diagram—Draw, chart, or graph, including labeling and a brief explanation or description for clarity

Q: Diagram the route from East Liniment Community College to your home at 11-22 46th Street.

A:

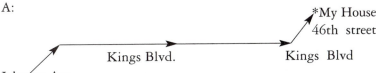

*My House
46th street

Kings Blvd.   Kings Blvd

Johnson Ave.
*East Liniment Community College

Evaluate—To examine something and then make a judgment about it

Q: Evaluate your decision to work part time and attend college full time.

A: My decision was both easy and difficult. My full-time job was well-paying and I never had to think about having enough money for new clothes, a movie, and eating in a restaurant. At the same time, opportunities for further advancement were limited. I realized that further education was the only solution to expanding my opportunities. My decision involved a compromise. It required that I cut back on non-essential purchases and plan a more disciplined budget. However, I am already realizing that the sacrifices I am making are well worth my efforts.

Explain—To make something understandable, to give reasons for something

Q: Explain why you decided to enroll as a student at East Liniment Community College.

A: I decided to enroll as a computer science major at East Liniment Community College for several reasons. I have always enjoyed mathematics and spend a lot of time trying to understand how the computer works. My talents seem to be strong in the areas of mathematics and technology. In addition, the job market in computer programming is wide open. I feel that when I graduate, I will have the opportunity not only to work in a field that I enjoy but also that I will be well compensated financially.

Identify/Name—To state something; to give the name of something

Q: Identify four students in your science laboratory.

A: John Jackson, Ludmilla Marcus, Edward Rodriguez, and Jane Simon are all students in my science lab.

Illustrate—To make something clear by giving examples

Q. Illustrate how studying mathematics can help you in your daily life

A. I was making a recipe that would yield six servings but I only wanted to make it for two people. I needed my math to figure out how to adjust the amounts of all the ingredients.

List—To present information in an itemized series or table

Q: List the nine stages of development from infancy to old age.

A: The nine stages of development are: infancy, early childhood, preschool, middle childhood, adolescence, early adulthood, middle adulthood, late middle age, late adulthood.

Paraphrase—To put something into your own words

Q: Paraphrase the following quote taken from your textbook. "Alveoli are air sacs that make up the lung tissue; within them, oxygen and carbon dioxide are exchanged between the lungs and blood."

A: The lungs are the organs where oxygen and carbon dioxide are exchanged with the blood. The specific structures in the lungs where the exchange takes place are called alveoli. These represent tiny air sacs.

React—To state your view of an issue and the reasons you feel the way you do

Q: React to the news that tuition will rise in the coming year

A: I am distressed and angry at the news of a rise in tuition. We students are already suffering financially, with the high cost of living in general, high tuition costs, the price of textbooks, and more. An increase in tuition may mean some students will have to work more hours and their studies will suffer. Some may have to drop out of school.

Summarize—State the important ideas in a condensed form, presenting only the main points or highlights

Q: Summarize the issues addressed by the two presidential candidates at the debate.

A: The major issues addressed by the presidential candidates in the debates included the future of social security, the future of Medicare, the possibility of prescription drug coverage, and tax rebates for childcare. Tax cuts and the budget deficit were also discussed.

Practice Using Direction Words

Directions: Read and study each direction word and its definition and example. When you are convinced that you know what each word requires, do the following exercise.

1. *Identify* three authors of reading selections on the topic of *culture* in this textbook.
2. *Illustrate* what is meant by the statement "Life is 10 percent what happens to you and 90 percent how you react to it."
3. *Describe* one of the other students in this class.
4. *Define* education.
5. *Paraphrase* the old saying "Genius is 90 percent perspiration and 10 percent inspiration."
6. *Explain* the value of good communication skills.
7. *Name* the instructors of the courses you are taking now.
8. *Compare* and *contrast* your experiences in high school and in college.
9. *Summarize* the requirements for your major as they are stated in the school catalog.
10. *List* three courses outside your major that you would like to take.
11. *React* to the statement "Every student in the United States should study a foreign language."
12. *Cite* three reasons that some college students drop out of school.

LEARNING STRATEGY VI—FIGURATIVE LANGUAGE

Figurative language is used so much in English that it is hard to imagine a conversation in which at least one example does not appear. "The line at the bursar's office was a zoo!" "The air conditioning broke down and the office was an oven." "My little brother is a pain in the neck!" Stevie Wonder sang, "You are the sunshine of my life. . . ." "Excuse me, I have a frog in my throat." "The bottom line is you can't pass this course if you don't pass the final exam."

One type of figurative language, the simile, is extremely common. Similes generally use the words *like* or *as*. Similes usually involve a simple comparison: "Whew! I worked like a dog last night!" "She eats like a horse, but stays as thin as a rail." "The news of the air crash spread like wildfire." "Searching for my dropped contact lens at the beach was like looking for a needle in a haystack." Forrest Gump observed that "Life is like a box of chocolates; you never know what you're going to get."

Another type of figurative language, the metaphor, is a bit more complex. Like the simile, it involves a comparison of one thing to another, but in a pure metaphor, the comparison is more complicated, more layered. Think about Shakespeare's *Romeo and Juliet.* As Romeo sees Juliet come onto her balcony at dawn, he says, "What light through yonder window breaks? It is the east and Juliet is the sun!" Romeo is comparing Juliet to the sun, but it is not a simple comparison. If Romeo compares his beloved to the sun, it is not the same as simply saying she is bright or warm. What does his metaphor make us think, make us feel? The sun is so many things: it gives light; it is bright; it gives warmth; it is beautiful; it is dependable. The sun is the giver of life! So, when Romeo says these scant four words, "Juliet is the sun," we learn a wealth of things about his feelings for her. Metaphor allows us to say a lot in few words; it makes our speech and writing so much more interesting.

Figurative Language in Poetry

Below are examples of figurative language written by famous poets. Explain what you think each poem means.

> *Hope is the thing with feathers*
> *That perches on the soul,*
> *And sings the tune without the words,*
> *And never stops at all.*
>
> —Emily Dickinson

> *A wicked whisper came and made my heart as dry as dust.*
>
> —Samuel Taylor Coleridge

> *Last summer you left*
> *my life quivering*
> *like a battlefield.*
> *I wore headaches like garments.*
>
> —Colleen McElroy

An aged man is but a paltry thing,
a tattered coat upon a stick, . . .

—William Butler Yeats

Metaphor in Prose

Here are some famous examples of metaphor by prose writers. Explain what each one means.

Hope is a good breakfast, but it is a bad supper.

—Francis Bacon

Speak softly and carry a big stick.

—President Theodore Roosevelt

A house divided against itself cannot stand.

—President Abraham Lincoln

What comparison is each of these writers making? What effect does the comparison have on the reader?

An Exercise in Understanding Figurative Language in Poetry

Below are two famous poems written by the great American writer Langston Hughes. Discuss each of the poems in view of what you have learned about figurative language.

ISLAND

Wave of sorrow,
Do not drown me now:

I see the island
Still ahead somehow.

I see the island
And its sands are fair:

Wave of sorrow,
Take me there.

HARLEM

What happens to a dream deferred?

Does it dry up
like a raisin in the sun?
Or fester like a sore—
And then run?

Does it stink like rotten meat?
Or crust and sugar over—
like a syrupy sweet?

*Maybe it just sags
like a heavy load.*

Or does it explode?

What comparisons does the writer make? What do you think his poems mean? Why do you think he used the comparisons he did?

An Exercise in Recognizing Figurative Language

Over the next few days, keep in mind what you have learned about figurative language. As you read the newspaper, magazines, listen to the radio, watch TV, and talk with friends, be aware of the many metaphors we use in everyday life. Keep a notebook with you to jot down the metaphors and similes you hear and read. When you have a good collection, create a chart like the one below. List the metaphors and similes in the left column and their sources in the right column. There are two examples in the chart to get you started. You should collect at least ten examples of your own.

Examples of Figurative Language	Sources
1. "The city woke up under a blanket of snow this morning."	The weatherman on Channel 4 said this on February 2nd at 6:20 p.m.
2. Cubs Sweep Series with White Sox	This was a headline in the sports section of the August 14th Chicago Tribune.
3.	
4.	
5.	
6.	
7.	
8.	
9.	
10.	
11.	
12.	

LEARNING STRATEGY VII—TEST-TAKING

The *test!* That word every student fears and dreads. Yet, in a way, a test is a great opportunity. It is the place where we can demonstrate, both to ourselves and to the instructor, that we have *learned,* that we know what we need to know. Most of us, however, are not good test-takers. We haven't learned the strategies of successful test-taking. Knowing these strategies can make a big difference in our performance.

Here are a few tips to improve your test-taking skills.

Before the Test

1. Study smart. Review the information in this textbook in Learning Strategy III. If you have marked your textbook chapters well, you have already gone a long way toward success on a test. You have decided what material is important and what is not. Review your marked text. Then, if you have class notes, reread them. Are some of the ideas you underlined in the text repeated in class notes? If they are, be sure to review them carefully.

   Did the instructor give you guidelines for studying? Remember, you have the right to ask your teacher what the exam will cover and what form it will take. If your instructor did not tell you, ask!

2. Study early. Don't wait until the night before. If you begin to study early you will avoid that panicky feeling that comes with last-minute cramming. Also, if you come across something you don't understand, you will have time to find the answer.

3. Take advantage of the practice tests that many textbooks offer. Or, your instructor may make old exams available to you. Getting comfortable with the format of the test will be a big step toward success. Test-taking is a skill—practice helps.

The Day of the Test

1. Come on time. (But don't come too early.) Arriving late to a test is a sure way to increase your anxiety, not to mention the time you lose. But if you arrive too early, you may become nervous as you wait. Try to arrive a few minutes before the test is scheduled to begin. Organize your belongings and get comfortable. Take deep breaths and visualize yourself doing well. After all, if you have studied well, there is no reason you won't perform well.

2. Come prepared. Bring a watch. Will you need your own paper? A calculator? A dictionary? Do you have a pencil or a pen?

3. Listen carefully to the instructor's (or monitor's) directions. If there is an answer form, make sure you know how to fill it out. Is it OK to guess? Or will wrong answers count against you?

4. Read all the directions on the test before you begin to answer.

5. Preview the entire test. How many questions are there? Compute how much time you should spend on each one. For example, an exam consisting of 40 multiple-choice questions with a 20-minute time limit means you have 30 seconds to spend on each item.

6. Don't spend too much time on one item. If you don't know the answer, don't waste time puzzling over it. Move on to the next question. If you have time at the end, go back to questions you did not know.

7. If you finish early, check over your answers. If you see an obvious mistake, change it. But beware—most studies show that your first answer is usually the correct one.

8. Don't let other test-takers distract you. Try to sit where you will not see other people, usually near the front of the room. Turn your chair toward the wall if you can. The more you insulate yourself from other people, the less distracted you will be. Sometimes another student will finish the test very early. Ignore it. You can't know why that person finished so quickly. Perhaps he or she did not study and simply gave up.

9. Learn from the results. When you get your test back, use it as a learning tool. Look at each item you got wrong and figure out why it was wrong. Did most of the questions you answered wrong come from information presented in class lectures? Perhaps you need to work on your note-taking skills. If most came directly from the text, you will know where to concentrate your studying next time.

GLOSSARY

abstract   An abstract word refers to a quality, condition, or idea that cannot be perceived by the senses. Abstract is the opposite of concrete. Examples of abstract words: love, happiness, justice, truth, fear.

allusion   An allusion is a reference to another idea, something the writer assumes the reader is familiar with.

analogy   An analogy is a comparison of one thing to another thing. Analogies are generally used to explain the nature of something unfamiliar to us by comparing it to something we already know. For example, in the novel *Being There,* author Jerzy Kosinski describes the economy by using the analogy of a garden; just as there are cycles (or seasons) in a garden, there are cycles (times of growth and times of stagnation) in the economy. Note that, while analogies can be helpful in understanding a difficult concept, they are not always *true.* (The economy and the garden are quite different things.) Other examples of analogies: comparing the human mind to a computer, the heart to a pump, life to a journey.

annotation   Annotation means marking the text by underlining, writing comments, noting questions, etc.

antonym   An antonym is a word that is opposite in meaning from another word. Examples of pairs of antonyms: hot /cold; high/low; sharp/dull.

argument   In discussions, an argument is a reason given to support a position or opinion.

concrete   Something concrete is something you can see, touch, hear, smell, or taste. Concrete is the opposite of abstract. Examples of concrete words: chair, wine, elephant.

connotation   Connotation refers to the emotional effect a particular word or phrase has on a person. Two words can have the same denotation, but different connotations. For example, *thin* and *skinny* have basically the same denotation, but different connotations. Likewise, *fat, chubby, heavy-set,* and *full-figured* all have the same basic meaning but arouse different feelings or attitudes in the mind of the listener or reader. Compare to *denotation.*

denotation   The denotation of a word is its literal, dictionary meaning.

exposition   Exposition is a form of writing whose purpose is to present information. It can take many forms. Exposition contrasts with narrative, which tells a story.

jargon   Jargon is the specialized language of a specific group or profession. The fields of law, medicine, and computers are well-known for their jargon. The jargon of a group is usually unfamiliar to people outside the group.

main idea   In an essay or article, the main idea is a brief statement of the author's main point or thesis.

metaphor   A metaphor is a figure of speech that compares one thing to another by saying that thing *is* the other. Shakespeare is the source of many of our most familiar metaphors: "All the world's a stage"; "What's in a name? . . . a rose by any other name would smell as sweet." Calderón de la Barca said "Life is a dream." Other familiar metaphors: "Life is just a bowl of cherries"; "Time is money."

narrative   Narrative is a form of writing that tells a story.

oxymoron   An oxymoron is a word or phrase that combines two opposites in meaning. Examples: "James Bond was a well-known secret agent"; "The menu offered fresh-frozen jumbo shrimp" (two oxymorons in one phrase). A famous oxymoron is the Greek word *sophomore,* which is a combination of two words: *wise* and *fool.*

paradox   A paradox is a statement that seems to contradict itself, but is nevertheless true. One of the most famous paradoxes in literature is the opening of *A Tale of Two Cities,* by Charles Dickens: "It was the best of times, it was the worst of times, it was the age of wisdom, it was the age of foolishness, it was the epoch of belief, it was the epoch of incredulity, it was the season of Light, it was the season of Darkness, it was the spring of hope, it was the winter of despair, we had everything before us, we had nothing before us, we were all going direct to Heaven, we were all going direct the other way . . ."

simile   A simile is a figure of speech in which a comparison is made using the words *like* or *as.* Examples: "I was as hungry as a bear"; "Her tears flowed like wine."

summary   A summary is a concise restatement in your own words of another writer's ideas.

symbol   A symbol is something (e.g., an object, a person, a word, a number) that stands for, or represents, something else.

synonym   A synonym is a word that means the same as another word. Examples of synonym pairs: old/elderly, doctor/physician, teacher/instructor, student/pupil.

thesis   In an essay, the thesis is a brief statement of the main point of the essay.

CREDITS

This page constitutes an extension of the copyright page. We have made every effort to trace the ownership of all copyrighted material and to secure permission from copyright holders. In the event of any question arising as to the use of any material, we will be pleased to make the necessary corrections in future printings. Thanks are due to the following authors, publishers, and agents for permission to use the material indicated.

Unit 1. 2: "What True Education Should Do" by Sydney J. Harris from *Chicago Daily News*, 1964. Reprinted by permission. **6:** "How to Mark a Book" by Mortimer Adler from *Saturday Review*, July 6, 1940. Reprinted by permission of the author. **11:** "The First Book" from *On the Bus with Rosa Parks*, W.W. Norton & Co., copyright © 1999 by Rita Dove. Reprinted by permission of the author. **12:** *Black Boy* by Richard Wright, chapter 8, p. 149-56. Copyright © 1937, 1942, 1944, 1945 by Richard Wright; renewed © 1973 by Ellen Wright. Reprinted by permission of HarperCollins Publishers, Inc. **19:** "Traveling" from *Just As I Thought* by Grace Paley. Copyright © 1998 by Grace Paley. Reprinted by permission of Farrar, Straus and Giroux, LLC. **21:** "Fire and Ice" by Robert Frost. Reprinted by permission of Henry Holt & Co. **23:** "Becoming Educated" from *Becoming Educated* by Barbara Jordan, pp. 89-93. Reprinted by permission. **27:** "An Unrelenting Drive, and a Harvard Degree" by Jacques Steinberg, *New York Times*, May 17, 2000. Copyright © 2000 by the New York Times Co. Reprinted by permission. **32:** "Long in Dark, Afghan Women Say to Read Is Finally to See," by Carlotta Gall, *New York Times*, Sept. 22, 2002. Copyright © 2002 by the New York Times Co. Reprinted by permission. **35:** "Overcoming an Invisible Handicap" by Thomas Cottle, *Psychology Today*, January 1980. Reprinted by permission of *Psychology Today*. Copyright © 1980 by Sussex Publishers, Inc. **39:** "The Teacher Who Changed My Life" by Nicholas Gage, *Parade Magazine*, Dec. 17, 1989. Copyright © 1989 Nicholas Gage. All rights reserved. Reprinted by permission of Parade Publications. **44:** "When Gadgets Get in the Way" by Lisa Guernsey, *New York Times*, Aug. 19, 2004. Copyright © 2004 by the New York Times Co. Reprinted by permission.

Unit 2. 51: "Culture" by Clyde Kluckhohn from *Mirror for Man: The Relation of Anthropology to Modern Life*, 1959. Reprinted by permission. **64:** "Values" by Ian Robertson from *Sociology*, 3rd ed., by Ian Robertson, Worth Publishers, New York, 1987. Reprinted by permission of the author. **70:** "Unity in Diversity" from *Sociology* by Donald Light and Suzanne Keller. Reprinted by permission of Random House, Inc. **77:** "Everyday People" by Matt Crenson, Associated Press, July 2000. Reprinted by permission. **82:** "Africa's Lost Tribe Hopes to

Respirator" by Elissa Ely, *The Boston Globe*, July 1989. Reprinted by permission.

Unit 6. 317: Chapter excerpt from *Sociology in Our Time*, 5th ed. by Diana Kendall. Copyright © Thomson Higher Education. **331:** Chapter excerpt from *Looking Out/Looking In: Interpersonal Communication*, 8th ed. by Ronald B. Adler and Neil Towne. Copyright © 1996 by Thomson Higher Education. **341:** Chapter excerpt from *Sociology in a Changing World*, 3rd ed. by William Kornblum. Copyright © 1994 by Thomson Higher Education. **363:** Chapter excerpt from *Contemporary Business*, 11th ed. by Louis E. Boone and David L. Kurtz. Copyright © by Thomson Higher Education. **384:** Chapter excerpt from *Understanding Computers Today and Tomorrow*, 10th ed. by Deborah Morley and Charles S. Parker. Copyright © by Thomson Higher Education.

Image Credits. 319: AP/Photo/Lawrence Journal-World, Mike Yoder. **322:** Gabe Palmer/© Mug Shots/CORBIS **364:** Materials courtesy of the U.S. Government. **387:** (right) © Smithsonian Institution Press. Photos: Pat Rawlings/SAIC/NASA. **394:** © google.com. **404:** (top) © 2005 Bank of America Corporation. All rights reserved. Used with permission. (bottom two) Used with permission of Ameritrade IP Company, Inc., all rights in the copyrightable content and trademarks are owned and reserved by Ameritrade IP Company, Inc., and that Ameritrade is a registered trademark of Ameritrade IP Company, Inc.

AUTHOR/TITLE INDEX